Fiscal Year 2014
The **Interior**
Budget in **Brief**
April 2013

Fiscal Year 2014
The Interior
Budget in Brief
April 2013

TABLE OF CONTENTS

TABLE OF CONTENTS

FOREWORD

BACKGROUND AND ORGANIZATION

This document highlights the programs of the Department of the Interior and its 2014 President's budget request. The **DEPARTMENTAL OVERVIEW** section summarizes budgetary resource requirements at the Department level. The **DEPARTMENTAL HIGHLIGHTS** section presents major Department-wide initiatives, program, and budget proposals. The **BUREAU HIGHLIGHTS** section presents a narrative summary of the budget request for each bureau and an in-depth comparison in tabular form of 2012-2014 budgetary resource estimates with brief descriptions of programmatic changes. The **APPENDICES** present tabular summaries of pertinent budgetary data. Appendix A is a Department-wide table, presenting the 2014 request with prior year amounts. Other appendices contain summaries of Interior initiatives and crosscutting programs including energy; water; youth; land acquisition; Everglades; oceans; maintenance and construction; recreation fees; grants and payments; receipt amounts; mineral revenue payments to States; and staffing levels.

USAGE AND TERMINOLOGY

All years references are fiscal years unless noted, and amounts presented reflect budget authority unless otherwise specified. Numbers in tables and graphs may not add to totals because of rounding. Numbers shown in brackets [ ] are displayed for informational purposes and are not included in totals.

At the time the budget was prepared, the *Department of Defense, Military Construction and Veterans Affairs, and Full-Year Continuing Appropriations Act, 2013* establishing a full year appropriation for the Department, was not yet enacted. In lieu of an enacted bill, the 2014 Budget in Brief displays 2013 funding as the annualized amounts established under the Continuing Appropriations Resolution for 2013, P.L. 112-175, which provided funding through March 27, 2013. These amounts are provided for reference as they do not reflect enacted legislation. Further, the 2013 amounts appearing under 2013 Full Year CR column do not reflect any adjustments required under the March 1, 2013, Sequester Order required by the *Balanced Budget and Emergency Deficit Control Act as amended by the Budget Control Act of 2011.*

For purposes of comparison, programs funded through the Interior, Environment, and Related Agencies appropriation display changes proposed in the 2014 budget request as against the 2012 enacted level. For this reason the order of the funding columns presented in this book for current authority differs from prior years in that the sequence is **2013 Full Year CR, 2012 Enacted**, and the **2014 Request**. The display of permanent funding is consistent with prior years, comparing the 2014 estimates to the current 2013 estimates, and showing 2012 actual authority.

Projects and programs funded in the Energy and Water Development Appropriation make comparisons against the annualized amount available for 2013 under P.L. 112-175. Bureau of Reclamation and Central Utah Project Completion Act funding is treated differently due to their emphasis on construction projects and funding changes can be significant across several years due to planned project schedules. For this reason, the more up-to-date comparison is provided.

The 2014 Budget in Brief differs from previous years in the use of the 2012 enacted amount for the prior year funding rather than 2012 actual. The 2012 enacted is used to facilitate comparison to the most recent enacted legislation available at the time the budget was prepared. In some cases both are provided, for example, in Appendix A, where the execution of fund transfers is required for display.

Fixed costs refer to costs that are unavoidable in the short term (e.g. cost of living pay increases, GSA-negotiated space rate costs, unemployment compensation, and government-wide changes in health benefits). Additional information on the basis for the amounts used in this document is provided in the note following Appendix A.

A listing of frequently used acronyms follows:

AGO	America's Great Outdoors
BIA	Bureau of Indian Affairs
BIE	Bureau of Indian Education
BLM	Bureau of Land Management
BOEM	Bureau of Ocean Energy Management
BSEE	Bureau of Safety and Environmental Enforcement
CUPCA	Central Utah Project Completion Act
DO	Departmental Offices
DWP	Department-wide Programs
FWS	Fish and Wildlife Service
IBC	Interior Business Center (formerly the National Business Center)
LWCF	Land and Water Conservation Fund
NIGC	National Indian Gaming Commission
NPS	National Park Service
NRDAR	Natural Resource Damage Assessment and Restoration
OIA	Office of Insular Affairs
OIG	Office of the Inspector General
ONRR	Office of Natural Resources Revenue
OS	Office of the Secretary
OSM	Office of Surface Mining Reclamation and Enforcement
OST	Office of the Special Trustee for American Indians
PILT	Payments in Lieu of Taxes
SOL	Office of the Solicitor
USGS	U.S. Geological Survey
USACE	U.S. Army Corps of Engineers
WCF	Working Capital Fund

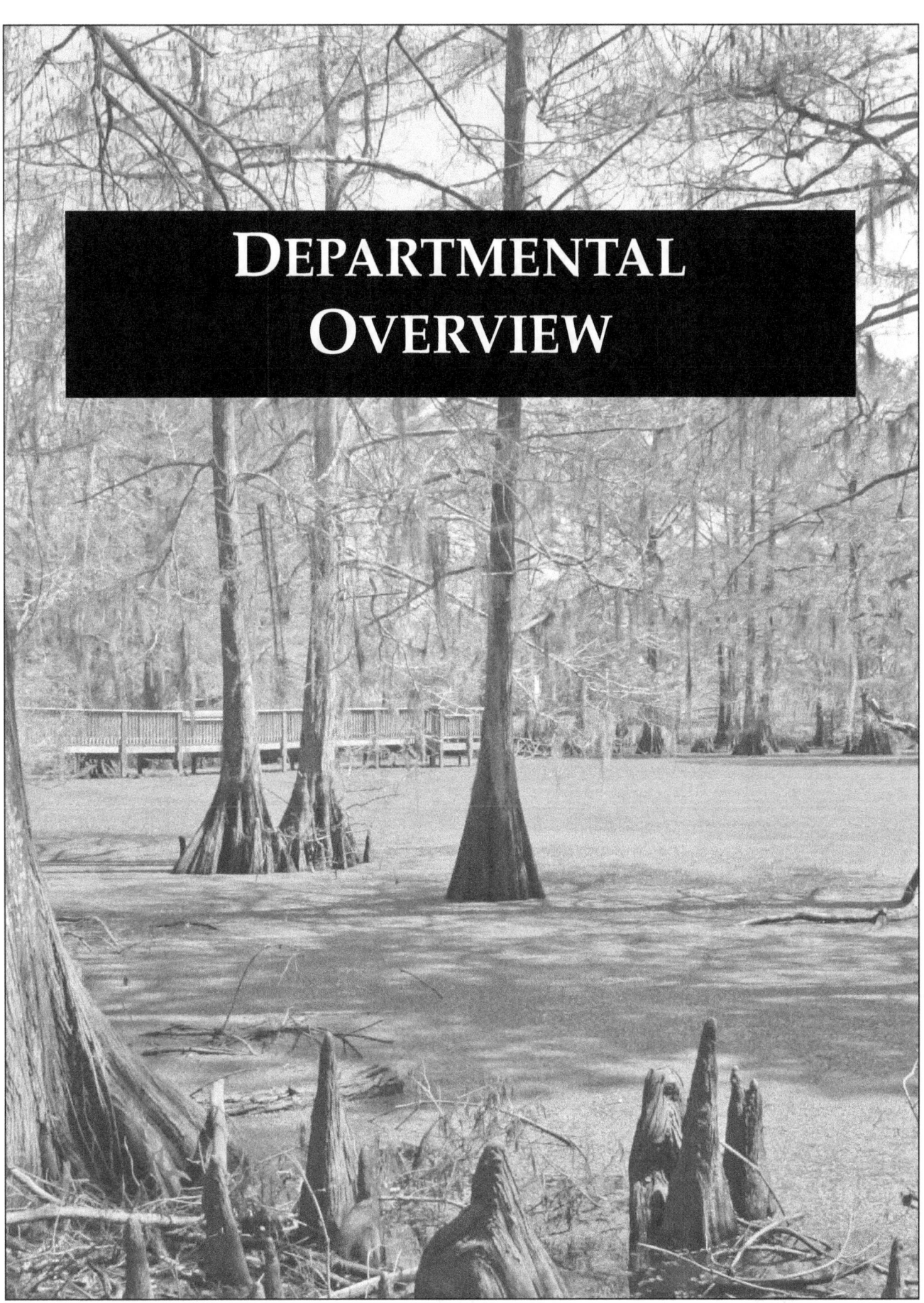

DEPARTMENTAL OVERVIEW

Introduction

 The last day of the Thirtieth Congress, March 3, 1849, was also the eve of President-elect Zachary Taylor's inauguration. The House of Representatives and the Senate were busy at work on two bills: the first, to find a formula for giving the newly acquired territory of California a civil government. The second, no less contentious, was also related to the recent enlargement of the national domain: legislation to create a Cabinet agency known as the Home Department, or Department of the Interior. The bill to create such a Department passed the House of Representatives on February 15, 1849. Two weeks later, the bill reached the Senate floor and late in the evening of March 3rd, the Senate voted 31 to 25 on the House-passed bill. President Polk was waiting in the Senate chambers and signed the bill creating a Department of the Interior.[1]

In 1849, when the Congress created the Home Department, it charged Interior with managing a wide variety of programs. In the last half of the 19th century, these programs ran the gamut of overseeing Indian Affairs, exploring the western wilderness, directing the District of Columbia jail, constructing the National Capital's water system, managing hospitals and universities, improving historic western emigrant routes, marking boundaries, issuing patents, conducting the census, and conducting research on the geological resources of the land.

Following the conservation movement at the beginning of the 20th century, there was an increasing sense of the fragile nature of this Country's natural resources. Accordingly, the Department's mission focused primarily on the preservation, management, understanding, and use of the great natural and cultural resources of the land.

Today, the Department manages the Nation's public lands and minerals including providing access to public lands and the Outer Continental Shelf for renewable and conventional energy; is the steward of 20 percent of the Nation's lands including national parks, national wildlife refuges, and the public lands; is the largest supplier and manager of water in the 17 western States and a supplier of hydropower energy; and upholds Federal trust responsibilities to Indian Tribes and Alaska Natives. It is responsible for migratory wildlife conservation; historic preservation; endangered species conservation; surface-mined lands protection and restoration; mapping, geological, hydrological, and biological science for the Nation; and financial and technical assistance for the Insular Areas.

Interior's budget covers a broad spectrum of activities, both to protect the Nation's resources and to ensure equity in their use. These activities include: operation of the National Park Service and the Fish and Wildlife Service; land management responsibilities of the Bureau of Land Management; delivery of quality services to American Indians and Alaska Natives; OCS management responsibilities of the Bureaus of Ocean Energy Management and Safety and Environmental Enforcement; research, data collection, and scientific activities of the U.S. Geological Survey; water management projects of the Bureau of Reclamation; regulatory responsibilities and reclamation activities of the Office of Surface Mining; and support for U.S. Territories and other Insular Areas.

[1] *Robert Utley and Barry Mackintosh, "The Department of Everything Else: Highlights of Interior History", 1988, pp 1-2.*

Departmental Overview

The Department of the Interior is helping to lead the United States in securing a new energy frontier, ushering in a conservation agenda for the 21st century, and honoring our word to the Nation's first Americans.

Ken Salazar, Secretary of the Interior
January 16, 2013

The Department of the Interior's mission affects the lives of all Americans. Simply put, Interior works to protect America's Great Outdoors and power the future. The Department serves as the steward for 20 percent of the Nation's lands, oversees the responsible development of 23 percent of U.S. energy supplies, is the largest supplier and manager of water in the 17 western States, maintains relationships with 566 federally recognized Tribes, and provides services to more than 1.7 million American Indian and Alaska Native peoples.

Interior operates through its component bureaus, each with different but complementary programs. Through its bureaus, Interior manages 401 units in the national park system, 561 national wildlife refuges, more than 245 million acres of land in the National System of Public Lands, and reclamation of nearly 322,000 acres of abandoned coal mine sites. Interior works to ensure America's spectacular landscapes, unique natural life, cultural resources, and icons endure for future generations. This Department tells and preserves the American story, and maintains the special places that enable the shared American experience.

Nearly every American lives within an hour's drive of lands or waters managed by Interior Department. In 2012, there were 483 million visits to Interior-managed lands. Recreational visits to Interior's lands had an economic benefit to local communities, particularly in rural areas, contributing an estimated $48.7 billion in economic activity in 2011. Through the America's Great Outdoors initiative, the Department is engaging local communities and young people to connect

to the outdoors, and work together to conserve and restore America's lands, water, and wildlife. The AGO initiative takes a strategic approach, focusing on landscapes of national significance, urban parks, wildlife refuge areas, rivers, and major water bodies.

Interior enables the safe and environmentally responsible development of conventional and renewable energy on public lands and the Outer Continental Shelf. The Department's oil and gas development activities accounted for nearly $9.7 billion of the roughly $13.7 billion in receipts generated by Interior's activities in 2012. For the past several years, Interior has targeted investments in America's energy future, particularly to encourage the development of renewable energy on the Nation's public lands and offshore areas where it makes sense. In 2009, there were no commercial solar energy projects on or under development on the public lands. From 2009 through March 2013, Interior authorized 37 renewable energy projects on or through the public lands which, if constructed, will have the potential to produce enough electricity to power more than 3.8 million homes.

Interior's mission requires a careful balance between development and conservation. The Department works to achieve this balance by working closely with its diverse stakeholders and partners to ensure its actions provide the greatest benefit to the American people. Central to this mission is the development and use of scientific information to inform decisionmaking. Scientific monitoring, research, and development play a vital role in supporting Interior's missions and Interior maintains a robust science capability in the natural sciences, primarily in the U.S. Geological Survey. An example of how this expertise is applied is the USGS current work as part of an interagency collaboration on hydraulic fracturing, which is aimed at researching and producing decision-ready information and tools on the potential impacts of hydraulic fracturing on the environment, health, and safety, including water quality and inducement of seismic activity.

The USGS provides exceptional support to Interior bureaus, however USGS alone cannot provide for all of Interior's scientific needs. The USGS and other Interior bureaus work collaboratively to find answers and to translate and apply scientific information and tools to important natural resource management questions. Science funding at the bureau and office level allows bureaus and offices to collaborate to produce and translate science into management-ready information, providing required resources to purchase studies, models, and expertise, and to hire scientists to help managers interpret the vast body of knowledge generated by USGS, universities, and other scientific institutions. These resources help answer imminent and important natural resource management questions and provide near-term solutions to address urgent and emerging issues such as the white-nose syndrome in bats.

Interior agencies work collaboratively to bridge gaps in knowledge, leveraging the complementary skills and capacity to advance the use of science to support management decisionmaking, ensure independent review of key decisions and science integrity, and adaptively use data to assist States, Tribes, and communities throughout the Nation. The Department's 2014 budget includes $18.6 million for hydraulic fracturing research within a total of $963.1 million for research and development in support of the Interior mission.

Achieving success in all of these important responsibilities on behalf of the American people is the Department's primary focus. The American people deserve nothing less.

Investing in America – Through the America's Great Outdoors initiative, the Administration is working to expand opportunities for recreation and conservation, through partnerships with States and others, and the promotion of America's parks, refuges, and public lands. The benefits extend beyond the conservation of natural resources and engagement of Americans with the outdoors. According to the Outdoor Industry Association, the American outdoor recreation economy provides an estimated 6.1 million jobs, spurs $646 billion in spending, and

brings $39.9 billion in Federal tax revenue and $39.7 billion in State and local tax revenue.

The AGO initiative is encouraging innovative partnerships in communities across the Nation, expanding access to rivers and trails, creating wildlife corridors, and promoting conservation while working to protect historic uses of the land including ranching, farming, and forestry. These efforts are based on donations reflecting the support of local communities to protect these areas and create more open space. For example, in 2012, the Department established the Sangre de Cristo Conservation Area, which will conserve a wildlife corridor in the Southern Rockies spanning 170,000 acres. When completed, the easement will represent the largest donation ever to the Fish and Wildlife Service.

In Montana, the Swan Valley Conservation Area connects the Canadian Rockies with the central Rockies of Idaho and Wyoming. The FWS established the Area in partnership with landowners who voluntarily entered their lands into easements. The new Area will protect one of the last low-elevation, coniferous forest ecosystems in western Montana that remains undeveloped and provide habitat for species such as grizzly bears, gray wolves, wolverines, and Canada lynx.

In 2012, the Department established the National Blueways System and the National Water Trails System under the AGO initiative. Recognition as a National Blueway for rivers and watersheds of national significance promotes and conserves economic, recreational, and natural values of healthy river systems from source to outlet and across watersheds. The NBS does not impose use limitations or regulatory requirements, but instead through collaborative efforts with others, recognizes and supports existing local and regional conservation, recreation, and restoration efforts by coordinating ongoing Federal, State, and local activities. The 410 mile long Connecticut River and its 7.2 million-acre watershed is the first river to be recognized as a National Blueway, followed by the recent designation of the White River in Arkansas and Missouri.

The new National Water Trails System network will increase access to water-based outdoor recreation in and around urban areas, provide national recognition and resources to existing local water trails, encourage community stewardship of local waterways, and promote tourism that fuels local economies across America. The water trails are a class of national recreational trails under the

National Trails Systems Act of 1986. Nine rivers were designated National Water Trails in 2012.

The 2014 budget includes $5.3 billion in current authority for AGO activities, an increase of $179.8 million above 2012. Funding is focused on land acquisition programs supported through the Land and Water Conservation Fund as well as land management operations, and other grant and technical assistance programs to promote conservation and improve recreational access. New in 2014, is expansion of the initiative to include $120.2 million for river restoration activities by the Bureau of Reclamation, $10.0 million for a revitalized and refocused Urban Parks and Recreation Resource grant program, and $3.0 million for a Historic Preservation Fund competitive grant program to support projects that help to tell the broader and diverse aspects of America's story. In addition to this current request, the Administration will submit a legislative proposal to permanently authorize annual funding, without further appropriation or fiscal year limitation, for the LWCF. This will provide an additional $141.0 million for Interior programs, $88.0 million for Federal land acquisition, and $53.0 million for recreational and conservation grants.

The 2014 budget continues a collaborative effort begun last year with the U.S. Forest Service in the Department of Agriculture to focus on the conservation and restoration of large landscapes and working lands, protecting ecosystems and the communities that depend on them. This approach works with partners at the local level to identify landscape areas or ecosystems for collaborative and leveraged conservation investments. Working jointly with the Forest Service, Interior has identified four focal landscape areas for targeted investment of $169.3 million in 2014.

A Stronger Energy Future – A stronger America depends on a growing economy that creates jobs. No area holds more promise than investments in American energy, clean, low cost, reliable, and secure energy supplies. Success depends on the Country's ability to pursue an all-of-the-above energy strategy. Interior's energy resource programs are at the forefront of this objective. The 2014 budget includes $771.6 million for renewable and conventional energy programs, an increase of $97.5 million above 2012.

Interior oversees onshore production of oil, gas, and coal on over 700 million acres of subsurface mineral estate. In 2012, more than 465 million barrels of oil were produced from Federal lands and waters, which resulted in over $6 billion in revenue for distribution to the States, Tribes, and the Treasury. Additionally, natural gas production on Federal lands and waters totaled more than 3.3 billion mcf and over $1.2 billion in revenue. Coal bed methane extracted from Federal lands totaled 600 million mcf of gas, generating over $240 million in revenue, and extraction of coal from Federal lands produced over 440 million tons of coal and nearly $800 million in revenue. The Department estimates the exploration and production of oil, gas, coal, hydropower, and minerals on Federal lands contributed nearly $275 billion to the U.S. economy in 2011.

Interior continues its effort to expand safe and responsible onshore energy development. In calendar year 2012, the Bureau of Land Management held 31 onshore oil and gas sales and 33 are planned in 2013. The BLM sales resulted in 1,707 parcels of land receiving bids in 2012, 30 percent more than in 2009. Onshore oil and gas leasing reforms put in place in 2010 resulted in fewer protests, less than 18 percent of 2,064 parcels offered in fiscal year 2012 were protested, the lowest since fiscal year 2003, reducing costs and speeding development. In 2014, the Department proposes a total of $127.1 million in current appropriations and offsetting fees for BLM's oil and gas program, representing an increase of $23.0 million in program capacity. This includes $48.0 million in proposed inspection fees, allowing for an increase of $10.0 million in BLM inspection and enforcement resources, along with a reduction of $38.0 million in requested appropriations for the program. The proposed onshore inspection fee is similar to the fee now charged to inspect offshore rigs and platforms.

The Department also plays a key role in efforts to strengthen the Nation's electric transmission grid. In 2012, Interior approved permits enabling more than 350 miles of transmission lines in seven states across Federal lands, including the 146 mile Pennsylvania-New Jersey Susquehanna-Roseland transmission line to improve electric service reliability in one of the most congested energy markets in the Country, and the 170 mile Sigurd to Red Butte transmission line in Utah, expected to provide enough energy to power over 400,000 American homes. This project is a key part of PacifiCorps' Energy Gateway Transmission Expansion to add about 2,000 miles of new transmission lines across the West.

Interior has been similarly active in supporting offshore production of oil and gas, while continuing to stress management and oversight reforms identified as a result of the Deepwater Horizon incident. At the end of 2012, more rigs were operating in the Gulf than in the previous two and a half years, equaling the number of rigs in the Gulf before the Deepwater Horizon oil spill. In 2012 alone, BSEE approved 112 new deepwater well permits, higher than in either of the two years preceding the Deepwater Horizon oil spill. At the same time, the Department has implemented safety and environmental management systems regulations; issued a new drilling safety rule to refine safety reforms and strengthen requirements; took steps to hold contractors accountable for their actions offshore; conducted the first full-scale capping stack deployment exercise to respond to a potential future well blowout scenario; and provided new guidance on oil spill response plans.

Interior released a new five-year program for offshore leasing last year, making areas containing an estimated 75 percent of the technically recoverable offshore oil and gas resources available for exploration and development. In March 2013, BOEM held the second Gulf of Mexico sale under the new OCS Plan, drawing 407 bids on 320 tracts covering more than 1.7 million acres offshore Alabama, Louisiana, and Mississippi, with high bids totaling $1.2 billion. In 2012, BOEM launched an assessment of energy resource potential off the coast of the Mid- and South Atlantic. The same year, Interior oversaw the first new exploratory activity in the Alaskan arctic in a decade, with Shell Oil Company beginning limited preparatory drilling activities in the Chukchi and Beaufort Seas under strict safety and environmental oversight. The 2014 budget includes a legislative proposal to implement an agreement reached in 2012 with the government of Mexico to open up previously off limits transboundary oil and natural gas reservoirs in the Gulf of Mexico. The 2014 budget includes $478.2 million for conventional offshore oil and gas activities.

Renewable energy, particularly solar and wind power, is a crucial and growing component of the Administration's all-of-the-above energy strategy. Among the significant results achieved for renewable power, since 2009, BLM has authorized more than 11,500 megawatts of energy on public lands and waters, established a road map for responsible solar development in the West designating energy zones, and flipped the switch on the first solar energy project to deliver power to the grid. The BLM also released the Final Environmental Impact Statement for a proposed 750 megawatt facility in Riverside County that would be one of the largest

solar energy projects on public lands in the California desert. The BLM is also moving forward on wind energy, with a proposed complex in Wyoming that would generate up to 3,000 megawatts of power, making it the largest wind farm facility in the U.S. and one of the largest in the world. The 2014 budget includes $29.1 million in BLM for onshore renewable energy programs.

Significant progress has been made to advance offshore wind energy. In 2012, BOEM issued the second non-competitive commercial wind lease off the coast of Delaware, and moved forward with first-ever competitive lease sales for wind energy areas off Virginia and Rhode Island/Massachusetts. These sales involve nearly 278,000 acres proposed for development of wind generation to produce electricity to power as many as 1.4 million homes. The 2014 budget includes $34.4 million in BOEM for offshore Renewable Energy development.

Water for a Growing America – Population growth, development, and a changing climate are creating growing challenges to the Nation's water supplies. In many areas of the Country, including the arid West, dwindling water supplies, lengthening droughts, and rising demand for water are forcing communities, stakeholders, and governments to explore new ideas and find new solutions to ensure stable, secure water supplies for the future.

Interior is tackling America's water challenges by providing leadership and assistance to States, Tribes, and local communities to address competing demands for water. Interior's programs are helping communities improve conservation and increase water availability, restore watersheds, and resolve long standing water conflicts. Interior is leading a national water conservation initiative, WaterSMART. The acronym stands for Sustain and Manage America's Resources for Tomorrow. WaterSMART is finding better ways to stretch existing supplies and helping partners plan to meet future water demands.

At the forefront of this effort is the Bureau of Reclamation. As the largest wholesaler of water in the 17 western States, Reclamation is working to stretch the Nation's limited water resources, reduce conflict, and facilitate solutions to complex water problems. Reclamation manages 476 dams and 337 reservoirs that deliver water to over 31 million people and one out of every five western farmers, irrigating ten million acres of farmland.

Since 2009, nearly $94 million in Federal funding has been awarded through Reclamation's WaterSMART grants for 158 projects, leveraging funding to implement more than $280 million in water management improvements across the West. WaterSMART supported projects, together with Reclamation's other water conservation activities funded through 2012, have contributed an estimated 616,000 acre-feet of water savings toward the Department's Priority Goal, enough water for more than 2.4 million people. WaterSMART also conserves energy, saving nearly 40 million kilowatt hours of electricity annually, enough power for 3,400 households. As part of WaterSMART, Reclamation is supporting 17 comprehensive water resource management studies across the West through the Basin Studies program to better inform water management decisions, including studies in Arizona, California, Colorado, Idaho, Kansas, Montana, Nebraska, Nevada, New Mexico, Oklahoma, Oregon, South Dakota, Texas, Utah , Washington, and Wyoming. This program provides leadership and tools to States, Tribes, and local communities to address current or projected imbalances between water supply and demand and to work toward sustainable solutions. The 2014 budget includes $35.4 million in Reclamation for WaterSMART activities.

The USGS is a key partner in Interior's WaterSMART initiative, by contributing research as part of its WaterSMART Availability and Use Assessment effort. The 2014 budget for the USGS includes $22.5 million for WaterSMART activities.

In 2012 USGS began a three year study of three focus areas in the Delaware River Basin, the Apalachicola–Chattahoochee–Flint River Basin, and the Colorado River Basin. The studies focus on water availability, investigating the components of a regional water budget to understand the amount entering and leaving each basin. This work contributed to *The Colorado River Basin Water Supply and Demand Study* released by the Department in December 2012, funded by Reclamation and the seven States in the Colorado River Basin. This first of a kind study projects an average imbalance in future water supply and demand greater than 3.2 million acre-feet by 2060. The study projects the largest increase in demand will come from municipal and industrial users, owing to population growth. The Colorado River Basin currently provides water to 40 million people, and the study estimates this number could double to nearly 76 million people by 2060, under a rapid growth scenario.

Fulfilling the Trust – This Administration has made it a top priority to help bring real and lasting change in Indian Country and to open a new constructive chapter of relations with Native Americans. The Administration has a comprehensive agenda to reform, repair, and rebuild Federal relations with Indian Country to ensure American Indians and Alaska Natives are offered the opportunities they deserve. This means respecting the inherent sovereignty of tribal nations and making sure the Federal government is honoring its commitments, fulfilling its trust responsibilities to tribal nations and individuals, providing resources, working cooperatively to build stronger economies and safer communities, and providing high quality education opportunities for Indian youth at schools funded by the Bureau of Indian Education.

Interior has worked diligently to restore tribal homelands. Since 2009, Interior has acquired more than 190,000 acres of land into trust and processed over 1,000 requests for land acquisitions that will allow for economic development, natural resource infrastructure, and health and housing projects to move forward as determined by the Tribes. The Secretarial appointed National Commission on Indian Trust Administration and Reform will help further these efforts as it undertakes a forward-looking, comprehensive evaluation of the Department's trust management.

One of the most significant recent developments regarding Interior's trust responsibilities was passage of the Claims Resolution Act of 2010, which ratified the $3.4 billion Cobell settlement agreement and four tribal water rights settlements. The Cobell settlement became final on November 24, 2012, following action by the U.S. Supreme Court and expiration of the appeal period.

Interior has launched implementation of a $1.9 billion Indian Land Buy-Back Program, authorized in the legislation, to purchase fractionated interests in trust or restricted land from willing Individual Indian Account holders at fair market value within a ten year period. The program enables tribal governments to use consolidated parcels for the benefit of their communities. Interior will rely on its extensive expertise and services, primarily in BIA and the Office of Special Trustee for American Indians, to implement the operational aspects, including valuations and acquisitions. As an added incentive to willing sellers, the Indian Land Buy-Back Program will fund up to $60.0 million for a scholarship fund for American Indian and Alaska Native students.

Departmental Overview

The entire program will be based on consultation with and participation of Tribes. Building on the Cobell settlement, the Administration has engaged Tribes in Nation-to-Nation negotiations on 59 additional settlements leading to over $1.1 billion in settlements to resolve long standing trust accounting and trust management claims.

Interior has also taken another step to give Tribes and individual Indians greater control over their own lands with the finalization of the most sweeping reform of Federal surface leasing regulations in more than 50 years. The new regulations remove bureaucratic red tape and streamline the approval for home ownership, expedite economic development, and spur renewable energy. As a result, individuals and Tribes will have the ability to do fundamental things on tribal lands, like buy a home or build a business.

The 2014 budget proposes an interim solution in the way in which funds are budgeted for contract support costs, which are important to the furtherance of self-governance and Indian self-determination. The 1975 Indian Self-Determination and Education Assistance Act, as amended, allows Tribes to implement programs previously administered by the Federal government through contractual arrangements. In turn, the Department pays tribal contractors for reasonable costs associated with the administration of those programs, known as contract support costs. Contract support costs funds are used by tribal contractors to pay a wide range of administrative and management costs, including but not limited to finance, personnel, maintenance, insurance, utilities, audits, communications, and vehicle costs. These funds allow Tribes to manage the Federal programs for which they contract, as well as eliminate the need for Tribes to use program funds to fulfill administrative requirements. The 2014 request for these costs is $231.0 million, an increase of $9.8 million above the 2012 enacted level.

In light of the Supreme Court's *Salazar* v. *Ramah Navajo Chapter* decision, the Administration is proposing Congress appropriate contract support costs funding to Tribes on a contract-by-contract basis. To ensure as much clarity as possible regarding the level of contract support costs funding, the Administration will provide Congress a contract-by-contract funding table for incorporation into the appropriations act. The Administration proposes this change as an interim step. The broader goal is to develop a longer-term solution through consultation with the Tribes, as well as streamline and simplify the

contract support costs process which is considered by many as overly complex and cumbersome to both Tribes and the Federal government.

Another area of emphasis reflected in the 2014 budget is a commitment to resolve tribal water rights claims and ensure Native American communities have access to use and manage water to meet domestic, economic, cultural, and ecological needs. Including funding for technical and legal support and for authorized settlements involving tribal waters, the 2014 budget request totals $159.6 million, which is an increase of $25.9 million over 2012. This includes a total of $135.3 million within the Bureaus of Reclamation and Indian Affairs to implement water rights settlements, an increase of $20.4 million above 2012. For communities benefiting from these settlements, a permanent water supply will vastly improve their quality of life and will offer greater economic security immediately as well as into the future.

To strengthen the Department's capacity to meet its trust responsibilities and more effectively partner with Tribes on water issues, $3.4 million in increases are provided in BIA's budget to support Water Management and Planning, Water Rights Litigation, and to conduct a comprehensive Department-wide evaluation to strengthen engagement, management, and analytical capabilities of the Indian Water Rights Office and other bureaus and offices that work on these issues. An increase of $766,000 in Reclamation's Native American Affairs Program and $1.0 million in the Cooperative Water Program at USGS will also strengthen technical analysis in support of water rights settlement work.

Interior is working to improve other areas of services in Indian Country. In education, Interior is working with the Department of Education to develop a national education reform agenda to better serve Indian children. The two agencies signed an agreement to bolster cooperation and coordination to better support Indian schools and serve Indian children. The budget includes $15.0 million to fund an elementary and secondary school pilot program based on the successful Department of Education turnaround schools model and concepts. Grants will be awarded to schools demonstrating the greatest need for the funds and the strongest commitment for using the funds to substantially raise the achievement of students.

Interior is putting more law enforcement officers in Indian communities, and improving training and equipment. Interior's revamped recruiting process for BIA law enforcement officers has increased the number of applicants for those positions by 500 percent, resulting in the largest officer hiring increase in BIA history. A pilot program of intense community policing on four reservations experiencing high crime rates saw promising results, a combined reduction of violent crime of 35 percent after the first 24 months. Now, 12 months later, crime continues to drop for a new combined reduction of 55 percent. Interior has expanded this successful pilot program to two additional reservations. The 2014 budget of $2.6 billion, includes $365.3 million for BIA's Public Safety and Justice programs, an increase of $19.0 million.

RESPONDING TO HURRICANE SANDY

As Hurricane Sandy left a wake of destruction across the Mid-Atlantic States and New England, the Department of the Interior mobilized resources to speed storm recovery on Federal and tribal lands in the impacted region and to support the Federal Emergency Management Agency in its efforts to assist States and local governments in the disaster area. At the peak, over 1,500 Interior employees supported response and recovery missions for Hurricane Sandy, through deployments and disaster recovery work.

The Disaster Relief Appropriations Act of 2013 appropriated $829.2 million for the Department to address funding needs relating to response, recovery, and mitigation of damages caused by Hurricane Sandy. The appropriation includes $469.2 million for response and recovery and to address damages to Interior parks, refuges, and facilities resulting from Hurricane Sandy. The bill also included $360.0 million for mitigation to restore and rebuild parks, including the Statue of Liberty shuttle dock shown below, refuges, and other Federal public assets and to support forward-looking projects to increase the resiliency and capacity of coastal habitat and infrastructure to withstand storms and reduce future damages.

BUDGET AUTHORITY AND RECEIPTS
(millions of dollars)

	2012 Enacted	2012 Actual	2013 Full Year CR	2014 Request
BUDGET AUTHORITY				
Current Appropriations	11,520	11,617	11,750	11,927
Rescissions	-86	-86	-4	-7
Supplementals	0	0	+852	0
Total, Current Appropriations	11,434	11,531	12,598	11,920
Permanent Appropriations	6,132	6,179	8,063	6,344
TOTAL	**17,566**	**17,710**	**20,661**	**18,265**
[Net discretionary BA]	*[11,266]*	*[11,393]*	*[12,441]*	*[11,741]*
RECEIPTS				
Outer Continental Shelf	7,881	6,645	6,845	6,995
Onshore Mineral Leasing	4,279	4,387	4,169	4,338
Other Offsetting Receipts	3,567	1,684	3,572	1,756
Other Receipts	781	988	954	962
TOTAL	**16,508**	**13,702**	**15,541**	**14,052**

SUMMARY OF MAJOR CHANGES

The Department's 2014 budget request totals $11.9 billion in current authority. This is an increase of $486.4 million over the 2012 enacted level. Of this, $10.9 billion is requested for programs funded by the Interior, Environment, and Related Agencies Appropriations Act. This is $513.2 million, or a 5.0 percent increase, compared to 2012. The 2014 request for the Bureau of Reclamation including the Central Utah Project Completion Act, funded in the Energy and Water Development Appropriations Act, is $1.0 billion in current appropriations, a reduction of $26.8 million and 2.5 percent when compared to the 2012 level.

Interior continues to generate more revenue for the U.S. Treasury than its annual appropriation. In 2014, Interior will generate receipts of approximately $14.1 billion and propose revenue and savings legislation estimated to generate more than $3.7 billion over the next decade. The 2014 budget also includes three mandatory spending proposals estimated at $8.1 billion in outlays over the next decade.

Bureau of Land Management – The 2014 request is $1.2 billion, an increase of $32.6 million over the 2012 enacted budget. This includes an increase of $23.5 million for BLM's two operating accounts, an increase of $10.3 million in BLM's request for current appropriations for Land Acquisition, and a reduction of $3.6 million that eliminates the Construction account.

To advance the America's Great Outdoors initiative, the request includes $8.0 million in programmatic increases for recreation and the National Landscape Conservation System to improve opportunities for recreation, education, and scientific activities while enhancing the conservation and protection of BLM-managed lands and resources. An additional $1.1 million will support interagency AGO projects to demonstrate ecosystem and landscape-scale conservation.

The BLM will continue to promote and facilitate the development of renewable energy on public lands,

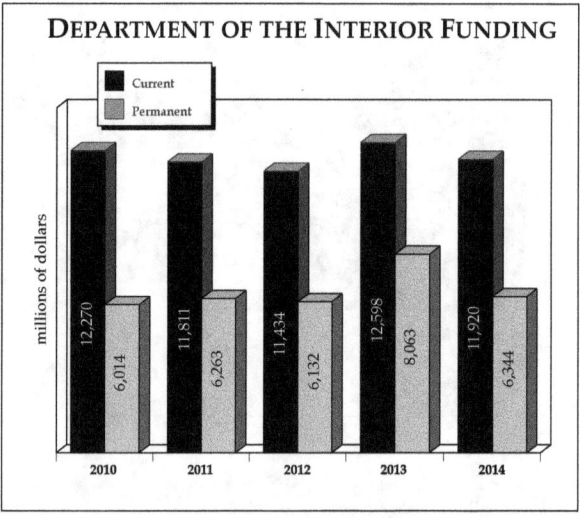

DEPARTMENT OF THE INTERIOR FUNDING

as part of the New Energy Frontier initiative. The 2014 budget includes a program increase of $9.1 million for renewable energy to support wind, solar, and geothermal energy, consisting of $7.1 million in new funding and a $2.0 million transfer of geothermal funds previously included within the Oil and Gas Management program. An additional $13.0 million in program increases is requested to strengthen management of the oil and gas program. These increases are offset by a proposal to shift the cost of oil and gas inspection and enforcement activity from current appropriations to inspection fees charged to industry, allowing for a reduction of $38.0 million in requested appropriations. The proposed inspection fees are estimated to generate $48.0 million, providing for a net $10.0 million increase in BLM's inspection and enforcement capability. There is an additional $6.0 million in the Lands and Realty Management program to support identification and designation of energy corridors in low conflict areas and site high voltage transmission lines, substations, and related infrastructure in an environmentally sensitive manner.

The 2014 budget features a $15.0 million increase to implement sage grouse conservation and restoration measures to help prevent the future listing of the species for protection under the Endangered Species Act.

The BLM funding for the Cooperative Landscape Conservation initiative increases by $3.3 million. This includes $2.5 million to support an integrated collaborative climate change adaptation effort to effectively plan for and respond to the impacts of climate change. An increase of $776,000 in Soil, Water, and Air Management will implement programs to improve the use of Rapid Ecoregional Assessments. The budget request also includes an increased investment of $2.8 million in the Youth in the Great Outdoors initiative.

Other program increases in the BLM budget include $3.5 million in the Oregon and California Grant Lands account to support the Secretary's Western Oregon Strategy, $2.0 million to implement recommendations of the recent National Academy of Sciences study of the Wild Horse and Burro program, $4.0 million in the Resource Management Planning program to support high priority planning efforts, $2.5 million in the Soil, Water, and Air Management program for applied science projects and information aimed at improving BLM understanding and management of public lands, $1.0 million in the Riparian Management program for increased science in sup-

port of program activities, and $500,000 for activities related to the Klamath Agreements authorized under existing law. The budget includes increases of $2.4 million and $2.0 million, respectively, in the Coal Management and Other Mineral Resources programs for inspection activities. An $8.2 million program increase is requested in the Bureau-wide Fixed Cost program to cover costs previously funded through program assessments. The budget includes a $1.3 million increase in Deferred Maintenance to support land mobile radio improvements and a $1.0 million increase in Administrative Support to fund the startup costs for a new congressionally-chartered charitable, non-profit foundation, the National BLM Foundation.

A $14.1 million program decrease is proposed for grazing permit renewal and monitoring in the Rangeland Management program. However, the impact of this decrease will be mitigated by a new grazing administration fee of $1.00 per animal unit month proposed on a pilot basis through appropriations language, estimated to raise $6.5 million in 2014. The 2014 budget reduces programmatic funding for the Alaska Conveyance program by $12.3 million from the 2012 level. The BLM will explore opportunities to further streamline the program. The impact of this funding reduction will be further mitigated by a legislative proposal to use a portion of oil and gas revenues from the National Petroleum Reserve-Alaska to fund land transfers in support of the Alaska Conveyance program. The budget also includes a reduction of $2.1 million in Information Technology Management.

Bureau of Ocean Energy Management – The 2014 operating request is $169.4 million, including $71.5 million in current appropriations and $97.9 million in offsetting collections. This is an increase of $11.9 million in net current appropriations above the 2012 enacted level.

The 2014 budget request includes program changes of $5.8 million above the 2012 enacted level to promote offshore conventional energy development that is safe and environmentally responsible. The request includes an increase of $1.3 million to support offshore renewable energy lease auctions. The request also includes an increase of $3.0 million for conventional energy development activities to develop baseline characterization and monitoring capabilities in the Gulf of Mexico, support the acquisition and processing of geophysical and geological data for the Atlantic OCS, and advance the use of technology to support the review of de-

SUMMARY OF MAJOR CHANGES
(millions of dollars)

INTERIOR, ENVIRONMENT, AND RELATED AGENCIES

Fixed Costs .... [+106.7]

BLM
AGO – Recreation, NLCS, and
  Demonstration Landscapes .... +9.1
Renewable Energy .... +7.1
Oil and Gas – Leasing, Oversight, and
  Environmental Studies.................................. +13.0
Oil and Gas Management Inspect. *(shift to fees)*.. -38.0
Oil and Gas Management Inspection Fees........ [+48.0]
Transmission Corridors Siting .... +6.0
Sage Grouse Conservation Activities................. +15.0
Land Acquisition *(current only)* .... +10.3
Grazing Permit Renewal and Monitoring......... -14.1
Grazing Administration Fees............................ [+6.5]
Alaska Conveyance .... -12.3

BOEM
Renewable Energy Auction Support................. +1.3
Conventional Energy...................................... +3.0

BSEE
Environmental Enforcement .... +4.2
Operations, Safety and Regulation.................... +14.2

OSM
Regulatory Grants.. -10.9
State Program Evaluations .... +4.0

USGS
Rapid Disaster Response .... +2.5
Alternative Energy... +4.0
Streamgages.. +7.2
Big Earth Data Initiative .... +9.0
3-D Elevation Program.................................... +11.0
Climate Science Centers.................................. +10.0
Hydraulic Fracturing...................................... +13.0
WaterSMART Availability and
  Use Assessment... +14.5
Ecosystems Restoration .... +15.5

FWS
Endangered Species.. +7.6
National Wildlife Refuge System .... +12.7
National Blueways System -
  Cooperative Watershed Management .... [+3.3]
Law Enforcement... +5.3
Science Support... +16.5
Aquatic Invasive Species .... +5.5
Cooperative Landscape Conservation................ +6.7
Construction .... -7.5
Land Acquisition *(current only)* .... +12.6
National Wildlife Refuge Fund......................... -14.0
Cooperative Endangered Species
  Conservation Fund *(current only)*...................... +8.3

NPS
Operations.. +19.5
  Natural Resource Projects............................. [+5.0]
  Invasives.. [+5.2]
  Cooperative Landscape Conservation........... [+6.0]
Heritage Partnership Programs........................ -8.4
State Conservation Assistance Program............. -5.2
Line-Item Construction Projects .... +5.3
Urban Parks Recreation and Recovery
  Grants Program.. +10.0

Indian Affairs
Trust Natural Resources Management .... +37.3
Trust Real Estate Services .... +7.7
Contract Support... +9.8
Klamath Basin Restoration Agreement .... +5.5
Public Safety and Justice................................. +17.4
Anti-Domestic Violence Program..................... +3.0
School Turnaround Pilot Program.................... +15.0
Tribal Colleges and Universities...................... +2.5
Post-Graduate Scholarships .... +3.0
Housing Improvement Program .... -12.6
Operations Streamlining................................. -19.7
Management Efficiencies................................. -13.8

Departmental Offices
Insular Affairs
  Technical Assistance.................................... +3.7
  Compact Impact.. -2.0
Office of the Special Trustee
  Historical Trust Accounting .... -7.0
  Trust Accountability .... -3.8

Department-wide Programs
Wildland Fire
  Hazardous Fuels Reduction .... -88.9
  Suppression - Regular and FLAME Fund .... +205.1
  Burned Area Rehabilitation............................ +3.0
Natural Resource Damage Assessment
and Restoration
  Restoration Support...................................... +3.6
  Oil Spill Preparedness.................................. +2.2

ENERGY AND WATER DEVELOPMENT

Bureau of Reclamation
Central Utah Project .... -25.4
Mni Wiconi Rural Water Supply Project........... -23.2
WaterSMART Program .... -20.5
Klamath Project... -7.7
Other Rural Water Supply Projects .... -6.3
San Joaquin River Restoration Fund................. +8.0
Central Valley Project, West San Joaquin
  Division, San Luis Unit .... +22.6
Indian Water Rights Settlements
  including Navajo-Gallup .... +28.2

velopment plans. The budget requests funding to be partially offset by fees to support the leasing of marine minerals such as sand and gravel needed to enhance the resiliency of coastal areas amid rising sea levels.

Bureau of Safety and Environmental Enforcement – The 2014 budget request is $222.1 million, including $98.2 million in current appropriations and $124.0 million in offsetting collections. This is an increase of $24.8 million in net current appropriations above the 2012 enacted level.

The 2014 budget includes an increase of $4.2 million for environmental enforcement activities to foster environmental compliance, and support inspection, investigation, and enforcement activities. The request also includes an increase of $14.2 million to increase operational safety capabilities, develop the National Offshore Training program for inspectors and engineers, and conduct research and development activities on critical safety systems associated with offshore oil and gas development. Funding is also requested to ensure the safety of oil and gas development in Alaskan waters and to enhance the use of technology in the Bureau's offshore inspection program.

Office of Surface Mining – The 2014 budget request for the Office of Surface Mining is $143.1 million, a decrease of $7.1 million from the 2012 enacted level. This includes a decrease of $10.9 million in grants to States and Tribes to encourage these regulatory programs to recover a larger portion of their costs from fees charged to the coal industry, and an increase of $4.0 million to provide additional technical support to State and tribal regulatory programs. The budget also includes increases for applied science to advance reclamation technologies. This request also proposes to finalize the transition of abandoned mine land reclamation from current to permanent funding.

Bureau of Reclamation – The 2014 budget request totals $1.0 billion, including the Central Utah Project Completion Act program. On a comparable basis to include CUPCA funding, this is a decrease of $26.8 million below the 2012 enacted level and $33.4 million below the 2013 Continuing Resolution, P.L. 112-175, annualized. Interior's 2014 budget proposes to consolidate the CUPCA program with Reclamation to allow the Department to evaluate the priority of the CUPCA program in the context of other water programs. The 2014 CUPCA request is $3.5 million, a decrease of $25.4 million from the

2013 Full Year Continuing Resolution. Reclamation's 2014 request also reflects the following: a reduction of $29.5 million in the Rural Water program, including a reduction of $23.2 million due to the completion of the construction of Mni Wiconi Project and a reduction of $6.3 million in other rural water supply projects; a reduction of $20.5 million in the WaterSMART Program; and a reduction of $7.7 million in the Klamath Project. These reductions are primarily in recognition of the economic conditions facing the Nation.

The 2014 budget includes some increases in programs such as $8.0 million for the San Joaquin River Restoration Fund to continue activities required by the settlement; $22.6 million for the Central Valley Project, West San Joaquin Division, San Luis Unit to support implementation of the San Luis drainage management plan; and the Indian Rights settlements. Funding for Indian water rights settlements in Water and Related Resources shows a reduction of $50.5 million, reflecting the shift of these funds to the requested new Indian Water Rights Settlements account. A $28.2 million increase in settlements funding is primarily in the Navajo-Gallup Water Supply Project with small decreases in the other settlements. Reclamation is requesting the establishment of an Indian Water Rights Settlements account in 2014 to assure continuity in the construction of the authorized projects and to highlight and enhance transparency in handling these funds.

The 2014 Water and Related Resources budget also contains $21.0 million for ongoing settlement operation and maintenance functions including the Ak Chin Indian Water Rights Settlement Act, San Carlos Apache Tribe Water Settlement Act, Animas-La Plata Project specified in Colorado Ute Settlement Act, and the Nez Perce/Snake River Water Rights Act, which is part of the Columbia/Snake River Recovery Project. These funds are proposed to remain in the Water and Related Resources account. The total for Reclamation's implementation of Indian water rights settlements in 2014 is $159.7 million, $99.7 million in current funding and $60.0 million in permanent authority.

U.S. Geological Survey – The USGS budget request is $1.2 billion, $98.8 million above the 2012 enacted level. The President's budget reflects the Administration's commitment to investments in research and development to support sound decisionmaking and sustainable stewardship of natural resources. This includes science, monitoring, and assessment activities critical to understand and manage the ecological, mineral, energy, and water resources which underlie the prosperity and well-being of the Nation. Highlights of the budget include increases for science priorities in ecosystem restoration, climate adaptation, invasive species, and earth observations, including streamgages, light detection and ranging, and managing critical data. The budget provides increased support to enhance sustainable energy development, address water resources challenges, and enhance America's Great Outdoors through the 21st Century Conservation Service Corps Youth initiative.

The USGS budget includes investments in important science programs to help meet societal needs. A program increase of $14.5 million above 2012 for WaterSMART will be used to develop regional water availability models, integrate and disseminate data through online science platforms, and support the National Groundwater Monitoring Network. A program increase of $7.2 million for the National Streamflow Information Program will fund more than 400 streamgages to strengthen the Federal backbone at high priority sites sensitive to drought, flooding, and potential climate change effects.

A program increase totaling $10.0 million above 2012 for the National Climate Change and Wildlife Science Center/Department of the Interior Climate Science Centers includes an increase of $3.5 million for grants focused on translational and applied science needed by resource managers for decisionmaking. An increase of $3.2 million will support coordination with other Federal climate science activities and ensure scientific results and products are made available to the public in a centralized, web-accessed format. An increase of $2.5 million will support applied science and capacity-building for tribal climate adaptation needs in each of the eight CSC regions. A program increase of $3.0 million above 2012 will enable completion of the national biological carbon sequestration assessment and development of tools in collaboration with other agencies to support biological sequestration activities on public lands.

The 2014 budget also provides a program increase of $11.0 million above 2012 for the 3-Dimensional Elevation Program to collect LIDAR data, used for a wide range of applications in mapping, agriculture, planning, and natural resources management. Data collection will be coordinated with other agencies to implement a national LIDAR program to enhance science and emergency response activities, resource and vulnerability assessments, ecosystem

based management, and tools to inform policy and management.

The budget includes a program increase of $13.0 million above 2012 to support the continuation of a hydraulic fracturing research and development effort with the Department of Energy and Environmental Protection Agency, to better understand and minimize potential environmental, health, and safety impacts of energy development involving hydraulic fracturing. New work will address issues such as water quality and quantity, ecosystem, community, and human health impacts, and induced seismicity. A program increase of $4.0 million above 2012 is also provided for science to support ecologically sound and sustainable development of renewable energy on Federal lands.

The 2014 budget includes a program increase of $9.0 million in Core Science Systems for the Big Earth Data initiative. This interagency initiative will improve access to and use of data from the satellite, airborne, terrestrial, and ocean-based Earth observing systems. These investments will provide benefits in natural resource management and hazard mitigation, by improving access to critical information.

Program increases totaling $15.5 million above 2012 in ecosystems activities will support a wide range of science, including ecosystems restoration work in the Chesapeake Bay, California Bay-Delta, Columbia River, Everglades, Puget Sound, Great Lakes, Upper Mississippi River, Gulf Coast, and Klamath Basin. Within this total, $3.0 million will support the science and integration of ecosystems services frameworks into decisionmaking and implementation of efforts to assess and sustain the Nation's environmental capital. A program increase of $2.4 million will address invasive species such as Asian carp, brown tree snakes, white-nose syndrome in bats, coral reef health, and other emerging invasives of national concern.

A program increase of $2.5 million above 2012 is requested to improve rapid response to natural disasters. Funding will improve the Federal government's capacity to provide timely and effective science and information to minimize potential risks posed by natural hazards. Funding will be invested in USGS monitoring networks for rapid response to earthquakes, volcanoes, landslides, tsunamis, floods, hurricanes, and other potential threats to people, infrastructure, and ecosystems.

Fish and Wildlife Service – The 2014 Fish and Wildlife Service budget includes $1.6 billion in current appropriations, an increase of $76.4 million above the 2012 level. This includes America's Great Outdoors initiative related increases of $68.9 million in the Resource Management account. There is a $3.9 million increase in the FWS North American Wetlands Conservation grants program. In 2014 funding for State and Tribal Grants remains at the 2012 level of $61.3 million. The budget also includes $1.2 billion available under permanent appropriations, most of which will be provided directly to States for fish and wildlife restoration and conservation.

In 2014, a total of $1.6 billion is proposed for FWS as part of the Administration's America's Great Outdoors initiative to help reconnect people with the Nation's vast natural resources. This includes $1.3 billion for operations, an increase of $68.9 million over the 2012 level. As part of this initiative, the request includes a program increase of $3.3 million to coordinate a landscape level conservation approach to river systems throughout the Country as part of the National Blueways System, a Department-wide initiative.

The 2014 budget also includes increases for programs funded through the Land and Water Conservation Fund, a vital component of the America's Great Outdoors initiative. The 2014 budget proposal includes $106.3 million for Federal land acquisition, of which $70.8 million, a program increase of $12.6 million, is in current funding and $35.5 million is in new permanent funding. In addition, the budget proposes a total of $84 million for the Cooperative Endangered Species Conservation Fund, of which $8.3 million is a program increase in current funding and $28.0 million is part of the LWCF permanent funding proposal. The 2014 Federal Land Acquisition program builds on efforts to strategically invest in interagency landscape-scale conservation projects while continuing to meet agency-specific programmatic needs.

The budget proposes an increase of $7.2 million for activities associated with renewable energy development. The request supports scientific research into the impacts of energy transmission and development infrastructure on wildlife and habitat. The research will identify potential impacts associated with the development of energy infrastructure and strategies to minimize the impacts on habitat and species likely to be impacted, including desert tortoise and sage grouse. This increase will enable FWS to participate more fully in priority landscape level planning and

assist industry and State fish and wildlife agencies as they plan for the siting of renewable energy projects and transmission corridor infrastructure.

The budget request for the Resource Management account continues support for key programs including $185.4 for Endangered Species, a program increase of $7.6 million; $499.2 million for the National Wildlife Refuge System, a program increase of $12.7 million; $68.3 million for Law Enforcement, a program increase of $5.3 million; $33.3 million for Science Support, a program increase of $16.5 million; $14.5 million for Aquatic Invasive Species, a program increase of $5.5 million; and $17.6 million for Cooperative Landscape Conservation, a program increase of $6.7 million.

The 2014 budget request continues the FWS commitment to ecosystem restoration by including $89.2 million composed of $16.0 million for the Everglades; $4.9 million to maintain 2012 funding for California's Bay-Delta; $10.2 million to maintain 2012 funding for the Gulf Coast; $10.3 million for the Chesapeake Bay; and $47.8 million for the Great Lakes.

Funding for the Cooperative Landscape Conservation activity is $17.6 million, an increase of $2.1 million, and funding for Science Support is $33.3 million, an increase of $16.6 million. The budget supports applied science directed at high impact questions to mitigate threats to fish and wildlife resources.

The 2014 budget proposes a reduction of $14.0 million for National Wildlife Refuge Fund payments to counties to offset local tax loss due to Federal land ownership. An estimated $8.0 million in permanent receipts collected and allocated under the program would remain available to counties for this purpose. The budget also reduces funding for construction by $7.5 million.

National Park Service – The 2014 budget request for NPS of $2.6 billion is $56.6 million above the 2012 enacted level. In 2014, a total of $2.5 billion is requested for NPS as part of the America's Great Outdoors initiative. This includes $2.3 billion for park operations, as represented by the Operation of the National Park System account, which is a total increase of $48.4 million over 2012. The 2014 request for operations funds fixed costs of $28.9 million and a net program increase of $19.5 million for NPS operations. Among the increases in operations is $6.0 million for Cooperative Landscape Conservation, $5.2 million to control invasive and exotic species at parks, $5.0 million to competitively fund the highest priority, non-recurring natural resource project needs at park units, $3.0 million to address white-nose syndrome in bats at parks, $2.1 million to fund operational needs at new park units, and $1.0 million for Youth funding to engage youth in the great outdoors through employment and educational opportunities.

The request for the Historic Preservation Fund is $58.9 million, a programmatic increase of $3.0 million compared to 2012 enacted. Grants-in-aid to States and Tribes are continued at the 2012 level and $3.0 million is provided for competitive grants targeted toward communities that are currently underrepresented on the National Register of Historic Places. Within the National Recreation and Preservation account, there are two programs tracked as part of the AGO initiative. Funding for the Rivers, Trails, and Conservation Assistance program is $10.1 million, essentially level with 2012, and funding for the American Battlefield Protection Program assistance grants is level with 2012 at $1.4 million.

Programs funded out of the Land and Water Conservation Fund are also a key component of the Administration's AGO strategy. The budget requests $100.4 million for the Land Acquisition and State Assistance account, a total decrease of $1.5 million. This includes $40.0 million for the State Conservation Grants program, a $5.2 million programmatic decrease, plus $60.4 million for NPS Federal land acquisition, a programmatic increase of $3.4 million. Of this amount, $12.1 million is for Federal acquisition projects at park units selected as part of a collaborative process with other Interior bureaus and the Forest Service, and $20.4 million is for projects to address core, NPS-specific mission priorities. The budget includes $10.0 million to revitalize the Urban Parks Recreation and Recovery program. In addition to this current request, the Administration will submit a legislative proposal to permanently authorize annual funding, without further appropriation or fiscal year limitation, for the LWCF. This will provide an additional $30.2 million for Federal land acquisition, $20.0 million for the State Conservation Grants program, and $5.0 million for UPARR grants in permanent funding in 2014.

Other funding includes a total of $52.0 million for the National Recreation and Preservation account. This reflects a programmatic reduction of $8.4 million from Heritage Partnership programs to encourage self-sufficiency for these non-Federal organizations. Funding for Construction totals $160.0 million, a total increase of $4.6 million. Of this amount,

programmatic changes include an increase of $5.3 million for line-item construction projects. Programmatic reductions include of $1.8 million from construction program management and operations, $760,000 from the housing improvement program, $228,000 from equipment replacement, $440,000 from construction planning, and $2.4 million from management planning.

Indian Affairs – The 2014 budget includes $2.6 billion for Indian Affairs programs, an increase of $31.3 million from the 2012 enacted level. This includes increases of $37.2 million for Operation of Indian Programs, excluding a proposed transfer of Contract Support Costs to a stand alone account. The budget also includes $2.9 million in Indian Land and Water Claim Settlements. The budget includes decreases of $16.5 million in the Construction account and $2.1 million in the Indian Guaranteed Loan program.

The budget proposes program increases of $37.3 million for the Trust land management programs and $7.7 million in real estate services to assist Tribes in the management, development, and protection of Indian trust land and natural resources. Additional funding is provided for science and technical support to Tribes for the sustainable stewardship and development of natural resources. The funding will support resource management and decisionmaking in the areas of energy and minerals, climate, oceans, water rights protection, endangered and invasive species, and resource protection enforcement. Of this funding, $2.5 million will focus on projects that engage youth in the natural sciences and establish an office to coordinate youth programs across Indian Affairs. The budget also includes $7.0 million, an increase of $5.5 million, for the Klamath land purchase agreement.

In 2014, Contract Support Costs and the Indian Self-Determination Fund are increased by $9.8 million for a total of $231.0 million for new and existing tribal 638 contracts. In response to the Supreme Court decision on contract support costs, the 2014 budget proposes to move both budget line items to an account separate from the Operations account.

Public Safety and Justice funding has a program increase of $17.4 million to support additional law enforcement and officers, detention corrections staff, resource protection officers, and tribal court operations. The budget also includes $3.0 million to address the needs of Indian communities with elevated levels of domestic violence. The BIA Human Services program will partner with the Law

Enforcement program to expand services to help stem domestic violence and care for its victims.

The budget supports student academic achievement in BIE funded schools by initiating a $15.0 million pilot program to turn around lower performing elementary and secondary schools, provides $2.5 million in increased funding to meet the needs of growing enrollment at tribal colleges, and boosts funding for scholarships by $3.0 million for post-graduate fellowship and training opportunities in the natural sciences.

The budget proposes to initiate payments for the Taos Pueblo Indian Water Rights Settlement enacted as part of the Claims Resolution Act of 2010. Funding for the Nez Perce/Snake River settlement was completed in 2013.

The budget proposes to eliminate the $12.6 million Housing Improvement Program. The $650.0 million Housing and Urban Development Native American Housing Block Grant serves the same population as HIP. Tribes who receive HUD funding are not precluded from using HUD funding to provide assistance to HIP applicants.

The 2014 request reflects a reduction of $19.7 million as the Bureau will undergo a consolidation in 2013 to streamline and improve oversight operations. The BIA will engage in extensive consultation with Tribes to identify strategies to ensure tribal needs and priorities are addressed. Following consultation, Indian Affairs will construct an implementation plan for a streamlined, cost-effective organization. The budget also includes $13.8 million in administrative savings from reductions to fleet, travel, contractors, and awards.

Departmental Offices and Department-wide Programs – The 2014 request for the Office of the Secretary is $268.9 million, an increase of $7.0 million from the 2012 enacted level. Of this, $121.1 million is for the Office of Natural Resources Revenue programs, an increase of $1.6 million above the 2012 enacted level and includes a program decrease of $380,000 in production verification and meter inspections and $653,000 in program efficiencies. The budget proposes an increase of $267,000 for minerals receipts modeling development to improve revenue estimation and reporting capabilities, and an increase of $800,000 for various science initiatives. Other changes include the proposed transfer of the Indian Arts and Crafts Board from the Office of the Secretary to the Bureau of Indian Affairs of

$1.3 million, a program decrease of $563,000 to valuation services, and a general reduction of $86,000.

The budget request for the Office of Insular Affairs is $92.0 million, a decrease of $12.3 million from the 2012 enacted level. The budget includes an increase of $766,000 to enhance the implementation of sustainable energy projects and $3.7 million for general technical assistance. The budget also includes $3.0 million, a reduction of $2.0 million, to help mitigate the impacts and costs of Compact migration. Funding of $13.1 million for the Palau Compact Extension is not requested for 2014 as it is expected the Compact will be authorized and funded in 2013.

The Office of Inspector General request is $50.8 million, a program increase of $984,000. Within this total, a program increase of $840,000 is for mission support, consisting of a $2.0 million increase for D.C. area office consolidation and a reduction of $1.2 million associated with administrative efficiencies.

The Office of the Special Trustee request is $139.7 million, $12.4 million below the 2012 enacted level. The 2014 budget decreases Executive Direction funding by $3.0 million and Program Operations and Support by $9.4 million. Within the total, program decreases of $7.0 million is from Historical Trust Accounting and $3.8 million is from Trust Accountability. Proposed funding for OST supports the Department's Indian fiduciary trust responsibilities.

The 2014 request for the Department-wide Wildland Fire Management program is $776.9 million. The net program increase of $194.2 million includes program increases of $205.1 million split between the Suppression Operations account and the FLAME Fund to fully fund the 10-year suppression average, and $3.0 million for the Burned Area Rehabilitation program. These program increases are partially offset by a net program reduction of $88.9 million in the Hazardous Fuels Reduction program. This net reduction includes an increase of $2.0 million to conduct a research study on the effectiveness of hazardous fuels treatments. The 2014 request for the Wildland Fire Management account also includes a cancellation of $7.0 million in prior-year balances.

The 2014 request for the Natural Resource Damage Assessment and Restoration Fund is $12.5 million, a net program increase of $6.1 million. The increase includes $3.6 million to support additional restoration work and $2.2 million for a Department-wide onshore Oil Spill Preparedness plan.

The Department's 2014 request for the Working Capital Fund appropriation is $62.0 million, an increase of $80,000 from the 2012 enacted level. Within this request is $58.0 million for the Financial and Business Management System to complete the deployment of the last bureau, Reclamation. The budget proposes an increase of $2.0 million to initiate the Department's Cultural and Scientific Collections Management initiative. Reductions include $5.0 million for the proposed transition of the Department's Information Technology Transformation Initiative from appropriated WCF to the WCF centralized bill, $2.5 million for the completion of the Department's Acquisition Improvement initiative in 2012, and a decrease of $496,000 from the Service First/Consolidations initiative.

LEGISLATIVE MANDATORY PROPOSALS

The 2014 budget includes 17 mandatory proposals. These proposals will be submitted to the Congress to collect a fair return to the American taxpayer for the sale of Federal resources, to reduce unnecessary spending, and to extend beneficial authorities of law. Revenue and savings proposals will generate more than $3.7 billion over the next decade. The 2014 budget also includes three mandatory spending proposals estimated at $8.1 billion in outlays over the next decade.

Land and Water Conservation Fund – The Department of the Interior will submit a legislative proposal to permanently authorize annual funding, without further appropriation or fiscal year limitation, for LWCF in the Departments of the Interior and Agriculture. During a transition to permanent funding in 2014, the budget proposes $600.0 million in total LWCF funding, comprised of $200.0 million permanent and $400.0 million current funding. Starting in 2015, the fully authorized level of $900.0 million in permanent funds will be authorized each year.

Payments in Lieu of Taxes – The authorization for permanent PILT payments was extended through 2013 as part of the Surface Transportation Extension Act of 2012. The 2014 budget proposes to extend authorization of the program an additional year through 2014, while a sustainable long-term funding solution is developed for the PILT Program. This proposal is estimated to outlay nearly $410 million in 2014. The PILT payments help local governments carry out vital services, such as firefighting and police protection, construction of public schools and roads, and search and rescue operations. The payments are made annually for tax exempt Federal lands administered by the Department, including BLM, FWS, NPS, as well as the Forest Service, Federal water projects, and some military installations. The proposal utilizes the current PILT payment formula, which is based on population, receipt sharing payments, and the amount of Federal land within an affected county.

Palau Compact – On September 3, 2010, the U.S. and the Republic of Palau successfully concluded the review of the Compact of Free Association and signed a 15-year agreement that includes a package of assistance through 2024. Under the agreement, Palau committed to undertake economic, legislative, financial, and management reforms. The conclusion of the agreement reaffirms the close partnership between the U.S. and the Republic of Palau to strengthen the foundation for economic development in Palau by developing public infrastructure and improving health care and education. Compact funding will also undertake one or more infrastructure projects designed to support Palau's economic development efforts. The Republic of Palau has a strong track record of supporting the U.S. and its location is strategically linked to Guam and U.S. operations in Kwajalein Atoll. Permanent and indefinite funding for the Compact expired at the end of 2009. The 2014 budget assumes authorization of permanent funding for the Compact occurs in 2013. The cost for this proposal is estimated at $189 million over the 2014 through 2023 period.

Federal Oil and Gas Reforms – The budget includes a package of legislative reforms to bolster and backstop administrative actions being taken to reform the management of Interior's onshore and offshore oil and gas programs, with a key focus on improving the return to taxpayers from the sale of these Federal resources. Proposed statutory and administrative changes fall into three general categories: 1) advancing royalty reforms, 2) encouraging diligent development of oil and gas leases, and 3) improving revenue collection processes. Royalty reforms include: evaluating minimum royalty rates for oil, gas, and similar products; adjusting onshore oil and gas royalty rates; analyzing a price-based tiered royalty rate; and repealing legislatively-mandated royalty relief for deep gas wells. Diligent development requirements include shorter primary lease terms, stricter enforcement of lease terms, and monetary incentives to get leases into production. Revenue collection improvements include simplification of the royalty valuation process, elimination of interest accruals on company overpayments of royalties, and permanent repeal of Interior's authority to accept in-kind royalty payments. Collectively, these reforms will generate roughly $2.5 billion in net revenue to the Treasury over ten years, of which about $1.7 billion would result from statutory changes. Many States will also benefit from higher Federal revenue sharing payments.

Helium Sales, Operations and Deposits – The Department will submit a legislative proposal to authorize the Helium Fund to continue activities supporting the sale of helium. Under the Helium Privatization Act of 1996, the Helium Fund is set to expire upon repayment of the helium debt, anticipated to occur the first quarter of 2014. This proposal will allow continued operation of the Helium program while facilitating a gradual exit from the helium market. To minimize impacts to the helium market, the proposal will gradually increase the sales price of helium while reducing the total volume of helium sold each year, until the amount in storage reaches 3 billion standard cubic feet. At that point, the remaining helium will be reserved for Federal users. The proposal would enable the sale of helium and related products and deposits of net proceeds to the Treasury. Additional revenues from this proposal are estimated at $480 million over the decade.

Transboundary Gulf of Mexico Agreement – The 2014 budget includes a legislative proposal to implement the Agreement between the U.S. and the United Mexican States Concerning Transboundary Hydrocarbon Reservoirs in the Gulf of Mexico, signed by representatives of the U.S. and Mexico on February 20, 2012. The Agreement establishes a framework for the cooperative exploration and development of hydrocarbon resources that cross the United States-Mexico maritime boundary in the Gulf of Mexico. The Agreement would also end the moratorium on development along the boundary in the Western Gap in the Gulf. The Agreement provides access to an area along the U.S.-Mexico boundary in the Gulf of Mexico roughly the size of Delaware, for exploration and production activities. The area is estimated to contain up to 172 million barrels of oil and 304 billion cubic feet of natural gas. The budget assumes bonus bid revenues from lease sales in this area will generate an estimated $50 million for the Treasury in 2014.

Return Coal Abandoned Mine Land Reclamation Fees to Historic Levels – The budget proposes legislation to modify the 2006 amendments to the Surface Mining Control and Reclamation Act, which lowered the per-ton coal fee companies pay into the AML Fund. The proposal would return the fees to the levels companies paid prior to the 2006 fee reduction. The additional revenue, estimated at $54 million over ten years, will be used to reclaim high priority abandoned coal mines.

Reallocate NPR-A Revenues to Priority BLM Alaska Activities – The budget proposes to temporarily halt revenue sharing payments to the State of Alaska from NPR-A oil and gas development to reallocate these resources to a new Alaska Land Conveyance and Remediation Fund. This fund would supplement current appropriations and address priority BLM program needs in Alaska, specifically the remediation of oil and gas legacy wells in NPR-A and the completion of remaining land title conveyances to the State of Alaska, individual Alaska Natives, and Alaska Native Corporations. The regular 50/50 Federal-State revenue sharing arrangement would resume once the work on these two Alaska-specific activities is complete. This approach of temporarily suspending revenue sharing payments is similar to the approach taken by Congress to address priority site remediation needs in the Naval Oil Shale Reserve No. 3 located in the State of Colorado.

Discontinue AML Payments to Certified States – The budget proposes to discontinue the unrestricted payments to States and Tribes certified for completing their coal reclamation work. These payments can be used for general purposes and no longer contribute to abandoned coal mine lands reclamation. While the Surface Transportation Extension Act of 2012 capped annual payments to each certified State and Tribe at $15.0 million, this proposal terminates all such payments, with estimated savings of approximately $327 million over the next ten years.

Reclamation of Abandoned Hardrock Mines – To address the legacy of abandoned hardrock mines across the U.S. and hold the hardrock mining industry accountable for past mining practices, the Department will propose legislation to create a parallel Abandoned Mine Lands Program for abandoned hardrock sites. The program would be financed through the imposition of a new AML fee on hardrock production on both public and private lands. The BLM will distribute the funds through a set allocation to reclaim the highest priority hardrock abandoned sites on Federal, State, tribal, and private lands. Additional revenue is estimated at $1.8 billion for the 2014-2023 period, while outlays for reclamation projects, which lag behind collections, are estimated at $1.3 billion over the same period.

Reform Hardrock Mining on Federal Lands – Interior will submit a legislative proposal to provide a fair return to the taxpayer from hardrock production on Federal lands. The legislative proposal will institute a leasing program under the Mineral Leasing Act of 1920 for certain hardrock minerals including gold, silver, lead, zinc, copper, uranium, and molybdenum, currently covered by the General Mining Law of 1872. After enactment, mining for these metals on Federal lands will be governed by the new leasing process and subject to annual rental payments and a royalty of not less than five percent of gross proceeds. Half of the receipts will be distributed to the States in which the leases are located and the remaining half will be deposited in the Treasury. Existing mining claims will be exempt from the change to a leasing system, but will be subject to increases in the annual maintenance fees under the General Mining Law of 1872. Holders of existing mining claims for these minerals could, however, voluntarily convert claims to leases. The Office of Natural Resources Revenue will collect, account for, and disburse the hardrock royalty receipts. The proposal is projected to generate revenues to the U.S. Treasury of $80 million over ten years, with larger revenues estimated in following years.

Net Receipts Sharing for Energy Minerals – The Department proposes to make permanent the current arrangement for sharing the cost to administer energy and minerals receipts. Under current law, States receiving significant payments from mineral revenue development on Federal lands also share in the costs of administering the Federal mineral leases from which the revenue is generated. In 2014, this net receipts sharing deduction from mineral revenue payments to States will be implemented as an offset to the Interior Appropriations Act, consistent with the provision included since 2010. Permanent implementation of net receipts sharing is expected to result in savings of $44 million in 2015 and $421 million over ten years.

Geothermal Energy Receipts – The Department proposes to repeal Section 224(b) of the Energy Policy Act of 2005. Prior to passage of this legislation, geothermal revenues were split between the Federal government and States, with 50 percent directed to States, and 50 percent to the Treasury. The Energy Policy Act of 2005 changed this distribution beginning in 2006 to direct 50 percent to States, 25 percent to counties, and for a period of five years,

25 percent to a new BLM Geothermal Steam Act Implementation Fund. The allocations to the new BLM geothermal fund were discontinued a year early through a provision in the 2010 Interior Appropriations Act. The repeal of Section 224(b) will permanently discontinue payments to counties and restore the disposition of Federal geothermal leasing revenues to the historical formula of 50 percent to the States and 50 percent to the Treasury. This results in savings of $4 million in 2014 and $48 million over ten years.

Federal Land Transaction Facilitation Act – The Department proposes to reauthorize this Act that expired on July 25, 2011, and allow Federal lands identified as suitable for disposal in recent land use plans to be sold using this authority. The sales revenues would continue to fund the acquisition of environmentally sensitive lands and administrative costs associated with conducting the sales.

Federal Migratory Bird Hunting and Conservation Stamps – Federal Migratory Bird Hunting and Conservation Stamps, commonly known as Duck Stamps, were originally created in 1934 as the annual Federal license required for hunting migratory waterfowl. Today, 98 percent of the receipts generated from the sale of these $15.00 stamps are used to acquire important migratory bird areas for migration, breeding, and wintering. The price of the Duck Stamp has not increased since 1991, while the cost of land and water has increased significantly. The Department proposes legislation to increase these fees to $25.00 per stamp per year, beginning in 2014. Increasing the cost of Duck Stamps will bring the estimate for the Migratory Bird Conservation account to $61 million. With these increased receipts, the Department anticipates additional acquisition of an estimated 7,000 acres in fee and an estimated 10,000 acres in conservation easement in 2014. Total acres acquired for 2014 will then be estimated at 28,000 in fee title and 47,000 in perpetual conservation easements.

Bureau of Land Management Foundation – The budget proposes legislation to establish a congressionally-chartered National BLM Foundation. This Foundation will provide an opportunity to leverage private funding to support public lands, achieve shared outcomes, and focus public support on the BLM mission. The Foundation will be established as a charitable, non-profit organization to benefit the public by protecting and restoring the BLM's natural, cultural, historical, and recreational resources for future generations. The National BLM Foundation would be similar to other existing foundations which benefit Federal programs, including the National Park Foundation, the National Fish and Wildlife Foundation, and the National Forest Foundation.

Recreation Fee Program – The Department of the Interior proposes to permanently authorize the Federal Lands Recreation Enhancement Act, which expires in December 2014. The Department currently collects over $200 million in recreation fees annually under this authority and uses them to enhance the visitor experience at Interior facilities. In addition, the Department will propose a general provision in the 2014 budget request to amend appropriations language to extend the authority through 2015.

OFFSETTING COLLECTIONS AND FEES

The budget includes the following proposals to collect or increase various fees, so industry shares some of the cost of Federal permitting and regulatory oversight.

Fee Increase for Offshore Oil and Gas Inspections
Through appropriations language, the Department proposes to increase inspection fees to $65.0 million in 2014 for offshore oil and gas drilling facilities subject to inspection by the Bureau of Safety and Environmental Enforcement. These fees will support BSEE's expanded inspection program to increase production accountability, human safety, and environmental protection.

New Fee for Onshore Oil and Gas Inspections
Through appropriations language, the Department proposes to implement an inspection fee in 2014 for onshore oil and gas activities subject to inspection by BLM. The proposed inspection fee is expected to generate $48.0 million in 2014, $10.0 million more than the corresponding $38.0 million reduction in requested appropriations for BLM, thereby expanding the capacity of BLM's oil and gas inspection program. The fee is similar to those already in place for offshore operations and will support Federal efforts to increase production accountability, human safety, and environmental protection.

Onshore Oil and Gas Drilling Permit Fee – The 2014 budget proposes to continue a fee for processing drilling permits through appropriations language, an approach taken by Congress in the 2009 and subsequent Interior Appropriations Acts. A fee of $6,500 per drilling permit was authorized in 2010, and if continued, will generate an estimated $32.5 million in offsetting collections in 2014.

Surface Mining and Reclamation Permit Fee – The 2014 budget continues an offsetting collection initiated in 2012, allowing the Office of Surface Mining Reclamation and Enforcement, to retain coal mine permit application and renewal fees for the work performed as a service to the coal industry. The fee will help ensure the efficient processing, review, and enforcement of the permits issued, while recovering some of the regulatory operating costs from the industry benefitting from this service. The fee, authorized by section 507 of SMCRA, will apply to mining permits on lands where regulatory jurisdiction has not been delegated to the States. The permit fee will generate $2.4 million in offsetting collections in 2014.

Grazing Administrative Fee – The 2014 budget proposes a new grazing administrative fee of $1 per animal unit month. The BLM proposes to implement this fee through appropriations language on a three-year pilot basis. The 2014 budget estimates the fee will generate $6.5 million in 2014, which will assist BLM in processing grazing permits. During the period of the pilot, BLM will work through the process of promulgating regulations for the continuation of the grazing fee as a cost recovery fee after the pilot expires.

Marine Minerals Administrative Fee – The 2014 budget proposes to establish an offsetting fee in the BOEM Marine Minerals program to recover costs associated with processing offshore sand and gravel mining permits. The fees are estimated to generate $470,000 in revenue in 2014, to offset the cost of the program, and would be implemented through existing regulatory authority under the Outer Continental Shelf Lands Act.

DEPARTMENT OF THE INTERIOR
FACTS

Land — Interior manages more than 500 million acres or about 20 percent of the land area of the United States, 700 million acres of subsurface minerals, and 53 million acres of submerged land in four Pacific marine national monuments. The Department has jurisdiction over an additional 1.7 billion acres of the Outer Continental Shelf.

Parks, Refuges, and Public Lands — Interior manages 401 units of the national park system, 561 national wildlife refuges, 72 fish hatcheries, and one historic fish hatchery as well as 21 national conservation areas and similarly designated areas, and 19 national monuments in BLM's National Landscape Conservation System.

People — Interior has about 70,000 employees located in approximately 2,400 locations across the United States, Puerto Rico, U.S. Territories, and Freely Associated States.

Volunteers — Interior benefits from approximately 332,000 volunteers who provide almost 9.6 million hours of service, valued at $209 million per year.

Conservation — About 322,000 acres of high-priority abandoned coal mine sites have been reclaimed through the OSM's Abandoned Mine Lands program. The FWS acts to protect over 2,055 endangered and threatened species; 1,143 are in the United States.

Revenues — Interior collects revenues from energy, minerals, grazing, timber, lands sales, and other revenue producing activities. Interior's estimated revenue projections in 2014 are $14.0 billion.

Water — The Department is the largest supplier and manager of water in the 17 western States. Reclamation manages 476 dams and 337 reservoirs that deliver irrigation water to 31 million people and one out of every five western farmers irrigating 10 million acres of farmland.

Energy — Interior manages lands, subsurface rights, and offshore areas that produce approximately 23 percent of the Nation's energy, including 18 percent of natural gas, 28 percent of oil, and 44 percent of coal. Federal lands also host projects that account for a significant portion of the Nation's renewable energy generating capacity for hydropower (17 percent), windpower (one percent), and geothermal energy (36 percent). Interior has approved solar energy projects totaling 54 percent of the Nation's installed solar energy capacity.

Visitation — Annually, more than 59 million visits are made to BLM public lands, nearly 287 million visits to national park units, more than 47 million visits to national wildlife refuges and fish hatcheries, and 90 million visits to Reclamation recreation sites.

American Indians — The Department maintains relationships with 566 federally recognized Tribes in the lower 48 States and Alaska, and provides support to a service population of more than 1.7 million people. The BIE provides education services to approximately 41,000 students in 23 States attending 183 elementary and secondary schools and dormitories and supports 31 BIE-funded community colleges, universities, and post-secondary schools. There are 85 BIA-funded corrections programs and 187 bureau and tribal law enforcement programs.

American Indian Trust — Interior has responsibility for the largest land trust in the world. Today, the Indian trust encompasses approximately 55 million surface acres and 57 million acres of subsurface mineral estates. On these lands, Interior manages over 119,000 leases for uses such as farming, grazing, and oil and gas production on behalf of individual Indians and Tribes. The Office of the Special Trustee manages nearly $4.4 billion of trust funds held in over 3,000 trust accounts for more than 250 Indian Tribes, and over 387,000 open Individual Indian Monies accounts.

Science – Interior provides unbiased, multi-discipline science for use in understanding, managing, and protecting the landscape, natural resources, and natural hazards. Data is available to the public from over 8,000 streamgages and 2,500 earthquake sensors. Over ten million satellite scenes have been downloaded from the Landsat archives since being made available at no cost in 2008 with three million downloaded in 2012 alone. Over 61,000 publications dating back to 1882 are available through the USGS publishing warehouse.

DEPARTMENTAL HIGHLIGHTS

America's Great Outdoors

From restoring national treasures like the Everglades and the Great Lakes to connecting young people with recreational activities, the Administration has pursued a 21ˢᵗ century conservation agenda that builds healthy communities, grows our economy, and safeguards our most cherished natural resources.

Nancy Sutley, Chair
Council on Environmental Quality
December 4, 2012

Throughout American history, the great outdoors have shaped the Nation's character and strengthened its economy. In the increasingly urbanized and plugged-in society of the 21ˢᵗ Century, the threat of a diminished connection between people and the outdoors has never been greater. President Obama launched the America's Great Outdoors initiative in April 2010 to address this challenge, charging his Cabinet, through the leadership of the Secretaries of the Interior and Agriculture, the Administrator of the Environmental Protection Agency, the Assistant Secretary of the Army for Civil Works, and the Chair of the White House Council on Environmental Quality, with developing a 21ˢᵗ Century conservation agenda. These leaders turned first to the American people to learn which conservation and outdoor recreation issues mattered most. Through over 105,000 written comments and in 51 listening sessions in cities and communities across the Country, Americans collectively expressed they care deeply about enjoying a shared outdoor heritage, and they have a vibrant vision of how best to protect it.

Led by this public dialogue, the Department of the Interior in partnership with other Federal agencies developed an action plan to implement the initiative. Together with farmers, ranchers, outdoor enthusiasts, hunters, anglers, business leaders, Tribes, States, and local governments, Interior is connecting Americans to the outdoors and expanding access; establishing and revitalizing great urban parks and community green spaces; conserving and restoring large landscapes and working lands and waters; and enhancing rivers.

There are few gifts we can give our children and grandchildren that are more important than conserving our Nation's natural, historic and cultural heritage, and providing ample opportunities for them to experience it first-hand. Working hand in hand with communities through the America's Great Outdoors initiative, we have undertaken and completed countless projects to promote conservation efforts, provide more outdoor recreational opportunities, and support economic growth and job creation. I know that, together, we can continue to add to this impressive list of accomplishments in the coming years.

Ken Salazar, Secretary of the Interior
December 4, 2012

2014 BUDGET SUMMARY

The 2014 President's budget request maintains the Interior Department's commitment to its stewardship of America's Great Outdoors with a current request of $5.3 billion. In addition to this current request, the Administration will submit a legislative proposal to permanently authorize annual funding, without further appropriation or fiscal year limitation, for the Land and Water Conservation Fund. This will provide an additional $141.0 million for

Interior programs, $88.0 million for Federal land acquisition, and $53.0 million for recreational and conservation grants. Together with the current request, a total increase of $320.8 million will be provided compared to the 2012 enacted level.

Funding in support of the AGO initiative is focused in four areas: land management operations including youth programs; programs funded through the Land

AMERICA'S GREAT OUTDOORS
(dollars in millions)

	2012 Enacted	2014 Current Request	2014 Permanent Request	2014 Total
LAND MANAGEMENT OPERATIONS				
Bureau of Land Management	1,072.2	1,095.8	0.0	1,095.8
Fish and Wildlife Service	1,226.2	1,295.1	0.0	1,295.1
National Park Service	2,236.6	2,284.9	0.0	2,284.9
Subtotal, Land Mgmt Operations	**4,535.0**	**4,675.8**	**0.0**	**4,675.8**
LAND AND WATER CONSERVATION FUND PROGRAMS				
Federal Land Acquisition	146.6	176.0	88.0	264.0
State Grants	44.9	40.0	20.0	60.0
Urban Parks and Recreation Recovery Grants..	0.0	10.0	5.0	15.0
Cooperative Endangered Species Conservation Fund*	25.0	56.0	28.0	84.0
Subtotal, LWCF Programs	**216.5**	**282.0**	**141.0**	**423.0**
OTHER GRANT PROGRAMS				
Partnership Program	100.6	104.5	0.0	104.5
Rivers, Trails, Conservation Assistance	9.9	10.1	0.0	10.1
Historic Preservation and Battlefield Grants	57.3	60.3	0.0	60.3
Subtotal, Other Grant Programs	**167.8**	**174.9**	**0.0**	**174.9**
RECLAMATION RIVER RESTORATION	**153.8**	**120.2**	**0.0**	**120.2**
TOTAL, AMERICA'S GREAT OUTDOORS	**5,073.1**	**5,252.9**	**141.0**	**5,393.9**

* In 2012, $25.0 million was appropriated by Congress from the LWCF. The total appropriation for the program was $47.7 million. The 2014 budget proposes to fund all of the CESCF from the LWCF.

and Water Conservation Fund, including Federal land acquisition and recreation and conservation grant programs in the Fish and Wildlife Service and National Park Service; historic preservation as well as technical assistance programs that promote conservation and improve recreational access, particularly in urban areas; and Reclamation's river restoration activities conducted in collaboration with local and basin-wide watershed partnerships.

Land management operations will receive $4.7 billion, an increase of $140.8 million compared to 2012. This request provides $1.1 billion to the Bureau of Land Management, $1.3 billion to FWS, and $2.3 billion to NPS for operations.

The budget includes a total current request of $400.0 million for LWCF programs that conserve lands and support outdoor recreation within Interior and the U.S. Department of Agriculture's Forest Service. Of this amount, Interior LWCF programs will receive $282.0 million, a total increase of $65.5 million compared to the 2012 enacted level. This includes $176.0 million for Federal land acquisition, $56.0 million for FWS Cooperative Endangered Species Conservation Fund grants, $40.0 million for NPS State Assistance grants, and $10.0 million for NPS Urban Parks and Recreation Recovery grants. With the permanent proposal, this is increased to $264.0 million for Federal land acquisition, $84.0 million for FWS CESCF grants, $60.0 million for NPS State Assistance grants, and $15.0 million for NPS UPARR grants.

Other assistance programs will receive an increase of $7.1 million for a total of $174.9 million: $104.5 million for FWS conservation grants, $60.3 million for NPS historic preservation grants, and $10.1 million for NPS Rivers, Trails, and Conservation Assistance.

Reclamation river restoration projects are funded at $120.2 million, a decrease of $33.6 million compared to 2012 and an increase of $10.7 above the 2013 Continuing Resolution, P.L. 112-175 annualized. This reduction is primarily due to the completion of the Red Bluff Fish Passage Improvement Project.

CONNECTING AMERICANS TO THE GREAT OUTDOORS

America's national parks, monuments, wildlife refuges, and national conservation areas and other outdoor spaces are treasured for their beauty, the recreational opportunities they provide, and for their value to our culture and history. Spending time in the outdoors provides Americans with many ways to stay active, allowing people to improve their physical and mental health, have fun and engage in new experiences, while experiencing the importance of conservation. The AGO initiative is increasing opportunities throughout the Country for Americans to connect to the great outdoors. Interior-managed Federal lands and waters offer millions of visitors wide-ranging opportunities to make a personal connection to the outdoors by providing a vast array of trails, roads, and facilities that support and promote a broad range of educational, recreational, and tourism opportunities. Interior is working to better inform the public about national recreational opportunities and make public lands, particularly urban lands and waters, more accessible to visitors. Additionally, engaging young people in conservation and outdoor recreation through employment, education, and volunteer activities continues to be a focal point of AGO that will cultivate a new generation of stewards to protect outdoor places.

In addition to its recreational, cultural, and historic value, America's outdoors provide vital jobs and economic benefits to communities across the Country. In 2012, the Outdoor Industry Association reported that, nationwide, recreation activities including hunting, camping, biking, and boating resulted in $646 billion in outdoor recreation spending each year, which in turn supported 6.1 million jobs. Much of this is spent in Interior's 401 national park units, 561 national wildlife refuges, and BLM's 21 national conservation areas and similarly designated areas, and 19 national monuments. Looking at data specific to Interior, across all sectors its activities contributed $384.8 billion to the Nation's economy and supported an estimated 2.4 million jobs. Of this impact, recreation and tourism contributed $48.7 billion and supported nearly 403,000 jobs.

The 2014 budget includes $4.7 billion to fund the operations that conserve and maintain these public lands, 41 percent of the Department's 2014 budget request, and an increase of $140.8 million over 2012 enacted. The following sections highlight the operational budget for each land management bureau in 2014.

LAND MANAGEMENT OPERATIONS

In 2014, the budget features program increases in the application of science on public lands. Across Interior, the budget includes an increase of $143.6 million for research and development, of which $45.4 million is funded within the three land management agencies and Reclamation. As a result of these investments, Interior will be able to address critical challenges in energy production and the management of ecosystems, invasive species, public lands, and water.

Specific examples of science increases, including those not identified in the government-wide summary of research and development, include a $21.1 million increase for invasive species control on Interior lands and waters, such as providing additional funds to control quagga and zebra mussels in parks in the West. The spread of quagga mussels to Lake Mead and Lake Mohave alone will potentially cost millions of dollars by clogging engines and encrusting boats and facility infrastructure, disrupting the food chain, reducing sport fishing, and littering beaches with shell debris. Preventing the further spread of invasive species such as these is a high priority for Federal, State, local, and tribal governments, as well as private landowners and companies.

The budget requests $4.5 million for the three land management bureaus and Reclamation to fund interagency AGO projects that demonstrate ecosystem and landscape-scale conservation in the Southwest Deserts, Crown of the Continent, and Grasslands of the Northern Great Plains landscapes. This increase supports an Administration initiative to establish regional interagency landscape conservation teams. These landscapes serve as demonstration sites and models for aligning, targeting, and better leveraging Federal resources to achieve more strategic landscape conservation outcomes. This increase will support coordinated research to enhance the models used to guide ecosystem restoration and improve ecosystem services while tackling such issues as invasive plants and species restoration. Coordinating efforts in these ecosystems will greatly contribute to species and habitat preservation in these areas.

Another example of the Administration's landscape-scale conservation efforts are the multi-agency efforts in support of Everglades restoration. Eliminating barriers to overland flow of water in the Everglades is one of the indisputable tenets of restoration; simply providing a particular volume of water to these wetlands will not attain restoration. Flows must mimic the natural water depths and flooding durations, be distributed across this landscape in a manner that best approximates historical flow patterns, and travel at sufficient speed to maintain the characteristic Everglades landscape, which is composed of dense sawgrass ridges next to broad sloughs. Only when all of these conditions are met will the natural system respond in a manner that will promote marsh conditions capable of supporting the unique flora and fauna of the Everglades.

United States Highway 41, the Tamiami Trail, has long been recognized as one of the primary barriers to flow of water through the ecosystem. The Modified Water Deliveries project provides modifications to Tamiami Trail through a one-mile bridging component, which will begin restoring more natural flow, but is insufficient to achieve restoration.

In 2010, NPS evaluated the feasibility of additional bridging for the Tamiami Trail in order to achieve more natural water flow and habitat restoration within the Everglades. In response to the NPS evaluation, Congress authorized NPS to implement this additional bridging, consistent with the feasibility study. The 2014 budget proposes that NPS make a one-time contribution of $30.0 million within its construction account to leverage funds from other sources to cover the remaining costs for the highest priority bridging component. The 2.6 miles of bridging is located at the deepest portion of Shark Valley Slough, an intermittent grass riverway that historically carried the largest volume of water into the Everglades National Park.

In 2014 Interior will continue its focus on engaging youth and young adults in land stewardship, recreation, and conservation. This initiative strives to employ, educate, and engage young people from all backgrounds to explore, connect with and preserve America's natural and cultural heritage. Secretary Salazar established youth employment as a Goal within the Department.

Bureau of Land Management – The 2014 BLM budget request for land management operations is $1.1 billion, a total increase of $23.5 million above the 2012 enacted level.

PROTECTING BATS FROM WHITE-NOSE SYNDROME

The white-nose syndrome is a disease responsible for unprecedented mortality for at least six ecologically and economically important species of bats in 22 U.S. eastern States and five Canadian provinces. Mortality from the disease at many sites reaches 95 percent. Named for the visible white fungus around the muzzles, ears, and wings of affected bats, this disease is caused by a previously unknown species of fungus Geomyces destructans that thrives in places of low temperature and high humidity such as caves where bats hibernate. While there is no evidence that G. destructans is pathogenic to humans, human activity can quickly spread this disease among bat populations.

Recent scientific research indicates that white-nose syndrome can easily expand its current range to affect bat populations throughout the Country.

Bats play an important role in North American ecosystems by consuming large amounts of insect populations. Bats also reproduce slowly; most species have only one pup per year. A reduction in bat populations could lead to increased numbers of insect pests resulting in damage to forests and agriculture, higher loads of environmental pesticides, and increased public health risks associated with diseases transmitted by insects.

The Fish and Wildlife Service, U.S. Geological Survey, National Park Service, and other Federal agencies have been working together with their tribal, provincial, State, and private sector partners to address this critical issue. In 2011, a national white-nose syndrome plan was published to mount a coordinated response. This plan outlines seven key elements: communications, data and technical information management, diagnostics, disease management, epidemiological and ecological research, disease surveillance, and conservation and recovery.

Scientists have increased their understanding of this new disease, but significant knowledge gaps remain. Current responses are focused on containing infestations through public education, restrictions on cave use, and implementing prevention and sanitation practices. There are no known treatments for white-nose syndrome. Populations that are free of the disease must be protected.

In 2014, an increase of $3.5 million for FWS and NPS will increase prevention and containment strategies. An increase of $1.5 million for USGS will enhance surveillance and diagnostic detection as well as develop management tools and a vaccine.

White-nose syndrome in bats, first documented in the winter of 2006-2007, has spread rapidly across the eastern United States and Canada, and has killed millions of bats in eastern North America. The fungus that causes the disease has been detected as far west as Oklahoma.

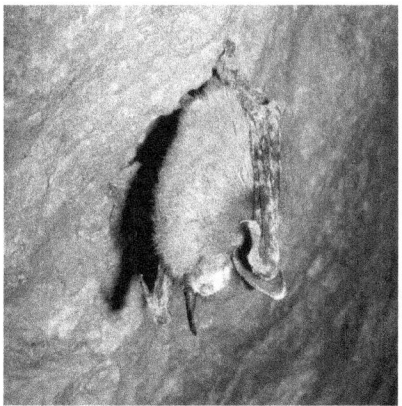

The 2014 BLM budget request includes important funding increases to help advance key goals of the President's AGO initiative. The request includes $8.0 million in programmatic increases to enhance BLM's recreation management program and operations in its National Landscape Conservation System. This includes a $2.0 million program increase in the Recreation Resources Management program for science support to improve recreation management practices and policies. A $6.0 million program increase in the National Monuments and National Conservation Areas program will allow BLM to strengthen law enforcement, enhance visitor safety and experiences, increase habitat conservation and restoration, and expand interpretation programs and products. These investments enhance and improve recreational access and opportunities, raise awareness of the value and benefits of AGO, and conserve and restore valuable natural and cultural resources.

The 2014 budget request also includes an increase of $1.1 million for BLM to participate in inter-agency AGO projects to demonstrate ecosystem and landscape-scale conservation. The BLM will collaborate with other AGO partners to advance community-based landscape-scale conservation in the Southwest Deserts, Crown of the Continent, and the Grasslands of the Northern Great Plains landscapes. In the Southwest Desert landscapes, the BLM will focus on restoring the Aravaipa Creek watershed and improve wildlife habitat values along the borderlands in southwestern New Mexico. For the Crown of the Continent landscape, BLM will support the work of the Crown Management Partnership to control invasive weeds. In the Grasslands of the Northern Great Plains landscape, BLM will work with partners to initiate projects to improve wildlife habitat, such as crested wheatgrass fields, to improve habitat for greater sage grouse, pronghorn antelope, and imperiled grassland birds.

YOUTH IN THE GREAT OUTDOORS

The Department of the Interior manages America's backyard, making sure that it is available for all young people to enjoy. The Youth in the Great Outdoors Initiative employs, educates, and engages young people from all backgrounds in exploring, connecting with, and preserving America's natural and cultural heritage. In 2014, Interior will continue its focus on engaging youth and young adults in land stewardship, recreation, and conservation. The budget requests an increase of $12.6 million across the Department for the Youth in the Great Outdoors initiative.

Through employment and educational opportunities offered by the Department, youth has a key role in creating a new energy frontier, tackling climate change issues, empowering Native communities, building trails, enhancing wildlife habitat, and restoring cultural and historic landmarks. As stewards of the Nation's lands, waters, cultural heritage, and tribal customs, Interior has a unique opportunity to reach out to under served populations to ensure these natural and cultural resources are enjoyed by all Americans. By investing in youth today, Interior can transform the lives of millions of young Americans while growing the next generation of conservation and community leaders.

YOUTH IN THE GREAT OUTDOORS
(dollars in millions)

	2012 Enacted	2014 Request	Change
Bureau of Land Management	8.6	11.4	+2.8
Bureau of Reclamation	3.8	3.8	0.0
U.S. Geological Service	2.2	3.2	+1.0
Fish and Wildlife Service	13.5	15.9	+2.4
National Park Service	13.6	14.7	+1.0
Indian Affairs	0.0	5.5	+5.5
TOTAL, DEPARTMENT OF INTERIOR	41.8	54.4	+12.6
[Recreational Fee Program]	[6.4]	[6.4]	[0]

The BLM will use a $1.0 million increase in Administrative Support to fund the start up costs for a new congressionally-chartered charitable, non-profit foundation. A legislative proposal to establish the National BLM Foundation is being submitted with the President's budget. The Foundation will help leverage private funding to support and supplement BLM management of public lands.

Fish and Wildlife Service – The 2014 budget request for the Resource Management account is $1.3 billion, a total increase of $68.9 million above the 2012 level. The budget request continues to advance key goals of the AGO initiative. The national wildlife refuge system has unique authorities and flexible programs that deliver landscape level conservation while at the same time providing outdoor recreation, hunting and fishing opportunities, and protecting wildlife populations. Annually, more than 47 million visitors come to refuges to hunt, fish, observe and photograph wildlife, and participate in environmental education and interpretive programs. The FWS operations generate nearly $4.2 billion in economic activity and create more than 34,000 private sector jobs nationwide. Millions of acres of refuge lands are owned outright and managed wholly by FWS to restore and protect habitat for fish and wildlife for the enjoyment of the American people.

The 2014 budget includes increases for the refuge system totaling $13.5 million above 2012 to enhance cooperative efforts to conserve wildlife and habitat. The refuges will use cost-sharing partnerships and other collaborations to support the recovery of species facing extinction while improving habitat for thousands of plants and animals. Partnerships have been instrumental to the success of the refuge system since its creation by President Theodore Roosevelt in 1903. In 2012, partnerships were critical to establishing the Nation's 556th refuge, the Everglades Headwaters National Wildlife Refuge and Conservation Area in Florida. The new refuge will eventually span 150,000 acres, help restore the flow of freshwater into the Everglades, and conserve habitat for charismatic species like the Florida panther.

The 2014 budget includes $9.4 million for a cross-programmatic partnership approach to complete planning, restoration, and management actions addressing current threats to endangered species on and around wildlife refuges. The Cooperative Recovery initiative works across FWS to better leverage and coordinate efforts to implement recovery actions more broadly to improve, recover, and ultimately remove species from the threatened and endangered species list. With nearly 300 listed species located in or around units of the refuge system, the ecosystems surrounding them provide important habitat for listed species and can provide essential connectivity for species conservation. The focus will be on implementing recovery actions for species near delisting, reclassifying species from endangered to threatened, or undertaking immediate actions that are needed for critically endangered species. The Endangered Species program will work with other FWS programs to identify, fund, and implement high-priority recovery projects, which will benefit multiple facets of its mission.

The FWS will administer funds to support a landscape level conservation approach to river systems throughout the Country under the Administration's National Blueways System. Rivers play a vital role in connecting Americans with the lands and waters that provide economic, recreational, social, cultural, and ecological value to their communities. The National Blueways System will provide a new emphasis on the unique value and significance of a locally-led headwaters to mouth approach to river management and create a mechanism to encourage stakeholders to integrate their land and water stewardship efforts. The budget request includes an increase of $3.3 million for the Cooperative Watershed Management program, an Administration-wide, collaborative program. For ease of administration, the new funding is requested in the FWS budget, however, Blueways projects will be selected through a multi-agency, joint decisionmaking process and will support conservation and outdoor recreation efforts to advance watershed stewardship. Also included for the refuge system is a program increase of $3.6 million for Challenge Cost Share projects to implement habitat restoration projects with local partners and volunteer groups. These funds will be used by refuges to conduct projects, small in cost, but with a big impact to improve habitat for wildlife use and remove barriers to species recovery.

The budget includes an increase of $16.6 million to develop scientific data to support landscape level conservation. Based on the latest science available, FWS will implement on-the-ground applications of scientific findings to address resource management challenges to develop successful wildlife and habitat management protocols. Information derived from inventory and monitoring efforts on wildlife refuges will help to establish baselines and determine the status and trends of fish, wildlife, and plants. Research funds will also be used to answer imminent and important natural resource management questions and provide near-term solutions to urgent and emerging issues such as the white-nose syndrome devastating bat populations across the Country. To effectively deliver its mission, FWS needs focused, applied science directed at high impact threats to natural resources to manage species to healthy and sustainable levels. The budget includes an increase of $1.5 million to address and mitigate the threats posed by white-nose syndrome. An additional $1.4 million is requested to research the impacts and identify mitigation strategies related to energy transmission corridors in the American West. This research will identify impacts to sage grouse and desert tortoise from foundational energy infrastructure such as overhead transmission lines and solar arrays.

The 2014 budget request continues support for visitor services at the 2012 level, to provide an essential connection for people to the great outdoors. Visitors will continue to enjoy premier outdoor recreation opportunities, such as fishing and wildlife photography, prevalent as a result of ongoing science-based wildlife and habitat management. The refuge system is among the Nation's treasures and its interpretive and environmental education programs provide visitors a deeper understanding of their natural surroundings and the role of the refuge system in landscape level conservation.

The FWS continues its effort to implement the important provisions of the Lacey Act. As the Nation's first Federal wildlife protection law, the Lacey Act remains an important tool in supporting conservation through reducing the importation and interstate transfer of injurious or illegal plants and animals. The request includes a program increase of $4.2 million for enforcement of the Lacey Act, to address technical challenges in wildlife science forensics, and support partnerships with foreign governments to reduce demand for illegal wildlife products.

National Park Service – The 2014 NPS budget request for operations is $2.3 billion, a total increase of $48.4 million above the 2012 enacted level. The 2014 request for operations funds fixed costs of $28.9 million and $40.0 million in program increases for NPS operations. These increases are partially offset with $20.6 million in program reductions to park operations and related programs. With these funds, NPS conserves and interprets resources as breathtaking as Grand Canyon National Park, thought provoking as the Manassas National Battlefield Park, and uplifting as the Brown v. Board of Education National Historic Site. The NPS shared the stories

and breathtaking beauty of these sites with nearly 287 million visitors in 2012. These visitors, in turn, provide economic benefits to local communities and the Nation as a whole. A recent study, prepared by Michigan State University, found that visitors to national parks generated $30.1 billion in economic activity, and supported an estimated 252,000 jobs nationwide.

In 2014, NPS will continue to engage visitors in the great outdoors and protect and interpret cultural and natural resources. Highlights of the 2014 budget request include program increases that will enhance critical resource stewardship activities, including an additional $5.2 million to control exotic and invasive species such as zebra and quagga mussels and $6.0 million for Cooperative Landscape Conservation, for a total request of $8.9 million. This Cooperative Landscape Conservation increase includes $5.0 million for climate change adaptive management tools and $1.0 million as part of a multi-bureau focus on biological carbon sequestration. The budget also provides a $2.0 million increase to the Repair and Rehabilitation program, for projects that improve the accessibility of NPS infrastructure, and that lead to greater water and energy efficiency at park units. A separate increase of $920,000 will provide additional educational and informational opportunities for visitors with visual or hearing impairments by creating accessible interpretive exhibits. The budget also proposes a $1.0 million increase to engage youth in the great outdoors through a combination of additional employment and educational opportunities. Other emerging management needs addressed in the 2014 budget include a $2.0 million program increase to enhance internal controls and improve accountability throughout the park system, and a $2.1 million program increase to fund operational

needs at new or recently expanded national park units such as César E. Chávez National Memorial, which was established in October 2012 to recognize the leadership of a man who brought sustained international attention to the plight of U.S. farm workers, and secured for them higher wages and safer working conditions through the establishment of the Country's first permanent agricultural union.

Spurring Growth and Innovation through Science

The 2014 budget for the Department of the Interior provides strong support for basic and applied science that addresses Interior's mission priorities, including $963.1 million for research and development, a 17.5 percent increase over the 2012 enacted level. This funding supports scientific monitoring, research, and analysis to assist decisionmaking in resource management and the special trust responsibilities of Interior and other federally-mandated and nationally significant programs. Investments in science promote economic growth and innovation, ensure American competitiveness in a global market, improve natural hazard preparedness, and improve the knowledge of U.S. strategic mineral supplies and water use and availability. Sustainable stewardship of natural resources requires strong investments in natural sciences research and development.

Science underpins all of Interior's efforts and provides the basis for informed resource management decisions and the protection of life and property. Specific activities supported include energy permitting, ecosystem management, oil spill restoration, Earth observations, such as water and wildlife monitoring, invasive species control, and tribal natural resource management. The budget for research and development includes increases totaling $143.6 million above 2012 enacted, across the Department.

Interior's mission requires a careful balance between development and conservation. The Department works to achieve this balance collaborating closely with its diverse stakeholders and partners to ensure its actions provide the greatest benefit to the American people. Central to this dialogue is scientific information. Research and development play a vital role in delivering Interior's mission and Interior maintains a robust capability in the natural sciences, primarily in USGS. An example of how this expertise is applied is USGS's current work as part of an interagency collaboration investigating the potential effect of hydraulic fracturing on water

quality and inducement of seismic activity, to produce decision-ready information and tools.

The USGS provides exceptional support to Interior bureaus, however USGS alone cannot provide for all of Interior's scientific needs. The USGS and other Interior bureaus must work collaboratively to find the answers needed for important natural resource management questions. Science funding at the bureau and office level allows bureaus and offices to participate more fully in that collaboration, providing required resources to purchase studies, models, and expertise, and to hire scientists to help managers interpret the vast body of knowledge generated by USGS, universities, and other scientific institutions. This science helps answer imminent and important natural resource management questions and provides near-term solutions to address urgent and emerging issues such as the white-nose syndrome in bats.

Interior agencies work collaboratively to bridge gaps in knowledge leveraging the complementary skills and capacity to advance the use of science to support management decisionmaking, ensure independent review of key decisions and science integrity, and adaptively use data to assist States, Tribes, and communities throughout the Nation.

Bureau of Reclamation – Reclamation's mission to manage, develop, and protect water and related resources in an environmentally and economically sound manner requires significant technical and scientific resources. For example, the 2014 budget provides $2.0 million for financial and technical support to the California Bay-Delta Federal Science Task Force. Funding will be used to address science gaps and to respond to issues raised by the National Academy of Sciences relating to FWS and the National Marine Fisheries Service biological opinions for the water operations in the Central Valley. The funds will be used to implement a collaborative science process that includes agencies as well as stakeholders in the development of adaptive management processes to support implementation of and possible revision to existing biological opinions. This collaboration and adaptive management will inform the Integrated Bay-Delta Conservation Plan biological opinion.

Bureau of Indian Affairs – The 2014 budget includes a $24.5 million increase in Natural Resources Management programs for analysis, and technical support activities to support the sustainable management of alternative and conventional energy sources and natural resources such as land, water, oceans, endangered and invasive species, and to support adaptation to a changing climate. An increase of $9.0 million for Cooperative Landscape Conservation will fund a wide array of conservation activities related to the management of Indian trust land and natural resource assets. Of the increase, $7.0 million will provide funding for coordination, technical support, and tools to enable tribal and trust land managers to analyze, evaluate, and participate in landscape-level conservation and management activities, utilize science to more effectively manage resources, and to develop reservation climate adaptation plans. Another $2.0 million of the increase will support the development of a tribal oceans program, including a competitive grant program to enable Tribes with ocean and coastal trust resources or harvest rights to more effectively manage those resources and perform ocean inventory and species vulnerability assessments, identify critical indicator species, establish monitoring protocols, and implement pilot mitigation and recovery projects. These tools are critically important for Tribes that rely on fisheries and other aquatic resources for their food and livelihoods, and ways of life.

In the Pacific Northwest, Tribes are witnessing declining fish returns in the upper reaches of rivers. In 1986 only six spring chinook returned to the White River, putting the viability of the run in question. The Puyallup Tribe has taken action to ensure juvenile spring chinook will find their way to the upper White River each year. The Puyallup Tribe is raising 250,000 spring chinook at their hatchery so they can stock acclimation ponds in the upper White River. The juvenile spring chinook will be fed by the Tribe for eight weeks while they are imprinted on the upper watershed creeks and then released to begin their journey to the ocean. The acclimation pond program has played a large role in the recovery of the spring chinook stock in the White River. Because of diligent hatchery management, the spring chinook population on the White River has slowly increased, with returns now normally in the thousands.

National Park Service – Long-term conservation of the critically endangered Kemp's Ridley sea turtle in relation to the effects of climate change is one facet of the NPS applied research efforts at Padre Island National Seashore, Texas. As the most important nesting beach for the Kemp's Ridley in the U.S. and part of the bi-national U.S.-Mexico Kemp's Ridley Recovery Plan, the NPS has the responsibility for protecting nesting females, nests, and hatchlings at the national seashore. Research at Padre Island focuses on providing park managers with information on the potential erosion of turtle nesting beaches and more frequent tidal inundation of nests associated

with climate change induced sea level rise that will impair progress in the recovery of this high-priority iconic park species. This project provides essential monitoring information on the Kemp's Ridley's use of park beaches and the turtle's reproduction within the park. The Kemp's Ridley is a native reptile to the park's marine waters and efforts to improve sea turtle protection are consistent with the NPS Ocean Park Stewardship Action Plan's strategy to improve the protection of ocean park resources.

Fish and Wildlife Service – Ensuring that the growth of wind power and natural gas and oil drilling is done in a manner that minimizes impacts to wildlife and their habitats requires knowledge about the project impacts to species of concern, including migratory birds, bats, bald and golden eagles, and other birds of prey. The FWS will invest resources in tools, methods, and techniques to improve decisionmaking about siting, designing, monitoring, and operating energy projects in ways that can best reduce mortality and other impacts on wildlife. Resources will be applied to determine the best mitigation methods, manage energy development-related data, determine how to monitor changes to species and habitats as a result of energy developments, and explore landscape-level cumulative effects. For example, FWS will fund development of geospatial information system applications to support risk analyses that will help to predict impacts on eagles relating to wind energy projects. These tools will assist FWS to better assess the effect of the project relative to other previously authorized projects in the local area.

NORTH ATLANTIC LANDSCAPE CONSERVATION COOPERATIVES

Landscape Conservation Cooperatives have, by design, a potentially large and beneficial role guiding strategic investments in conservation, restoration, and infrastructure. The Cooperatives are developing shared science capacity to make better conservation decisions in the face of change, including prioritization of projects to increase resiliency against impacts caused by major storm events, sea-level rise, and other climate-related changes.

These Cooperatives are self-directed, regional collaborations of agencies and organizations that have recognized the importance of working together and utilizing science to design landscapes that can sustain natural and cultural resources. The North Atlantic LCC encompasses the Atlantic seaboard and Atlantic coastal watersheds from Virginia north to Maine and the Atlantic Provinces of Canada and southern Quebec. The partnership includes 13 States plus the District of Columbia, Fish and Wildlife Service, U.S. Geological Survey, National Oceanic and Atmospheric Administration, National Park Service, U.S. Forest Service, Environmental Protection Agency, Canadian Wildlife Service, United South and Eastern Tribes, and several non-governmental organizations. The North Atlantic LCC also coordinates with and integrates the priorities of existing regional partnerships such as the Atlantic Coast Joint Venture, Atlantic Coastal Fish Habitat Partnership, Northeast Association of Fish and Wildlife Agencies, and Mid-Atlantic Regional Council on the Oceans.

These partners and partnerships, working through the North Atlantic LCC, have invested in the development of a number of tools to assess the impacts of various stressors on species, habitats, systems, and ecological functions, such as stream flow. In the wake of Hurricane Sandy, these and other tools will help to guide decisions about actions to improve the resiliency of natural systems and communities. The LCC partners, along with Climate Science Centers, are also developing better projections of future impacts from sea-level rise and intense storms to beaches, marshes, other coastal systems, and the fish and wildlife species using these systems along the Atlantic coast. These projections will support assessments of the likely persistence of systems under various management scenarios as well as the services provided by maintaining them. For example, management actions that increase the persistence of coastal marshes in the face of storms and sea-level rise will maintain the ability of these systems to help protect adjacent communities and infrastructure from coastal flooding and provide habitat to migratory birds and other species that depend on marshes.

The LCCs present an opportunity for Department of the Interior bureaus and other Federal agencies responsible for responding to Hurricane Sandy to work with partners to identify common issues and goals, reduce redundancy, and utilize science to guide strategic investments to help coastal systems and communities recover and be more resilient in the future.

To better understand white-nose syndrome in bats and its movement and distribution across the landscape, the USGS Fort Collins Science Center and FWS have collaborated to develop a data tracking system for information on infected bat specimens. The USGS scientists are working with FWS to develop a single, secure, web-based system to support implementation of common methodologies and protocols across agencies and organizations. This geospatially oriented data management system will track specimens from the point of collection through analysis by centralizing all partner data into a single repository. The data will conform to integrity standards by allowing users to enter, verify, and report their data remotely using a secure internet connection. The white-nose syndrome disease tracking system will provide wildlife managers and researchers with near real-time access to data, which can be used to evaluate seasonality of disease effects, identify distribution patterns through geospatial analyses, and forecast potential risk areas.

Bureau of Ocean Energy Management – The BOEM's Marine Minerals Program manages Outer Continental Shelf sand, gravel, and shell resources. These resources are critical for the long-term success and cost-effectiveness of many shore protection, beach nourishment, and wetlands restoration projects along the Gulf and Atlantic coasts. Investments are needed in this program to ensure adequate capability to protect and improve natural resources and the environment locally, regionally, and nationally. Demands for sand and gravel and other resources from the OCS are constant and require an ongoing set of information about the availability of these resources based on very specific parameters including location on the OCS, texture, size, and color. In order to make scientifically sound decisions about the use and environmental impacts of OCS marine minerals, BOEM must first have an understanding of the marine mineral resources currently on the OCS. To conduct this critical scientific analysis, $1.0 million is requested for comparative, long-term environmental studies to understand seafloor habitat, ecosystem functions, and the resilience of inner shelf sand bodies. These studies will allow BOEM to make informed, environmentally responsible leasing decisions that more consistently align with project timelines.

In the aftermath of Superstorm Sandy that caused massive beach erosion along the east coast, BOEM received an unprecedented number of requests from other Federal agencies, States, and communities for sand and gravel needed to rebuild beaches and construct dunes to improve protection from future storms. The Bureau is improving its ability to respond to coastal disasters and is among the Federal agencies reaching out to States that experienced significant beach and dune damage from the storm. Preliminary assessments suggest the greatest needs for OCS sand resources are in distinct coastal segments in New Jersey, New York, and North Carolina. The BOEM has worked previously with coastal Atlantic States to identify and quantify potential OCS sand resources that could be used for shore protection projects. The MMP has the capability to identify OCS sand resources needed in the Hurricane Sandy recovery efforts. The Bureau will use and supplement as needed existing environmental analyses conducted over the past 20 years to respond quickly to requests for OCS sand resources for beach nourishment projects. In November 2012, the U.S. Army Corps of Engineers, Philadelphia District, asked BOEM to participate in the environmental review of USACE proposal to use OCS borrow areas for the Long Beach Island Storm Damage Reduction Project in central New Jersey. The BOEM has since begun working with USACE in the preparation and review of environmental documents to help support recovery efforts. As Atlantic States rebuild their communities, BOEM will lend the expertise of the MMP to this important recovery effort.

Bureau of Safety and Environmental Enforcement The BSEE will use a requested $2.0 million increase to invest in its Emerging Technologies program to promote safety and environmental compliance of offshore oil and gas activities and investigate new technologies, procedures, and materials for the promotion of safe, pollution-free operations, the prevention of oil pollution, and the improvement of oil spill response and cleanup. The BSEE will contract with universities and other entities with expertise to identify and develop best available standards technology and make this information available to industry to inform energy and mineral operations ranging from the drilling of oil and gas exploration wells in search of new reserves to the removal of platforms and related infrastructure once production operations have ceased. The requested research will help to inform the BSEE regulations, notices to lessees, and industry standards.

Office of Surface Mining Reclamation and Enforcement – After cessation of underground mining, groundwater infiltrates into and fills mine voids. This filling over time creates underground reservoirs or pools that are hydrostatically connected and can cover several square miles of area. Discharges from these pools often have water quality issues that degrade streams and groundwater and cost hundreds of millions of dollars to treat. Treatment must be continued for decades and addresses the symptom and does not resolve the source of degradation. With an increase of $400,000 in 2014, OSM will fund projects to investigate water quality and quantity interaction between adjacent underground mines, mines and surface water systems, and the mines and adjacent aquifers. Improving the reliability of modeling underground mine abandonment is essential to treat water pollution, prevent unchecked discharges or mine pool blowouts, and establish requirements for mining operators to responsibly deal with these types of potential problems before mine closures.

Bureau of Land Management – The Great Basin is facing increasing drought, fire, and invasive species issues, is well-suited for the development of renewable energy, and will soon have the benefit of a rapid ecoregional assessment for climate-related information and science. There is an existing interbureau collaboration regarding sage grouse habitat, and engagement from the Great Basin Landscape Conservation Cooperative, the Northwest and Southwest Climate Science Centers, and NOAA's Regional Integrated Sciences and Assessment program. Aligning Bureau and interagency resources and actions in this region will provide a model for regional climate adaptation coordination that can be exported to the large landscape demonstration areas of the AGO initiative and may inform the eventual expansion of the AGO portfolio. One of the projects BLM is proposing for 2014 is a regional coordination pilot to help integrate and focus interagency and intergovernmental decisions for managing the risks associated with large-scale change agents.

There will be four phases to this project. The first phase will be a compilation and assessment of the different types of planning decisions that are currently being made by the Federal, State, local, and tribal resource management agencies in the region. The second phase will crosswalk these decisions with the national climate adaptation plans that are being developed for fish, wildlife, and plants, and with the national strategies that are being developed to address wildland fire, invasives, and drought. The third phase will be to develop proposals to improve the coordination and integration of regional decisionmaking in four critical areas: 1) identifying

---

HIGHLIGHTING INVASIVE SPECIES INITIATIVES

Invasive species pose one of the greatest threats to the ecological, economic, and cultural integrity of America's landscapes. The Department's management of invasive species cuts across a number of priorities such as climate change adaptation, America's Great Outdoors, ocean policy, the arctic, traditional and alternative energy development, improved information management, and meeting tribal trust responsibilities. The Administration's budget for 2014 recognizes that certain non-native species cause great harm to the economy, environment, and in some cases, to human health directly. These invasive species can be plants, animals or microorganisms. They can displace native plant and animal communities, increase wildfires, damage critical water and power infrastructure, increase the cost of natural resource conservation, and threaten human livelihoods. Invasive species, such as cheat grass, Asian carp, quagga and zebra mussels, and invasive plant and animal pathogens, have altered entire landscapes and harmed Interior lands, waters, and infrastructure. The 2014 budget builds on existing efforts across a number of Interior bureaus to more pro actively address problems caused by invasive species through prevention, management, and research efforts. The Administration proposes targeted budget increases in 2014 for the Bureau of Reclamation, U.S. Geological Survey, Fish and Wildlife Service, and National Park Service that will enhance Interior's response to the serious threat of invasive species.

Invasive species harm fragile ecosystems and degrade public lands and waters in multiple ways. The 2014 budget for the USGS Ecosystems mission area includes an increase of $5.4 million for research on key invasive species and priority ecosystems where the impacts have been significant. The 2014 budget also directs additional funding to address research and monitoring for new and emerging invasive species of national concern. If invasive species can be found before they spread, ecosystem damage and control costs can be greatly reduced or eliminated. In addition, USGS is developing and adapting advanced technologies to enhance its ability to detect and control invasive species.

---

core areas, corridors and potential refugia for fish, wildlife and plant species and priority areas for development, 2) managing the risks associated with catastrophic fire, 3) managing the risks associated with invasive plants and animals, and 4) managing the risks associated with prolonged drought. The fourth phase will include sharing lessons learned with LCC, CSC, and RISA networks.

This project will promote interagency climate change adaptation planning in the Great Basin, and also identify interagency coordination and integration opportunities that are transferable to other regions of the Country and will help the cooperatives strategically focus their investments.

U.S. Geological Survey – The 2014 budget invests in key areas of USGS research to examine contamination of the environment, collect elevation data, and improve understanding about the impacts of energy on wildlife. The USGS research is documenting with increasing frequency that many chemical and microbial constituents not historically considered as contaminants are present in the environment on a global scale. The 2014 budget includes an increase of $2.0 million to study emerging contaminants, commonly derived from municipal, agricultural, and industrial wastewater sources and pathways.

These newly recognized contaminants represent a shift in traditional thinking as many are produced industrially yet are dispersed to the environment from domestic, commercial, and industrial uses. For example, biosolids, sludge from wastewater treatment plants have a very high nutrient value, but are a potential source of pharmaceuticals and other emerging contaminants to the environment. Contaminants may enter the environment through septic tanks, municipal effluent, hospital waste, and poultry, swine, dairy, and cattle operations.

One example of a new contaminant threat is the impact of estrogen on fish in the Shenandoah and Potomac Rivers. The USGS research has determined exposure to estrogen reduces production of immune-related proteins in fish. This suggests certain compounds, known as endocrine disruptors, may make fish more susceptible to disease. This research may provide new clues for why intersex fish, fish kills, and fish lesions often occur together in the Shenandoah and Potomac Rivers. The study revealed largemouth bass injected with estrogen produced lowered levels of hepcidin, an important iron-regulating hormone in mammals also found in fish and amphibians. The research suggests estrogen-mimicking compounds may make fish more susceptible to disease by blocking production of hepcidin and other immune-related proteins that help protect fish against disease-causing bacteria. The USGS researchers have previously found intersex occurring in fish in the Potomac and Shenandoah Rivers. Because other studies have shown estrogen and estrogen-mimicking compounds can cause intersex, the co-occurrence of the fish lesions, fish kills, and intersex in these two rivers suggested to USGS scientists that estrogen-mimicking compounds could be involved in the fish lesions and fish kills in addition to being a possible cause of intersex traits.

The 3-D Elevation Program initiative will systematically collect enhanced elevation data using Light Detection and Ranging and other technologies over the United States during an eight-year period. The 3-D elevation data is important to natural hazard scientists working on the identification of earthquake faults, farmers looking for high resolution elevation data for planting decisions, and emergency response managers as a critical input for estimating flood risks. Based on a 2012 study, there are 602 mission-critical activities of 34 Federal agencies, the 50 States, selected local and tribal governments, and private and other organizations that would benefit from enhanced elevation data for uses, including the State of Alaska, where aviation safety can be improved with more accurate elevation data to navigate through Alaska's many rugged mountains and active volcanoes. The Nation will receive up to $13.0 billion annually in new benefits from enhanced availability of this elevation data.

In the push to develop new forms of sustainable energy, the wind power industry is at the forefront. Recent evidence shows that certain species of bats are particularly susceptible to mortality from wind turbines. Bats are beneficial consumers of harmful insect pests, and migratory species of bats cross

LDCM LAUNCH AND FIRST IMAGES

The National Aeronautics and Space Administration and the Department of the Interior's U.S. Geological Survey released the first images from the Landsat Data Continuity Mission satellite, which was launched February 11, 2013. The satellite's Operational Land Imager and Thermal Infrared Sensor instruments observe each image simultaneously. The USGS Earth Resources Observation and Science Center in Sioux Falls, South Dakota, processes the data. Since launch, LDCM has been going through on-orbit testing. The mission operations team completed its review of all major spacecraft and instrument subsystems, and performed multiple spacecraft attitude maneuvers to verify the ability to accurately point the instruments.

The two LDCM sensors collect data simultaneously over the same ground path. The OLI collects light reflected off the surface of Earth in nine different regions of the electromagnetic spectrum, including bands of visible light and near-infrared and short-wave-infrared bands, which are beyond human vision. The TIRS collects data at two longer wavelength thermal infrared bands that measure heat emitted from the surface. By looking at different band combinations, scientists can distinguish features on the land surface. These features include forests and how they respond to natural and human-caused disturbances, and the health of agricultural crops and how much water they use. Data from LDCM will extend a continuous, 40-year-long data record of Earth's surface from previous Landsat satellites, an unmatched, impartial perspective that allows scientists to study how landscapes all across the world change through time.

After its checkout and commissioning phase is complete, LDCM will begin its normal operations in May. At that time, NASA will hand over control of the satellite to USGS, which will operate it throughout its planned five-year mission life. The satellite will be renamed Landsat 8. The USGS will process data from OLI and TIRS and add it to the Landsat Data Archive at the USGS Earth Resources Observation and Science Center, where it will be distributed for free via the Internet.

The LDCM captured this image on March 18, 2013, the first day that OLI observed Earth from space. This natural color Landsat scene was created using data from OLI spectral bands 2 (blue), 3 (green) and 4 (red), and it emulates the true colors the human eye would see from space. The data was collected at the same time as the TIRS data.

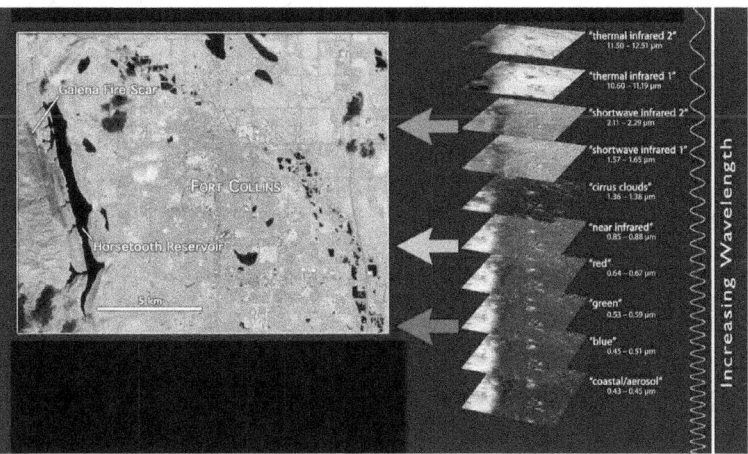

international and interstate boundaries. Mortality caused by white-nose syndrome in bats is already becoming a major threat to the viability of many bat species, and so the potential impacts of wind energy need to be mitigated. The 2014 request includes an increase of $2.0 million for the USGS to increase science to inform decisions related to wildlife impacts from development of renewable energy infrastructure.

LAND AND WATER CONSERVATION FUND

*The Land and Water Conservation
Fund today is helping us meet the goals
of President Obama's America's Great
Outdoors initiative to foster a 21st century
vision for conservation and outdoor
recreation. We are working in partnership
with communities across America to use the
revenues from the energy resources we take
out of the ground to build a lasting legacy of
parks, trails, and open spaces.*

**Ken Salazar, Secretary of the Interior
March 30, 2012**

In 1965, Congress created the Land and Water Conservation Fund to embody its bipartisan commitment to safeguard natural areas, water resources, cultural heritage, and to provide recreation opportunities to all Americans. The LWCF is based on a simple concept: take revenues from the depletion of one resource, offshore oil and gas, and use them to conserve parks, wildlife refuges, forests, open spaces, trails, and wildlife habitat. Every State, and nearly every county in the Nation, has benefited from this program. And all this is done without spending a single tax dollar.

This program has enjoyed a broad base of support over the years, however the requirements for carrying out successful conservation and recreation projects and programs have changed greatly. Conserving large landscapes requires collaboration among all stakeholders, including private landowners, conservation and recreation groups, and local, State, tribal, and Federal governments. America's Great Outdoors calls for broad collaboration around locally driven priorities and more efficient and coordinated ways of investing in, restoring, and managing the Country's natural and cultural resources.

The 2014 budget proposes a total of $400.0 million in current funding for LWCF activities. Of this, $282.0 million is for Interior programs, and $118.0 million is for the U.S. Forest Service. In addition, the budget features a landmark legislative proposal for a multi-year strategy leading to full funding for the LWCF in 2015, not subject to annual appropriations. For 2014, the Administration proposes a one-third permanent and two-thirds current funding structure.

The 2014 permanent request through LWCF includes $141.0 million for Interior, plus an additional $59.0 million for the Forest Service for a total request of $200.0 million. Total proposed LWCF funding from both components in 2014 is $600.0 million, of which $423.0 million supports Interior programs and $177.0 million supports Forest Service programs.

The Administration is focused on maximizing LWCF's performance and outcomes. In addition to increased rigor on monitoring and evaluation of the LWCF grant programs, the Administration launched a Collaborative LWCF initiative in the 2013 budget that enables the Federal land management agencies to establish and leverage funding towards national priorities. In addition to the Collaborative LWCF initiative, other programs funded through LWCF, agency core acquisition programs and grants to States through Forest Legacy, Cooperative Endangered Species Conservation, Urban Parks and Recreation Recovery, and State Conservation Assistance grants, round out a multi-faceted approach to land and water conservation through local, State, and Federal action.

Permanent Funding for LWCF – Despite national support for LWCF—its benefits, widespread popularity, and success at developing a highly strategic collaborative component, effective implementation of the program is constrained by long standing challenges. Uncertainty about annual current appropriations prevents the agencies, and local and State partners, from engaging in the multi-year planning that landscape conservation and effective collaboration with local communities requires. Annual planning driven by the budget process can favor funding individual projects that are urgent and involve the most motivated willing sellers, but which may not be the most strategic in terms of advancing broader conservation objectives.

Land available for acquisition from willing sellers exceeds available LWCF funding, leaving many landowners who wish to sell their properties to the United States for the public's enjoyment with a choice: wait indefinitely for an LWCF appropriation to come through, or sell to another party who may not share the vision for placing the land in the public trust. These challenges are made more complex as they also impact the partner groups that work with agencies to protect critically important habitat and recreation areas who are hampered by the lack of certainty and irregularity of annually appropriated funding. The chronic uncertainty and underfunding of LWCF has made it increasingly challenging for

Federal, State, and local managers to use this tool to address the development threats facing the Nation's most important open spaces, pristine habitats, and cultural sites, the lands and waters that provide communities with recreational areas and preserve their history. Many program partners are ready to bring resources to the table and leverage the Federal investment, but lose interest as a result of long delays and more attractive offers from developers.

The Administration proposes to address these challenges by pursuing full and permanent funding for LWCF programs. Permanent funding will increase financial certainty needed to build local and community partnerships in conservation and optimize valuable investments by leveraging other Federal and non-Federal funds. Permanent appropriations will support the efficiencies demonstrated by the Collaborative LWCF program and enable a more predictable, transparent and inclusive process. Permanent funding will also finally achieve the original intent of the LWCF Act: to dedicate a meaningful portion, $900.0 million, of the royalties private companies pay to access the Nation's offshore oil and gas reserves to preserving the Nation's lands and waters for the benefit of all Americans and future generations.

Federal Land Acquisition – In 2014, the Federal land acquisition request funded through the LWCF totals $356.2 million. Of the total, $264.0 million is for Interior and $92.2 million for the Forest Service. Within this total, Interior funds the Office of Valuation Services with current funding of $12.2 million and permanent funding of $6.0 million to provide appraisal support valuations of lands and minerals in support of land acquisition and other programs. Mission-specific core land acquisition priority projects and program management across both agencies is funded at $187.0 million. In 2014, the Administration proposes targeting the remaining $169.3 million for an Interior-Forest Service collaborative land acquisition program to support strategic interagency landscape-scale conservation projects that also meet agency specific acquisition needs. Interior requests $112.2 million for its three bureaus, NPS, FWS, and BLM, and the Forest Service requests the remaining $57.0 million.

Collaborative Land Acquisition Projects – The Collaborative LWCF program serves as a model for LWCF programs to invest in the most ecologically important landscapes and in projects with a clear strategy to reach shared goals grounded in science-based planning. Through Collaborative LWCF, the

Interior bureaus and Forest Service jointly direct funds to projects that will achieve the highest return on Federal investment, and coordinate land acquisition planning with government and local community partners. The Collaborative LWCF program is designed as a nationwide competition in which individual landscape proposals are scored against ecological and technical criteria to form a ranked list of priority landscape projects that is submitted with the President's budget request to Congress.

Landscape proposals are prepared by interagency teams, with appropriate involvement of Federal and non-Federal partners with equities in the landscape. Often the proposals are the product of years of extensive Federal, State, and local engagement and have the support of dozens of stakeholder organizations. A Federal Technical Committee scores the proposals, and a Federal National Selection Committee comprising the directors and chiefs of the four agencies, as well as senior leadership from the two Departments, agrees on final funding recommendations. The National Selection Committee represents the government's most senior and experienced conservation leaders with oversight for the agencies' respective LWCF programs. The National Selection Committee considers a full range of factors in final decisions, including: leveraging opportunities with other Federal and non-Federal funding sources; the strength and maturity of partnerships and degree of local support; and existing and emerging Administration priorities, which impact the landscapes under consideration for investment in any given year.

For 2014, the Secretaries of the Interior and Agriculture and the National Selection Committee chose landscapes for Collaborative LWCF investment through a rigorous merit-based evaluation process. After evaluating and prioritizing multiple ecosystems, they selected four landscapes for 2014 funding:

- Crown of the Continent in Montana.
- Florida-Georgia Longleaf Pine in Florida, Georgia, and South Carolina.
- Southwest Deserts in California.
- National Trails System in the United States.

The Collaborative LWCF program focuses multi-agency and partner effort investing in these ecologically important and threatened landscapes to ensure they remain resilient in the face of development pressures and global change. While efforts continue to protect individual tracts of land with other

LWCF components, the Collaborative component makes timely and smart investments in strategic conservation on a landscape-scale focusing on select areas for acquisition by multiple Federal agencies in concert with State and local efforts that can achieve outcomes in a short time frame of two to three years. These coordinated efforts will protect large areas to maximize ecosystem values, support at-risk species, and prevent ecosystem decline or collapse, thereby precluding the need for more expensive restoration and regulatory solutions. The proposed Federal investments in these landscapes will leverage significant private commitments to land and water conservation that build on community-based efforts and fulfill the needs for open space, recreation, and preserve historical uses.

Crown of the Continent – The Crown of the Continent landscape spans the Rocky Mountains, which extend through the northwest part of Montana and parts of Canada. The Collaborative LWCF request will support community-based conservation efforts to build resiliency in ecological systems and communities, enabling this landscape to continue to support a full range of native biodiversity in the face of global change. Building ecological resiliency includes maintaining intact, interconnected landscapes and restoring fragmented or degraded habitats.

Since the mid-1990s, a very broad base of citizens, organizations, user groups, and local, Federal, and tribal governments have worked together in support of the Federal acquisition of key private lands in a shared vision for the Crown. The agencies have engaged in long standing collaborations with non-government organization partners, local community groups such as the Blackfoot Challenge and Rocky Mountain Front Landowner Advisory Group, and State and county government officials, to tailor a Federal conservation strategy and acquisition program that achieves a synergy between private rights, open space, traditional land uses, and conservation.

A full suite of native forest carnivores are found within the Crown, including wolves, wolverines, pine martens, fishers, bobcats, and black and grizzly bears. The planned acquisitions will protect threatened and endangered wildlife, fish, and plant habitats and connectivity while fostering watershed health, in support of the conservation goals of the State Wildlife Action Plan, Partners in Flight, Endangered Species Recovery Plans, Forest Management Plans, and agency general management and departmental level strategic plans.

The request supports working farms, ranches, and forests through the use of conservation easements in lieu of fee acquisition on many tracts. The proposed acquisitions will also benefit local economies by supporting and expanding opportunities for big game hunting. The landscape is home to a number of large game species, including antelope, elk, deer, and moose which range throughout the acquisition area and can be hunted within some fee ownership acquisitions. Hunting provides recreational opportunities and vital revenue to local communities. In addition, investing in the Crown's wealth of water, wildlife, and recreation resources, including 40 new access points and increased opportunities for local tourism, will support the economic well-being and quality of life for local residents.

The 2014 budget proposes a total of $15.6 million in Interior Collaborative LWCF funding and $31.0 million in Forest Service Collaborative LWCF funding for Crown of the Continent.

Florida-Georgia Longleaf Pine – The Florida-Georgia Longleaf Pine landscape is located in Georgia, Florida, and South Carolina. The Collaborative LWCF request for the Longleaf Pine landscape is crucial to the ecological well being and recovery of the diminishing longleaf pine ecosystem in the South. Longleaf pines, which once covered up to 98 million acres of the Southeast have been reduced to about three million acres, much of it in poor condition. The acquisitions funded in this request address the most critical needs of each agency in support of the shared priorities of longleaf pine ecosystem conservation and restoration and endangered and threatened species recovery. The lands selected for this proposal are the highest priority for each unit to protect critical habitat, improve management, protect private lands from wildfire, and leverage the efforts of conservation partners.

Federal agencies drew from wildlife habitat gap analyses, recovery plans, other State and Federal natural resource assessments and initiatives, and local government and general public input, to develop a plan for land acquisition that targets the most critical conservation needs, including acquisitions within three of the 16 Significant Geographic Areas identified in the *America's Longleaf Restoration Initiative Range-wide Conservation Plan.* The initiative is a collaborative effort of multiple public and private partners supporting range-wide efforts to restore and conserve longleaf pine ecosystems, led by a 33-member Partnership Council representing non-government organizations, State and Federal agencies, industry, and private landowners. Members such as these have forged enduring partnerships that have conserved natural landscapes for many years while building strong political support for conservation.

The 2014 budget proposes a total of $12.9 million in Interior Collaborative LWCF funding for the Longleaf Pine landscape in current funding. An additional $6.7 million is requested within the Forest Service budget. Interior's request will fund projects local communities identified as priorities through America's Great Outdoors, including the Santee Basin in South Carolina and the Waccamaw Blue Trail in South Carolina, in addition to other significant habitats within the ecosystem. It will also protect significant cultural lands, including the Gullah Geechee Corridor, an area intrinsically linked to the cultural heritage of African Americans in the Southeast. The project supports local economies by protecting highly prized natural landscapes for outdoor recreation and tourism. The working forest component further enhances economic vitality of local communities by providing forest products that support local economies.

Southwest Desert – The Southwest Deserts landscape area, which covers the California deserts garners broad national, regional, and local community support with conservation goals rooted in years of

partnership between a wide variety of government agencies and non-government organizations, and informed by multiple conservation and recreation plans for the area. In the Southwest Deserts, the Federal government is working with Local and State partners to ensure conservation and community outcomes are achieved alongside development initiatives. Diverse and increasing demands are being put on this landscape causing immediate and escalating demands, which drive community-based efforts to conserve resources.

Federal agencies with responsibilities in the landscape and State and non-government organizations partners have a long history of working together through the Desert Managers Group, LCC, the Coachella Valley Multiple Species Habitat Conservation Plan Team, and the Desert Renewable Energy Conservation Plan Action Team. The DRECP constitutes an important component of California's renewable energy planning and involves multiple Federal and State agencies working together to identify areas for biological conservation. This Collaborative LWCF request will directly support work being done through the DRECP, achieving habitat protection and recreational opportunities in alignment with renewable energy development.

Prior Federal investments in this area have led to important resource protection successes, a reflection of the strong partnerships in the area that continue to leverage Federal dollars. Because pressures on the land are increasing, Federal funding remains critical as local, State and Federal agencies work together to ensure conservation and community needs are addressed as development advances. The 2014 Interior budget proposes $40.3 million for Southwest Deserts landscape projects, of which $28.6 million is current and $11.8 million is permanent funding. The 2014 Forest Service budget proposes an additional $10.4 million for Southwest Deserts landscape projects.

National Trails – The Collaborative LWCF request for National Trails will benefit the Country's world-class system of 30 National Scenic and Historic Trails totaling over 54,000 miles in length, traversing 49 States and every ecological biome in the Nation. The national trails system winds through wilderness, rural landscapes, and historic and cultural corridors. These long-distance trails, stretching for hundreds or thousands of miles each, connect with 70 wildlife refuges, 80 national parks, 90 national forests, and 100 major metropolitan areas. They protect crucial conservation areas and wildlife migration corridors and provide education, recreation, and fitness for all ages. The budget request will support acquisitions to improve safety, access, connectivity, and integrity for 11 trails in 17 States.

Each national trail is a collaborative venture in the conservation, interpretation, and responsible public use of important elements of the Nation's natural and cultural heritage. The National Trails System Act enacted by Congress in 1968, created a broad partnership directing BLM, NPS, and the Forest Service to work in partnership with States, local units of government, land trusts, and private landowners, to protect lands and structures along these trails, enabling them to be accessible to the public. As established by law, the administration and management of these trails requires interagency collaboration, and significant LWCF investment to protect them for public appreciation. The collaborative nature of the national scenic and historic trails means that a financial investment by any of the partners has the potential to be greatly leveraged by contributions from other partners, including State agencies, local governments, and land trusts.

Federal investment does not just help to buy land to protect critical resources, it also sets the stage for citizen and community involvement in national trail stewardship. Federal investment in these trails stimulates citizen engagement in public resource stewardship and volunteerism, connects citizens with the Nation's natural and cultural heritage, and strengthens communities across the land. Few Nations on earth have national trails systems, and none has one as extensive, diverse, and inspiring. The 2014 Interior budget proposes $43.4 million for National Trail landscapes in permanent funding. The 2014 Forest Service Budget requests an additional $8.9 million for the National Trails system. This request will protect and enhance the fragile, vulnerable, inspiring, and irreplaceable resources associated with these national trails.

To be successful, we must be thoughtful, strategic, and community-oriented in our approach to conservation. We are focused on targeting conservation investments to critical needs, relying on the best available science and planning tools to identify high-value opportunities that will produce measurable outcomes. Through LWCF, we are making conservation decisions informed by this kind of rigorous science-based analysis, but we are doing something more: realizing the added value of collaboration. Smart collaboration—within the Federal government and with States, Tribes, and non-governmental partners—better enables us to meet the needs of communities, achieve agency missions, and build stable, resilient ecosystems.

Rhea Suh
Assistant Secretary - Policy,
Management and Budget
March 18, 2013

Interior Core Land Acquisition Projects – The 2014 request of $264.0 million for Federal land acquisition includes $79.4 million for mission-specific, core funded projects. Of the amount proposed for core project funding, $52.5 million is requested as current appropriations and $26.8 million is proposed as permanent appropriations. The core land acquisition projects emphasize accomplishment of bureau-specific missions and priority land management requirements. The three Interior land management bureaus consider multiple factors to determine and prioritize lands and easements for acquisition. These criteria include the mission value of planned acquisitions, feasibility of acquiring and operating the lands, the availability of willing sellers, the risk of imminent development of property, and the participation of partners. A list of the 2014 proposed core projects are included in Appendix F of this book. Detailed information about each project can be found within the specific bureau budget justification in the Land and Water Conservation Fund or land acquisition section.

In addition to the core project request, Interior requests an additional $45.2 million in current appropriations to support Federal Land Acquisition through land protection planning, purchase of inholdings, emergency projects, donations, exchanges, hardship cases, relocations, and acquisition management.

The 2014 budget for NPS also includes $9.0 million in current appropriations for American Battlefield Protection program land acquisition grants, equal to the 2012 enacted level. These matching grants provide much needed resources to States and local governments to preserve and protect threatened Civil War battlefield sites outside the national park system. Private non-profit entities may also apply in partnership with a State or local agency. These grants support the fee simple acquisition of land, or the acquisition of permanent, protective interests in land, at Civil War battlefields listed in the Civil War Sites Advisory Commission's 1993 *Report on the Nation's Civil War Battlefields*.

Bureau of Land Management Core Projects – In 2014, BLM requests $16.1 million for core land acquisition projects. Of this, $5.5 million is requested in current funding to include: $2.0 million for California Coastal National Monument in California, Point Arena; $1.7 million for Canyons of the Ancients National Monument in Colorado; and $1.8 million for the Lower Salmon River Area of Critical Environmental Concern/Special Recreation Management Area lands in Idaho. The remaining $10.6 million is proposed as permanent funding to include: $1.1 million for Agua Fria National Monument and Ironwood Forest National Monument in Arizona; $600,000 for Dominguez-Escalante National Conservation Area in Colorado; $1.0 million for Henrys Lake Area of Critical Environmental Concern in Idaho; $3.0 million for Cascade-Siskiyou National Monument and Crooked National Wild and Scenic River in Oregon; $4.0 million for Red Cliffs National Conservation Area in Utah; and $900,000 for the North Platte River Special River Management Area in Wyoming.

The BLM's requested acquisitions would establish a number of publicly accessible sites along the California coast to improve the interpretation of the resource and recreational value of the California Coastal National Monument. This request includes several core projects, which would provide access for hunters and anglers as an additional benefit, including: Cascade-Siskiyou NM; Crooked National Wild and Scenic River; Dominguez-Escalante NCA; Henrys Lake ACEC; Lower Salmon River ACEC/SRMA; and, North Platte River SRMA.

The access of hunters and anglers to the public lands is often frustrated by complicated checkerboard land ownership patterns. Hunting and angling access easements alleviate some of these challenges and provide better access to valuable public recreation opportunities.

Fish and Wildlife Service Core Projects – In 2014, FWS requests $37.7 million for core projects. Of this, $26.7 million is requested in current funding to include: $5.0 million for Cache River National Wildlife Refuge in Arkansas; $5.0 million for Everglades Headwaters National Wildlife Refuge and Conservation Area in Florida; $2.0 million for Flint Hills Legacy Conservation Area in Kansas; $3.0 million for Neches River National Wildlife Refuge in Texas; and $11.7 million for Dakota Grassland Conservation Area and Dakota Tallgrass Prairie Wildlife Management Area in North and South Dakota. The remaining $11.1 million is proposed as permanent funding for core projects to include: $2.0 million for Grasslands Wildlife Management Area and San Joaquin River National Wildlife Refuge in California; $1.0 million for Blackwater National Wildlife Refuge in Maryland; $567,000 for Northern Tallgrass Prairie National Wildlife Refuge in Minnesota; $900,000 for John H. Chafee National Wildlife Refuge in Rhode Island; $1.0 million for Lower Rio Grande Valley in Texas; $1.0 million for the Upper Mississippi River National Wildlife Refuge that touches the four States of Iowa, Illinois, Minnesota, and Wisconsin; and $4.6 million for the Silvio O. Conte National Fish and Wildlife Refuge in the four States of Connecticut, Massachusetts, New Hampshire, and Vermont.

National Park Service Core Projects – In 2014, NPS requests $25.6 million for core projects. Of this, $20.4 million is requested in current funding to include: $319,000 for Sand Creek Massacre National Historic Site in Colorado; $5.3 million for Sleeping Bear Dunes National Lakeshore in Michigan; $1.8 million for San Antonio Missions National Historic Park in Texas; $2.8 million for Virgin Islands National Park in the Virgin Islands; $5.5 million for Civil War Sesquicentennial Units; and $4.7 million for Greenways and Blueways. The remaining $5.2 million is proposed as permanent funding for core projects to include $1.5 million for Saguaro National Park in Arizona and $3.7 million for Santa Monica Mountains National Recreation Area in California.

LWCF Grant Programs – Federal land acquisition through the LWCF is complemented by matching grants that fund State and local activities. Four grant programs are proposed to be supported through LWCF in 2014: the NPS State Conservation Assistance grants and Urban Parks and Recreation Recovery grants, the FWS Cooperative Endangered Species Conservation Fund grants, and the Forest Service's Forest Legacy grants.

State Conservation Assistance Grants – Administered by NPS, this program provides matching grants to States and through States to local governments, for the acquisition and development of public outdoor recreation areas and facilities. The program helps create and maintain high quality recreation areas and facilities and stimulates investments in the protection and maintenance of recreation resources across the United States. The benefits to local communities are many. Access to outdoor recreation sites and greenways has been shown to improve overall mental health, increase physical activity, and connect people to nature as well as foster a greater sense of community. As documented in the *National Recreation and Park Association's Synopsis of 2010 Research Papers*, urban trees in the lower 48 States, many of which are located in parks, remove an estimated 783,000 tons of pollution per year, with an estimated annual value to society of $5.6 billion. The State Conservation Assistance program itself has a clear and noticeable economic impact. The most recent study published that looks at the economic impact of Interior programs, *The Department of the Interior's Economic Contributions, FY 2011*, found Federal investment of $37.1 million for State Conservation Assistance grants resulted in a Nationwide economic impact of $120.0 million and supported 803 jobs.

Most of the grants awarded to States have gone to locally sponsored projects to provide close-to-home recreation opportunities readily accessible to Americans across all walks of life and physical abilities. Land and Water Conservation Fund assisted parks touch the lives of people living in more than 98 percent of American counties. Each State has the flexibility to ensure the highest State and local priorities are addressed. In 2012, LWCF grants supported the creation of 32 brand new parks, helped acquire 2,439 acres, and enhanced 311 parks with new or rehabilitated facilities. Overall, 314 communities benefitted from these grants. For example, a recent grant assisted the Texas Parks and Wildlife Department in acquiring 17,639 acres of Devils River Ranch at the confluence of the Devils River and Amistad Reservoir, helping the State protect a total of 37,000 acres including 24 river miles. Public recreation opportunities span an unprecedented range from remote wilderness to family-friendly river access for fishing, hunting, and paddling. However, not all grants are focused on land acquisition. The City of Bremerton, Washington's Lions Park was in need of renovation. The 1970s-era design at this park resulted in much of the 1,900 feet bordering Puget Sound being covered in pavement, and blocked stunning views with non-native trees. In re-thinking the park, the City of Bremerton removed more than 2.5 acres of asphalt, restored the shoreline, and redeveloped park infrastructure with sustainable elements including porous paving, green roofs, rain gardens, and a nature-themed playground. The Federal investment, less than 30 percent of the project, was matched with grants from the Lion's Foundation and the State.

In 2014, the budget proposes $40.0 million in current funding for State Conservation Assistance, a programmatic decrease of $5.2 million compared to the 2012 enacted level. Included within this request is $36.4 million to be allocated to States through the traditional formula based process. An additional $3.6 million will be allocated to administer the new grants, as well as monitor grant assisted sites to ensure they are not converted to non-recreational uses.

The Administration's proposal to permanently authorize annual funding for LWCF, without further appropriation or fiscal year limitation, will provide an additional $20.0 million for State Conservation Assistance grants in 2014.

Urban Parks and Recreation Recovery Grants – The 2014 budget requests $10.0 million in current funding to revitalize the UPARR program, through the LWCF. Established in November 1978, by P. L. 95-625, the UPARR grants program was designed to provide matching grants to select physically and economically distressed urban communities to revitalize and improve recreation opportunities. This program provides grants directly to local governments to rehabilitate existing indoor and outdoor recreation facilities; demonstrate innovative ways to enhance park and recreation opportunities; and develop local Recovery Action Program Plans to identify needs, priorities, and strategies for revitalization of the total recreation system. This program, like the NPS State Conservation Assistance grants program, aligns with the AGO goal of creating and enhancing a new generation of safe, clean, accessible urban parks, and community green spaces. This proposal is also part of a broader, renewed focus by Interior to develop strategies to improve the integration of agency programs and park units to impact urban economies and the quality of life for urban residents, expanding opportunities for all.

Funding for UPARR grants has not been appropriated since 2002. However, since its inception, $307.1 million has been appropriated for grants to improve and protect more than 1,520 recreational sites in distressed urban communities nationwide, and to help create and launch new innovative programming. The UPARR rehabilitation grants have been used to completely overhaul inner-city outdoor playgrounds, parks, ball fields, and tennis and basketball courts. The grants also have enhanced other recreation facilities such as recreation centers and indoor pool facilities that were unsafe and in many cases closed. For example, a 2002 grant to the City of Detroit, Michigan completely restored and enhanced Peterson Playfield, which had deteriorated to the point where the recreation facilities were unsafe. All the main recreation opportunities of the park, including the ball fields, tennis courts, and basketball courts were restored. Additionally, new, accessible playground equipment for disabled children and a water spray-ground were installed. Today, Peterson Playfield is a major athletic and community hub, used by all ages for everything from tennis and Little League to walking. In 2014, the grants will be targeted at rehabilitating primarily outdoor-oriented neighborhood parks, especially those with active recreation opportunities; directly connecting with and engaging underserved communities and youth; removing barriers and improving access to make parks easier to use; and involving and expanding public and private partnerships.

The Administration's proposal to permanently authorize annual funding, without further appropriation or fiscal year limitation, for LWCF would provide an additional $5.0 million for UPARR grants in 2014.

Cooperative Endangered Species Conservation Fund Grants – Because more than half of all species cur-rently listed as endangered or threatened spend at least part of their life on privately owned lands, the Department recognizes that success in conserving species will ultimately depend on working coopera-tively with landowners, communities, and Tribes to foster voluntary stewardship efforts. States play a key role in catalyzing these efforts.

The CESCF, authorized by the Endangered Species Act and funded through the LWCF, provides grants to States and Territories to participate in a wide array of voluntary conservation projects to benefit candidate, proposed, and listed species on non-Federal lands. The 2014 budget includes $56.0 million in current funding for CESCF grants. These funds would be leveraged with State funds for the development of habitat conservation plans, acquisition of lands to support habitat conservation plans and facilitate species recovery, as well as grants for States to improve the status of species through public education and outreach, habitat restoration, species status surveys, and captive propagation.

For example, a grant awarded in 2012 to California will fund the acquisition of nearly 1,351 acres of important biological core habitat areas for the threat-ened coastal California gnatcatcher. The purchases will also benefit numerous other listed and unlisted species covered by the Carlsbad Habitat Manage-ment Plan, including the least Bell's vireo, California least tern, western snowy plover, and several plant species. The proposed land acquisition supports a large, landscape-level conservation initiative that will greatly enhance the conservation goals of the Carlsbad HMP by securing key regional wildlife linkages and preserving core habitat in the three targeted areas. The parcels proposed for acquisition support a mosaic of high quality, native riparian and upland habitats.

The Administration's proposal to permanently authorize funding, without further appropriation or fiscal year limitation, for LWCF will provide an additional $28.0 million for CESCF grants in 2014.

AN AGO URBAN AGENDA FOR
THE 21ST CENTURY

The President's America's Great Outdoors initiative has helped connect Americans to the treasured outdoor spaces in their communities, including the more than 80 percent of Americans who live in urban areas.

Lisa Jackson, Administrator
Environmental Protection Agency
December 4, 2012

Parks and green spaces improve a community's economy, health, quality of life, environment, and social cohesion. In cities and towns across the Country, parks generate tourism and recreation dollars and improve investment and renewal. Parks and green spaces also have social value as places where people of all ages can come together to relax and recreate at little or no cost.

However, in some communities, the nearest park is miles away and cannot be visited using public transportation. Even in communities with ample open space, a lack of modern, well maintained facilities, or affordable, reliable transportation and safe pedestrian routes can deter people, especially youth and families, from enjoying the outdoors.

Interior bureaus are working with partners in cities across the Nation, replacing old infrastructure and hardscape with buildings and roads that are functional as well as truly green; increasing the number of parks and trails to improve public health; planting rain gardens, increasing tree canopy, and building landscape elements that trap pollutants and silt to address stormwater management issues; restoring habitat for urban wildlife; and helping cities monitor water quality, address contaminants, and implement the research that forms the underpinning of these urban greening efforts.

The Rocky Mountain Greenway is an outstanding example of what can happen when strong Federal, State, local, and private partnerships align to improve access and connections to the great outdoors. Completion of the Rocky Mountain Greenway, first proposed by Secretary Salazar and Colorado Governor John Hickenlooper in May 2011, will result in a comprehensive trail system connecting three national wildlife refuges, Rocky Mountain Arsenal, Two Ponds, and Rocky Flats, to Rocky Mountain National Park and hundreds of miles of trails in the Denver metropolitan area.

This Greenway will provide Denver area residents and visitors greater access to rivers, parks, open spaces, and other outdoor wildlife-dependent recreation opportunities. The national wildlife refuges will anchor the trail network and offer additional birding, hiking, fishing, and environmental education opportunities. A portion of this effort is being funded through a Federal Transit Administration's Transit in Parks program grant. This grant, a proposal developed by the Rocky Mountain Greenway partnership, which includes the State of Colorado, Fish and Wildlife Service, local municipalities, and nongovernmental organizations, will provide for the initial design and construction of the western trail link, connecting Rocky Flats and Two Ponds National Wildlife Refuges to the Greater Denver trail system. Building on these efforts such as the Rocky Mountain Greenway, Interior is developing a comprehensive vision of urban conservation for the 21st Century.

This focus on urban areas will require Interior to realign some of its thinking and priorities. In 2013, Interior will prepare a new report, *AGO Urban Agenda for the 21st Century*, that identifies existing Interior assets and activities in and near cities and recommends ways to increase the urban presence. Interior will also identify 20 AGO urban projects, highlighting cutting edge efforts to increase recreational opportunities, urban wildlife and habitat, greenspace, and green infrastructure, to be completed during 2013 in cities across the Nation. The report will look for the first time across the bureaus to better align resources, identify priorities, and create a comprehensive vision for urban conservation, recreation, and restoration.

The 2014 budget will request $10.0 million in current funding to revitalize the Urban Parks and Recreation Recovery program. An additional $5.0 million for this program is proposed as permanent funding through the Land and Water Conservation Fund, providing a total of $15.0 million. This increase will provide targeted support to economically distressed urban communities for the rehabilitation of critically needed recreation facilities. From 1979 through 2008, the UPARR program awarded approximately 1,500 grants to 380 local jurisdictions in 43 States, the District of Columbia, and Puerto Rico. These grants addressed the diverse needs of urban areas, including rehabilitating playgrounds, ball fields, and recreational trails; converting non-recreational facilities into recreation centers; and development of recreation plans. In 2014, the UPARR program will focus on rehabilitating primarily outdoor-oriented neighborhood parks, removing barriers and making parks easier to access, and involving and expanding public and private partnerships.

NATIONAL BLUEWAYS AND AMERICA'S GREAT OUTDOORS

The National Blueway designation recognizes that strong, diverse partnerships are the best way to address the modern-day threats to our Nation's most important rivers, and the White River is an outstanding example of that approach. The River is the recreational and economic lifeblood of communities from the Ozarks to the Mississippi. River users and river lovers of all stripes have banded together to protect the White River watershed and maintain this magnificent resource for the region—and for the Nation.

David Hayes, Deputy Secretary of the Interior
January 9, 2013

In May 2012, Interior established the National Blueways System to recognize and support locally-led efforts to sustain the economic, recreational, and natural values of rivers and watersheds of national

significance. A National Blueway includes the entire river from headwaters to mouth as well as the river's watershed. The designation does not establish a new protective status or regulation, but is intended to recognize and support existing local and regional conservation, recreation, education, and restoration efforts by coordinating ongoing Federal, State, and local activities.

The first National Blueway is the 410 mile-long Connecticut River and its 7.2 million acre watershed. Covering parts of Connecticut, Massachusetts, New Hampshire, and Vermont, the watershed includes the Silvio O. Conte National Fish and Wildlife Refuge, sub-boreal forests, floodplains, a major migratory pathway, and a globally recognized wetland. The Connecticut River is also an important economic resource to the 2.4 million residents and 396 communities in the watershed. Annually, 1.4 million people enjoy the recreational opportunities presented by the watershed, including National Recreation Trails, scenic byways, Wild and Scenic Rivers, and National Natural Landmarks. These and other recreation opportunities contribute an estimated $1.0 billion to local economies, according to the Trust for Public Land.

Inclusion in the National Blueways System recognizes and supports exemplary river system stewardship efforts to enhance abundant conservation, environmental education, recreation, and economic opportunities by over 40 organizations, including the Friends of the Silvio O. Conte Refuge, the Connecticut Watershed Council, the Connecticut River Museum, and the Marine Biological Laboratory in Woods Hole, Massachusetts. Collaborating Federal agencies include the Department of Agriculture's Natural Resources Conservation Service and Forest Service, and the U.S. Army Corps of Engineers. Benefits are already starting to emerge from this designation including better coordination among the many groups that share similar programs and goals, but may not have worked together given the size of the watershed.

In January 2013, Interior announced the Nation's second National Blueway, the White River watershed. Flowing over 700 miles from its headwaters in the Ozarks to its mouth at the Mississippi River, the White River drains a watershed spanning 17.8 million acres across 60 counties in Arkansas and Missouri. It is home to 1.2 million people who rely on the economic benefits that recreation, tourism, agriculture, and commerce along the river provide to watershed communities. The White River is an important part of the wildlife-related economies of Arkansas and Missouri, which State-wide, accounted for $1.8 billion and $2.8 billion, respectively. Public and private landowners in the watershed have already conserved more than 3.2 million acres of land for the benefit of people and wildlife.

The White River National Blueway was nominated for recognition as a National Blueway by 26 diverse stakeholder groups including the National Wildlife Refuge Association, The Nature Conservancy, Ducks Unlimited, The Conservation Fund, the National Audubon Society, the Arkansas Canoe Club, the Missouri Department of Conservation, the Arkansas Game and Fish Commission, the Arkansas Natural Heritage Commission, the cities of Augusta and Clarendon, Arkansas, and local businesses. Federal partners include the U.S. Army Corps of Engineers, Department of Agriculture, Department of the Interior, and the Lower Mississippi Valley Joint Venture. In conjunction with this designation, FWS also announced it approved an expansion of the acquisition boundary of the Cache River National Wildlife Refuge, one of the White River's main tributaries, that will protect floodplain habitat. Additionally, USACE announced it will move forward with the Lower Cache River Basin Restoration Project, increasing fish and wildlife habitat. Other partners including the USDA and local groups are working with the agricultural community to minimize nutrient pollution and erosion through efforts such as planting trees, optimizing the management of pasture land, and mapping out better ways of handling waste generated by chicken producers.

In 2014, the President's budget proposes a $3.3 million Cooperative Watershed Management Program administered by FWS on behalf of a multi-agency committee to support watershed partnerships such as the Connecticut and White River National Blueways and their important role in watershed stewardship. The CWMP supports the formation and expansion of locally led watershed groups and development of multi-stakeholder watershed management projects. These funds will be awarded via a joint decisionmaking process of the National Blueways Committee. The program will provide candidate and designated National Blueways partnerships with financial assistance to support strategic watershed coordination, collaboration, partnership development, regional planning, implementation, and project delivery.

Additionally, the budget request includes LWCF funding to acquire refuge lands within the watersheds of the two National Blueways. This includes $4.6 million to acquire and conserve 3,700 acres as part of the Silvio O. Conte NFWR. This acquisition will protect important fisheries and wildlife habitat including grassland and northern boreal forest tracts. The budget also proposes $5.0 million to acquire an estimated 1,920 acres at the Cache River NWR. These tracts contain a variety of habitats, and their acquisition will contribute greatly to habitat conservation efforts in this area.

RIVER RESTORATION

Bureau of Reclamation – In 2014, Reclamation's river restoration programs are included in the AGO initiative. The Reclamation's 2014 budget request for river restoration is $120.2 million, a decrease of $33.6 million below the 2012 enacted budget and an increase of $10.7 million above the 2013 Continuing Resolution annualized, primarily due to the completion of the Red Bluff Fish Passage Improvement Project in the 2012 budget.

Reclamation's river restoration programs directly support the goals of the AGO program, through local and basin-wide collaboration in watershed partnerships. Reclamation's river restoration helps reduce environmental conflicts and litigation, as evidenced by the San Joaquin River Restoration Program, where 18 years of litigation was settled by committing to restored water flows and the reintroduction of salmon to the River, as well as certainty on water and power delivery to customers. Restoration programs support tribal needs, restoring fisheries affected by water and power operations as demonstrated by the Trinity River Restoration program which is re-establishing the physical process and rescaling the Trinity River as a foundation for fishery recovery. Restoration programs also develop valuable conservation skills for young people working on projects as is demonstrated by the Lower Colorado River Multi-Species Conservation Program among others. The 2014 budget includes $26.0 million for the San Joaquin River Restoration Program, $14.0 million for the Trinity River Restoration program, another $4.0 million for the San Joaquin and Trinity restoration programs within the Central Valley Project Restoration fund, and $18.2 million for the Lower Colorado River Multi-Species Conservation Program.

Reconstruction of dams, coastlines, and lakes that limited the availability of fish and other natural resources depended upon for food, recreation, conveyance, economic vitality, and quality of life are bringing communities back together. The Red Bluff Fish Passage Improvement Project, the culmination of over 40 years of effort, was initiated as a means to find a balanced solution to improve fish passage and the reliability of irrigation water deliveries. Reconstruction of the Red Bluff Diversion Dam, which had been an obstacle for fish migration, has resulted in the gates being opened permanently. A new fish screen and pumping system will divert water from the Sacramento River into the Tehama-Colusa and Corning Canals while ensuring safe fish passage. The 2014 budget includes $1.9 million for ongoing operations and maintenance of the Red Bluff Fish Passage Improvement Project.

Partnering with people and communities helps enforce the objectives of AGO by restoring, protecting, and cultivating waterways in an effort to reconnect people with the Nation's cultural, natural, and economic resources. The Glen Canyon Dam Adaptive Management program has brought together diverse interests in a collaborative partnership to restore and protect the river while maintaining dam operations. The program's Adaptive Management Work Group, led by the Department of the Interior, has representation from Reclamation, FWS, NPS, BIA, Colorado River Basin States, environmental groups, recreation interests, and contractors for Federal power from Glen Canyon Dam. The AMWG makes it possible to bring all these varied interests to a consensus on how to protect downstream resources and strike a wise balance on river operations. Another example of a cooperative partnership is the Columbia/Snake Salmon Recovery Program Tributary Habitat Activities' Yankee Fork Off-Channel Habitat Restoration Project located in Idaho. To support the YFOHRP, Reclamation is partnering with local, State and tribal governments, landowners, and others to improve habitat in support of salmon and steelhead trout, enhance river recreation that support jobs in tourism and outdoor recreation, and build relationships that will strengthen the State of Idaho. The 2014 budget includes $3.5 million for the Glen Canyon Dam Adaptive Management Program and $18.0 million for the Columbia/Snake Salmon Recovery Program Tributary Habitat Activities.

Recovery of endangered species and their habitat is another goal of river restoration. Restoring species to their native habitat and ensuring water is fit for habitation is important to the survival of human and plant and animal populations. The Upper Colorado River Endangered Fish Recovery Program and San Juan River Basin Recovery Implementation Program were put into operation as measures to recover populations of endangered fish and to improve water development to meet current and future needs. These recovery programs have taken a cooperative approach to recovering endangered species, avoiding litigation, and ensuring ESA compliance. Benefits of the recovery programs are instream flow protection and habitat restoration, which are expected to result in healthier riverine and riparian environments, improving the quality of life for humans in adjacent communities and

USGS GeoForce – Funding Scientific Field Experiences for Youth Attending Minority-Serving High Schools

The U.S. Geological Survey contributes to Interior's Youth in the Great Outdoors initiative by engaging youth through meaningful hands-on work experience, training, professional mentoring, and graduate research in the natural sciences. The 2014 budget includes an additional $1.0 million for USGS to hire additional youth and invest in the science, technology, engineering, and mathematics education that is critical to achieving the USGS mission now and in the future.

The USGS will use this new funding in 2014 to expand support for efforts such as GeoForce, a program to encourage students from minority-serving high schools in rural South Texas and inner-city Houston, to take on the challenges of a rigorous math and science curriculum, to pursue higher education in these fields, and to enter the high-tech workforce.

GeoFORCE students from Texas met with the Assistant Secretary for Water and Science, Anne Castle at Great Falls, Virginia. These high school students are finishing their fourth summer of geologic field experiences and 100 percent are heading off to university. The USGS scientists are proud to help mentor this outstanding class and support them on a pathway to a career in science.

benefiting national parks, wildlife refuges, and public lands frequented by outdoor recreationists and nature enthusiasts. The 2014 budget includes $6.1 million for the Upper Colorado River Endangered Fish Recovery Program and $2.4 million for the San Juan River Basin Recovery Implementation Program.

Other ongoing efforts in river restoration in 2014 include: $10.2 million for the Middle Rio Grande Endangered Species Collaborative Program; $4.6 million for the Gila River Basin Native Fishes Conservation Program, Colorado River Basin Project, Central Arizona Project; $9.7 million for the Platte River Recovery Implementation Program; and $1.7 million for other smaller programs.

Other Partnership Programs

From conserving working landscapes from Montana to Florida, to creating a new generation of dynamic and accessible urban parks from New York to Los Angeles, to establishing a network of national water trails and blueways, we have worked closely for the last three years with States, local communities, and other partners to preserve America's natural heritage and open up more opportunities for outdoor recreation.

Ken Salazar, Secretary of the Interior
September 12, 2012

Partnerships are a key component of Interior's delivery of programs. Partnerships underpin nearly every program and provide a critically important connection to local communities, interested constituencies, and diverse populations. They are key to the success of the AGO initiative. In communities across the Nation, Interior works with State, local, and tribal governments, local communities, non-governmental organizations, and citizens to realize the wide-ranging benefits of a revitalized connection to the outdoors. Recognizing that no single entity, Federal, State, tribal, local, or private, is able to provide the resources necessary to achieve the Nation's conservation goals, the Department, through FWS and NPS, administers technical assistance programs and a number of grant programs that are leveraged with partners.

Conservation Grants – Interior's 2014 budget includes $104.5 million, an increase of $3.9 million above the 2012 enacted level for FWS conservation grant programs. These grants are in addition to the $56.0 million current request for the Cooperative Endangered Species Conservation Fund through the LWCF, described above.

North American Wetlands Conservation Act Grants – The NAWCA grant program provides grants throughout the United States, as well as in Canada and Mexico, for the conservation of waterfowl and other wetland-associated migratory birds. For the past twenty years, NAWCA funds have been invested in the continent's most vital wetland ecosystems, the key for sustaining species and important to hunters and anglers. Projects are funded based on the significance of the wetland ecosystems and wildlife habitat to be conserved, migratory bird species benefited, partner diversity, non-Federal contributions leveraged, and the long-term value of the conservation work proposed. The FWS budget includes $39.4 million for these grants in 2014, an increase of $3.9 million. This request, along with non-Federal partner matches, will enable the NAWCA program to continue to select and fund wetland protection, restoration, and enhancement projects such as the Bird Island Cove Estuarine Habitat Restoration Project in Texas and the Thousand Acre Marsh Wetland Protection Project in Delaware that were funded in 2012, along with 22 other projects.

State and Tribal Wildlife Grants – This grant program assists States, the District of Columbia, Commonwealths, Territories, and Tribes in protecting fish and wildlife populations along with their habitat, including non-game species. The Tribal Wildlife Grants provide a competitive funding opportunity for federally recognized tribal governments to develop and implement programs for the benefit of wildlife and their habitat, including species of Native American cultural or traditional importance, and species that are not hunted or fished. In 2012, 23 Tribes in 17 States used Tribal Wildlife Grants to fund a wide range of conservation projects ranging from salmon restoration to invasive species control.

For State Wildlife Grants, all funded activities must link with species, actions, or strategies included in each State's Wildlife Action Plan. These plans collectively form a nationwide strategy to prevent wildlife from becoming endangered and are unique compared to many prior conservation plans because of broad participation and an open planning process. By working with stakeholders and other members of the community, State fish and wildlife agencies translate pressing conservation needs into practical actions and on-the-ground results. Through this program, FWS has been able to assist States to improve efforts to conserve native flora and fauna and encourage multi-State projects.

The budget includes $61.3 million for grants to help conserve and recover imperiled fish and wildlife, level with the 2012 enacted budget. To target a sizable share of the funds toward national conservation objectives, the 2014 request includes $44.1 million to be awarded based on a statutory formula, $13.0 million to be awarded competitively to States, and $4.3 million to be awarded competitively to Tribes. The work conducted with competitive grant funding focuses on projects with the most significant conservation benefits such as:

- Baseline surveys on species, such as sea turtles, and assessments of how species have been impacted by climate change and other environmental stressors across State boundaries.

- Protection of species' habitat across boundaries or Species of Greatest Conservation Need habitat areas, thereby increasing the ability for multiple States to protect habitats through cooperative projects among State fish and wildlife agencies to support viable populations at the broader ecological scale.

Neotropical Migratory Bird Conservation – These grants support projects that benefit neotropical migratory birds that breed in the U.S. and Canada and winter in Latin America. The more than 340 species of neotropical migratory birds include plovers, terns, hawks, cranes, warblers, and sparrows. The populations of many of these birds are in decline, and some are currently protected as threatened or endangered under the Endangered Species Act. The 2014 FWS request includes $3.8 million for Neotropical Migratory Bird Conservation grants, level with 2012. This funding will support nearly 30 projects such as the Arctic Shorebird Demographics Network II project and the Targeted Grazing Management to Conserve the Sprague's Pipit project that were funded in 2012.

Rivers and Trails – The NPS budget request includes $10.1 million for the NPS Rivers, Trails, and Conservation Assistance program to help communities increase and improve recreational opportunities. This amount is nearly the same as the 2012 enacted level.

Working in communities across the Nation, this program provides expertise and experience to help citizens and community groups achieve on-the-ground conservation successes and urban renewal through their projects. From urban promenades to trails along abandoned railroad rights-of-way to wildlife corridors, the rivers and trails program promotes the creation and restoration of diverse greenways, as well as river conservation activities spanning downtown riverfronts to regional water trails and stream restoration. One recent example was the assistance provided to the Rails-to-Trails Conservancy in New York to provide technical assistance to help create an all-season recreational trail alongside a lightly used rail corridor to connect the communities of Norwood and Norfolk, New York. The Norwood-Norfolk Central School District applied for this grant because the New York Department of Transportation would not allow sidewalks to be built alongside the only road that connects the two communities to their shared school facilities. This trail will give students and staff an opportunity to safely walk or bike to school. In 2014, NPS will initiate 80 new community-based, on-the-ground partnership projects and continue to assist more than 100 additional communities and partners to create or improve 1,900 trail miles, conserve or provide access to over 1,000 miles of rivers and waterways, and conserve or restore over 40,000 acres of park and natural areas.

Historic Preservation and Battlefield Protection Grants – America's great outdoors are endowed with a vast collection of natural and cultural features that reflect both community and national character. As economic pressures, development, and other factors threaten the sustainability of heritage resources, locally led partnership initiatives can guide efforts to preserve these unique places. Working with State and local partners, NPS plays a vital role in sustaining local efforts to preserve the Nation's cultural history through a variety of programs that

---

APPLYING SCIENCE TO ASIAN CARP PREVENTION AND CONTROL

The spread of Asian carp from the Mississippi River system into the Great Lakes is one of the most acute threats facing the Great Lakes and its multi-billion dollar fishing industry. Since 2010, there has been an aggressive focus by the Administration to push the Asian carp invasion further from the Great Lakes, but more effort is needed on the lower Illinois, upper Mississippi, Ohio, Missouri, and other river systems. The 2014 budget builds on Asian carp prevention and control and management efforts already underway, in the U.S. Geological Survey and Fish and Wildlife Service.

In 2010, USGS began conducting research as part of the Asian Carp Regional Coordinating Committee. This Committee is charged with developing a control program to prevent Asian carp from becoming established in the Great Lakes. The USGS research is essential to developing tools to fight the spread of Asian carp. Tremendous progress has been made by USGS, including predicting tributaries that might provide suitable habitat for Asian carp spawning, developing selective toxicants, and testing water guns and CO_2 barriers. Completing this research is a critical step toward focusing monitoring and control efforts. The 2014 USGS budget includes a $3.0 million increase, as compared to the 2012 enacted budget, of which $1.0 million is included in the 2013 operating plan for Asian carp research in the Great Lakes and the Upper Mississippi River. This effort will augment current support to provide scientific information and methodologies to better prevent, detect, and control Asian carp, and enable research that transfers technology to managers for field use both within and outside the Great Lakes Basin.

The 2014 FWS budget includes a program increase of $5.9 million above the 2012 level to address the threat posed by Asian carp to the Great Lakes. Of this amount, the FWS will allocate $5.0 million to support eDNA labs within FWS Fish Technology Centers to increase early detection capabilities. This funding will also support rapid assessment, containment, response, and control outside the Great Lakes in high-risk ecosystems and habitats, a critical element of the National Asian Carp Management and Control Plan. The remaining increase of $903,000 is for traditional gear sampling as part of a comprehensive surveillance and monitoring program. The effort complements FWS activities to prevent other invasive species from establishing and becoming another costly crisis that harms wildlife, habitat, and the American people.

---

address historic preservation needs nationwide. The 2014 budget request includes $60.3 million for two NPS historic preservation grant programs. Of this amount, $58.9 million is for the NPS Historic Preservation Fund, a $3.0 million increase over the 2012 funding level. This includes $46.9 million for grants-in-aid to States and Territories and $9.0 million to Tribes, level with 2012 enacted for these two grant programs. These grants assist State and Tribal Historic Preservation Offices in their efforts to protect and preserve their historic resources and carry out other activities pursuant to the National Historic Preservation Act and other laws.

The $3.0 million increase will be used to establish a competitive grants program under the HPF to survey and nominate properties associated with communities currently under-represented in the National Register of Historic Places and National Historic Landmarks. State, local, and tribal communities and preservation organizations would be eligible to compete for these grants in collaboration with State and tribal historic preservation offices.

The National Register of Historic Places is the official list of the Nation's historic places worthy of preservation. Authorized by the National Historic Preservation Act of 1966, the National Register of Historic Places is part of a national program to coordinate and support public and private efforts to identify, evaluate, and protect America's historic and archeological resources. Currently, 86,000 entries are included in the National Register of Historic Places, with approximately 1,600 nominations received annually. However, current estimates place the combined representation of African-American, American Latino, Asian-American, American Indian, Native Alaskan, and Native Hawaiian sites on the National Register of Historic Places and among National Historic Landmarks at less than eight percent of the total listings.

Grants will be awarded to applicants who propose surveys of communities currently under-represented, demonstrate the professional capability and capacity to conduct the surveys and prepare the nominations, and have incorporated extensive community engagement.

The NPS American Battlefield Protection program grants are funded at $1.4 million, equal with the 2012 level. These grants, which complement the American Battlefield Protection program land acquisition grants funded through the LWCF, assist in the preservation and protection of America's significant battlefields. These grants support efforts in site identification and documentation, planning, interpretation, and educational projects. In 2012, this grant program awarded 27 grants, including one to the Connecticut River Museum to study a War of 1812 raid by the British on Pettipaug Neck, a safe harbor for American privateers. The raid resulted in the greatest American loss of ships of the entire war. This project will survey and document the raid and delineate the battlefield boundaries. These data will then be used for a National Register nomination.

ON-THE-GROUND RESULTS

People across the Country are coming together to protect and preserve the places that nurture our souls, provide opportunities for recreation, and power our economies. We know that an investment in conservation now is a direct investment into our Nation's economy, and one that will benefit generations to come.

Ken Salazar, Secretary of the Interior
March 2, 2012

Conservation in America has reached a crossroads, needs have never been greater amid resources never more scarce. An ecological and fiscal imperative exists to plan conservation action at a landscape- and watershed-scale. Because large landscapes are often comprised of Federal, State, tribal and private working lands, collaboration between and among Federal agencies and State and local partners is critical. And because solutions are most durable when they are owned by communities, Federal agencies increasingly seek to catalyze and bolster local conservation efforts. More than at any time before, alignment of Federal, State, and private resources and authorities toward community-based conservation goals at meaningful ecological scales are proving essential to success.

In recent years, Federal agencies have generally excelled in adopting this cross-jurisdictional approach as evidenced by agency-specific landscape- and watershed-scale conservation initiatives. What was lacking, however, was an institutional means to coordinate these initiatives across the Federal agencies to better align investments and authorities. A significant focus of the AGO initiative has been to address this challenge.

Nine Federal agencies — BLM, Reclamation, FWS, NPS, NRCS Forest Service, NOAA, the Advisory Council on Historic Preservation, and USACE, recently committed, through a Memorandum of Understanding, to continue efforts to demonstrate this community-based landscape- and watershed-scale conservation model across seven geographic areas: Southwest Deserts, Crown of the Continent, Great Plains Grasslands, Longleaf Pine, New England Forests and Waters, Connecticut River Watershed, and the White River Watershed.

A complementary, Cabinet-level MOU between Interior, USDA, and USACE was recently signed committing these agencies to continued support of the National Blueways System in particular, to enhance river-oriented outdoor recreation and education, natural resource stewardship, and sustainable economic development at a watershed-scale.

In 2012, Interior reached significant milestones in translating the AGO vision into on-the-ground action. Accomplishments include:

- Interior, USDA, and USACE established a new America the Beautiful Pass that allows the men and women in the U.S. Armed Forces and their families to visit more than 2,000 national parks, national forests, wildlife refuges, and other public lands without paying entrance or amenity fees.

- Interior continued its efforts to promote veteran hiring. Overall, 16 percent of employees hired were veterans, of which five percent were service disabled veterans.

- Interior provided 19,175 jobs for young Americans, ages 15-25, an increase of 20 percent above 2009 levels. Since Secretary Salazar established youth employment as a Priority Goal within the Department, Interior has employed more young people each year above 2009 levels, 36 percent in 2010 and 30 percent in 2011.

- Interior and USDA investments in Youth Conservation USACE programs increased participation by 20 percent in 2012 above 2011 levels.

- Interior and the Department of Education signed an historic agreement to expand outdoor learning access for an estimated 54 million students and teachers.

- The President designated four new National Monuments to protect unique American natural, cultural, and historic sites and promote local economic growth: Fort Monroe in Virginia, Chimney Rock in Colorado, and Fort Ord and Cesar Chavez in California.

- Interior, USACE, the Departments of Commerce and Tranportation, and EPA established a new National Water Trails System, a new network that will increase access to water-based outdoor recreation in and around urban areas, provide national recognition and resources to existing, local water trails, encourage community stewardship of local waterways, and promote tourism that fuels local economies across America. The water trails will be a class of national recreational trails under the National Trails System Act of 1986. Nine rivers were designated National Water Trails in 2012: the Alabama Scenic Water Trail, Atlanta's Chattahoochee River National Recreation Area Water Trail, Bronx River Blueway, Hudson River Greenway Water Trail, Kansas River Water Trail, Mississippi River National River and Recreation Area Water Trail, Mississippi River Water Trail-Great River Water Trail section, Okefenokee Wilderness Canoe Trail, and Willamette River Water Trail.

- Interior and the City of New York signed an unprecedented agreement between NPS and the City of New York Department of Parks and Recreation, documenting how the two agencies will cooperatively manage 10,000 acres of Federal and city-owned parks in and around Jamaica Bay to promote visitation, education programs, scientific research, and opportunities for outdoor recreation.

- Interior, USDA, USACE, and Commerce re-launched the recreation.gov website with dramatic improvements and expanded content, helping millions of visitors plan travel, find outdoor resources, and explore national parks, lands, waters, and historic and cultural sites.

- Reclamation released nearly 2,000 tagged chinook salmon at various locations in the San Joaquin River. The efforts are part of research studies to collect data that will help the San Joaquin River Restoration

Program understand how juvenile chinook salmon may move through the San Joaquin River and bypass system and also adult spawning habitat use in the River. These study efforts mark the first time a number of adult fall-run chinook salmon are in the river near Friant Dam and, possibly, the first documented successful spawning of salmon in the River in many decades.

- Reclamation's San Juan River Habitat Restoration Program in New Mexico restored 6.5 miles of secondary channel and six acres of backwater habitat for endangered species. Additionally, the Platte River Recovery Implementation Program acquired nearly 1,248 acres of land for habitat during 2012 and acquired up to 4,800 acre-feet of water per year to help increase flows for endangered species.

Additionally, Interior and its partners made significant progress on the 101 AGO projects identified by Governors and stakeholders in all 50 States, published in 2011 in a report titled *America's Great Outdoors Fifty-State Report*. The initial success of this process inspired the designation of additional projects throughout the 50 States, for a total of 130 Interior AGO priority projects. By the end of 2012, 95 percent of the 130 projects had achieved a tangible outcome, with the remaining five percent on track to do so in 2013. Interior instituted a process to select additional projects for 2013, including continuing the best of the multi-year, collaborative efforts from 2012.

Enjoying and protecting the Nation's lands and waters is an American value that crosses regional, demographic, and political lines. Interior is proud of these shared accomplishments, but looks forward to what can be achieved in the future through these partnerships. As noted earlier, the 2014 President's budget includes an increase of $3.3 million to provide candidate and designated National Blueways partnerships with financial assistance to support strategic watershed coordination, collaboration, partnership development, regional planning, implementation, and project delivery. Complementary Federal land acquisition projects will protect important habitat within the watersheds of the Connecticut River and White River National Blueways, both of which are part of the seven geographic areas addressed in the AGO demonstration landscapes.

The budget requests $4.5 million for the three land management bureaus and Reclamation to target three areas in the AGO landscape portfolio: the Southwest Deserts, Crown of the Continent, and the Grasslands of the Northern Great Plains landscapes. This increase will support coordinated research to enhance the models used to guide ecosystem restoration and improve ecosystem services while tackling such issues as invasive plants and species restoration. A portion of the funding, $1.0 million, will support efforts by the National Fish and Wildlife Foundation to build capacity with community partners to help collaboratively conserve large landscapes.

An example of the type of work these projects will support is in the Grasslands of the Northern Great Plains landscape. This landscape covers about 180 million acres across Montana, Nebraska, North Dakota, South Dakota, Wyoming, and two Canadian provinces. Native prairie is among the most endangered ecosystems on the planet. Over the past two decades, States such as Iowa and Minnesota, have lost all but one percent of the native prairie with an accelerated loss in the last three to five years. Large contiguous blocks of native prairie still remain but the prairies are being plowed and prairie wetlands are being drained for agricultural purposes. These landscapes have an incredible diversity of grasses and plants, used by many fish and wildlife for their food and cover. With a 2014 request of $1.4 million, FWS will use a portion to address these threats in partnership with the NRCS to restore and enhance native grassland in this area and recover imperiled prairie species, such as the Dakota skipper, a small butterfly. These strategic funding increases will help not only to maintain current, ongoing partnerships but will foster the development of new partnerships to benefit conservation across this Nation.

NATIONAL COUNCIL TO BUILD
21ST CENTURY CONSERVATION SERVICE CORPS

A Memorandum of Understanding, signed by the Secretaries of the Interior, Agriculture, Commerce, and Labor, as well as the EPA Administrator, Chair of the President's Council on Environmental Quality, CEO of the Corporation for National and Community Service and Assistant Secretary of the Army Civil Works establishes a national council to guide implementation of the Obama Administration's 21st Century Conservation Service Corps. The 21CSC is a national collaborative effort to put America's youth and returning veterans to work protecting and restoring America's great outdoors.

A recommendation of the President's America's Great Outdoors initiative, the 21CSC expands efforts of the Administration to increase job opportunities for young people. It builds on existing partnerships with youth conservation corps across the United States to engage thousands of young Americans in hands-on service and job training experiences on public lands and community green spaces.

The 21CSC assists young people, including diverse low-income, underserved and at-risk youth, as well as returning veterans, to gain valuable training and work experience while accomplishing conservation and restoration work on public lands, waterways, and cultural heritage sites. The 21CSC contributions range from helping restore parks and beaches in the wake of Hurricane Sandy to leading visitor interpretation programs in national forests and refuges.

The National Council will support the 21CSC by enhancing partnerships with existing youth corps programs around the Nation, stimulating existing and new public-private partnerships, and aligning the investment of current Federal government resources.

For additional information, visit:
http://www.doi.gov/21csc

For a copy of the MOU, visit:
http://on.doi.gov/UZma3a

The President's America's Great Outdoors initiative is helping to connect Americans with the recreational, economic, and health benefits of our nation's extraordinary natural resources. The 21CSC will help prepare the leaders of the future by providing youth with valuable opportunities for recreation, career development, and service to their community and their Nation.
Nancy Sutley, Chair
White House Council on Environmental Quality

Building on the legacy of President Roosevelt's Civilian Conservation Corps during the Great Depression in the 1930s, 21CSC will help build and train a workforce who represent the diversity of America while creating the next generation of environmental stewards and improving our public lands.
Ken Salazar, Secretary
Department of the Interior

By coordinating resources across the Federal family and working with partners, 21CSC will accomplish important restoration work, provide more job and training opportunities, expand educational opportunities for youth, and create meaningful pathways to careers, all while reconnecting America's youth with the great outdoors.
Tom Vilsack, Secretary
Department of Agriculture.

The 21CSC is a great example of how innovative partnerships are utilizing government resources more efficiently and effectively. The Labor Department is committed to working with our partners to provide young people with valuable training opportunities that can form the foundation of lifelong careers.
Hilda Solis, Secretary
Department of Labor

Our Federal lands and waters are vital to the health and well-being of Americans. The 21CSC will expand the USACE' capacities to conserve and maintain these areas, and provide youth and veterans with meaningful work, education, and exposure to the outdoors.
Jo Ellen Darcy, Assistant Secretary
U.S. Army Corps of Engineers

We here at Commerce plan to use 21CSC to expand NOAA's existing habitat conservation programs to provide technical training to veterans and youth so they can develop expertise in the conservation sector.
Rebecca Blank, Acting Secretary
Department of Commerce

As we see every day in AmeriCorps, young people bring extraordinary energy, passion, and talent to public service. This partnership is a win all-around: it expands opportunity for young people, taps the leadership skills of veterans, improves our public lands, and puts a new generation on a lifelong path of service.
Wendy Spencer, CEO
Corporation for National and Community Service

America is home to some of the most beautiful outdoor spaces in the world. The 21CSC will not only help our young people and returning heroes feel more of a connection to those spaces, but it will also ensure our treasured outdoors are preserved for generations to come.
Lisa Jackson, Administrator
Environmental Protection Agency

New Energy Frontier

The Administration has implemented a true all-of-the-above approach to American energy, with renewable energy from sources like wind and solar doubling since the President took office, while at the same time domestic oil and gas production has increased each year.

Ken Salazar, Secretary of the Interior
October 23, 2012

On May 7, 2012, Secretary of the Interior Ken Salazar "flipped the switch" on the Enbridge Silver State North solar project, the first large-scale solar energy facility on U.S. public lands to deliver power to American consumers. Located 40 miles south of Las Vegas, Nevada, Silver State North is a 50 megawatt plant that will use photovoltaic technology to generate enough power for nearly 9,000 Nevada homes. Constructed on 618 acres of public land managed by the Bureau of Land Management, the solar project underwent full environmental analysis and public review. The BLM worked closely with Federal, State and local partners, members of the environmental and conservation community, and interested stakeholders to protect wildlife and advance this environmentally sound project. This milestone is in line with the Administration's broad commitment to expand production of all sources of American made energy, including renewable sources such as wind and solar.

Innovation and technology are helping to create a new energy frontier in America. The Department of the Interior is an integral part of that effort as the steward of the Nation's public lands. Interior manages one-fifth of the Nation's landmass and 1.7 billion acres of the Outer Continental Shelf, and has the resources to help America responsibly produce more energy at home. Oil and gas development on Federal lands and waters presently account for nearly 23 percent of the Nation's energy supply. Under Interior's stewardship, responsible domestic energy development, both conventional and renewable, has made significant contributions to the Nation's energy security and to the clean energy economy of the future.

Just four years ago, in 2009, there was not a single commercial solar energy project on or under development on Federal lands. Since then, Interior has authorized 37 renewable energy projects on or through the public lands, which if fully developed, will provide more than 11,500 megawatts of power, enough to power more than 3.8 million homes, according to developer estimates.

At the end of 2012, domestic crude oil production was higher than at any time since 1992 and natural gas production was at its highest level ever.

PARTNERSHIPS ARE ADVANCING THE NEW ENERGY FRONTIER

These renewable energy projects reflect the Obama Administration's commitment to expand domestic energy production on our public lands and diversify our Nation's energy portfolio.

Ken Salazar, Secretary of the Interior
March 13, 2013

In March 2013, Secretary Salazar joined with California Governor Edmund Brown, Jr. to announce the approval of three major renewable energy projects that, when built, are expected to deliver 1,100 megawatts to the grid, enough to power more than 340,000 homes, and help support more than 1,000 jobs through construction and operations.

Working together, the State of California and the Department of the Interior have established a unique partnership in support of the State and Federal government's clean energy goals. Since 2009, the aligned Federal and State permitting and environmental review processes have advanced five gigawatts of wind, solar, geothermal, and transmission projects on public lands in California, and more than 15 gigawatts State-wide.

Interior and California agencies are also engaged in the Desert Renewable Energy Conservation Plan, a mutual landscape-level planning effort to streamline renewable energy development in appropriate areas in the California desert, while at the same time conserving important natural resources and natural communities for species protection and recovery. A draft of the plan is expected to be complete in 2013.

The approved projects underwent extensive environmental review and public comment. The companies agreed to undertake significant mitigation efforts to minimize impacts to wildlife, water, and historical, cultural, and other resources. State and Federal agencies have set up a joint compensation fund operated by the National Fish and Wildlife Foundation to help mitigate impacts. The projects will displace an estimated 800,000 metric tons of greenhouse gases each year, equivalent to more than 150,000 cars, while generating tens of millions of dollars in construction payroll, local housing demand, increased tax revenue, and purchases of local goods and services during construction and operation.

- The McCoy Solar energy project, located nearly 13 miles northwest of Blythe, California, was proposed by McCoy Solar, LLC, a subsidiary of NextEra Energy Resources, LLC. The 750 megawatt photovoltaic solar facility would be one of the largest solar projects in the world, and as proposed would encompass about 7,700 acres of BLM-managed lands and 477 acres of private land. Because BLM worked closely with the developer to reduce the footprint, the project will occupy only 4,394 acres. McCoy Solar has agreed to purchase more than 4,500 acres of habitat to protect the desert tortoise, burrowing owl, and Mojave fringe-toed lizard species. The project is expected to employ nearly 500 workers during peak construction and provide 34 permanent jobs. When operational, the facility would generate enough clean power for an estimated 225,000 homes in southern California. A 12.5 mile generation transmission line would connect the project to Southern California Edison's Colorado River Substation.

- The Desert Harvest Solar Farm, proposed by EDF Renewable Energy, formerly enXco, on a site six miles north of Desert Center, California, will encompass nearly 1,208 acres of BLM-managed lands for the 150 megawatt photovoltaic facility. The project's infrastructure will be concentrated with that of a nearby solar project, minimizing new ground disturbance. The BLM added requirements to ensure the plant will not contribute to overdraft of the local groundwater basin. When operational, the facility will generate enough electricity to power an estimated 45,000 homes in southern California. The project also includes an on-site substation and 230 kilovolt line to the Red Bluff Substation, which will connect the project to the Southern California Edison regional transmission grid.

- The Searchlight wind energy project will be built on 18,949 acres of BLM-managed land near Searchlight, Nevada, 60 miles southeast of Las Vegas. The permanent footprint of the 200 megawatt project will be approximately 160 acres. The Western Area Power Administration is proposing to construct, operate, and maintain a new switching station to connect the project to the existing power grid. When built, the project will provide enough electricity to power nearly 70,000 homes. The facility will create an estimated 275 peak construction jobs, 15 full and part-time operational jobs, and generate an estimated $18.6 million in property and sales tax revenue for local government.

For more information on BLM's approved and pending renewable energy projects, visit http://www.blm.gov/wo/st/en/prog/energy/renewable_energy.html.

Foreign oil imports now account for less than half of the oil consumed in America, the lowest level since 1995. Most of the domestic boom is coming from onshore production from shale rocks underlying private lands. At the same time, however, oil production on Federal lands rose seven percent in 2012 over the previous year, the largest single-year production gain in the past eight years. Offshore there were 37 deepwater floating rigs drilling in the Gulf at the end of 2012, up from 26 at the beginning of the year. The Department's Bureau of Safety and Environmental Enforcement approved 112 new deepwater well permits in 2012, the most since 2005, when these data began to be tracked electronically.

These resources are a significant driver of U.S. economic development and employment. The Department estimates that in 2011, oil, gas, coal, hydropower, wind power, geothermal power, solar power, and other mineral activities on Interior-managed lands and offshore areas supported nearly 1.5 million jobs and $275 billion in economic activity. Excluding hydropower, the Energy Information Administration projects increased generation from renewable energy in the electric power sector. This will account for 33 percent of the overall growth in electricity generation from 2010 to 2035. According to the Bureau of Labor Statistics, employment in electric power generation, transmission, and distribution is expected to decline by 0.9 percent each year for the next ten years. The Bureau predicts, however, green energy, especially wind and solar, will account for a larger share of the U.S. energy supply. As these sectors expand, the need for both high- and low-skilled workers to construct, maintain, and operate plants will grow.

Interior's focus on America's energy future supports an all-inclusive approach, one that responsibly develops not only conventional but also renewable resources on the Nation's public lands. Interior's resource programs are working to achieve a responsible balance between reducing reliance on imported oil and broadening the Nation's energy portfolio, while also ensuring that it chooses the right places to develop and enforcing strong safety standards in development.

Responsible and Accountable Energy Development – In 2014, the Department will continue to advance a suite of reforms to get the best return for the taxpayer, encourage diligent development, and strengthen revenue collection processes. These efforts will capitalize on the reorganization of the former Minerals Management Service, completed in 2012, into the Bureau of Ocean Energy Management, Bureau of Safety and Environmental Enforcement, and Office of Natural Resources Revenue within the Office of the Secretary. Together these reforms will promote maximum transparency in agency decisions and processes, a priority for this Administration and the Secretary.

As the steward for the development of the Nation's oil and gas resources, Interior is keenly aware of its responsibilities to the American taxpayer. In 2012, Interior disbursed $12.2 billion in revenue generated from energy production on public lands and offshore areas, a $1 billion increase over the previous year, and in line with increased production taking place across the Country. The revenues were distributed to Federal, State, and tribal accounts, providing important funding to local economies and supporting critical restoration, conservation, and preservation projects. Interior transferred $6.6 billion directly to the U.S. Treasury, making the Department's mineral revenue disbursements one of the Nation's largest sources of non-tax revenue.

To promote transparency and equity within energy markets, Interior is leading the Administration's effort to implement the Extractive Industries Transparency Initiative. The EITI requires governments to publicly disclose their revenues from oil, gas, and mining assets, and for companies to make parallel disclosures regarding payments. Working with industry and the public, the Department established a multi-stakeholder group to oversee the design and implementation of EITI within the U.S. Signing onto the global standard that EITI sets will help ensure

---

STRENGTHENING ACCOUNTABILITY AND TRANSPARENCY

The U.S. Extractive Industries Transparency Initiative Multi-Stakeholder Group is piloting a new approach to participatory government, bringing representatives from industry, government, and the public together to develop new ways to bring greater transparency to the revenue that is generated and collected from extractive processes of the Nation's natural resources.

The EITI is a voluntary, global effort designed to increase transparency, strengthen the accountability of natural resource revenue reporting, and build public trust for the governance of these vital activities. Each Nation's EITI reporting requirements is country-specific and developed jointly by a multi-stakeholder group comprised of members of the public, government, and companies through a multi-year, consensus-based process.

Participating countries publicly disclose revenues received by the government for oil, gas, and mining development, while companies make corresponding disclosures regarding these same payments to the government. Both sets of data are reviewed and reconciled by a mutually agreed upon independent third party, and results are then released in a public report. The goals under EITI complement the top to bottom reforms of Interior's natural resource management undertaken over the last three years.

At the inaugural meeting of the U.S. EITI Multi-Stakeholder Group in February 2013, Samantha Power, Senior Advisor to the President and Senior Director for Multilateral Affairs and Human Rights, described the U.S. EITI as a critical tool in the fight against corruption, an effective weapon to ensure greater transparency and empower citizens.

American taxpayers are receiving every dollar due for the extraction of these valuable public resources.

In 2012, Interior established a new Priority Goal targeting onshore oil and gas operations to ensure taxpayers are receiving revenues owed for production and that operations are safe and environmentally responsible. Although the Priority Goal focuses on the onshore inspection and monitoring program, milestones and deliverables will be used to gauge the reduction of risks in other areas of production and revenue collection. Interior established this goal to produce tangible results in an area identified for improvement by the Government Accountability Office.

2014 BUDGET SUMMARY

The 2014 request for the New Energy Frontier initiative totals $607.5 million in current funding. This is an increase of $46.3 million over the 2012 level. In addition, the Department will manage $164.2 million in funding for conventional energy activities from fees and permanent sources, including fees charged for inspections, applications for permits to drill, and funding from the Permit Processing Improvement Fund established by Section 365 of the Energy Policy Act. Spending from fees and permanent funding increases $51.2 million from the 2012 level, reflecting a proposal to expand onshore oil and gas inspection activities and offset the BLM's inspection program costs to the taxpayer with fees from industry. Total funding for the New Energy Frontier initiative in 2014 is $771.6 million, an increase of $97.5 million over the 2012 level.

The 2014 request for New Energy Frontier programs includes $99.9 million for renewable energy activities, a $26.4 million increase over the 2012 level. Combined current and permanent funding for conventional energy and compliance activities totals $671.7 million, an increase of $71.0 million over the 2012 level. New Energy Frontier funding in 2014 maintains the Department's emphasis on strategic investments to advance renewable energy development, encourage domestic energy production, enhance environmental enforcement functions, expand training and electronic inspection capabilities, and fund operational safety improvements.

NEW ENERGY FRONTIER
(dollars in millions)

	2012 Enacted	2014 Request	Change
RENEWABLE ENERGY			
BLM	19.7	29.1	+9.4
BOEM	33.0	34.4	+1.4
RECLAMATION	0.8	1.1	+0.3
USGS	5.9	9.9	+4.0
FWS	7.0	14.1	+7.2
BIA	6.0	8.3	+2.3
OIA	1.1	3.0	+1.9
Subtotal	**73.5**	**99.9**	**+26.4**
CONVENTIONAL ENERGY AND COMPLIANCE			
BLM	125.5	147.9	+22.4
BOEM	127.8	135.0	+7.3
BSEE	197.4	222.1	+24.8
USGS	25.1	39.8	+14.7
FWS	3.1	3.4	+0.3
BIA	2.5	2.5	0.0
ONRR	119.4	121.1	+1.6
Subtotal	**600.7**	**671.7**	**+71.0**
TOTAL	**674.2**	**771.6**	**+97.5**

The 2014 request also assumes several legislative and administrative proposals related to energy programs; these are described more fully in the Departmental Overview. In particular, the request includes a package of oil and gas program reforms that combines administrative reforms with legislative changes, including several new proposals as well as proposals submitted with the 2013 request. These proposals include royalty reforms, changes to encourage diligent development of oil and gas leases, and improvements to revenue collection processes. In total, this package of reforms is estimated to save $2.5 billion over the period 2014-2023, of which the legislative components are estimated to save $1.7 billion.

Developing Renewable Energy

In just over four years, we have advanced 37 wind, solar, and geothermal projects on our public lands–or enough to power more than 3.8 million American homes. These projects are bolstering rural economies by generating good jobs and reliable power and strengthening our national energy security.

Ken Salazar, Secretary of the Interior
March 13, 2013

In delivering new energy to America, Interior, working with Federal partners, States, and local communities, is guided by the fundamental belief that renewable energy development, where promoted and sited in a thoughtful way, can fully contribute to conservation and protection of the environment. Interior has continued to responsibly and aggressively develop renewable energy resources, to date authorizing 37 renewable energy projects on public lands since 2009, and laying the groundwork to hold the first-ever auctions for commercial wind development in the Atlantic. This year, the Department will complete groundbreaking milestones to offer additional commercial lease sales for Wind Energy Areas offshore New Jersey, Maryland, and Massachusetts, and analyze a lease request to develop cutting-edge floating wind turbines in Federal waters off Maine. Other demonstration projects are proposed off Virginia and Oregon. In addition, in 2013 BOEM is reviewing a mid-Atlantic wind energy transmission line that has the potential to eventually bring up to 7,000 megawatts of offshore wind energy capacity to the grid.

The Secretary's efforts to expand domestic energy have produced groundbreaking projects. In 2009, Interior established the first regulatory framework for offshore renewable energy development and in 2010, launched a "Smart from the Start" development strategy to identify wind energy areas using a coordinated, focused approach with extensive environmental analysis, public review, and large-scale planning. In 2012, Interior identified six wind energy areas on the Atlantic coast with the greatest wind potential and fewest development conflicts. In 2012, the Department issued the second commercial wind lease off Delaware and will move forward with the first ever competitive lease sales for wind energy areas off Virginia and Rhode Island/Massachusetts. These sales have the potential to support

Onshore Oil and Gas Development Priority Goal

GOAL:
Improve production accountability, safety, and environmental protection of oil and gas operations through increased inspection of high-risk oil and gas production cases.

METRIC:
By September 30, 2013, the Bureau of Land Management will increase the completion of inspections of Federal and Indian high-risk oil and gas cases by nine percent over 2011 levels, the equivalent of covering as much as 95 percent of the potential high-risk cases. In fiscal year 2014, BLM is targeting to maintain inspections of the potential high-risk cases.

Renewable Energy Priority Goal

In the Energy Policy Act of 2005, Congress set a goal of approving 10,000 megawatts of non-hydro renewable energy by 2015. The BLM achieved that milestone in 2012, beating the Energy Policy Act target by three years. The Department and BLM have not allowed early achievement of the Energy Policy Act goal to lead to complacency. Interior recommitted itself to aggressively advancing the Administration's alternative energy goals by establishing a Renewable Energy Priority Performance Goal for 2010 through 2014. It will increase approved capacity authorized for renewable solar, wind, and geothermal energy resources affecting Interior-managed lands, while ensuring full environmental review, to reach 15,429 megawatts. The Department will successfully meet this goal if a majority of the energy projects designated as priority projects for 2012 and 2013 are approved.

an estimated 4,000 megawatts of wind generation, enough electricity to power 1.4 million homes.

In 2012, the Department made significant achievements to advance responsible development of renewable energy on public lands. Using a structured, scientific process, Interior released guidelines designed to help wind energy project developers avoid and minimize impacts of land-based wind projects on wildlife and their habitats. The voluntary guidelines are the result of a five-year process that included multiple opportunities for public review and comment. The guidelines were also informed by the Wind Turbine Guidelines Advisory Committee, established in 2007, which is comprised of diverse stakeholders, including Federal and State agencies, Tribes, the wind energy industry, and conservation organizations. These voluntary guidelines also will help developers identify additional steps and review processes and permits that may be needed to ensure compliance with Federal laws such as the Migratory Bird Treaty Act, the Bald and Golden Eagle Protection Act, and the Endangered Species Act.

The Department also:

- Formed two more Federal/State Renewable Energy Task Forces with the States of Hawaii and South Carolina. These task forces facilitate communication and cooperation, among Interior, other State, local and Federal agencies, and Tribes, concerning renewable energy development in Federal waters offshore the two States.

- Created a roadmap for smart solar development onshore by finalizing the Western Solar Energy Plan, which provides a blueprint for utility-scale solar energy permitting. The Plan covers six western States and establishes 17 solar energy zones, totaling an estimated 285,000 acres of public lands, with access to existing or planned transmissions that will serve as priority areas for commercial-scale solar development.

- Expanded a partnership with the Defense Department by signing a historic Memorandum of Understanding to strengthen the Nation's energy security and reduce military utility costs. The MOU encourages appropriate development of renewable energy projects on public lands withdrawn (set aside) for defense-related purposes, and other onshore and offshore areas near military installations. Nearly 13 million of the 16 million acres that have been withdrawn over the years for military use are located in the West and are high in wind, solar, and geothermal resources.

- Approved five new renewable energy projects in 2012, including a 350 megawatt solar energy project on tribal trust land of the Moapa Band of Paiute Indians in Clark County, Nevada. The project marks a milestone as the first-ever, utility-scale solar project approved for development on tribal lands, and is one of the many steps the Administration has taken to help strengthen tribal communities. This project is expected to generate enough power for an estimated 100,000 homes.

- In Wyoming, Interior approved the Chokecherry-Sierra Madre wind energy project, the largest proposed wind energy project in the U.S. to date, and one of the largest in the world. This project will use 1,000 turbines to produce 3,000 megawatts of power, enough to power nearly one million homes.

- Approved construction of the transmission line for First Solar's Campo Verde solar energy project, which will cross public lands southwest of El Centro, California. The 139 megawatt solar energy project is expected to support more than 250 jobs through construction and operations, generate $17.5 million in local tax revenue over the life of the facility, and provide an estimated $239 million of financial benefits to local, county, and State economies. At full capacity, when built, the Campo Verde solar facility will produce enough electricity to power nearly 40,000 homes.

- Identified 373 existing Bureau of Reclamation canals and conduits with the combined potential to generate an additional 365,000 megawatt hours of hydropower annually, enough to power more than 30,000 homes. This finding builds upon the 191 existing Reclamation dam and reservoir sites identified in 2011 with a potential of 1.2 million megawatt hours annually, enough to power more than 104,000 households each year.

The Department of the Interior's New Energy Frontier initiative includes $99.9 million for renewable energy activities, an increase of $26.4 million above the 2012 enacted level. The funding requested is critical to advance development of vast wind resources along the Atlantic coast and to conduct the necessary environmental work to allow responsible construction of renewable energy power generation and transmission facilities on and through the public lands, particularly those that tie to established transmission corridors.

Bureau of Land Management – In 2013 and 2014, BLM will continue to facilitate and promote the development of renewable energy resources on the vast public lands it manages in the West, lands that are rich in renewable energy resources and potential, including wind, solar, geothermal, and biomass. The BLM lands also serve as corridors for energy transmission infrastructure, a function that is vital to the Nation's overall ability to efficiently and effectively utilize energy and power. The BLM is focused on developing renewable energy in an accelerated but responsible manner, ensuring the protection of signature landscapes, wildlife habitats, and the cultural resources of the public lands. In its pursuit of renewable energy development, BLM works closely and collaboratively with local communities, States, Tribes, industry, conservationists, and other interested stakeholders to develop utility-scale renewable energy projects in the right way and in the right places, to avoid or minimize conflicts with other public land uses.

The 2014 request continues to provide strong support for BLM's contributions to the New Energy Frontier initiative in the responsible development of renewable and conventional energy. The budget request provides a $7.1 million program increase for Renewable Energy to support planning efforts and studies aimed at identifying additional renewable energy development zones or leasing areas and implementation of renewable energy plans scheduled to be completed in 2013 for Arizona, California, and Nevada. The increase will enable BLM to prepare and offer the first competitive solar energy lease sales and allow BLM to continue ongoing program management responsibilities associated with geo-

thermal energy development by replacing permanent funding previously provided for this purpose through the Geothermal Steam Act Implementation Fund, which has expired. The request also reflects the realignment of $2.0 million in geothermal funds from the Oil and Gas Management program to the Renewable Energy Management program, which BLM executed in its 2013 Operating Plan.

Bureau of Ocean Energy Management – The Secretary has delegated to BOEM the Energy Policy Act of 2005 authority to grant leases, easements, or rights-of-way for activities on the OCS related to production, transportation or transmission of energy from renewable sources. In 2012, BOEM completed the first lease under Interior's Smart from the Start initiative, which facilitates environmentally responsible offshore wind development along the OCS by identifying wind energy areas in a coordinated, focused approach with extensive environmental analysis, public review, and large-scale planning. Continuing this momentum, BOEM issued proposed sale notices for the sale of commercial wind energy leases in the Virginia and Rhode Island/Massachusetts offshore wind energy areas, and passed another milestone for renewable energy development by issuing a Determination of No Competitive Interest for the proposed Mid-Atlantic offshore wind energy transmission line. If constructed, it would be the first such major offshore transmission line in the United States.

The BOEM request includes $34.4 million, an increase of $1.4 million from the 2012 enacted level, for renewable energy development activities such as the siting and construction of offshore wind farms on the OCS, as well as other forms of renewable energy such as wave and current. The funds will be used to continue the Department's commitment to the thoughtful development of renewable energy resources for the Nation.

Bureau of Reclamation – The 2014 request allocates $1.1 million for a pilot initiative to increase renewable generation by exploring how renewable energy technologies, including solar, small hydropower, and hydrokinetics, can be integrated into Reclamation projects. Reclamation will continue efforts to: optimize its hydropower projects to produce more energy with the same amount of water; investigate hydro pump-storage projects that can help integrate large amounts of different renewable resources such as wind and solar into the electric grid; and work with Tribes to assist them in developing renewable energy sources. These important projects will assist in the production of cleaner, more efficient renewable energy.

Fish and Wildlife Service – The 2014 FWS renewable energy request includes $14.1 million, an increase of $7.2 million over the 2012 level, to expand capability to fulfill endangered species consultation requirements for renewable energy projects. The request includes a program increase of $1.4 million for scientific research into the impacts of energy transmission and development infrastructure on wildlife and habitat. The research will identify potential impacts associated with the development of energy infrastructure and develop strategies to minimize the impacts on habitat and species likely to be impacted, including the desert tortoise and sage grouse.

The FWS Endangered Species Consultation program will utilize the findings, and a requested program increase of $1.5 million, to conduct environmental reviews associated with proposed renewable energy projects. The request includes a program increase of $2.8 million for conservation planning assistance and $750,000 for migratory bird conservation and monitoring that will enable FWS to cooperate with Federal, State, tribal, and local governments and the renewable energy industry to ensure priority landscape level planning considers the impacts on wildlife and habitat. Application of biological expertise and pro-active consultation and cooperation will limit lengthy delays as project planning nears completion and should minimize legal challenges that might hinder project development.

The FWS will help ensure the Nation's energy development occurs in an environmentally responsible manner, consistent with wind power industry guidelines issued in 2012, and reflective of the Department's long standing commitment to wildlife conservation. The request includes a program increase of $750,000 for law enforcement activities that address the impact of energy development on wildlife and habitat.

Indian Affairs – The 2014 request provides $8.3 million, an increase of $2.3 million above the 2012 enacted level, for renewable energy projects on tribal lands. More than 50 renewable energy projects are ongoing on an estimated 35 reservations. This, however, is barely tapping the potential that exists in Indian Country for renewable energy development. The BIA has identified 267 reservations with renewable energy potential, but the resources on these reservations have not yet been fully determined.

The potential for hydroelectric power on these reservations is significant. A tremendous need exists to quantify the potential on individual reservations to gain a better understanding of how to best develop these resources where Tribes have expressed an interest in doing so. The budget includes an increase of $1.9 million to complement existing program activities to complete technical and engineering studies associated with renewable energy projects. These studies will be used to complete feasibility and financial packages and to start the environmental permitting. Concurrent with assessment of these resources, BIA will also determine the needs and interests of the Indian communities and, in accordance with community interest, work with Tribes to bring these resources to the production stage. Developing these resources has the potential to create green jobs in Indian Country while also helping to alleviate chronic unemployment on Indian reservations.

The BIA is working with several Tribes on hydro-generation projects, providing assistance with the planning of facilities using existing dams. Many reservations have feasibility and environmental studies under review. Detailed planning is required for resource potential, fish disturbance, and potential environmental impact if these projects are to be successful. Currently, most activity is in northern California, and there is potential for future projects within the BIA Rocky Mountain Region. Tribes with the best potential are in the northwest, Rocky Mountains, and Great Plains, and they include Rocky Boy's, Flathead, Crow, Cherokee, Pyramid Lake, Wind River, as well as several northern California Tribes.

U.S. Geological Survey – The 2014 USGS budget includes $9.9 million for renewable energy activities, an increase of $4.0 million over the 2012 enacted level. The increase would fund research to support permitting decisions for alternative energy strategies on Federal lands. The increase would also fund research to provide information on species, populations, habitats, and energy technology

FIRST EVER COMMERCIAL SOLAR ENERGY PROJECT ON AMERICAN INDIAN TRUST LANDS

In June of 2012, Interior approved a 350 megawatt solar energy project on tribal trust land of the Moapa Band of Paiute Indians in Clark County, Nevada, the first ever, utility-scale solar project approved for development on tribal lands. This low impact photovoltaic facility will sit on nearly 2,000 acres of the Tribe's 71,954 acre reservation, located 30 miles north of Las Vegas. The project is expected to generate 400 jobs at peak construction and 15-20 permanent jobs.

In early 2011, the Moapa Band of Paiutes came to the Interior Department with its development partner, K Road Power, to propose plans and after initial discussions, the Bureau of Indian Affairs recommended the project be included on the Department's Priority Project list of renewable energy projects.

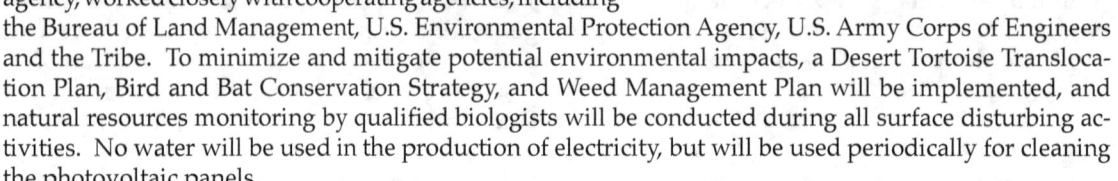

Since that initial meeting, the project has exemplified what can be achieved when the Federal government, Indian Tribes, and private partners work together in pursuit of a common goal. The BIA, through its Western Regional Office, served as the lead agency on the project. Heightened coordination between the BIA and its Federal partners allowed the Department to complete its review within 14 months.

In evaluating the proposed project's compliance with the National Environmental Policy Act, BIA, as the lead Federal agency, worked closely with cooperating agencies, including the Bureau of Land Management, U.S. Environmental Protection Agency, U.S. Army Corps of Engineers and the Tribe. To minimize and mitigate potential environmental impacts, a Desert Tortoise Translocation Plan, Bird and Bat Conservation Strategy, and Weed Management Plan will be implemented, and natural resources monitoring by qualified biologists will be conducted during all surface disturbing activities. No water will be used in the production of electricity, but will be used periodically for cleaning the photovoltaic panels.

The project will generate lease income for the Tribe, create new jobs and employment opportunities for tribal members, and connect the existing tribally-owned Travel Plaza to the electrical grid, decreasing its dependence on a diesel powered generator. The procurement of construction materials and equipment is expected to generate additional sales and use tax revenues for the county and the State.

Collaborating with the Department of Energy's Office of Indian Energy on this project and other projects, interagency efforts are underway to complement and coordinate tribal energy development. The Department of Energy has been providing technical assistance to the Tribe related to distributed hybrid and renewable energy options for its community and facilities.

so the impacts of energy development on natural populations can be assessed and modeled as part of providing decision support tools.

Office of Insular Affairs – In 2012, OIA awarded funding for a wind turbine pilot project in Guam as well as energy efficiency improvements to a number of Government of Guam buildings. These activities are consistent with the 2011 U.S. Department of Energy, National Renewable Energy Laboratory recommendations for initial energy efficiency, renewable energy assessments, and a strategic plan for implementation and deployment. Funding also is being used by the Guam Energy Office to develop an energy code curriculum to train building industry professionals on the importance of following Guam's recently developed Tropical Energy Code.

The budget provides $3.0 million, $1.9 million above the 2012 level, for sustainable energy projects. The Empowering Insular Communities program supports the development and implementation of sustainable energy strategies in all four U.S. territories: American Samoa, Guam, the Commonwealth of the Northern Mariana Islands, and the U.S. Virgin Islands. Strengthening the energy foundations in the islands will reduce their dependence on costly oil imports, help stabilize critical energy services, and attract investment in the local economies.

CONVENTIONAL ENERGY DEVELOPMENT

Today, drilling activities in the Gulf are back to pre-spill levels. And the U.S. is now positioned as a global leader in offshore oil and gas safety. That's good for domestic production and good for the industry as a whole.

Ken Salazar, Secretary of the Interior
April 24, 2012

Over the past several years, Interior has reformed the Nation's onshore and offshore oil and gas programs to expand domestic energy production in a safe and environmentally responsible way. Deepwater Horizon shook Americans' confidence in offshore energy development. Interior moved quickly and aggressively to strengthen safety standards and environmental protections and put in place assurances that companies drilling in deepwater areas are prepared to deal with a blowout.

As part of a comprehensive set of reforms, the Department divided the three conflicting missions of the Minerals Management Service into strong and separate organizations.

At the end of 2012, more rigs were operating in the Gulf than in the previous two and a half years, equaling the number of rigs in the Gulf before the Deepwater Horizon oil spill. Since 2010, the Department issued over 1,800 drilling permits, including 146 new deepwater and 161 new shallow water permits.

In 2012, the Department released a new five-year program for offshore leasing, making areas containing an estimated 75 percent of the technically recoverable offshore oil and gas resources available for exploration and development. Interior oversaw the first new exploratory activity in the Alaskan arctic in a decade under strict safety and environmental oversight. Also in 2012, the Administration reached agreement with the government of Mexico to open up previously off limits transboundary oil and natural gas reservoirs in the Gulf of Mexico. When approved by Congress, this agreement would make accessible nearly 1.5 million acres of the United States OCS, believed to contain as much as 172 million barrels of oil and 304 billion cubic feet of natural gas. In March 2013, Interior held the second sale under the new OCS Plan, the first of five Central Gulf of Mexico lease sales that will be held under the program. The sale generated more than $1.2 billion in high bids.

At the same time, Interior advanced reforms to ensure offshore oil and gas production can continue to expand safely and responsibly. In 2012, the Bureau of Safety and Environmental Enforcement implemented regulations for safety and environmental management systems, issued a new drilling safety rule to refine safety reforms and strengthen requirements, took administrative action to hold contractors accountable for their actions offshore, collaborated with the U.S. Coast Guard to provide consistency in OCS regulation to promote compliance, and participated in the first full-scale industry

capping stack deployment exercise to help prepare for the possibility of a future deepwater blowout.

Onshore, the Department implemented leasing reforms bringing the public into the leasing process earlier, so fewer leases end up in court. Interior has worked to resolve controversies on some of the largest oil and gas projects in the West, including more than 3,500 new wells on Anadarko's Greater Natural Buttes project in Utah, while at the same time safeguarding air quality and assuring the protection of critical wildlife habitat. In December 2012, Secretary Salazar issued a Secretarial Order to promote the co-development of oil and gas and

SCIENCE, RESEARCH, AND INNOVATION IN ENERGY

Science, research, and innovation continue to play a vital role in Interior's efforts to further expand oil and gas production in the U.S. and make sure it's done safely and responsibly. Improvements in technologies like hydraulic fracturing are responsible for greatly increasing the Nation's capacity to develop America's abundant unconventional resources in recent years. Hydraulic fracturing is an oil and gas well development process that involves injecting water under high pressure into a bedrock formation to increase oil and gas flow to a well from petroleum-bearing rock formations.

Through a close collaboration across the government to streamline research efforts, Interior, through the USGS, with the U.S. Department of Energy and the Environmental Protection Agency, is working to meet the critical need of increasing public understanding and public confidence of these technologies in order to continue safe and responsible exploration and production for many decades to come.

The USGS is conducting studies to assess the amount of water required for hydraulic fracturing as well as the impacts of withdrawing water from the local environment. On-the-ground projects are currently proposed or ongoing in more than 15 States to establish baseline water quantity and quality measurements and assessments.

Hydraulic fracturing, directional drilling, and other advanced technologies have enabled the production of oil and gas from rock formations that previously could not be developed. As a result, unconventional resources like shale gas and shale oil are among the fastest growing energy sources in the United States. Unconventional gas now accounts for well over 60 percent of the U.S. gas supply. The USGS has long assessed the amount of oil and gas yet to be discovered using standard industry practices and geologic knowledge at the time of the assessment. High volume hydraulic fracturing coupled with directional drilling is now commonplace; and the USGS has completed many unconventional energy resource assessments of actively producing formations, such as the Marcellus Shale and Bakken Shale, as well as frontier areas such as Alaska, that  are only just now being explored for shale oil or shale gas. Assessments are important not only to help predict the amount of oil and gas that might be available in the future but also to allow land and resource managers to plan and prepare for potential future oil and gas development prudently.

The USGS conducted research that associates deepwell fluid injection, a process sometimes used to dispose of produced waters or flowback waters from hydraulic fracturing and gas production, with the triggering of earthquakes. Earthquakes may occur when the injected fluid reaches a critically stressed fault. Deepwell fluid injection is a technique in which wastewater, typically produced waters from the petroleum formation and flowback from the fracking operation, is injected back into the Earth for storage. The USGS is researching the factors that control the generation of injection-induced earthquakes and maintains information regarding the potential earthquake hazards associated with deepwell fluid injection.

potash resources in New Mexico, addressing a long standing source of serious conflict regarding the sequencing of production of these resources.

In November 2012, BLM held its second annual oil and gas lease sale in the National Petroleum Reserve - Alaska, offering nearly 4.5 million acres for development. In February 2013, the Department finalized the Integrated Activity Plan Record of Decision for the National Petroleum Reserve, providing a roadmap to facilitate appropriate energy development and conservation in the right places.

Interior finalized a new plan in March 2013 to promote research, demonstration, and development of oil shale and tar sand resources on public lands in Colorado, Utah, and Wyoming. BLM signed two leases for RD&D oil shale proposals in Colorado, to encourage industry to develop and test technologies aimed at developing oil shale resources on a commercial scale.

The Department is also part of a multi-agency research and development effort with the Department of Energy and the Environmental Protection Agency to better understand and minimize potential environmental, health, and safety impacts of energy development involving hydraulic fracturing. New work will build on existing efforts and address issues such as water quality and quantity; ecosystem, community, and human health impacts; and induced seismicity. Continued support for this collaboration is included in the 2014 budget.

Other Department actions taken in 2012 to advance the safe development of conventional energy sources on public lands and waters include:

- Groundbreaking steps to assess the conventional energy resource potential in the Mid- and South Atlantic with the release of a draft Programmatic Environmental Impact Statement. This milestone advances BOEM's regionally-tailored approach to OCS exploration and development, consistent with the OCS Oil and Gas Leasing Program for 2012-2017.
- New initiatives to expedite safe and responsible development of domestic energy resources on U.S. public lands and Indian trust lands in the Dakotas, Montana, and States across the Country as part of BLM's ongoing efforts to ensure efficient processing of oil and gas permit applications. The Bureau is implementing new automated tracking systems that are expected to reduce the review period for drilling permits by two-thirds and expedite the sale and processing of Federal oil and gas leases. The new system will track permit applications through the entire review process and quickly flag any missing or incomplete information, greatly reducing the back-and-forth between BLM and industry applicants currently needed to amend paper applications.

- Released a new estimate for potential additions to domestic oil and gas reserves from reserve growth in discovered, conventional accumulations in the United States. The USGS estimates the mean potential of undiscovered, conventional reserve additions for the United States total 32 billion barrels of oil, 291 trillion cubic feet of natural gas, and 10 billion barrels of natural gas liquids, an estimated ten percent of the overall U.S. oil and gas endowment.

- Approved a land-into-trust application from the Three Affiliated Tribes of the Fort Berthold Reservation, the first in a series of necessary approvals that will enable the Tribes to build the first U.S. refinery in decades, supporting American made energy, including domestic resources from the Bakken Formation, while also creating jobs.

The 2014 budget request for current and permanent conventional energy and minerals programs is $671.7 million, an increase of $71.0 million above the 2012 level, to support environmentally sound and safe development of conventional energy resources on public lands and the OCS. This includes an increase of $32.0 million to continue aggressive implementation of reforms within BOEM and BSEE.

Bureau of Land Management – Federal onshore oil and gas resources are vital components of the Nation's energy portfolio. In May, 2010, BLM implemented leasing reforms to establish a more orderly, open, and environmentally sound process for developing oil and gas resources on public lands that has resulted in a significant decline in the number of protests. In fiscal year 2012, only 18 percent of BLM's oil and gas leases were protested, down from 47 percent in 2009.

The 2014 request enhances BLM's ability to support oil and gas development on Federal lands. The request for Oil and Gas Management includes a $10.0 million increase to continue implementation of the important leasing reforms first instituted in

May 2010 and restores base funding for oil and gas oversight to 2011 levels.

The budget also proposes to expand and strengthen BLM's oil and gas inspection capability with revenues from new fees on industry. The BLM is taking steps to improve its oil and gas inspection capabilities. The Bureau has transitioned to a risk-based inspection strategy and will continue to expand its implementation. This strategy will help ensure the highest risk cases are inspected each year. The budget proposes $48.0 million in new inspection fee collections, which will offset a proposed reduction of $38.0 million in appropriated funds, providing for a net increase of $10.0 million for inspection and enforcement activities. The additional funds will enable BLM to conduct defensible and timely lease parcel environmental analyses and correct deficiencies identified by GAO in its February 2011 report, which designated Federal management of oil and gas resources, including production and revenue collection, as high-risk.

Bureau of Ocean Energy Management – The 2014 BOEM budget includes $135.0 million for conventional energy activities, an increase of $7.3 million over the 2012 level. Within this total, $63.8 million is provided for environmental assessments, including $700,000 to support necessary baseline environmental characterization and monitoring activities, and $1.1 million to establish an air quality regulatory program in Alaska. The 2012 Consolidated Appropriations Act transferred jurisdiction for air quality monitoring from the Environmental Protection Agency to the Department for OCS sources located offshore the North Slope Borough of the State of Alaska. The new jurisdiction includes both the Beaufort Sea and Chukchi Sea OCS planning areas, or Arctic OCS. With this statutory change in place, Interior, through BOEM, now has responsibility for thoroughly reviewing the potential air quality effects of new offshore operations in these arctic areas, in addition to areas of the Western and Central Gulf of Mexico where BOEM already has jurisdiction. The bureau is undertaking an integrated effort across regions and in close coordination with the EPA to implement this new authority and enhance the program overall.

In 2014, BOEM requests $1.5 million to implement ePlans, a web-based plan submittal and workflow information technology application. The submittal, review, and approval of an OCS Plan are critical steps for offshore lease holders before any operations can commence. This effort to modernize an important component of BOEM's IT infrastructure will achieve significant gains for both the rigor of analysis and the efficiency of plan review, including projected reductions of 30 to 40 percent in review processing time. The automation of this system also will yield significant savings for industry, and increase coordination and opportunities for data-sharing across Federal and State agencies.

Bureau of Safety and Environmental Enforcement
The 2014 request for BSEE includes $222.1 million for conventional energy activities, an increase of $24.8 million over the 2012 level. The request continues strong support for responsible development of offshore oil and gas resources, and the reforms put in place to strengthen regulatory and oversight capability, and foster environmental compliance, inspection, investigation, and enforcement programs.

The Environmental Enforcement program fosters environmental compliance, inspection, investigation, and enforcement programs to assure the highest level of environmental standards for all offshore energy activities. The 2014 request proposes a $4.2 million increase to hire, train, equip, and support a cross section of critical staffing to conduct environmental inspections, Safety and Environmental Management System audits, and investigations. It also will take enforcement actions and evaluate the effectiveness of environmental mitigation measures.

The 2014 request will focus significant increases of $15.2 million for Operations, Safety and Regulation, including program increases of $2.5 million to support the anticipated growth in exploration, development, and production activities on the Alaska OCS, and $1.0 million to streamline the permitting process to support development of a modern electronic system to manage the permitting process. Additional increases are proposed of $1.4 million to research requirements for well structure integrity and $2.0 million for offshore safety systems and operations. As the industry pushes into deeper water and drills more high-pressure/high-temperature wells, BSEE's safety and enforcement protocols must be kept up-to-date. The BSEE will use this increase to keep pace with industry's advancement and ensure the integrity of state-of-the-art equipment and operations. These increases are partially offset by $3.0 million in additional estimated inspection fee collections. Inspection activities also will benefit from a program increase of $3.7 million to support the new National Offshore Training program. The program will provide contemporary learning and development opportunities to BSEE's inspectors and engineers. Courses are designed to enhance safety and environmental stewardship by using the best science and technology to evaluate, protect, and preserve the human, marine, and coastal environments.

The reorganization of the former Minerals Management Service separated the conflicting missions and strengthened oversight of offshore energy development. The request includes a program increase of $4.0 million for BSEE to sustain the necessary level of support services, recruit and retain new inspectors, engineers, and scientists, and conduct additional environmental and technological studies.

Office of Natural Resources Revenue – Through ONRR, the Interior Department seeks to ensure the full and fair return of royalties and other monies owed to the American people from the production of energy and mineral resources, both onshore and on the OCS. This includes ensuring that revenue due to the public is received, accounted for, and appropriately distributed. The means of collecting royalties, rents, and other revenues must be transparent and robust. Revenue distributions, which totaling $12.2 billion in 2012, benefit States, Tribes, individual Indian mineral royalty owners, and U.S. Treasury accounts.

The creation of ONRR on October 1, 2010 as part of the reorganization of the former Minerals Management Service provided an opportunity for a top to bottom review to improve management and oversight of revenue collection and disbursement activities for the Department. The ONRR is focused on implementing priority initiatives aligned to ensure the Department is collecting the government's share of revenue from oil and gas produced on Federal lands, consistent with recommendations made by the Government Accountability Office, Interior's Office of Inspector General, and other external organizations. The Office consistently receives clean audit opinions from annual audits performed by independent auditors.

The 2014 request includes $121.1 million for ONRR's receipts management programs, a $1.6 million increase above the 2012 enacted level, including $1.5 million for fully funded fixed costs. All of the funds requested support conventional energy activities within the New Energy Frontier initiative.

U.S. Geological Survey – The 2014 request for USGS is $39.8 million for conventional energy programs. The request includes an increase of $13.0 million to support an interagency research and development

effort with the Department of Energy and the Environmental Protection Agency to understand and minimize potential environmental, health, and safety impacts of energy development through hydraulic fracturing. Hydraulic fracturing is a process that uses high pressure fluid to create fractures in rock layers to produce petroleum, natural gas, coal seam gas, or other substances. The energy from the injection of a highly-pressurized fluid creates new channels in the rock, which can increase the extraction rates and ultimate recovery of unconventional fossil fuels. The 2014 budget supports the research to understand and address potential impacts on water quality and availability, induced seismicity, earthquakes, ecological effects, and human and community effects, as well as assessment and characterization research in various USGS base programs.

Fish and Wildlife Service – The 2014 request of $3.4 million for FWS conventional energy activities includes a program increase of $250,000 to complement renewable energy funding for law enforcement activities that will help ensure the development of oil, gas, and electricity transmission is consistent with wildlife and habitat conservation. Specific efforts will include educational outreach to energy developers and land management agencies, compliance assistance and monitoring, and investigative work to document violations of law in circumstances where known mitigation measures have not been adopted.

As part of President Obama's all-of-the-above energy strategy, Interior is committed to expanding safe and responsible oil and gas development on public lands and Indian trust lands. With the help of new technology, the Bakken in North Dakota is generating impressive energy production for our Country and creating thousands of American jobs, as well as substantial royalty revenues for the State, Tribes, and taxpayers. By upgrading and improving our oil and gas drilling permit processing systems and technologies, we believe we can improve efficiencies while ensuring thorough reviews for safety and compliance.

Ken Salazar, Secretary of the Interior
April 3, 2012

Indian Affairs – The Office of Indian Energy and Economic Development is working closely with tribal nations to explore and develop conventional energy resources on Indian Trust lands where Tribes are interested in developing these resources. Together, the Office and Tribes are further defining, quantifying, and developing tribal energy resources for industrial scale energy production. The Department estimates energy and mineral development on Indian lands in 2012 supported over $16.0 billion of economic activity and nearly 120,000 jobs related to trust resources. In the last three years, this Office assisted Indian mineral owners in the negotiation of 55 leases for oil, gas, renewable energy, and aggregate materials development on approximately 3.1 million acres. The 2014 request includes $2.5 million for conventional energy and audit compliance, the same as the 2012 enacted level, to support tribal leasing activities on reservations.

Prior to 2006, the Three Affiliated Tribes of the Fort Berthold Reservation had not leased any of their lands for oil and gas exploration for over 25 years. At the request of the Tribes, Indian Affairs staff has been evaluating the oil and gas potential for the Tribes. From 2005 to 2013, IEED assisted the Tribes in the negotiation of lease agreements with oil and gas companies. These lease agreements have allowed the Tribes to share in the success of the oil and gas leasing boom in the Bakken Formation in the Williston Basin. Increased focus from Indian Affairs to approve leases in a timely fashion with a hands-on approach to technical as-sistance helped stimulate oil and gas development in the area. In 2011, over 200 drilling permits and associated rights-of-ways were approved in the area. In 2012, the number of drilling permits and associated rights-of-way permits has risen to over 300. Drilling activity is expected to increase through 2013, with the development rate leveling off to 200 wells per year over the next five years. Nearly 1,000 wells are expected to be drilled to initially develop the Bakken Formation with an additional 1,000 wells drilled to complete full development of the Bakken and Three Forks Formations over the next ten to 20 years.

To provide better coordination and collaboration among interagency staff to respond to increased demand for oil and gas permits in certain regions, Indian Affairs is developing teams to provide technical staff to assist as demand increases. The teams include expert specialists in realty services and environmental compliance, as well as petroleum engineers. The first team is already working on the Fort Berthold Reservation and has provided a solution to the increased workload. A new team is in the initial stages of becoming operational at the Uintah and Ouray Reservation in Utah. Plans are being developed to place a team at the Navajo Regional Office for future lease sale activities of Navajo lands in New Mexico. This concept will be used at other reservations where IEED is seeing an increase in energy development activity.

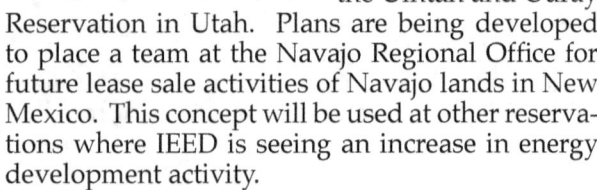

Water Challenges

WaterSMART is a perfect example of the value of strong partnerships that bring Interior together with local water and conservation managers to create sustainable water supplies in the West.

Ken Salazar, Secretary of the Interior
March 21, 2012

The health, security, economic, and ecological well-being of the American people depend on adequate supplies of clean water. Water is needed to stay healthy, produce energy, grow food, advance the economy, and engage in recreation. On a more basic level, water is vital to maintaining healthy ecosystems. The amount of water available to support people, the economy, and the environment is finite. As the need for water continues to grow, available supplies will be increasingly strained, risking the depletion of shared natural resources and raising the potential for conflict.

America's water resource challenges are varied and increasing. Aging water infrastructure, population growth, depletion of groundwater resources, impaired water quality, increasing demand for human and environmental uses, and climate variability and change all play a role in determining the amount of available fresh water.

Water shortages and conflicts among competing uses have become more commonplace in many areas of the United States, even in normal water years. Prolonged drought and increasing demands for water are exacerbating the challenges facing water managers, and traditional approaches no longer meet today's needs. As competition for water resources grows, so does the need for information and tools to aid water resource managers.

State governments and a complex array of laws and ownership regimes govern water allocation and use, but the Federal government has a role to play by providing leadership and support for sustainable water stewardship.

The Administration places a priority on ensuring clean and safe water supplies and on restoring and protecting ecosystems. Federal agencies must work together with State and local governments, Tribes, industry, the agricultural sector, and other non-governmental partners to achieve these goals. These integrated efforts will lead to improved strategies and results to better protect the Nation's water resources.

> *Imbalances between water supply and demand are increasing in intensity, geographical scope, and complexity. The WaterSMART program is designed to help secure and stretch existing water supplies, provide tools that support better management of water, and advance research and projects that contribute to water sustainability.*
>
> *Anne Castle*
> *Assistant Secretary – Water and Science*
> *March 22, 2013*

WATERSMART
SUSTAIN AND MANAGE AMERICA'S RESOURCES FOR TOMORROW

Interior continues to implement the multiple components of the WaterSMART program, established by Secretary Salazar in 2010. The goals of the program are to secure and stretch water supplies for use by existing and future generations to benefit people, the economy, and the environment, and identify adaptive measures needed to address climate change and future demands. The Program's successes are showcased in *WaterSMART – A Three-Year Progress Report*, published in October 2012.

In 2012, the Department of the Interior focused efforts to promote sustainable water strategies, and improve water management through science, collaboration, and cooperation. These approaches are demonstrated by efforts underway to examine water resources in the Colorado River Basin and other basins, the U. S. Geological Survey Water Census, and the Cooperative Watershed Management program. Comprehensive basin-wide approaches such as these will be critical to assessing water needs, evaluating the availability of and risks to water supplies, and planning for the impacts of reduced availability and increasing demands in collaboration with Interior's partners. The Colorado River Basin was selected as a study pilot area for coordinated strategies in water management as part of the WaterSMART initiative.

Spanning parts of the seven Basin States of Arizona, California, Colorado, Nevada, New Mexico, Utah, and Wyoming, the Colorado River Basin is one of the most critical sources of water in the West. The Colorado River and its tributaries provide water to nearly 40 million people for municipal use, irrigate nearly 5.5 million acres of land, and are the lifeblood for at least 22 federally recognized Tribes, seven national wildlife refuges, four national recreation areas, and eleven national parks. Hydropower facilities along the Colorado River provide more than 4,200 megawatts of generating capacity, helping to meet the power needs of the West and offset the use of fossil fuels. The Colorado River is also vitally important to meeting Mexico's agricultural and municipal water needs, and serves as host to a variety of endangered species.

The challenges and complexities of ensuring a sustainable water supply and meeting future demand in an over-allocated and highly variable system such as the Colorado River have been recognized and documented in several studies conducted by the Bureau of Reclamation, USGS, and the Basin States over the past several decades. Looking ahead, concerns regarding the ability of the Colorado River system to meet future needs are even more apparent, given the likelihood of increasing demand for water throughout the Basin coupled with projections of reduced supply due to climate change.

Colorado River Basin Water Supply and Demand Study – Completed in December 2012, the purpose of the study was to define current and future imbalances in water supply and demand in the Basin and the neighboring areas of the Basin States that receive Colorado River water over the next 50 years, through 2060, and to develop and analyze adaptation and mitigation strategies to resolve those imbalances. Of particular importance, the Colorado River Basin Study provides the participants an opportunity to collaborate on scenario planning. Developed with input from a broad range of Basin Study participants, the water supply and demand scenarios incorporate key factors that drive future uncertainty. These factors include changes in natural systems including climate, demographics and land use, technology and economics, and social and governance structures. The Study did not result in a decision on how future imbalances should be addressed. Rather, the Study provides a common technical foundation and identifies a range of potential challenges and solutions that may be considered to resolve them. The Study —including a discussion of the methodologies—is available at www.usbr.gov/lc/region/programs/crbstudy.html.

Other On-going Basin Studies – Throughout 2013, Reclamation will continue the strong partnerships with local water and conservation managers working together on comprehensive water studies in the Los Angeles Basin in California; the Pecos River Basin

COLORADO RIVER BASIN WATER SUPPLY AND DEMAND STUDY

On December 12, 2012, Secretary of the Interior Ken Salazar announced the release of a study that projects water supply and demand imbalances throughout the Colorado River Basin and adjacent areas over the next 50 years. The Colorado River Basin Water Supply and Demand Study, the first of its kind, also includes a wide array of adaptation and mitigation strategies proposed by stakeholders and the public to address the projected imbalances.

This Study is one of a number of ongoing basin studies that Reclamation is undertaking through Interior's WaterSMART program....These analyses pave the way for stakeholders in each basin to come together and determine their own water destiny. This Study is a call to action, and we look forward to continuing this collaborative approach as we discuss next steps.

Anne Castle, Assistant Secretary – Water and Science
December 12, 2012

Authorized by the 2009 SECURE Water Act, the Study analyzes future water supply and demand scenarios based on factors such as projected changes in climate and varying levels of growth in communities, agriculture, and business in the seven Colorado River Basin States of Arizona, California, Colorado, Nevada, New Mexico, Utah, and Wyoming.

The average difference between supply and demand is projected to be greater than 3.2 million acre-feet by 2060, according to the Study. One acre-foot of water is approximately the amount used by a single household of four people in a year. The Study projects the largest increase in demand will come from municipal and industrial users, owing to population growth. The Colorado River Basin currently provides water to some 40 million people, and the Study estimates this number could nearly double to 76.5 million people by 2060, under a rapid growth scenario.

The Study includes over 150 proposals from study participants, stakeholders, and the public that represent a wide range of potential options to resolve supply and demand imbalances. Proposals include increasing water supply through reuse and desalinization methods and reducing demand through increased conservation and efficiency efforts. The Study does not determine how future imbalances should or will be addressed. Reclamation intends to work with stakeholders to explore in-basin strategies, rather than proposals—such as major trans-basin conveyance systems—that are not considered cost effective or practical.

Through the Colorado River Basin Study, the Basin States have taken established partnerships to a higher level, providing huge benefits to the States.

Kay Brothers
Deputy General Manager of Engineering and Operations (retired)
Southern Nevada Water Authority

The ability to share the collective wisdom and experience of water managers representing the seven Basin States, the Tribes, the Federal government, and NGOs benefits all of the States involved.

Ted Kowalski, Interstate and Federal Section Chief
Colorado Water Conservation Board

Throughout the course of the three-year Study, eight interim reports were published to reflect technical developments and public input. Public comments were encouraged on the final Study and were summarized and posted to the website for consideration in future basin planning activities.

in New Mexico; the Republican River Basin in Colorado, Kansas, and Nebraska; the Sacramento-San Joaquin River Basins in California; and the Upper Washita River Basin in Oklahoma.

National Water Census – Another key component of Interior's water sustainability strategy is to inform the public and decisionmakers about the status and changes over time of the Nation's freshwater resources. Through the WaterSMART program, the USGS has developed and begun implementation of the WaterSMART Availability and Use Assessment program—known as the National Water Census. The Census will provide a more accurate picture of the quantity and quality of the Nation's water resources for beneficial uses and a basis for improved forecasting of water availability for future economic, energy production, and environmental uses. The concept of a Census is consistent with the SECURE Water Act, which calls for the establishment of a WaterSMART Availability and Use Assessment within USGS.

The Census includes a series of studies, focused on selected large watersheds, where there is a desire on the part of watershed stakeholders to conduct a comprehensive technical assessment of water availability with the best available tools. These Geographic Focus Area Studies help to assess water availability in these watersheds and provide opportunities to test and improve approaches for future studies.

Throughout 2013, USGS will finalize the framework within which the Census will be conducted and continue Geographic Focus Area Studies of water availability and use in the Colorado, Delaware, and Apalachicola-Chattahoochee-Flint River Basins:

- *Colorado River Basin* – While surface water in the Colorado River Basin is carefully regulated and monitored, other components of the water budget are less well understood. Through stakeholder consultations and as a result of issues identified during the Colorado River Basin Water Supply and Demand Study, USGS identified the following major components of the Basin water budget for investigation: 1) estimation of current water use—in particular the consumptive use of water—and historical and future trends in water use, 2) assessments of evapotranspiration and dynamic variation in snowpack water content on a regional and yield of water scale, and 3) estimation of groundwater discharge to

> The Census is a great example of leveraging resources for both the benefit of regional water management and the WaterSMART Availability and Use Assessment. The Delaware River Basin Commission is getting invaluable assistance in the form of customized work products that advance our long-term Strategy for Sustainable Water Resources, and the U.S. Geological Survey is getting very specific integrated water resource management feedback from a data rich Basin that will inform and ground truth the National Water Census—to ensure that it is a value added to water managers across the Nation.
>
> **Robert Tudor**
> **Deputy Executive Director**
> **Delaware River Basin Commission**
>
> **WaterSMART – A Three Year Progress Report**, published October 2012

streams and rivers. Better quantification of these components of the Basin water budget will inform water managers of water sources and movement and enhance their ability to make resource management decisions. For example, preliminary studies by USGS indicate that somewhere between 20 and 60 percent of the surface water flow in the upper Basin is derived from groundwater discharge. Identification of stream reaches that receive large amounts of groundwater discharge will be a major effort in the upper portion of the Colorado River Basin during the Geographic Focus Area Study.

- *Apalachicola-Chattahoochee-Flint River Basin* – Increased water use for municipal and industrial supplies, power generation, and agriculture has led to conflict over water resources in the Apalachicola-Chattahoochee-Flint River Basin among Alabama, Florida, and Georgia. Competition over water is not limited to the State borders since during drought conditions, competition among all water users can become pronounced. The Apalachicola-Chattahoochee-Flint Geographic Focus Area Study, currently underway, will provide information for water managers including enhanced water use information and linked surface water and groundwater models. This information also provides input to ecological models to predict changes in fish and mussel populations, including endangered and threatened species, in streams that flow into main stem rivers. Together, the databases and models can be used to make better decisions regarding future growth and water use, and potential effects on water availability for diverse uses.

- *Delaware River Basin* – The Delaware River Basin covers parts of the four States of Delaware, New Jersey, New York, and Pennsylvania. The Basin has the largest inter-basin withdrawal of water east of the Mississippi River and provides water to over 15 million people. The information, databases, and products developed as a part of the Delaware River Basin Geographic Focus Area Study will inform the Delaware River Basin Commission's strategy for a sustainable future water supply. Products will include: 1) a database of water withdrawal, use, and return flow information for watersheds that will be accessible to basin water resource managers; 2) a web-based tool developed using index streamgages of daily streamflow from 1960 to 2010 to estimate flows for ungaged streams in the Basin; 3) an evaluation of water needs for the Basin's aquatic ecological systems including an updated decision support system for sections of the River to evaluate and adapt reservoir release flow to enhance habitat and the development of tributary response relations for interacting aquatic species; and 4) an easy to use hydrologic model of the non-tidal portions of the watershed tributaries to evaluate potential impacts from future population, land use, or water demand scenarios.

Cooperative Watershed Management and the National Blueways System – In 2012, Interior established the Cooperative Watershed Management program in the Bureau of Reclamation under authority from the Omnibus Public Land Management Act of 2009. This program has been very successful in building locally based support. A solicitation in 2012 to allocate $250,000 generated 30 proposals requesting a total of $1.7 million in Federal funds. Expansion of this program has allowed Interior to broaden its reach to better meet the objectives of the Department's National Blueways System and encourage partnerships that will sponsor projects to conserve river resources like those of the Connecticut River.

In May 2012, the Secretary of the Interior established the National Blueways System to recognize and support locally led efforts to sustain the economic, recreational, and natural values of rivers and watersheds of national significance. The designation does not establish a new protective status or regulation, but provides recognition and support for existing local and regional conservation, recreation, restoration efforts, and coordination of ongoing Federal, State, tribal, and local activities in the watershed. The 2014 budget proposes $3.6 million Department-wide, $3.3 million in the Fish and Wildlife Service, and $250,000 in the Cooperative Watershed Management program in Reclamation to expand this important program supporting landscape-scale collaborative conservation with watershed partnerships. The $3.3 million in the FWS budget will be used to provide candidate and designated National Blueways partnerships with financial assistance to support partnership coordination and watershed projects. Funds will be available to land management bureaus in the Department including BLM, Reclamation, FWS, and the National Park Service as grants and cooperative agreements. Projects will be selected via a joint decisionmaking process of the National Blueways Committee, consisting of members from these land management bureaus.

WATERSMART
(dollars in millions)

	2013 Full Yr CR [1/]	2012 Enacted	2014 Request	Change from 2012	Change from 2013
BUREAU OF RECLAMATION					
WaterSMART Grants	24.5	12.2	12.0	-0.2	-12.5
Basin Studies	6.0	4.9	4.7	-0.2	-1.3
Cooperative Watershed Management	0.3	0.2	0.3	0.0	0.0
Shared Investment Water Innovation Program	0.0	0.0	1.0	+1.0	+1.0
Title XVI Water Reclamation/Reuse Program ..	20.3	24.7	14.0	-10.7	-6.3
Water Conservation Field Services	4.9	5.0	3.4	-1.6	-1.4
Subtotal, Reclamation	**55.9**	**47.1**	**35.4**	**-11.7**	**-20.5**
U.S. GEOLOGICAL SURVEY					
Fisheries	0.5	0.5	1.9	+1.4	+1.4
Land Change Science	0.6	0.5	0.6	+0.1	0.0
Contaminant Biology	0.0	0.0	1.0	+1.0	+1.0
Toxic Substances Hydrology	0.0	0.0	1.8	+1.8	+1.8
Groundwater Resources	2.7	2.7	4.5	+1.8	+1.8
National Water Quality Assessment	1.1	0.0	3.3	+3.3	+2.2
Hydrologic Research and Development	0.0	0.0	0.3	+0.3	+0.3
Hydrologic Networks and Analysis	5.4	4.3	6.6	+2.3	+1.2
Cooperative Water Program	1.5	0.0	2.0	+2.0	+0.5
National Cooperative Geologic Mapping	0.0	0.0	0.2	+0.2	+0.2
National Geospatial Program	0.2	0.0	0.2	+0.2	0.0
Subtotal, U.S. Geological Survey	**12.0**	**8.0**	**22.5**	**+14.5**	**+10.5**
TOTAL, WATERSMART PROGRAM	**67.9**	**55.1**	**57.9**	**+2.8**	**-10.0**

[1/] *2013 Full Year Continuing Resolution, P.L. 112-175, annualized.*

2014 BUDGET SUMMARY

Water and energy are linked....Water is necessary to generate power, while energy is required to store, move, and treat water. Water saved is energy earned, and energy saved is water earned.

Michael Connor, Commissioner
Bureau of Reclamation
October 11, 2012

Interior's 2014 budget request includes $57.9 million for the WaterSMART program, including $35.4 million for Reclamation and $22.5 million for USGS.

Bureau of Reclamation – The Department is the largest supplier and manager of water in the 17 western States. Reclamation manages 476 dams and 337 reservoirs that deliver water to over 31 million people. These facilities deliver water to one in every five western farms for about ten million acres of irrigated land. Reclamation is also the Nation's

second largest producer of hydroelectric power, generating 40 billion kilowatt hours of energy each year from 58 power plants, including five plants owned by Reclamation but operated by other entities. Hydropower is the Nation's primary source of renewable energy. Reclamation is improving operational efficiencies at existing hydropower generation facilities and looking into the integration of hydropower production with other renewable resources. In addition, Reclamation's facilities provide substantial flood control, as well as many recreational and fish and wildlife habitat benefits. Reclamation has an important role in providing leadership and assistance to States, Tribes, and local communities to address competing demands for water.

The Department's 2014 budget request includes $35.4 million for water sustainability efforts through Reclamation, a decrease of $11.7 million from 2012 and $20.5 million below the annualized 2013 Continuing Resolution, P.L. 112-175, in recognition of the constrained fiscal environment. In 2014, Reclamation will continue implementing the existing WaterSMART components, including the WaterSMART Grants, Basin Studies program, mation will continue to award competitive grants that require a minimum 50 percent non-Federal cost-share and which may include the following:

- Water and energy efficiency improvements that save water, increase energy efficiency and the use of renewable energy in water management, address endangered species and other environmental issues, and facilitate transfers to new uses. WaterSMART recognizes the connection between energy and water use and emphasizes the need to continue to develop sources of renewable energy.

- Pilot and demonstration projects to address the technical and economic viability of treating and using brackish groundwater, seawater, impaired waters, or otherwise creating new water supplies within a specific locale.

- System optimization reviews that assess the potential for water management improvements and identify specific ways to implement those improvements.

- Projects to develop tools to more efficiently manage water resources in a changing climate.

Reclamation generally funds new water conservation projects that can be completed within two or three years to encourage near-term impacts on water savings. Reclamation considers water conservation, the use of water markets, and improved efficiency as crucial elements of plans to address western water issues. With leveraged water sustainability grants, the 2014 budget continues the important investment in increasing conservation and advancing the efficient use of water in the West.

With the funding requested in 2014, Reclamation anticipates initiating 27 new WaterSMART Grant projects, including those that will contribute to the Priority Goal for Water Conservation. Reclamation will also continue to develop the WaterSMART Clearinghouse website—a tool for sharing water conservation information with the public and water resources managers—to help coordinate and integrate sustainable water strategies.

Basin Studies – The Department's budget request includes $4.7 million for Reclamation's Basin Studies program. The 2014 request is a decrease of $194,000 from 2012 and $1.3 million from the 2013 Full Year Continuing Resolution. In 2014, Reclamation will continue the following activities:

Title XVI Water Reclamation and Reuse program, Cooperative Watershed Management program, and Water Conservation Field Services program—and a new Shared Investment Water Innovation program.

WaterSMART Grants – The 2014 budget request includes $12.0 million for WaterSMART Grants, a decrease of $233,000 from 2012 and $12.5 million from the 2013 Continuing Resolution annualized. Recla-

> *The Basin Studies program is perhaps the most valuable component of the WaterSMART in that it leverages Reclamation funding and the extensive expertise of its water professionals in a collaborative effort with equally knowledgeable State and local water interests to identify practical, implementable solutions to existing or anticipated shortages. The Basin Studies conducted to date have advanced the state of knowledge about the dynamics of each particular watershed and brought to bear the collective expertise of interested stakeholders to formulate constructive actions to address imbalances.*
>
> *Anne Castle*
> *Assistant Secretary – Water and Science*
> *March 22, 2013*

- Conduct state-of-the-art projections of future water supply and demand on a basin-wide scale, analyses of how the basins' existing water and power operations and infrastructure will perform in the face of changing water supplies and needs, develop recommendations on the optimization of operations and infrastructure to supply adequate water in the future, and perform trade-off analyses of the options identified. Funding also will continue for SECURE Water Act feasibility studies, initiated in 2013. Through the feasibility studies, Reclamation will collaborate with willing States, Tribes, and local water management entities on a 50/50 cost-share basis to evaluate the implementation of adaptation strategies developed in basin studies or equivalent studies to address demand and supply imbalances, including those caused by the effects of climate change. The feasibility studies are selected through a competitive process to ensure that studies that best meet program goals are funded. Reclamation will not seek authorization or appropriations for projects identified in the feasibility studies.

- Continue West-wide climate risk assessments to provide a baseline of water supply, demand, and operations risks and impacts associated with climate change. This information will provide a consistent foundation for basin studies across the western States and support the Landscape Conservation Cooperative partnerships. Through this activity, Reclamation will assess the climate change risks to water supplies and demands, and identify impacts to Reclamation's operations to better support development of adaptation options through future basin studies. In 2014, this will include an analysis of how climate projections can be incorporated into Reclamation planning processes such as feasibility studies, among others. The information developed through these assessments will be communicated with partners through the LCC partnerships and other venues.

- Participate in and support the Desert and Southern Rockies LCC partnerships. These partnerships between Interior and other Federal agencies, States, Tribes, non-governmental organizations, and other stakeholders develop and share applied science tools and approaches that support resource management at the landscape scale. The LCC partnerships leverage the resources and expertise of the partners and work across jurisdictional barriers to focus on natural resource issues specific to a particular ecosystem or landscape. In 2014, Reclamation and FWS will continue to work with LCC partners to evaluate the science and technical capabilities needed to support the Desert and Southern Rockies partnerships, including: 1) building and expanding on existing applied science tools and capabilities and identifying gaps that can be addressed through the Department's Climate Science Centers, universities, and other sources; 2) providing support for adaptation and conservation efforts by various partners in the LCCs, including facilitating data sharing, developing and implementing adaptive management techniques and monitoring plans; and 3) identifying and implementing potential new adaptation strategies to address climate change impacts.

In 2014, Reclamation and its partners will fund one or two basin studies in the western U.S. and one new West-wide climate risk impact assessment, identified as vulnerability assessments under the Priority Goal for Climate Change.

Cooperative Watershed Management – In 2014, Reclamation anticipates awarding four to six projects totaling $250,000 for the establishment and expansion of existing watershed groups through the Cooperative Watershed Management program. Reclamation also will participate in the Department's National Blueways System.

Shared Investment Water Innovation Program – In 2014, Reclamation anticipates initiating a new external water resources grants program of $1.0 million for research and development of new technologies such as water reuse, desalination, water conservation, water infrastructure, and hydropower generation that can help solve complex water problems.

Title XVI Water Reclamation and Reuse Program – Reclamation's budget request in 2014 includes $14.0 million for the Title XVI Water Reclamation and Reuse program, a major component of the WaterSMART strategy. The 2014 level for Title XVI is a decrease of $10.7 million from 2012 and $6.3 million below the 2013 annualized Continuing Resolution. Title XVI projects will identify and investigate opportunities to reclaim and reuse wastewater and naturally impaired ground and surface water in the 17 western States and Hawaii. Title XVI provides authority for project sponsors to receive Federal funding on a cost-shared basis for planning, design, construction, and pre-construction activities. Only Congressionally authorized Title XVI projects are eligible to receive funding for design and construction activities.

Title XVI projects have the potential to stretch water supplies using time-tested methodologies and piloting new concepts. By making use of recycled and reused water, these projects spur significant investments, creating long-term water supplies for communities, and avoiding the need to develop new supplies. Federal investments in Title XVI projects, including all projects funded since 1992, made available an estimated 295,000 acre-feet of water in 2012. The 2014 budget includes $14.0 million for distribution, on a competitive basis, to those authorized projects that best reduce existing diversions, address specific water supply issues in a cost-effective manner, resolve and address environmental and water quality concerns, and meet other program goals.

Water Conservation Field Services – The 2014 Reclamation budget request includes $3.4 million to provide small scale, cost-shared financial assistance at the local level for water conservation planning activities, on-the-ground efficiency improvements, and demonstration projects. Applicants must compete for funding that is capped at $100,000 per project. The 2014 budget is a decrease of $1.6 million from 2012 and $1.4 million below the 2013 Full Year Continuing Resolution.

U.S. Geological Survey – The USGS provides a broad range of expertise in geography, geology,

hydrology, biology, and data integration that is used by Federal agencies, Tribes, States, local communities, and others in water management and science. The USGS data and analyses of water quality and quantity help resource managers develop, regulate, and monitor management practices to ensure the continued availability of water resources.

The need to quantify, forecast, protect, and secure fresh water sources to meet demands now and into the future was recognized when Congress established a National WaterSMART Availability and Use Assessment program in 2009. The last assessment of the availability and use of water resources in the United States was completed in 1978—over 30 years ago. The collection of new and continuing assessment data of the Nation's water resources is needed to ensure future water supplies.

The 2014 budget request includes $22.5 million for the USGS WaterSMART Availability and Use Assessment program—known as the National Water Census. This is a $14.5 million increase from 2012 and $10.5 million from the 2013 Full Year Continuing Resolution. An interdisciplinary science approach will be used to implement this assessment.

Regional Estimates of Baseflow and Recharge – Any water budget analysis for water availability has to consider groundwater as a critical component. However, regional groundwater availability studies will not be completed for more than a decade and are focused on only 40 of the 62 priority principal aquifers of the United States. During the intervening time–and for those areas that are not slated for regional groundwater availability studies—baseflow and recharge estimates are needed for basin focused water budget analyses under WaterSMART. In 2014, the Groundwater Resources Program will develop regional techniques for these estimates.

Ecological Water Science – The USGS will advance understanding of wildlife and habitat water needs by classifying streams across the Nation based on their hydro-ecological type, systematically examining ecological responses to hydrologic alterations, developing flow alteration, and ecological response relationships for each type of river or stream. Efforts in 2011 and 2012 concentrated on the classification system for streams and supported ecological water needs work in the geographic focus areas—the Apalachicola-Chattahoochee-Flint River Basin, Colorado River Basin, and Delaware River Basin. In 2013 and continuing into 2014, USGS is working to complete the classification system and develop a means to link hydrologic data to biological databases to allow for the systematic analysis of ecological responses to hydrologic alteration.

Water Quality Assessment – In 2013 and continuing into 2014, USGS will work to better understand how natural and human-induced variability in water quality and quantity are linked; develop ways of assessing the degree to which these linkages influence water availability for human uses and ecosystem services; and improve understanding of the cause and effect linkages between water quantity and quality. This involves integrating water quality and quantity information and relating it to the human and ecological needs for the water.

Geographic Area Focus Studies – In 2014, USGS is continuing its geographically focused studies of water availability and use in the Colorado River Basin States of Arizona, California, Colorado, Nevada, New Mexico, Utah, and Wyoming; the Delaware River Basin States of Delaware, New Jersey, New York, and Pennsylvania; and the Apalachicola-Chattahoochee-Flint River Basins in the States of Alabama, Florida, and Georgia.

National Groundwater Monitoring Network – Section 9507(b) of the SECURE Water Act authorizes the National Groundwater Monitoring Network, a groundwater monitoring program for each major aquifer system located in the U.S. The Network will bring comparable monitoring data together from disparate sources to close spatial data gaps and evaluate national-scale groundwater levels, quality, and rates of change. In 2013, USGS began implementation of the Network. With additional funds in 2014, USGS will:

- Provide day-to-day management of the Network and provide guidance to data providers.

- Transition from a pilot-scale Network data portal to a production-scale portal.

- Use hydrologic information and modeling tools currently available and being developed for selected major aquifers, as part of the Groundwater Resources Program groundwater availability studies, to identify monitoring locations to enhance the national network.

- Incorporate groundwater level and groundwater quality data from selected wells and springs into the Network in consultation with State, tribal, and local entities.

- Establish a National Program Board composed of Network data providers.

- Begin expansion of the Groundwater Climate Response Network to improve understanding of the effects of global climate change on groundwater recharge and availability.

Information Management – Managing the various data streams and integrating this information into a cohesive picture is a major effort of WaterSMART. The USGS is developing a system to use historical streamgage data to estimate stream flows at stations that do not have streamgages, and to make the data available to the public. Efforts begun in 2013 and continuing into 2014 will concentrate on storing, integrating, and providing information about water budget components within a defined watershed.

Streamflow Estimation and Hydrologic Stressors – The USGS researchers are developing a system to allow decisionmakers access to critical water budget information for water availability analyses. Streamflow is one of the most critical components of a water budget. Future efforts will concentrate on storing, integrating, and serving information about water budget components within a defined watershed. The goal is a web-based system in which the user can access all information on daily streamflows, recharge, precipitation, evapotranspiration, storage, and monthly water use characteristics for that watershed and all associated watersheds that may impact its characteristics. The same system will be used to develop the water budget and access information on historical trends in water budget components. One integrating tool of the WaterSMART web system is the USGS National Hydrography Dataset. The NHD provides USGS scientists with a means of relating information about hydrologic stressors, like water withdrawals and return flows, to the stream network. In 2014, USGS will begin to populate that information into NHD and relate it to streamflow estimation models.

Water use information, which delineates the direct hydrologic stressors caused by human water withdrawals and return flows, is critical to WaterSMART's water budget analyses. This information, collected mostly at State, regional, and local levels, must be obtained on a geospatially site-specific scale to be fully useful in WaterSMART analyses. More work is required to develop improved methods of sampling, estimating, aggregating, and presenting water use data. Research into new methods that use remote sensing and spatial datasets in water use estimation is needed. The Cooperative Water Program will work directly with State, tribal, regional, and local cooperators to maximize use of their water use datasets in water availability and use assessments. Priority will be placed on irrigation and self-supplied industrial water use. The USGS will integrate this information with decision support tools to facilitate its use in water resource management decisionmaking.

RESOLVING LAND AND WATER CLAIMS

Today's agreement signifies not only another major milestone in progress toward the Navajo-Gallup Water Supply Project, but also the high priority the Obama Administration has placed on completing the project to deliver clean running water to Navajo communities—many for the first time.

Ken Salazar, Secretary of the Interior
September 27, 2012

The 2014 budget request for Indian water settlements demonstrates the Administration and Department's strong commitment to resolving tribal water rights claims and ensuring that Tribes have access to use and manage water to meet domestic, economic, cultural, and ecological needs. Including funding for technical and legal support and for authorized settlements involving tribal waters, the 2014 budget request totals $159.6 million, which is an increase of $25.9 million over 2012 and $35.8 million above the 2013 Full Year Continuing Resolution annualized.

To strengthen the Department's capacity to meet its trust responsibilities and more effectively partner with Tribes on water issues, increases totaling $5.2

CROW TRIBE-MONTANA WATER RIGHTS COMPACT

Secretary of the Interior Ken Salazar, Crow Chairman Cedric Black Eagle, and Montana Governor Brian Schweitzer signed the compact on April 27, 2012—marking a major milestone in implementing the Crow Tribal Water Rights Settlement Act of 2010, which is part of the Claims Resolution Act of 2010. The signing of the Compact authorized $460.0 million and calls for the Bureau of Reclamation to plan, design, and construct a municipal, rural, and industrial water system for the Tribe and to rehabilitate and improve the Crow Irrigation Project.

The Obama Administration is proud to be a party to the Crow-Montana Compact. Signing the Compact...demonstrates the Administration's continued commitment to resolving Indian water rights and providing settlements that truly benefit Indian Tribes....The Compact not only ensures delivery of a much-needed safe supply of water for the Crow community, but will also bolster their economic security.

Ken Salazar, Secretary of the Interior
April 27, 2012

Water is life. This Compact ensures that Crow people will have water and the necessary infrastructure for generations to come.

Cedric Black Eagle, Chairman
Crow Tribe Apsáalooke Nation
April 27, 2012

million over 2012 are provided in the budgets of the Bureau of Indian Affairs, Reclamation, and USGS. This includes increases totaling $3.4 million for BIA to support Water Management and Planning, Water Rights Litigation, and to conduct a comprehensive Department-wide evaluation to strengthen engagement, management, and analytical capabilities of the Indian Water Rights Office and other bureaus and offices that work on these issues. An increase of $766,000 in the Reclamation Native American Affairs Program and $1.0 million in the Cooperative Water program at USGS are to strengthen technical analysis in support of water rights settlement work.

The 2014 budget request includes $135.3 million for authorized settlements, including $35.7 million in BIA's budget and $99.7 million in Reclamation's budget. This is an increase of $20.4 million from 2012 and $30.4 million from the 2013 Continuing Resolution annualized.

In 2012, the Department continued moving forward to implement four Indian water rights settlements, signed into law in December 2010, as part of the Claims Resolution Act of 2010 and the ongoing Navajo-Gallup Water Supply project authorized in Title X of the Omnibus Public Land Management Act of 2009. The four settlements provide permanent water supplies and offer economic security for the Taos Pueblo of New Mexico; the Pueblos of Pojoaque, Tesuque, San Ildefonso, and the Nambé involved in the Aamodt settlement in New Mexico; the Crow Tribe in Montana; and the White Mountain Apache Tribe in Arizona. Together, these Acts authorize funding to settle claims to complete and improve reservation water systems, rehabilitate irrigation projects, construct a regional water system, and codify water sharing arrangements with neighboring communities.

The Claims Resolution Act of 2010 authorized the establishment of trust funds for each of the Tribes to manage the development of these projects. Reclamation has primary responsibility for constructing the water systems, while the Bureau of Indian Affairs is responsible for funding the trust funds.

Bureau of Reclamation – In 2014, Reclamation's budget includes $18.2 million for projects that are part of the Claims Resolution Act settlements, including $2.0 million for the White Mountain Apache Settlement, $7.5 million for the Crow Settlement, $4.0 million for the Taos Pueblo Settlement, and $4.7 million for the Aamodt Settlement.

The 2014 budget proposes establishment of a separate Indian Water Rights Settlements account within Reclamation to highlight and segregate these funds to enhance transparency in managing and budgeting settlement construction funds. This proposal would establish an account that parallels the BIA Land and Water Claim Settlements account. The account will include the four settlements discussed above, as well as $60.5 million for the Navajo-Gallup Water Supply Project authorized in 2009. The Navajo-Gallup Project will provide reliable and sustainable municipal, industrial, and domestic water supplies from the San Juan River to 43 Chapters of the Navajo Nation including the Window Rock, Arizona area;

the city of Gallup, New Mexico; the Navajo Agricultural Products Industry; and the southwestern portion of the Jicarilla Apache Nation Reservation in New Mexico.

The 2014 Reclamation budget also contains $21.0 million for ongoing settlement operation and maintenance functions including the Ak Chin Indian Water Rights Settlement Act, San Carlos Apache Tribe Water Settlement Act, Animas-La Plata Project specified in the Colorado Ute Settlement Act, and Nez Perce/Snake River Water Rights Act, which is part of the Columbia and Snake River Recovery Project.

Bureau of Indian Affairs – The 2014 budget includes $35.7 million for the BIA Land and Water Claim Settlements account, which will fund ongoing settlements including:

- *Shoshone-Paiute Tribes of the Duck Valley Reservation Settlement* – The Omnibus Public Land Management Act of 2009 authorizes $60.0 million over five years for the Shoshone-Paiute Tribes of the Duck Valley Reservation Water Settlement. The budget includes $12.0 million for this settlement.

- *Navajo Nation Water Resources Development Trust Fund* – The Omnibus Public Land Management Act of 2009 authorizes $50.0 million over ten years for the Navajo Nation Water Resources Development Trust Fund. The BIA 2014 budget includes $6.0 million—the fifth payment to satisfy this requirement.

$43.0 MILLION AGREEMENT FOR NAVAJO-GALLUP WATER SUPPLY PROJECT

Secretary of the Interior Ken Salazar and Navajo Nation President Ben Shelly announced a $43.0 million financial assistance agreement for design and construction of a portion of the Navajo-Gallup Water Supply Project. The leaders broke ground in June 2012 on the historic project, which, when completed, will have the capacity to deliver clean running water to a potential future population of approximately 250,000. This milestone is one in a series of steps that are part of the larger Navajo-Gallup Water Supply Project.

- *Navajo-Gallup Water Supply Project* – The budget includes $7.8 million for San Juan Conjunctive Use Wells and San Juan River Navajo Irrigation Project Rehabilitation, which are part of the Navajo-Gallup Settlement.

- *Taos Pueblo Indian Water Development Fund* – The budget includes $8.8 million for the first current payment of the Taos Pueblo Indian Water Rights Settlement. This Settlement authorizes the Department to provide a total of $38.0 million to be funded through 2016.

- The budget request also includes $1.0 million for other smaller Indian land and water settlements.

REGIONAL WATER ISSUES

The Department is engaged in water resource and supply activities across the West in areas such as the Klamath Basin, the Colorado River, and California's Bay-Delta.

Klamath Basin – Two agreements designed to restore the Klamath River Basin while also sustaining the communities that rely on the resources of the Basin were approved and signed by a broad cross section of stakeholders. The Klamath Hydroelectric Settlement Agreement, to which the Interior Department is a party, called for a study of the potential removal of four privately owned hydroelectric facilities on the Klamath River. Under this Agreement, congressional action is needed before the Secretary may make a determination whether facilities removal will advance restoration of the salmonid fishery and is in the public interest. The Klamath Basin Restoration Agreement, which the Department has not signed, seeks to restore the communities of the Basin through a series of restoration actions combined with a water agreement for lake levels, river flows, and irrigation needs. Although the Department is not a party to the Klamath Basin Restoration Agreement and would require congressional authorization before becoming a party, a number of restoration and water supply enhancement actions called for under the agreement are authorized under existing law.

The 2014 budget includes $63.4 million for activities in the Klamath Basin across the Department. Of this amount, $52.8 million continues traditional activities including operation of irrigation projects, fisheries management, operation of national wildlife refuges, and other resource enhancements and management actions. In addition to these traditional activities,

Interior is using current authorities to support projects listed in both the Klamath Basin Restoration and Hydroelectric Settlement Agreements including: $7.0 million for BIA to fund acquisition of former reservation lands of the Klamath Tribe to support economic and cultural activities; $3.6 million in the FWS budget, of which $1.6 million will be used for fish related monitoring and modeling—such as fish population, water temperature, hydrology, water quality, fish disease, stock assessments, fish and watershed habitat planning, restoration projects, and projects to improve in stream flows for fish. While actual grant projects have yet to be selected, FWS estimates $2.0 million will be leveraged from the Cooperative Endangered Species Fund for habitat acquisition.

The Department coordinates its efforts with the Department of Agriculture's U.S. Forest Service, the National Oceanic and Atmospheric Administration's National Marine Fisheries Service, the States of California and Oregon, Native American Tribes, and non-governmental organizations.

U.S. AND MEXICO SIGN HISTORIC COLORADO RIVER WATER AGREEMENT

The Colorado River is the lifeblood of local communities from the peaks of Rocky Mountain National Park to the mouth at the Sea of Cortez, supplying water for millions of Americans, irrigating our farms, and helping to power our cities and towns....The Department of the Interior recognizes the many challenges facing the Colorado River, and this bi-national agreement demonstrates our shared commitment to cooperation and partnership to protect and promote its future.

Ken Salazar, Secretary of the Interior
November 20, 2012

Colorado River – On November 20, 2012, Secretary Salazar joined the U.S. and Mexico delegations in San Diego, California, at an official signing ceremony of Minute 319 to the 1944 Treaty with Mexico – a historic bi-national agreement to guide future management of the Colorado River through 2017. A Minute is a rule, agreed to by all parties, which clarifies the Treaty where the original wording was vague or silent on an issue. The five-year agreement approved by both governments provides for a series of joint cooperative actions between the United States and Mexico. Elements of the agreement include:

- Implementing efforts to enhance water infrastructure and promote sharing, storing, and conserving water as needed during both shortages and surpluses.

- Establishing proactive basin operations by applying water delivery reductions when Lake Mead reservoir conditions are low in order to deter more severe reductions in the future.

- Extending humanitarian measures from a 2010 agreement, Minute 318, will allow Mexico to defer delivery of a portion of its Colorado River allotment, storing the water in Lake Mead, while it continues to make repairs to earthquake-damaged infrastructure.

- Establishing a program of Intentionally Created Mexican Allocation whereby Mexico could temporarily reduce its order of Colorado River water, allowing that water to be delivered to Mexico in the future.

- Promoting the ecological health of the Colorado River Delta.

Minute 319 became effective immediately. Many of the projects and programs outlined in the agreement will be implemented through the Bureau of Reclamation.

Another historic milestone was achieved on the Colorado River in November 2012 when Secretary Salazar triggered the first "high-flow experimental release" at Glen Canyon Dam, under a new experimental long-term protocol to better distribute sediment to conserve downstream resources, while meeting water and power needs and allowing continued scientific experimentation, data collection, and monitoring on the Colorado River. The new protocol calls for experimental releases from the Dam through 2020 to send sediment downstream to rebuild sandbars, beaches, and backwaters. The rebuilt areas will provide key wildlife habitat, enhance the aquatic food base, protect archeological sites, and create additional camping opportunities in the Canyon.

The new protocol is built on more than 16 years of scientific research and experimentation conducted under the Glen Canyon Dam Adaptive Management Program. In partnership with stakeholders in the Colorado River Basin, the Department translated the research into a flexible framework that enables scientists to determine, based on the best available data, when the conditions are right to conduct these releases to maximize the ecosystem benefits along the Colorado River corridor in Glen Canyon National Recreation Area and Grand Canyon National Park. The River outlet tubes of the Glen Canyon Dam were opened, releasing additional flows that continued for nearly five days based on the parameters specified in the protocol. Through the foundation laid by the protocol, annual experiments can be conducted through 2020 to evaluate the effectiveness of multiple high flow experimental releases in rebuilding and conserving sandbars, beaches, and associated backwater habitats that have been lost or depleted since the Dam's construction and operation. The protocol identifies the conditions under which a high flow release will likely yield the greatest conservation and beneficial use of sediment deposited by inflows from Colorado River tributaries as a result of rainstorms, monsoons, and snowmelt.

As mentioned above, Reclamation and FWS are leading the Southern Rockies and Desert LCCs. These partnerships were created to address the landscape impacts of change on America's water, land, and other natural and cultural resources and to ensure resource managers have the applied science tools they need to adapt to climate change and threats that cross political boundaries. Significant interest by other Federal, non-Federal and tribal partners exists in participating in these LCCs. The Steering Committee for the Desert partnership has 28 members, including ten Federal partners, five States, seven non-governmental organizations, five Tribes, and one Mexican partner. The Steering Committee for the Southern Rockies partnership has 25 members, including ten Federal partners, seven State agencies, six non-governmental organizations, and two Tribes.

As a result of the Desert and Southern Rockies LCC partnerships, the Department has been able to initiate and support projects that will make important contributions to the Colorado River Basin. These include a project with Arizona Game and Fish to develop a spatial fisheries database and a decision tool that can be used by both wildlife and water managers to forecast the spread of invasive species across the landscape. Another example is a project led by The Nature Conservancy that builds on the Colorado River Basin Study to develop a decision support tool for incorporating ecological flows into water management models used for Basin-wide water supply planning. Additionally, the New Mexico Office of the State Engineer will improve crop coefficients for the Middle Rio Grande by assessing actual crop water use through remote sensing technologies that estimate the evapotranspiration of individual crops within the Basin utilizing Landsat satellite data. Updated decisionmaking models, based on climatic change and other water limiting factors, improve the accuracy of the calculation of water used by crops. The results from this project will provide local, State, tribal, and Federal water managers with a better estimate of future water demand.

Finally, Colorado River restoration efforts are being advanced through the Bureau of Reclamation's Upper Colorado River and San Juan River Recovery programs and the Lower Colorado River Multi-Species Conservation program. These efforts are making significant strides in recovering listed and native fish species and protecting current and future water uses within the Colorado River Basin.

California Bay-Delta – The Sacramento–San Joaquin River Delta is a regional, State, and national treasure. It is an integral part of an ecosystem dependent on more than 750 wildlife species and more than 120 species of fish. As a migratory corridor for numerous species, the Bay-Delta hosts two-thirds of the State's salmon and nearly half of the waterfowl and shorebirds along the Pacific flyway. The Bay-Delta spans five counties and is home to more than 500,000 people. It is a place of great scenic beauty, historic towns, productive farms, close-knit communities, and varied recreation.

The Bay-Delta is the hub of the Nation's largest water delivery system and one of the most important estuary ecosystems. The Bay-Delta provides drinking water to 25 million people and sustains nearly $400 billion of annual economic activity, including a $28.0 billion agricultural industry and a robust set of recreational opportunities. It irrigates more than seven million acres of farmland on which 45 percent of the Nation's fruits and vegetables are grown. It supports a thriving commercial and recreational fishing industry that contributes hundreds of millions of dollars annually to the California economy.

In July 2012, the Governor of California, the Secretary of the Interior, and the Assistant Administrator for Fisheries, National Oceanic and Atmospheric Administration outlined revisions to the proposed Bay-Delta Conservation Plan. The revised Plan, along with a full range of alternative proposals, underwent a rigorous public environmental review completed in late 2012. The parties expect

---

CALIFORNIA AND THE OBAMA ADMINISTRATION OUTLINE A PATH FORWARD FOR THE BAY-DELTA CONSERVATION PLAN

A healthy Delta ecosystem and a reliable water supply are profoundly important to California's future....This proposal balances the concerns of those who live and work in the Delta, those who rely on it for water, and those who appreciate its beauty, fish, waterfowl, and wildlife.

Edmund Brown Jr.
Governor, State of California
July 25, 2012

As broken and outdated as California's water system is, we are also closer than ever to forging a lasting and sustainable solution that strengthens California's water security and restores the health of the Delta....Through our joint Federal-State partnership, and with science as our guide, we are taking a comprehensive approach to tackling California's water problems when it comes to increasing efficiency and improving conservation. With California's water system at constant risk of failure, nobody can afford the dangers or costs of inaction.

Ken Salazar, Secretary of the Interior
July 25, 2012

Our proposed changes to the BDCP reflect important improvements in shaping a comprehensive strategy to fix a broken system. Because this is a complicated issue and we do not have all the answers today, we will continue to evaluate and refine the proposal. We call upon the many participants throughout California to join us in staying focused on science-based solutions.

Dr. Jane Lubchenco
Under Secretary of Commerce for
Oceans and Atmosphere and
NOAA Administrator
July 25, 2012

to issue a draft Bay-Delta Conservation Plan and corresponding Environmental Impact Report and Environmental Impact Statement for public review in the spring of 2013.

Population growth, habitat loss, and ongoing threats to levee stability and water supply have harmed the California Bay–Delta, threatening the health and economies of California communities. The revised approach, captured in the revised Bay-Delta Conservation Plan and EIS, is grounded in science, designed to help restore fish populations, protect water quality, and improve the reliability of water supplies for all water users who receive deliveries from State and Federal projects. It improves on key aspects of previous proposals and offers a strong governance model, financing options, a scientific review process, and a conservation strategy that includes a new water conveyance facility to move water and help restore the health of the ecosystem. The Conservation Plan is coordinated by six Federal agencies and calls for the restoration of tens of thousands of acres of marshes, wetlands, and habitat, and the construction of a new water conveyance system to move water from north of the California Bay-Delta to water users in the Central Valley and the southern part of the State.

Between 2009 and 2013, Interior has invested nearly $800 million in major water projects in the region, including construction of the Delta-Mendota Canal/California Aqueduct Intertie to relieve conveyance limitations, allow for maintenance and repair activities, and provide the flexibility to respond to Central Valley Project and State Water Project emergency water operations. Other recent accomplishments include the Red Bluff Diversion Facility; Contra Costa fish screens; a large number of water reuse and water conservation projects; feasibility studies, reports, and environmental documentation for potential storage projects; and seismic safety improvements at Folsom Dam. The 2014 budget for Reclamation includes $153.7 million for California Bay-Delta, an increase of $23.6 million from the 2013 Full Year Continuing Resolution, primarily for implementation of the San Luis drainage management plan. The budget also includes $10.6 million for USGS and $4.9 million for FWS.

Reclamation is proposing $37.0 million in the 2014 budget for its California Bay-Delta Restoration account, $2.9 million below the 2013 Full Year Continuing Resolution. The funds will support implementation of the Bay-Delta Conservation Plan as modified by the Interim Federal Plan. This account focuses on the health of the Bay-Delta ecosystem and improving water management and supplies.

San Joaquin River Restoration Program – Beginning in late 2009, the Department reinstated flows in a 330-mile stretch of California's San Joaquin River, much of which had been dry for over 60 years. The 2014 budget supports the settlement of *Natural Resources Defense Council* v. *Rodgers*. The Settlement included a provision to establish the San Joaquin River Restoration Fund to implement the two primary goals of the Settlement, which are to restore and maintain fish populations and to avoid adverse water impacts. Reclamation is proposing $26.0 million in current funding in 2014 for this effort. The increase for San Joaquin River Restoration program implementation will ensure that significant progress will occur on several key settlement requirements: 1) construction work on the Arroyo Canal fish screen and Sack Dam fish passage high priority infrastructure projects; 2) flow and seepage management projects necessary to mitigate damage and potential liability; 3) the Friant-Kern Canal capacity restoration project; and 4) the Mendota Pool Bypass and Reach 2B Channel and structural improvements project, a key component of the San Joaquin River Restoration program and America's Great Outdoors.

RIVER RESTORATION PROJECT

In February 2013, the Bureau of Reclamation awarded a $3.6 million construction contract for the Battle Creek salmon and steelhead restoration project for the construction of a fish barrier and weir that will allow a constant five cubic-feet-per-second of minimum flow in Baldwin Creek, downstream of the Darrah Springs State Trout Hatchery.

The key to success on such a complex issue as this restoration project is collaboration and cooperation at all levels....Reclamation has worked diligently with local and national stakeholders and agencies to find ways to improve native fish habitat. This project will do that.

Michael Connor, Commissioner
Bureau of Reclamation
February 7, 2013

The five cubic-feet-per-second will provide the necessary flows for suitable salmon and steelhead habitat in the Creek, while the barrier weir is to protect the Hatchery from various pathogens that could be transmitted from infected anadromous fish. Construction is planned to be completed by year-end.

The restoration project will increase threatened and endangered Chinook salmon and Central Valley steelhead trout populations by restoring nearly 42 miles of habitat in Battle Creek and six miles of habitat in its tributaries, while maintaining renewable energy production at the Battle Creek Hydroelectric Project.

Strengthening Tribal Nations

And over the next four years, as long as I have the privilege of serving as your President we're going to keep working together to make sure the promise of America is fully realized for every Native American.

President Barack Obama
December 5, 2012

The Strengthening Tribal Nations initiative is a comprehensive multi-year effort to advance the President's commitments to American Indians and Alaska Natives to improve conditions throughout Indian Country. Informed by consultation with the Tribes and reflective of tribal priorities, Interior's 2014 budget continues the initiative with a focus on improving self-determination for tribal nations, the safety of Indian communities, trust resource management, and post secondary, elementary, and secondary education.

The 2014 budget request for Indian Affairs is $2.6 billion, $31.3 million above the 2012 enacted level. Included within this amount are increases for natural resources, public safety, other key programs, and fixed costs offset by reductions that show a commitment to improved operations and efficiency savings and other programmatic reductions.

Programmatic increases of $119.7 million in the budget request for the Strengthening Tribal Nations initiative include support for:

- Public safety programs to apply lessons learned from successful law enforcement pilot programs and increases in staff at detention centers.

- Sustainable stewardship and development of natural resources in Indian Country.

- Post secondary education and funding for an elementary and secondary education pilot program based on the Department of Education's turnaround schools model and concepts.

- Real estate and economic development-related increases to foster economic opportunities on reservations.

INDIAN AFFAIRS
(dollars in millions)

TOTAL INDIAN AFFAIRS FUNDING

2012 Enacted	2,531.3
2014 Request	2,562.6
Change	+31.3

CHANGES

Strengthening Tribal Nations	**+119.7**
Advancing Nation-to-Nation Relationships	+10.3
Protecting Indian Country	+24.9
Improving Trust Land Management	+61.3
Advancing Indian Education	+23.2
Achieving Better Results at Lower Costs	**-104.5**
Consolidations	-19.7
Administrative Savings	-13.8
Transfer of Indian Arts and Crafts Board	+1.3
Program Reductions	-72.3
Fixed Costs	**+16.1**

ADVANCING NATION-TO-NATION RELATIONSHIPS

I am also hopeful because of the rising generation who I have seen embrace the responsibility of following in your footsteps.

President Barack Obama
December 5, 2012

In December 2012, President Obama hosted the fourth White House Tribal Nations Conference at the Department of the Interior. The President, key cabinet officials, and senior advisors met with representatives of 566 federally recognized Tribes to discuss a wide range of issues. Topics at the conference included:

- Strengthening Tribal Communities – Economic Development, Housing, Energy, and Infrastructure.

- Protecting Our Communities – Law Enforcement and Disaster Relief.

- Securing Our Future – Cultural Protection, Natural Resources, and Environmental Protection.

- Building Healthy Communities, Excellence in Education, and Native American Youth.

- Strengthening and Advancing the Government-to-Government Relationship.

The White House Tribal Nations Conferences have led to many successful achievements including the launch of a formal consultation process in December 2011 by Secretary Salazar. The process is governed by a new consultation policy created through cooperative work with tribal representatives implementing

the President's direction in a November 2009 Executive Order requiring all Federal agencies to commit to regular and meaningful consultation. Interior has a long history of consultation with Tribes, but this new policy establishes requirements and guidelines that apply to all Interior officials and managers to promulgate best practices and achieve effective consultation with Tribes.

In 2012, Interior created a new framework for better consultation with Alaska Native Corporations. These entities were created by the Alaska Native Claims Settlement Act of 1971, to receive land and monetary compensation in settlements of aboriginal land claims by Alaska Natives. The policy is designed to ensure corporation officials are at the table and engaged when it comes to the matters that affect them and builds on the Department's existing tribal consultation policy.

Indian Affairs is also taking a wholesale look at the current regulations addressing how Indian groups apply for and receive Federal recognition as an Indian Tribe. Indian Affairs expects to distribute a draft for review by Tribes, as well as non-federally recognized Indian groups, with the goal of publishing a proposed rule by the end of 2014. The revisions will address both the application process and the criteria for Federal recognition.

The 2014 budget continues to propose language to clarify the Department's authority to take Indian land into trust and amend the Indian Reorganization Act of 1934, thereby reducing significant delays. In 2009, the Supreme Court held in *Carcieri* v. *Salazar* that the Secretary of the Interior may acquire land in trust for an Indian Tribe under Section 5 of the IRA only if the Tribe was under Federal jurisdiction in 1934. The proposed language would make clear the IRA applies without regard to whether a federally recognized Tribe was under Federal jurisdiction in 1934. Such an amendment would restore two long standing policies of the United States, to assist all Tribes in securing tribal homelands under the IRA, and to ensure federally recognized Tribes are treated equally under the law.

The 2014 budget proposes an interim solution in the way in which funds are budgeted for contract support costs, which are important to the furtherance of self-governance and Indian self-determination. The 1975 Indian Self-Determination and Education Assistance Act, as amended, allows Tribes to implement programs previously administered by

the Federal government through contractual arrangements. In turn, the Department pays tribal contractors for reasonable costs associated with the administration of those programs, known as contract support costs. Contract support costs funds are used by tribal contractors to pay for a wide range of administrative and management costs, including but not limited to finance, personnel, maintenance, insurance, utilities, audits, communications, and vehicle costs. These funds allow Tribes to manage the Federal programs for which they contract, as well as eliminate the need for Tribes to use program funds to fulfill administrative requirements. The 2014 request for these costs is $231.0 million, an increase of $9.8 million above the 2012 enacted level.

In light of the Supreme Court's *Salazar* v. *Ramah Navajo Chapter* decision, the Administration is proposing that Congress appropriate contract support costs funding to Tribes on a contract-by-contract basis. To ensure as much clarity as possible regarding the level of contract support costs funding, the Administration will provide Congress a contract-by-contract funding table for incorporation into the appropriations act. The Administration proposes this change as an interim step towards a more comprehensive solution. The broader goal is to develop a longer-term solution through consultation with Tribes, as well as streamline and simplify the contract support costs process, which is considered by many as overly complex and cumbersome to both Tribes and the Federal government.

SECRETARIAL COMMISSION ON TRUST ADMINISTRATION AND REFORM

I want to thank you for your hard work and dedication to how we might continue to reform the trust management and administration process and ensure the United States never again encounters the type of failures raised in Cobell and related litigation.

David Hayes, Deputy Secretary of the Interior
September 6, 2012

The Commission on Indian Trust Administration and Reform was established by Secretary Salazar to empower Indian Nations and strengthen Nation-to-Nation relationships. The Commission was tasked to conduct a comprehensive evaluation of the Department's management and administration of nearly $4.4 billion in American Indian trust assets and offer recommendations to improve processes to achieve trust administration that is more responsive, accountable, transparent, and customer-friendly.

The Commission developed draft documents that address several complex, long standing issues such as the Federal trust responsibility and conflict of interest protocols, and issued draft memoranda concerning trust models and a compilation of reform recommendations. In particular, the Commission is focusing on management and oversight, improving coordination and services, and fiduciary management of trust assets.

The Commission initiated an extensive outreach campaign through tribal consultation to provide American Indians and Alaska Natives with opportunities to provide input on the activities and recommendations of the Commission. During 2012, the Commission convened three public meetings in different locations across the Nation. It hosted three public webinar meetings. The Commission also held two events for college students and young adults to provide dialogue about the Federal government's handling of trust assets for American Indians and Alaska Natives.

For more information about the Commission and its work, please visit the Interior Department website at http://www.doi.gov/cobell/commission/index.cfm.

INDIAN LAND BUY-BACK PROGRAM

The Cobell Settlement Agreement was approved by Congress as the Individual Indian Money Account Litigation Settlement in the Claims Resolution Act of 2010. The Settlement was finalized on November 24, 2012, following action by the U.S. Supreme Court and expiration of the appeal period. The $3.4 billion Settlement addresses the Federal government's responsibility for trust accounts and trust assets maintained by the United States on behalf of more than 300,000 individual Indians. Part of the Settlement, $1.5 billion, is being used to compensate class members for their historical accounting, trust fund, and asset mismanagement claims regarding the Individual Indian Money accounts held in trust by the Federal government.

The remaining part of the Settlement establishes a $1.9 billion fund to consolidate fractionated ownership of land interests in Indian Country. The Land Buy-Back Program provides to individuals, in possession of fractionated interests in parcels of land, cash payments for their land interests. The Settlement gives the Department of the Interior ten years to expend the funding to acquire, at fair market value, fractional interests in trust or restricted land from willing sellers. Lands acquired through the program will remain in trust or restricted status and be consolidated for beneficial use by tribal communities.

As an additional incentive to participate in the Land Buy-Back Program, the Settlement authorizes up to $60.0 million to be set aside for an Indian Education Scholarship Fund for American Indian and Alaska Native students when individuals sell fractional interests under the Land Buy-Back Program. On March 12, 2013, Secretary Salazar announced the selection of the American Indian College Fund to administer the student scholarship fund, with a fifth of the annual scholarships to be awarded by the American Indian Graduate Center.

Given its size, limited duration, and importance of the Land Buy-Back Program, an office was established in the Office of the Secretary, subject to the oversight of the Deputy Secretary, to facilitate coordinated engagement and accountability within the Department and to streamline projects and the prioritization of resources.

Goals of the Land Buy-Back Program:

- Reduce the number of fractional interests in trust or restricted lands, giving priority to the most highly fractionated tracts of land in accordance with the Settlement.
- Increase the number of trust or restricted acres in tribal land bases by focusing on cost-effective acquisitions of fractional interests, which will promote tribal sovereignty and self-determination.
- Increase the number of trust or restricted tracts in which the Tribe has majority ownership in order to facilitate economic development or other uses.
- Target fractionated tracts that are amenable to cost-efficient valuation techniques.
- Consult with Tribes to realize opportunities for tribal participation and assistance and to identify and accommodate tribal acquisition priorities to the fullest extent practicable.
- Provide clear information and guidance to individual Indian land owners of fractional interests about the opportunity to voluntarily participate in the Land Buy-Back Program.
- Manage administrative expenses in the most cost-efficient manner possible, in a way that facilitates effective, long-term trust management and systems integration.

PROTECTING INDIAN COUNTRY

...I have prosecuted violent crimes from Indian reservations, so I know the importance of a safe environment for children and other tribal citizens.

Kevin Washburn
Assistant Secretary - Indian Affairs
September 14, 2012

Improving public safety and promoting safer Indian communities is a top priority for the President and tribal leaders. The 2014 budget includes increased resources to build on recent successes achieved through targeted efforts to reduce crime in Indian Country. The Department's success at four reservations is captured in the President's Priority Goal to reduce violent crime in Indian Country.

The goal was established in 2009 and set expectations for 2010 and 2011 to achieve a significant reduction in violent criminal offenses of at least five percent within 24 months on four targeted tribal reservations—Rocky Boys in Montana, Standing Rock in North Dakota, Mescalero Apache in New Mexico, and Wind River in Wyoming. The Bureau of Indian Affairs strategy included community policing, tactical deployment, and critical interagency and intergovernmental partnerships. Significant law enforcement staff and resources were deployed in these four communities, including more officers on the street, training of tribal law enforcement officers, modern equipment, after school and community engagement programs, and extensive monitoring to understand both the source of crime and successful program strategies. Through an adaptive management approach, law enforcement and community policing strategies were re-evaluated for effectiveness and modified to reduce crime. Measurements of specific crime trends and the sharing of best practices through community partnerships and with other law enforcement entities were used to gauge progress and strengthen the initiative.

At the end of the 24-month goal period on September 30, 2011, the BIA Office of Justice Services recorded an average 35 percent decrease in violent crime across the four reservations. These efforts were the result of concerted and coordinated efforts by BIA resources in law enforcement, corrections, and courts working closely with tribal leadership and community engagement. Additional results were

STRENGTHENING TRIBAL NATIONS PRIORITY GOAL

By September 30, 2013, in addition to continued efforts at four targeted tribal reservations that have achieved reductions of at least five percent in violent criminal offenses, achieve significant reduction in violent criminal offenses of at least five percent within 24 months on two additional targeted tribal reservations by implementing a comprehensive strategy involving community policing, tactical deployment, and critical interagency and intergovernmental partnerships.

Targeted Communities

- Rocky Boys Reservation, MT
- Standing Rock Reservation, ND
- Mescalero Apache Reservation, NM
- Wind River Reservation, WY
- San Carlos Apache Tribe, AZ
- Rosebud Sioux Tribe, SD

Performance for 2014

By the end of 2014, the reduced level of violent crime achieved in the initial four communities is expected to be maintained and a five percent reduction in violent criminal offenses from 2011 is targeted to be achieved in the two communities added in 2012.

achieved by the 36 month mark of September 30, 2012, as the reservations experienced a remarkable 55 percent decrease in violent crime across all four Priority Goal sites.

Specifically, the initiative resulted in a 75 percent decrease in violent crime at Mescalero, a 67 percent reduction in violent crime at Rocky Boys, and a 28 percent reduction in violent crime at Standing Rock. At Wind River, a seven percent increase in violent crime was recorded over the two year period, but a reduction of 56 percent was achieved by the end of the third year. Even though comparable strategies were deployed at this site, the expected reductions in crime were delayed due to additional need for community outreach and communications to capture the public's trust for BIA and law enforcement and overcome the geographic challenges of Wind River's larger land base.

CRIME REDUCTION BEST PRACTICES HANDBOOK: MAKING INDIAN COMMUNITIES SAFE

The BIA Office of Justice Services compiled a handbook to share strategies and best practices that were instrumental in the success of a pilot program on four reservations to reduce violent crime. The goal of the pilot program was to reduce crime by five percent. The strategies implemented and practiced by the law enforcement agencies operating on the four reservations resulted in a combined reduction of violent crime by 35 percent.

The OJS created an approach to crime reduction that combines elements of short-term enforcement actions with longer term prevention. Strong working relationships with Tribes, community service providers, other law enforcement entities, and the community at large were essential to the approach. The handbook includes an overview of the crime-reduction strategies of the pilot program and how they interrelate to achieve the overall goal of reduced violent crime. The handbook identifies methods to implement each strategy and specific challenges the strategy addressed.

The best practices identified in the handbook are intended as guidelines for the 187 law enforcement entities operating throughout Indian Country. The handbook covers strategies that achieved positive outcomes but also describes strategies that were less successful on these four reservations. Law enforcement programs are directed to review all strategies to determine which are applicable to their situation.

Based on the demonstrated effectiveness of this initiative, BIA expanded the program to two additional reservations beginning in 2012 and continuing through 2013. The additional Tribes are the San Carlos Apache Tribe in Arizona and the Rosebud Tribe in South Dakota. The law enforcement programs, including police services, corrections, and court services on each of these reservations are tribally run. The BIA allocated increased funds within 2012 to these two locations to address staffing shortfalls, training, equipment, and other needs. At both locations, the Tribes are in the process of hiring police officers, creating and implementing strategies for effective community policing, and garnering collaboration from community members.

The BIA completed a community assessment at both locations, as well as an initial analysis of crime data to identify current and historic crime trends, criminal relationships between suspects and locations, patterns, and points of origin for criminal activity. This analysis provided an accurate portrait of the base crime rate or crime rate profile for each location that enabled completion of an effective crime reduction plan for each reservation. The plans are now being implemented as management personnel are prioritizing their law enforcement response to begin reducing the crime rate at each location most effectively. At the one year mark, the two new sites have experienced a 22 percent increase in reported crime, which was not unexpected given the trends of the initial pilot sites. The BIA will continue to support the efforts of all six programs in 2014 with funding, technical assistance, monitoring, and feedback.

Law Enforcement Operations – The 2014 budget request continues support for Criminal Investigations and Police Services at $199.7 million reflecting a $5.5 million program increase above the 2012 enacted level. The increase will be used to hire additional tribal and bureau law enforcement personnel. The 2014 budget includes a program decrease of $2.6 million for Law Enforcement Special Initiatives. The BIA will realign funding to priority needs within law enforcement operations and maintain high priority operations.

Detention Center Operations – The 2014 budget includes $96.9 million for detention center operations at tribal and BIA operated facilities, a program increase of $13.4 million. The funding will be used for staffing, training, and equipment to increase capacity. Sufficient capacity to hold and process detainees is necessary for effective law enforcement

DON'T SHATTER THE DREAM CAMPAIGN

The BIA Office of Justice Services is committed to assuring holidays are a time of celebration for tribal nations, not a time of pain and sadness caused by impaired driving related motor vehicle accidents. As with the rest of the Nation, alcohol impaired driving is a problem across Indian Country. During the winter holiday season, the BIA OJS mobilizes Indian Country law enforcement during its annual *Don't Shatter the Dream* impaired driving campaign.

In its campaign, OJS law enforcement reminds communities that holiday celebrations can lead to increased drinking and driving, which when combined with inclement winter weather can be a recipe for disaster. Like all campaigns against drinking and driving, the campaign reminds people if plans involve consuming alcohol to always designate a sober driver and make sure to buckle up.

YOUR DECISION TO DESIGNATE **A SOBER DRIVER IS KEY** TO PRESERVING OUR HERITAGE.

DON'T SHATTER THE DREAM.

and to support efforts to combat crime in Indian Country. This increase will also be used to fund operations at seven newly constructed detention facilities, either recently completed in 2012 or scheduled for completion in 2013 or 2014.

Tribal Courts – The Tribal Law and Order Act of 2010 addresses inequities in the ability of Tribes and tribal courts to support adequate crime control in Indian Country. The Act allows tribal courts to impose greater sentences and fines to individuals who commit crimes within tribal jurisdictions. The Act also gives tribal courts greater discretion when administering tribal justice and encourages the courts to hear more cases because sentencing will have a greater impact on violators. In support of the enhanced capabilities given to tribal courts in the Tribal Law and Order Act, the 2014 budget includes $24.4 million, a program increase of $1.0 million above the 2012 enacted level, for the Tribal Courts program. The 2014 funding will be used for judges, prosecutors, public defenders, court clerks, probation officers, juvenile officers, other court support staff, training and related operations, and administrative costs for tribal justice systems and Courts of Indian Offenses.

Social Services – The 2014 budget includes a $3.0 million programmatic increase in Human Services to address domestic violence in Indian communities. Domestic violence has become an increased public safety crisis in parts of Indian Country and, consistent with the recent reauthorization of the Violence Against Women Act of 1994, the proposed increase will begin to address the problem with a new initiative in 2014. The funds will allow Indian Affairs to develop a comprehensive plan to address the needs of Indian communities with victims of domestic violence. A partnership between the BIA Human Services program and the Law Enforcement program will help create a centered focus on tribal locations with high levels of domestic violence cases. The goals of the initiative include: expanding family services related to domestic violence; improving teamwork between law enforcement and social services to more rapidly address instances of domestic violence; and improving coordination of services with other related partners addressing domestic violence in Indian Country.

COMBATING VIOLENCE AGAINST WOMEN IN INDIAN COUNTRY

I applaud Congress's reauthorization of the Violence Against Women Act. Tribal leaders, tribal law enforcement, and tribal courts are all too familiar with this type of violence. It is shameful for far too long, many American Indian women victims came to accept that there was nothing they could do when their abuser was non-Indian.

Kevin Washburn, Assistant Secretary – Indian Affairs
March 7, 2013

On March 7, 2013, in the Sidney R. Yates Auditorium in the Department of the Interior, President Obama signed a bill that strengthened and reauthorized the Violence Against Women Act. The landmark law, first enacted in 1994, provides a comprehensive approach to violence against women by combining tough new provisions to hold offenders accountable with programs to provide services for the victims of such violence. The legislation advances the progress the Nation has made in combating violence against women by providing greater protections against homicide, rape, assault and battery in the home, workplace, and on school campuses across the Country.

The reauthorized Act includes important new provisions for the communities of federally recognized Tribes on Indian lands. The legislation provides stronger protections and greater resources to States and Indian Tribes to make women and vulnerable populations safer. American Indian women experience among the highest domestic violence victimization rates in the Country and more than half of all married Indian women have non-Indian husbands. The legislation eliminates legal loopholes that prevented the arrest and prosecution of non-Indian men who commit domestic violence against Indian women on Federal Indian lands.

The legislation recognizes and affirms inherent tribal jurisdiction over non-Indians in domestic violence cases. The legislation provides tools to tribal governments to more effectively address the problem of domestic violence on Indian reservations and to tribal justice systems to more effectively protect Indian women from abuse. Under the newly enacted law, tribal courts have the ability to enforce protection orders against non-Indians, regardless of where the order originated, and to prosecute any individual who stands accused of domestic violence on a Federal Indian reservation. The 2014 budget includes an increase of $3.0 million to target issues of domestic violence in Indian Country.

IMPROVING TRUST LAND MANAGEMENT

This reform will expand opportunities for individual landowners and tribal governments to generate investment and create jobs in their communities by bringing greater transparency and workability to the Bureau of Indian Affairs leasing process.

Ken Salazar, Secretary of the Interior
November 27, 2012

The BIA's trust programs assist Tribes in the management, development, and protection of Indian trust land and natural resources on 55 million surface acres and 57 million acres of subsurface mineral estates. These programs assist tribal landowners to optimize the sustainable stewardship and use of resources, providing many benefits such as revenue, jobs, and the protection of cultural, spiritual, and traditional resources.

Taking land into trust is one of the most important functions Interior undertakes on behalf of Indian Tribes. Homelands are essential to the health, safety, social, and economic welfare of the tribal governments. In 2012, Interior acquired 37,971 acres of land in trust on behalf of Indian Tribes and individuals and approved 299 fee-to-trust applications. Over the last four years, Indian Affairs has processed more than 1,000 separate applications and acquired over 196,600 acres of land in trust on behalf of Indian Tribes and individuals.

Indian Affairs is striving to increase the economic utilization of Indian lands. On January 4, 2013, Federal leasing regulations for the 55 million surface acres the Federal government holds in trust for Tribes and individual Indians were finalized. The new regulations will further encourage and speed up economic development in Indian Country. The Department took a meaningful step forward by finalizing the sweeping reform of antiquated, one-size-fits-all Federal leasing regulations for the 55 million surface acres the Federal government holds in trust for Tribes and individual Indians. The rule identifies specific processes, with enforceable timelines, through which BIA must review leases. The regulation establishes separate, simplified processes for residential, business, and renewable energy development, so that, for example, a lease for a single family home is distinguished from a large solar energy project.

As a follow up to its work overhauling regulations addressing residential, business, and wind and solar resource leasing on Indian land, Indian Affairs is revising its regulations to address rights-of-way on Indian land. Indian Affairs expects to distribute a draft revised rule to tribal leaders for discussion and publish a proposed rule by the end of 2014. The goal of the revisions is to streamline the process for obtaining BIA approval of rights-of-way and to modernize the regulations to address both the types of rights-of-way needed and the technology available in the 21st century.

Trust - Natural Resources Management – The primary function of the Trust - Natural Resources Management program is to assist Tribes in the management, development, and protection of Indian trust land and natural resource assets. The 2014 budget includes $189.2 million, a program increase of $34.4 million for these programs primarily managed by Tribes.

* *Supporting Natural Resource Stewardship with Science and Technical Support* – The 2014 budget includes a $24.5 million increase for research, analysis, and technical support activities to support the sustainable management and development of alternative and conventional energy sources and natural resources such as land, water, oceans, endangered and invasive species, and to support adaptation to a changing climate. An increase of $9.8 million for Cooperative Landscape Conservation will fund a wide array of conservation activities related to the management of Indian trust land and natural resource assets. Of the increase, $6.5 million will provide funding for coordination, technical support, and tools to enable tribal and Trust land managers to analyze, evaluate, and participate in landscape-level conservation and management activities, utilize science to more effectively manage resources, and develop reservation climate adaptation plans. Another $2.0 million of the increase will support the development of a tribal oceans program, including a competitive grant program to enable Tribes with ocean and coastal trust resources or harvest rights to more effectively manage those resources and perform ocean inventory and species vulnerability assessments, identify critical indicator species, establish

APPLICATION OF SCIENCE AND LANDSCAPE-SCALE TOOLS STIMULATE NATURAL RESOURCES PROTECTION AND ECONOMIC DEVELOPMENT IN INDIAN COUNTRY

The Bureau of Indian Affairs natural resources programs assist American Indians and Alaska Natives in developing conservation and management plans to protect and preserve their natural resources on trust land and shared off-reservation resources. The program provides support for tribal natural resources programs under tribal contracts and direct implementation, covering millions of acres of Indian land viable for farming and grazing by livestock and game animals, forestry, fisheries and hatcheries, water resources, and mining for subsurface minerals. Bureau staff provide oversight and technical assistance to tribal programs at the agency level.

Science is an important component of developing conservation and management plans, which require analysis of base data at the local level. Plans require inventories of resources as well as other salient data such as land evaluations and available infrastructure for program development, conservation planning, and water rights claims settlements. Interior and Tribes apply science and landscape-scale tools to generate, promote, and implement sustainable conservation techniques for long-term growth and resiliency.

The agriculture program, for example, funds range inventories and range utilization surveys to identify vegetative cover, range condition, precipitation zones, current forage utilization, and establish the season of use as necessary for farming and grazing plans that maintain or improve the ecological health of the land. Plans apply scientific methods in preparing and designing land leveling, farm drainage, cropping patterns, crop varieties, application of irrigation water, farm pond specifications, wind and water erosion control, fencing, stock water engineering, and soil and water management necessary to prevent flooding, siltation and agricultural related pollutants, and agricultural pest, noxious weed, and invasive species control.

monitoring protocols, and implement pilot mitigation and recovery projects. These tools are critically important for Tribes that rely on fisheries and other aquatic resources for their food and livelihoods, and ways of life. Of the total $24.5 million increase, $2.5 million will focus on projects that engage youth in the natural sciences and will establish an office to coordinate youth programs across Indian Affairs.

- *Rights Protection Implementation* – This program supports the implementation of Federal court orders resulting from decisions in off-reservation treaty rights litigation. The program assists Tribes in developing conservation management plans and codes governing off-reservation conservation enforcement that protect fisheries and wildlife, which are key to preserving food sources and a way of

life for Indian Tribes. It also assists Tribes in areas where technical assistance is needed to implement treaty rights including harvest management, population assessment, habitat protection, stock enhancement, and public information. The budget request includes a program increase of $7.5 million. Of this amount, $3.5 million will be for implementation of off-reservation rights protection, and the remaining $4.0 million will fund research to more fully understand and enhance resource management associated with the program.

- *Tribal Management Development Program* – The primary purpose of this program is the management of tribal fish and game programs on Indian reservations. The budget includes a program increase of $2.0 million to support this economically and culturally significant

WILD RICE RESTORATION AND MANAGEMENT – USING SCIENTIFIC TOOLS TO MITIGATE NATURAL DISASTERS

Since 1990, the Great Lakes Indian Fish and Wildlife Commission and its cooperators established more than 1,200 acres of wild rice beds in Wisconsin alone, increasing the off-reservation abundance of this critical resource by about 25 percent. The Commission worked with the Wisconsin Department of Natural Resources to create an inventory of more than 300 waters supporting rice, and is working to develop the first cooperative wild rice management plan for the Wisconsin ceded territory. Cooperative management activities also extend into the Minnesota and Michigan ceded territories.

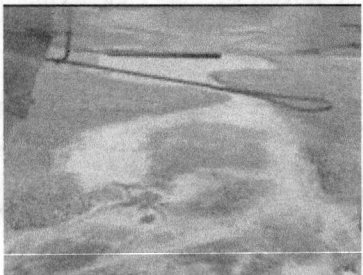
Figure 1: Pre-flood developing wild rice beds.

Figure 2: Post flood, all harvestable rice lost.

In the spring of 2012, the Fond Du Lac people lost the entire annual harvest of wild rice due to record flooding. Subsistence and cultural resources are particularly vulnerable to natural disasters, which have the potential to undermine successes and good efforts across the full spectrum of natural resource programs. The application of science to landscape conservation issues will generate critical knowledge and understanding of how to adapt to the changing landscape, prepare for and mitigate future natural incidents, and sustain and grow the healthy, resilient ecosystems which are integral to the fabric of Indian culture and life ways.

program. Many reservations and Indian communities are being impacted by cutbacks in State and other sources of funding that assist with game and hatchery programs. These economic realities combined with increased effects on fish and wildlife populations caused by overuse, climate change, and increased development are impacting tribal resources. This program is primarily contracted to Tribes and all management objectives are set by the respective tribal governments.

- *Invasive Species* – Tribal and BIA land managers, like all land managers, face a rising spread of invasive species and the detrimental impact of these species on natural landscapes. The budget includes a program increase of $3.0 million from the 2012 level. The funding will allow tribal and BIA land managers to more fully understand the invasive species challenges they face, and support tribal programs that control, manage, and eradicate harmful plant and animal species from reservations. Increased emphasis will be placed on coopera-

tion with adjacent land owners and operators and on long-term pest management strategies.

Trust - Real Estate Services – The Real Estate Services activity supports BIA responsibilities in the areas of trust services, probate, and land titles and records. Trust management also incorporates programs that coordinate and support the Department's trust reform improvement efforts. The budget request is $128.9 million, which includes a program increase of $7.7 million to support these programs.

- *Trust Services* – The Klamath Basin Hydroelectric Settlement Agreement was signed in February 2010 and is intended to enable the recovery of salmon and other species threatened by low river flows, poor water quality, and pollution. The Agreement calls for a study of the potential removal of four privately owned dams on the Klamath River; however, under the Agreement, congressional action is needed before the Secretary may make a determination whether, based on the

JOINT FISHERIES MANAGEMENT IN THE GREAT LAKES

The Bureau of Indian Affairs fulfills Indian trust responsibilities by enabling Tribes to meaningfully exercise their treaty fishing, hunting, and gathering rights.

The Great Lakes Indian Fish and Wildlife Commission is an active partner in fisheries management on Lake Superior. In 2011, its member Tribes harvested over 700,000 pounds of fish from the 1842 treaty ceded territory in Michigan alone. To sustain this important resource, the commission participates in joint fisheries management through the Great Lakes Fishery Commission.

In 2011, the Commission monitored populations of non-native, parasitic sea lamprey in seven Lake Superior tributaries; monitored 80,000 feet of gill net fishing; conducted fish assessments for important species like whitefish, lake trout, and lake sturgeon; monitored the rate at which sea lamprey wound native fish; developed models to determine harvest quotas; and shared fishery data through inter-governmental committees to enhance joint management of fisheries resources on a lake-wide basis. In addition, Commission officers patrolled 890,000 acres of ceded waters and enforced tribal fishing codes established to protect the fishery. In a Lake Superior study, surgically implanted micro-processors obtained temperature and depth data for lake trout, providing new insight into interactions with parasitic sea lamprey, an invasive species that preys on fish. Analysis showed that without sea lamprey, forty-two percent more fish would have been available for commercial and recreational fisheries in 2011.

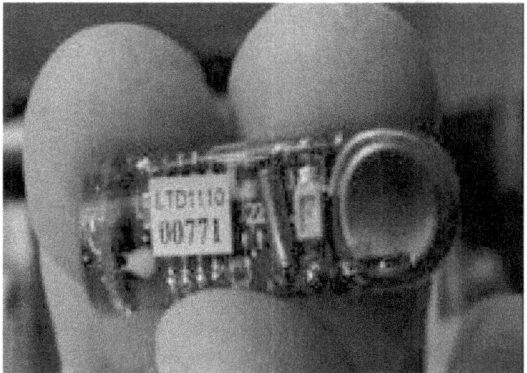 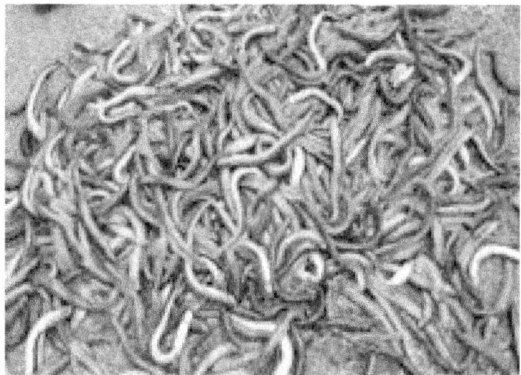

The Tribes have a long history of contributions to fishery conservation on the Great Lakes, of particular note is the successful restoration of lake trout in Lake Superior to self-sustainability.

studies, removal is in the public interest. The Klamath Basin Restoration Agreement, which the Department has not signed, restores the natural resources of the Basin while seeking to provide as much certainty as possible for water supplies needed by the irrigation community. Although the Department is not yet a party to the Agreement pending congressional authorization, a number of restoration/water supply enhancement actions important to the Interior mission are also related to the Klamath Basin Restoration Agreement and are authorized under existing law. The budget request for Trust Services includes a program increase of $5.5 million to support the objec-

tives of the Agreement including grants for economic development.

- *Litigation Support/Attorney Fees* – The 2014 request includes a program increase of $1.5 million for Litigation Support/Attorney Fees. The funding will enhance tribal participation in litigation, negotiation, or administrative proceedings to protect, defend or establish tribal rights and protect tribal trust resources guaranteed through treaty, court order, statute, executive order or other legal authorities. The increased funding would be allocated among a broad range of issues, including environmental matters pertaining to the protection and restoration of tribal trust resources, boundary disputes, and treaty rights such as hunting, fishing, or gathering rights.

- *Real Estate Services* – The 2014 request includes a $688,000 increase to assist BIA staff to address new workload demands associated with the Administration's New Energy Frontier priorities, including the negotiation and documentation of solar energy leases and transmission projects sited on Indian lands nation-wide. The funds will allow BIA to better manage the workload associated with the review of related long-term surface leases and assignments, subleases, and encumbrances.

- *Indian Land and Water Claim Settlements* – The Indian Affairs budget proposes $35.7 million for ongoing Indian land and water settlements, including $8.8 million for the first current payment for the Taos Pueblo Indian Water Settlement. Prior payments for this settlement were paid using permanent funds in 2011. In addition to the Indian Affairs Settlement funding, the Bureau of Reclamation's 2014 request includes $99.7 million for authorized settlements. The total increase for water settlements between the two bureaus is $20.4 million.

- *American Indian Water Evaluation* – The 2014 budget includes $1.0 million in funding to undertake a comprehensive evaluation to improve Federal engagement in Indian water issues. The evaluation will analyze options for developing Interior's engagement and management, enhancing water management and conflict resolution outcomes, and overcoming budgetary, legal, and policy challenges.

ADVANCING INDIAN EDUCATION

Education is key to the fabric of healthy communities….But we need to do better when it comes to meeting the academic and cultural needs of our American Indian and Alaska Native students across the Nation. These tribal consultations will be critical in developing the most effective framework to raise the bar for Indian Country education.

Ken Salazar, Secretary of the Interior
April 16, 2012

The 2014 budget request advances the Department's continuing commitment to American Indian educa-

tion. The Secretary's initiative to advance American Indian education recognizes its strategic role in the long-term health and vitality of Native American communities and is a vital component of the broader initiative to strengthen tribal communities. Advancing Indian education addresses the full spectrum of educational needs in Indian Country from elementary through post-secondary and adult education. One critical component is an education reform effort aimed at increasing the academic achievement of students in bureau-funded schools, who currently achieve at significantly lower levels in reading and math than the national norms.

The BIE elementary and secondary school system has 183 academic or resident only facilities located on 64 reservations in 23 States. During the 2011-2012 school year, BIE-funded schools served nearly 48,000 individual K-12 Indian students and residential boarders, which equated to an average daily membership of approximately 41,000 students due to transfers, absences, and dropout rates. Total funding for school operations from Federal sources for BIE-funded schools was nearly $1 billion in 2012, including $795.5 million from BIE and $203.6 million from the Department of Education. Many of the communities served by BIE schools are characterized by below average literacy rates, low incomes, and high unemployment. Elementary and secondary schools range in size from 11 to more than 1,000 students, representing over 250 Tribes with different cultural backgrounds. The 2014 budget includes $802.8 million for BIE programs, a program increase of $6.7 million from the 2012 enacted level, which does not include funding from the Department of Education.

Following tribal consultations across the Country to seek input on best practices to improve Indian education, Interior and the Department of Education formed a partnership to implement the White House Initiative on American Indian and Alaska Native Education. This Initiative seeks to close the achievement gap between Indian students and non-Indian students; decrease the alarmingly high dropout rates of American Indian and Alaska Native students; and help preserve and revitalize Native languages, histories, and cultures. The Initiative commits Federal agencies to work closely with tribal governments and use the full range of education expertise, resources, and facilities to achieve the Initiative's goals.

Additionally, Interior and the Departments of Education and Health and Human Services signed a Memorandum of Agreement to work together and encourage programs and projects to include instruction in and preservation of Native languages. In summary, the Agreement's seven goals are to conduct analysis of barriers; identify research on Native language retention and revitalization; identify best practices and disseminate this information; review Federal funding mechanisms that best allow integration of languages; assess current training offered by agencies; ensure grantees provide strong programs; and look for additional agencies who have an interest in the Agreement and its activities.

The BIE budget for 2014 proposes a new $15.0 million pilot program based on the Department of Education's turnaround school program. Grants will be awarded to schools that demonstrate the strongest commitment for using the funds to substantially raise the achievement of students.

Learning beyond high school is also critical to a successful life and career; 80 percent of new jobs in the competitive global economy require post-secondary education such as a college degree or vocational training. To address this need, BIE operates two post-secondary schools, administers operating grants to 27 tribal colleges and universities and two tribal technical colleges, and promotes post-secondary opportunities with scholarships to approximately 32,000 students.

Tribal Grant Support Costs – The BIE 2014 budget request includes $48.3 million, a $2.0 million pro-

---

THE VISION FOR BUREAU OF INDIAN EDUCATION SUCCESS

The BIE's mission is to provide quality educational opportunities from early childhood through life in accordance with a Tribe's needs for cultural and economic well being and in keeping with the wide diversity of Indian Tribes as distinct cultural and governmental entities.

Maximize Student Achievement – Teaching students effectively is the number one priority for BIE. Effective instruction is a critical element in turning BIE schools around. The BIE has increased the number of School Improvement Grants to encourage school turnaround models across BIE schools.

Advance Indian Education through Self-Determination – Self-determination and self-governance are an integral part of advancing Indian education. Over the past year, BIE consulted with tribal governments and their leaders on topics such as the Johnson-O'Malley student count, the Indian Affairs Administrative Assessment, and the P. L. 100-297 grant assurance form. Consultations have resulted in agency-wide collaborative efforts in the areas of education, language, culture, and economic development.

Optimize School Operations – To support the President's commitment to provide every student even footing when it comes to education, BIE has expressed a desire to adopt the Common Core State Standards, as have 46 States and the District of Columbia, to allow BIE to pursue a unified system of standards, assessments, and accountability rather than using the standards, assessments, and average yearly progress definitions of 23 different States.

Improve School Facilities – Indian Affairs provides funds for facility programs for 183 academic and resident only campuses. From 2002 through 2012, $2.0 billion has been invested in construction, improvement, and repair projects that have reduced the number of schools in poor condition from more than 120 to 63. This includes 42 complete school replacements and 62 major renovations, which are either completed, funded or under construction.

Seek Partners – The BIE signed eleven Memoranda of Understanding, Memoranda of Agreement, and cooperative agreements with other Federal agencies, tribal colleges, and tribal governments to increase access to new programs and initiatives as well as build capacity at tribal colleges and within tribal governments. The BIE recently partnered with Teach for America to increase BIE-funded schools' access to highly qualified teachers in hard-to-fill locations in the BIE system.

PARTNERS IN INDIAN EDUCATION

The Obama Administration is committed to ensuring Native American students receive an academically rigorous, culturally appropriate education that will prepare them to be productive citizens and leaders in their communities and help build safer, stronger, healthier, and more prosperous Indian communities.

Native American children experience some of the highest levels of poverty in the United States, which greatly impact their academic and life options. Recently, the Bureau of Indian Education developed an agreement with Teach for America. The mission of Teach for America is to provide qualified teachers, expand educational opportunities, and eliminate educational inequity in low income communities by promoting student achievement at the highest levels. The goal of the partnership is to help Indian students in BIE-funded schools reach their full potential and to foster culturally responsive teaching that serves as a national model. The Agreement with BIE is part of Teach for America's Native Achievement Initiative launched in 2010.

gram increase, for the Tribal Grant Support Costs program. The BIE currently funds 125 tribally controlled schools and residential facilities. Grant support funding helps to cover administrative and indirect costs incurred by Tribes operating contract and grant schools. Expenses typically include fiscal audits, personnel, property and procurement management, office services and record keeping, insurance, security, and legal services.

Tribal Colleges and Universities – The 2014 budget provides $69.8 million, a program increase of $2.5 million for Tribal Colleges and Universities to assist in the economic development of tribal communities as a result of increasing enrollment. Economic development is important to improve the quality of life in Native communities. Significant economic improvement can occur when community members have the requisite skills and knowledge required to support economic expansion. Tribal Colleges and Universities address the needs of some of the most economically depressed regions in Indian Country and are successfully overcoming long standing barriers to Indian higher education. They provide local communities with the resources and facilities to teach community members the skills they need to be successful and to support tribal plans for development. Tribal college faculty and administrators often serve as mentors and community role models

that contribute to development in a myriad of areas unique to each community.

Scholarships – The 2014 budget includes program increases of $3.0 million for Post Graduate Science Scholarships, $610,000 for Scholarships and Adult Education, and $100,000 for Special Higher Education Scholarships. The Post Graduate Science Scholarships are provided to enhance science educational opportunities for eligible American Indians and Alaska Natives at the highest levels of education. The Scholarships and Adult Education program enables Tribes to design educational programs that fit the needs of their specific communities. The Adult Education program supports adults in their efforts to obtain a General Education Development certificate and provides basic skills training needed to acquire job placement. Scholarship grants are awarded by Tribes to provide financial aid to eligible American Indians and Alaska Native students attending accredited post-secondary institutions. The Special Higher Education Scholarships program provides supplemental financial assistance to Indian students for graduate level study. Emphasis is placed on students pursuing education in professional areas of need to tribal communities such as law, education, medicine, natural resources, engineering, business administration, and social work.

BIE Evaluation – The 2014 budget includes $2.0 million to contract for a formal, independent evaluation of the BIE school system. This evaluation will focus on both structural issues of the system and the outcomes achieved by BIE schools. The evaluation will also assess the funding flexibility given to Tribes related to BIE funding.

ACHIEVING BETTER RESULTS AT A LOWER COST

Improved Management – Over the last few years, Indian Affairs has taken significant steps to reduce the administrative costs associated with the wide range of services delivered through its programs. In addition to cost-saving measures such as information technology standardization and infrastructure consolidation, Indian Affairs has identified opportunities to reduce costs and improve efficiency through streamlining and consolidations. The 2014 budget request includes a reduction of $19.7 million to reflect anticipated cost cutting proposed in 2013. Inherent in any consolidation is the need to identify and eliminate duplicative or overlapping functions and processes, identify more efficient ways to conduct business, and reduce associated positions. In 2013, Indian Affairs will use early retirement and voluntary separation incentives to manage full time employment reductions along with other position management techniques. Such an ambitious undertaking can only be successful with the full support and participation of the Tribes. To this end, Indian Affairs has engaged in extensive consultation with the Tribes to identify strategies to ensure tribal needs and priorities are addressed.

In addition to savings from consolidations, the 2014 budget includes reductions of $13.8 million including savings of $1.0 million in anticipated management efficiencies for non-self-determination contracts, $1.2 million from improved fleet management, $2.1 million from employee performance awards, and $9.5 million from travel reductions.

Indian Arts and Crafts Board – The budget also proposes a realignment for Indian programs within the Department. The 2014 Indian Affairs budget includes an increase of $1.3 million to reflect the transfer of the Indian Arts and Crafts Board from the Office of the Secretary to Indian Affairs. This will allow Indian Affairs to oversee the implementation of the Indian Arts and Crafts Act of 1990, as amended. The Act contains both criminal and civil provisions to combat counterfeit activity in the Indian arts and crafts market. The Board also manages three museums in the Plains Region dedicated to the promotion, integrity, and preservation of authentic Indian art and culture. Consolidation of the Indian Arts and Crafts Board within Indian Affairs provides opportunities to improve the oversight and execution of Indian cultural activities.

Program Reductions – The 2014 budget request includes $72.3 million in program decreases. Included is a reduction of $2.6 million for Law Enforcement Special Initiatives reflecting decreased participation in activities such as intelligence sharing. In administrative related activities, the budget reduces $7.1 million for Information Resources Technology as standardization occurs. The request includes a decrease of $16.5 million for the Indian Student Equalization Program in education, offset by a $15.0 million increase for a turnaround school pilot. The Agriculture and Economic Development programs are reduced by $566,000 and $543,000 respectively. In the Construction account, the request includes a decrease of $17.8 million for Replacement School Construction as the program will focus on addressing the building conditions of existing school facilities. The budget also includes a $2.1 million reduction for the Indian Guaranteed Loan Program while Indian Affairs seeks to improve performance and conducts a results-oriented independent evaluation to determine how to achieve its intended objectives through Indian Affairs or other Federal loan programs.

Program Elimination – The budget proposes to eliminate funding for the Housing Improvement Program. This $12.6 million program serves the same population as the $650.0 million Housing and Urban Development's Native American Housing Block Grant program. Tribes who receive HUD funding are not precluded from using that funding to provide assistance to HIP applicants.

Management Effectiveness

Interior's mission is vast in terms of our economic impact, physical presence, our direct impact on the American public. We have an obligation to the American taxpayer to look for better ways to get things done to deliver our mission more effectively.

Rhea Suh
Assistant Secretary – Policy, Management and Budget
November 15, 2012

The Obama Administration continues to challenge Federal agencies to make the Nation's government more effective—to deliver more to the taxpayers and manage Federal resources more responsibly. To meet this challenge agencies are reviewing programs for savings opportunities, eliminating lower priority and under achieving programs, encouraging employees to identify savings opportunities, and investigating new ideas to increase the effectiveness and efficiency of government operations. The Administration's efforts focus on the following strategies with the highest potential to achieve meaningful performance improvement within and across Federal agencies:

- Focusing on agency top priorities.
- Cutting waste.
- Reforming contracting.
- Closing the information technology gap.
- Promoting accountability and innovation through open government.
- Attracting and motivating top talent.

The Department of the Interior is working aggressively to meet the Administration's challenge on management and performance-based alignment of priorities and resources, and the progress is reflected in the 2014 budget. Interior's 2014 budget:

- Manages for results by defining core mission priorities, with deliberate strategies, performance measures, and priority goals as the basis for a multi-year strategic plan and annual operating plans.

- Reflects a comprehensive review of programmatic priorities and consideration of Government Accountability Office and Inspector General input on high risk areas and management challenges.

- Sustains the savings achieved through the Administration's Campaign to Cut Waste, maintaining the $217.0 million in administrative savings realized from 2010 through 2013 in areas such as supplies, travel, and advisory services.

- Continues to implement Department-wide policy changes to more effectively manage conferences, travel and relocation, information technology, and use strategic sourcing.

- Reflects efforts to enhance Federal contracting and acquisition policies and procedures to ensure taxpayers get the best value possible including increased competition and high levels of small business contracting.

- Transforms the delivery of information technology services to a more consolidated, secure, and customer-oriented business model.

- Fully funds fixed cost increases balancing these requirements with programmatic priorities.

- Reflects ongoing efforts to improve management of asset inventories by reducing lease and real property costs and in financial management, by reducing improper payments, accelerating payments, maintaining a clean audit opinion, and ensuring a robust set of internal controls.

- Reflects business decisions to consolidate functions and review the potential for organizational improvements to achieve greater efficiencies. This includes consideration of Government Accountability Office input on duplicative programs.

Cuts, Consolidations, and Savings – Interior's use of strategies to evaluate program performance and identify duplication, overlaps, and inefficient program delivery is improving the alignment of resources with priorities and meeting the challenge of fiscal transparency and accountability. Efforts are underway throughout the Department to identify ways to improve alignment of programs to improve effectiveness and efficiency and to leverage resources. In areas like land acquisition these efforts pay dividends by improving conservation outcomes while advancing partnerships and collaboration. Continuing efforts to achieve efficiencies and savings drive the need to propose reductions and elimination of programs that are lower priority or serve constituencies that could be addressed through other Federal programs. The 2014 request includes more than $600.0 million in programmatic reductions to offset support for operational requirements including programmatic and fixed costs.

Fixed Costs – The 2014 budget request fully funds $106.7 million of increases in fixed costs. Fully budgeting for these costs ensures transparency and reduces the erosion of program performance over time. These costs, limited to a set of costs based on an agreement with the Interior Appropriations Subcommittee, include space rental and associated security charges; workers and unemployment compensation; and centralized administrative and business systems, services, and programs financed through the Working Capital Fund. The request assumes a 1.4 percent increase in health benefits; a one-half percent pay raise adjustment for 2013; and a one percent pay raise adjustment for 2014. The Department does not include other payroll related increases in its fixed costs or increased costs related to postage, fuel, and other consumables. Significant elements of the increase in 2014, as compared to 2012, are $18.9 million for an additional paid day, $13.5 million for 2013 pay raise adjustments, $41.0 million for 2014 pay raise adjustments, $26.1 million for the employer share of health benefits, $6.1 million for Working Capital Fund programs, and $7.6 million in rent.

MANAGING FOR RESULTS

In 2010, the Department completed a new five-year strategic plan that simplifies Interior's objectives and outlines five mission areas with discrete goals, strategies, and measures to assess performance.

Interior's Strategic Plan lays the framework for the integration of programs, allocation and alignment of resources to achieve key goals, and collaboration and coordination with stakeholders. Performance measures in the Plan are used to gauge progress and assess the Department's performance. The following five mission areas provide the framework for the Department's overarching stewardship responsibilities and define long-term areas of focus:

- Provide natural and cultural resource protection and experiences.

- Sustainably manage energy, water, and natural resources.

- Advance government-to-government relationships with Indian Nations and honor commitments to Insular Areas.

- Provide a scientific foundation for decisionmaking.

- Build a 21st Century Department of the Interior.

Building upon the Department's Five-Year Strategic Plan, Interior is working to expand the practical use of performance information to help planning, decisionmaking, budget formulation, and transparency, in accordance with the Government Performance and Results Act Modernization Act of 2010. The Strategic Plan presents long-term goals across the Department and includes performance measures being used to track and

INTERIOR'S INCLUSIVE WORKPLACE STRATEGY

On August 16, 2010, Secretary of the Interior Ken Salazar issued an Inclusive Workplace Statement to all employees of the Department of the Interior. This statement communicated his commitment to employing the best people to do the best job possible. Secretary Salazar noted that achieving a diverse workforce and creating an inclusive culture are integral to Interior's success.

Secretary Salazar and Assistant Secretary for Policy, Management and Budget, Rhea Suh, also issued an Inclusive Workplace Strategy directing each Interior bureau to develop its own inclusivity and diversity action plan. Together, the Secretary's direction and bureau strategies form a framework for improvement and accountability. Leaders and managers are held accountable for implementing their plans to make Interior the best place to work in America, where all of its employees are respected, quality of work life is valued, and people have the opportunity to reach their potential. A crucial aspect of Interior's Inclusive Workplace Strategy is that all employees see themselves engaged in the initiative. The strategy is based, in part, on the premise that the behaviors and actions that support diversity and inclusion will come through the conviction and overt actions of all employees.

Interior's diversity efforts are sustainable because they assess the entire system, including the infrastructure and processes surrounding the diversity and inclusion change process. Just as Interior uses sound science to manage and sustain America's natural resources, the Inclusive Workplace Strategy employs a data driven approach to assess the current state of diversity and inclusion and to identify and remove barriers to diversity at all levels of the workforce.

Interior's Inclusive Workplace Strategy aims at transforming workforce diversity training and education from traditional anti-discrimination compliance to having a laser focus on organizational development and talent management. Among Interior's many initiatives for building and sustaining an inclusive workplace is the institution of a Diversity Change Agent program. This program is comprised of a cadre of fully committed and trained diversity change agents who affect and mobilize stakeholders and lead efforts to educate the workforce about diversity: what it is, why it is important, and how to guide people toward achieving it. The work of the diversity change agents extends the reach of Interior's equal employment opportunity and human resources professionals. Change agents keep diversity front-of-mind by initiating job-relevant conversations that position diversity as a continuing mission critical issue rather than a one-time training event.

demonstrate progress. Interior will release an Annual Performance Plan and Report for the 2014 Budget which includes supporting information on the annual achievement of the goals in the Strategic Plan and accomplishments.

The Department is using Priority Goals to achieve the President's key objectives. Progress toward achieving these Priority Goals is regularly reviewed among members of senior management through quarterly status reviews chaired by the Deputy Secretary. The quarterly and annual assessment of performance, funding, and necessary reforms to achieve these goals promotes improved communication and coordination, alignment of program activities, and helps to resolve impediments to success. All of

these efforts are helping to improve performance, accountability, and transparency across Interior.

Top 2014 priorities remain consistent with goals established in 2009 and first presented in the 2010 budget. These goals set out to achieve change in renewable energy development, water conservation and sustainable water management, the use of climate change adaptation to improve resource management, youth employment and engagement, and safety of Indian communities. A sixth Priority Goal was added in 2012 to promote and track improvements in the management of Interior's oil and gas resource programs. This goal recognizes the important high risk categorization by the Government Accountability Office for the Department's oil and gas programs and incorporates GAO's recommendations and Inspector General corrective actions.

CUTTING WASTE AND ACHIEVING EFFICIENCIES

The challenging economic situation makes it incumbent upon Federal agencies to bear in mind their role as stewards of taxpayer dollars with responsibility to ensure a high return on spending and intolerance for waste and abuse.

Over the years, Interior has kept pace with inflationary increases and programmatic requirements by streamlining and improving the efficiency and effectiveness of programs, driving cost cutting to reinvest in program performance. Internal reviews and those performed by GAO, the OIG, and others are used to focus on opportunities and improve best practices. Interior is instituting major restructuring to achieve savings in areas like information technology. The Information Technology Transformation is going to achieve improved information technology support while reducing cost by consolidating infrastructure across the Department. Other ongoing efforts, while not as large in scale or scope, will also achieve significant benefits. These include increasing the use of shared services to achieve economies of scale, facility co-location to reduce Interior's footprint, creating acquisition centers of excellence to improve contracting expertise and reduce duplication, recycling and reuse, fleet and equipment life-cycle management to maximize efficiency, and many other administrative business management practices. Nonetheless, Interior continues to examine opportunities where innovative ideas could result in cost avoidance and savings and improved efficiency and effectiveness.

In three separate Executive Orders, President Obama outlined a challenge to Federal agencies to improve performance and reduce waste, fraud, and abuse across government. In response, Interior developed a plan to reduce administrative spending by $217.0 million by the end of 2013. The implementation plan focuses on reducing travel, and certain areas of acquisition, printing, and supplies. It is fully integrated and leverages the Department's on-going initiatives in administrative areas including strategic sourcing and facilities downsizing, and Interior's sustainability initiative to reduce greenhouse gas emissions and improve facilities and fleet efficiency. To ensure accountability, Interior assigned savings targets to each bureau, developed an internal tracking process to monitor quarterly progress toward

efficiency savings goals, and continues to work in an integrated fashion to pursue key program, policy, and process reforms.

To achieve the $217.0 million savings goal by the end of 2013, the Department is building on savings efforts launched in 2011 and 2012. Between 2010 and 2012, Interior achieved $128.0 million in administrative savings. Another $89.0 million is planned for 2013. The 2014 budget sustains three years of targeted

---

REACHING INTERIOR'S SAVINGS GOAL

The Department of the Interior will achieve $217.0 million in savings from 2010-2013 as follows:

Travel	-$47.0 million
Advisory and Assistance Services and Other Contractual Services	-$100.0 million
Supplies and Equipment	-$70.0 million

---

administrative cost savings efforts and supports the continuation of aggressive organizational solutions to achieve greater savings in the future.

Interior's strategy capitalizes on the implementation of Department-wide policy changes in travel and relocation, strategic sourcing, and information technology consolidation. The Department's 2014 request continues to support these reforms. Interior's Campaign to Cut Waste initiative has expanded to include improved management of conference activities, support service reductions, and other efforts underway to reduce spending and achieve more effective and sustainable use of fleet, assets, space, acquisition, and information technology.

Travel and Conferences – Interior is charged with managing America's vast natural and cultural resources, spanning a geographic area from Palau, the western-most Pacific outpost, to the U.S. Virgin Islands, the eastern-most Caribbean station. Over 70,000 employees, along with more than 280,000 volunteers, carry out Interior's mission from more than 2,400 operating locations. Due to the vast footprint of the Department's operations, including the most remote locations in the Country, much of the travel performed is mission-essential. Extensive travel is often required for management of public lands and resources including law enforcement activities, volcano and earthquake monitoring, migratory bird inventories, and firefighting. Conducting law enforcement on vast public lands and in Indian communities can require driving hundreds of miles. Transportation of Indian children to and from schools located in rural areas can accumulate significant mileage. Interior's missions and activities, by their very nature require travel to evaluate the status of resources, gather data, share technologies, and conduct outreach with partners and stakeholders. A new, more expansive tribal consultation policy requires travel to ensure adequate effort is made to assess the views and concerns of Indian Tribes. In addition, much of Alaska is not accessible by ground vehicles and remote locations in the lower 48 States require the extensive use of aircraft.

Despite significant mission-related travel, from 2011 to 2012, Interior reduced travel spending from $196.0 million to $174.0 million, a decrease of over 11 percent. Working with the Chief Financial Officers' Council within Interior, the Department is continuing to examine and update travel policies and procedures, deploy bureau travel best practices, and ensure consistency in approval levels. Interior will continue to strongly encourage use of technology alternatives such as video conferences, teleconferences, web tools, and telepresence.

The Department is working to modernize, expand, and leverage video conferencing facilities to optimize investments in technology. Interior is leveraging data from GovTrip, the government wide electronic travel system, to monitor travel across the Department to ensure achievement of goals, and identify candidate locations for technology solutions that could help to reduce travel.

Interior's programs, people, and facilities are located in communities large and small and deliver services through partnerships that engage citizens, groups, and businesses. Many of Interior's missions involve resources that are not limited by the boundaries of Federal lands, so land managers work in partnership with their neighbors. Thus, extensive collaboration is essential for effective execution of Interior's mission; and Interior partners with States, local communities, Tribes, non-governmental organizations, universities, and others to ensure successful mission delivery. Conferences are a commonly used means for communication, training, information sharing, and staying current with technology and science. In addition, Interior's geographically dispersed activities necessitate the use of conferences to ensure effective and consistent policy implementation. Conferences are an important way to conduct training, often offering a less costly alternative to classroom or commercially offered training, particularly in highly technical areas, scientific fields, and for education programs. Conferences are also a means to share unique skills and knowledge that may not be available elsewhere.

In accordance with the Office of Management and Budget's memorandum, *Eliminating Excess Conference Spending and Promoting Efficiency in Government*, Interior implemented policies requiring prior approval from the Deputy Secretary or his designee for: 1) conferences funded or sponsored by another entity at which 15 or more Interior personnel will be attending; and 2) Interior funded or sponsored conferences at which 30 or more attendees will be present and half or more are in travel status. These policies require that travelers abide by Federal lodging and per diem limits, direct the use of Federal facilities, discourage speaker fees and other additive costs, direct minimal attendance, and require internal controls to ensure conference activities are effectively managed. Bureaus and offices have certified that effective internal controls are in place to manage conference activities and spending. The Department instituted annual planning and a robust process for coordination, review, and monitoring of conferences and conference sponsorships.

Management Support Services Contracts – The Department has set a goal to reduce spending on Management Support Services contracts by 20 percent from 2010 levels by the end of 2013. This goal is an important component of the Campaign to Cut Waste and the *Executive Order on Delivering an Efficient, Effective, and Accountable Government*. The MSS contracts are comprised of twelve OMB-designated

Product Service Codes that include activities such as engineering and technical services, acquisition planning, information technology services, and program management.

Acquisition Improvement – Interior continues to strengthen its acquisition program and promote efficiencies throughout the Department. Emphasis on buying smarter and encouraging innovation in contracting helps the agency achieve its many missions effectively and efficiently. Activities that provide savings and efficiencies include:

- Participation in the Federal Strategic Sourcing Initiatives.

- Achieving savings through agency Strategic Sourcing Initiatives such as IT hardware, office supplies, and multi-function copier devices.

- Advancing the use of the FedBid reverse auction program for commodity purchases and requiring the use of e-buy procurements, to the maximum extent possible, where reverse auctions are not suitable.

- Identifying and implementing new acquisition initiatives.

- Delivering a new Acquisition 101 training course.

Collectively, these activities will promote efficient spending, reduce the cost of acquiring common commodities, achieve savings, reward innovative performance, and provide greater awareness of proper acquisition procedures.

Vehicle Fleet – Interior has an extensive fleet composed of 23,882 government-owned and 9,938 leased vehicles used to carry out its diverse missions throughout the United States. The fleet is critical in the delivery of mission essential activities, including fire-fighting, management and protection of lands and resources, conducting scientific work and monitoring, and providing services to Indian communities. Interior is committed to maintaining an efficient fleet. Between 2005 and 2011, Interior reduced its vehicle fleet by 3,500 vehicles or nine percent, despite increases in law enforcement and other activities that require vehicles. Despite this achievement, Interior continues to manage toward additional efficiencies. Interior began a compre-

hensive review of its fleet operations in 2012 and utilizes annual Vehicle Allocation Methodology as a tool to identify opportunities to share vehicles across bureaus and offices; develops vehicle disposal plans for under-utilized vehicles; and uses its sustainability goals to drive improved use of alternative fuel vehicles. These efforts resulted in a three percent reduction in fleet vehicles during the past year.

Real Property Cost Savings and Innovation – In response to Presidential direction to eliminate waste by disposing of excess assets and reducing real estate and leased space occupancy, Interior implemented a Real Property Cost Savings and Innovation Plan in 2010 and updated its Plan in 2011 and 2012. This plan has the added benefit of supporting sustainability goals and reducing the Department's energy and water usage and greenhouse gas emissions. The plan outlined an ambitious set of goals to achieve savings by eliminating government-owned real property assets, where possible and practical, and reducing the use of leased and GSA provided space. Through the enhanced utilization of owned and leased space, disposition of unused assets, and colocation/consolidation efforts, the Department set a goal and achieved savings and cost avoidance totaling $166.0 million during 2010 – 2012. With the completion of the Real Property Cost Savings and Innovation Plan in 2012, Interior began implementing the new Freeze the Footprint initiative. Planning is underway now to identify how Interior bureaus and offices will limit facilities by freezing the current square footage of office and warehouse space. This effort will continue to improve utilization and control spending associated with real property through development and implementation of Real Property Strategic Plans.

Information Technology Transformation – One of the most significant undertakings to improve management effectiveness within the Department is the IT Transformation initiative. In December 2010, Secretary Salazar signed Secretarial Order 3309 to transform Interior's information technology into an agile, reliable, and cost-effective service that more effectively allows employees to better support Interior's mission.

Interior is in its second year of implementing the multi-year IT Transformation initiative and is applying a new business model for consolidated delivery of information technology services. The implementation phase of Interior's IT Transformation started in January 2012 and will continue over the next three years. An implementation plan

provides milestones and schedules for completing projects in service areas. Efforts are underway to complete workforce planning and detailed design in order to consolidate services in five major service areas. The Department's Chief Information Officer is leading these efforts in collaboration with bureau information technology coordinators. A senior team of bureau and Departmental management executives are providing oversight for this effort to ensure a smooth transition.

As plans mature they will guide implementation of the IT Transformation Strategic plan led by Interior IT Transformation service teams. To date, the teams have undertaken the following:

- *Workplace Computing/End User Services* – Interior implemented an enterprise wide BisonConnect e-mail, calendaring, and collaboration service. This marks the first Department-wide e-mail service, replacing multiple e-mail systems that did not communicate effectively. This team also developed and established agency-wide policy related to mobile computing and the use of personally owned devices laying the groundwork for initiatives slated for 2014.

- *Telecommunications* – Interior completed optimization of the Enterprise Services Network–the Department's communications backbone–and transitioned the agency from the FTS2001 to the Networx enterprise service contract.

- *Enterprise Hosting* – Interior continues Federal data center consolidation. Efforts to date are ahead of schedule resulting in the consolidation of 42 data centers. Interior's hosting team released a Request for Proposal for Cloud Hosting Services and expects to award a foundational cloud services contract to support hosting including hosting for the Financial and Business Management System.

- *Information Assurance/Risk Management Services* – An enterprise continuous monitoring strategic plan will be used in 2013 and

2014 to implement improvements in IT security including continuous monitoring and deployment of systems to automatically block unauthorized leakage of Personally Identifiable Information and other sensitive data.

- *Enterprise Service Desk* – Efforts continue to consolidate and improve services and response times for the Interior enterprise service help desk and provide support for e-mail. Interior issued a solicitation to get independent assistance to research best practices for expansion and improvement of enterprise service desk capabilities and services across the agency.

With a strong focus on IT Transformation, planning and development are underway for multiple Department-wide services including wireless managed services, voice services, and expansion of mobile capabilities.

The budget request for Interior's Working Capital Fund includes $5.0 million to support IT Transformation initiatives. Funding is critically important to invest in developing the five new service areas while consolidation, workforce planning, and transition from bureau-hosted services to centrally-hosted services is underway. Funding would be used for:

- *Workforce Planning and Change Management, $1.5 million* – IT Transformation will consolidate programs, services, infrastructure, and support from multiple bureau hosted environments to a single, centralized location. Significant realignments and reorganizations like this are more successful when adequate planning and change management are conducted in advance. Funding is needed to ensure an orderly transition from bureau-provided services to centrally-provided services in hosting, telecommunications, risk management, service desk, end user services, and the associated policy, planning and compliance efforts that support these services.

- *Data Center Closure, Migration and Consolidation, $2.4 million* – This investment is needed to consolidate over 12,000 servers located in 407 decentralized data centers. Funds will be used for migrating equipment, data, and applications to cloud-based hosting services and consolidated data centers, decommissioning bureau and office legacy systems, and closing existing centers. When IT Transformation is complete, Interior will have reduced the number of data centers by 45 percent—ahead of the Federal government's goal of a 40 percent reduction.

- *Strategic Sourcing for Enterprise Service Desk, Cellular, Enterprise Software, and Hardware, $335,000*–This funding will be used to develop requirements and contract vehicles that can be used to support the acquisition of wireless services, software, and hardware. The use of strategic sourcing vehicles can result in savings as lower costs can be negotiated on higher volumes of purchasing. Currently, the Department is utilizing strategic sourcing vehicles managed by other agencies for hardware, but is planning for future needs. Included in this investment is funding for an enterprise service desk function, which will replace dozens of bureau and office help desks. This will be launched as a managed service at the Department level.

- *Records Management, $765,000* – This funding will be used to acquire tools that are needed for electronic records management. This would create capability for all Interior bureaus and offices to access, search, and retrieve electronic data from e-mail and electronic documents. This information would be available in a records repository and would greatly expedite document production and responses to Freedom of Information Act requests. This solution is critically important for the Department to discontinue the current practices that involve paper records and costly and inefficient print and file requirements. There is an electronic forms component that will allow Interior to consolidate and standardize thousands of duplicative forms and terminate costly software licenses required for redundant forms systems.

OPEN GOV–Interior is committed to the principles of an open, transparent, collaborative, and participatory government. The Department continued its efforts to publish high value datasets to the public through Data.gov. To date, Interior has published 122,637 datasets, second only to the Department of Commerce. Interior is working closely with the Data.gov team to provide direct support for enhancements to the Data.gov catalog, supporting Office of Management and Budget requirements pertaining to open data.

Of the thousands of datasets Interior has made available, many are widely used across the Country by a broad array of organizations for countless purposes. This includes nationally authoritative data describing river and stream flow and quality; data describing topography and land cover; and aerial and satellite imagery that gives users the ability to look back in time and study the changing landscape of the Country over the last few decades. Aside from traditional uses in the natural resources management and academic communities, many businesses, including industry innovators like Microsoft, Google, and ESRI, rely on these datasets to build and improve commercial mapping products used by millions of citizens every day.

The Department serves as the Federal leader in the development and refinement of the government-wide Geospatial Platform, www.geoplatform.gov, an interagency initiative led by the Assistant Secretary for Water and Science and the Department's Geospatial Information Officer. The Geospatial Platform is an activity of the interagency Federal Geographic Data Committee, a body comprised of over 30 agencies led by OMB and the Department of the Interior. The Platform is a shared, cloud-based geospatial data and technology environment that will be used by all Federal Geospatial Data Committee partners to help them more efficiently and effectively utilize and share geospatial tools, data, and maps. By leveraging shared infrastructure and pooled investments, the Platform will help agencies reduce their individual investments in geospatial data and technology. As of 2013, the geospatial platform has been formally introduced as one of the Federal government's e-Government shared IT services.

The Department is developing a landscape decision tool. Working with Interior bureaus and partners including the U.S. Forest Service, the Department will use this tool to support land management decisionmaking by allowing employees to use geospatial data from Federal, State, and local governments and non-government entities to map locations for many purposes including restoration, land acquisition, and siting renewable energy projects. The tool will avoid duplication by publishing information across the Department and by integrating with the Geospatial Platform in order to share information and access government-wide data resources.

Information Technology Investment Management Reforms – Since the inception of the iStat Investment Review process in late 2010, Interior has used this process to conduct deep dive reviews of its IT systems and applications. The Department is conducting iStat reviews of IT investments to assess performance against a set of operational, funding, and schedule metrics. The reviews recalibrate projects and result in more focused implementation and operations and, in some cases, reduced system scope, redirection, and more defined requirements. This has resulted in changes in planned investments and the modification of plans to improve functionality and reduce costs. In addition, the Department has begun developing functional road maps to compare IT applications across defined functional areas in order to identify duplication and redundancy in IT investments.

As a result of the Department-wide Facilities Management Systems iStat review, Interior has taken significant action to resolve conflicts and align bureau-specific systems, and has taken definitive steps toward standardization of systems used to help manage facilities. Based on the review, efforts are underway to move all five bureaus using these systems to a consolidated platform and a road map to guide future investments is being developed.

Interior Business Center – In 2012 and 2013, the Department realigned functions formerly within the National Business Center to improve customer service and accountability. The Department's shared service provider was renamed the Interior Business Center and is narrowing its focus to three major lines of business: Acquisition Services, Financial Management Services, and Human Resources Services. The realignment of functions was based on a strategic assessment of the IBC's service offerings. The assessment recommended IBC narrow its focus to a core set of complementary shared services with clear benefit to Interior, achieve major performance improvements over the next two years, and pursue opportunities to expand services and deliver strategic value over the next three to five years.

As part of the IT Transformation implementation plan, the Information Technology Directorate will transfer from IBC to the Office of the Chief Information Officer in 2014. This Directorate provides hosting services for Interior business systems including the Financial and Business Management System and the Federal Personnel and Payroll System. The IBC Customer Support Center will also transfer to OCIO in 2014. The CSC provides help desk support for all IBC service offerings and FBMS. The 2014 budget for the Working Capital Fund reflects the transfer of these two groups from IBC to OCIO.

LOOKING FORWARD

Interior recognizes the need to manage effectively and efficiently, to operate within constrained budgets, and increase reform efforts to better align and deliver services to the American people. This commitment sets the stage for a series of actions underway in 2013 and proposed in the 2014 budget. These actions are taking place on the broad landscape of Interior programs and reflect focused management.

Service First – The Department operates out of over 2,400 locations and manages over 146,000 physical assets, second only to the Department of Defense. While effective program delivery relies on close coordination at the local level and a field level presence, alignment of operational models, standardization of administrative and support functions, centralization of common services, and other actions can be taken to improve efficiency, cut costs, and avoid future cost increases. The goal of the Service First initiative is to maximize resource sharing across bureaus and offices to improve service delivery and operational effectiveness and efficiency. Through Service First, Interior will rationalize its regional boundaries and locations, consolidate functions that can be conducted in a more centralized manner, create Centers of Excellence to create economies of scale, co-locate bureaus and offices to the greatest extent possible, and foster innovative service delivery models.

Service First began as a partnership authority between the Bureau of Land Management and U.S. Forest Service. Congress provided Service First authority so these agencies could conduct projects, planning, permitting, leasing, contracting, and other activities, either jointly or on behalf of one another; co-locate in Federal offices and facilities leased by an agency of either Department; and promulgate special rules as needed to test the feasibility of issuing unified permits, applications, and leases. The Secretaries of the Interior and Agriculture may make reciprocal delegations of their respective authorities, duties, and responsibilities to promote customer service and efficiency. Service First has effectively demonstrated that leveraging and taking a more strategic approach to operations can save costs and result in more seamless service to the public. In 2012, the Service First partnership authority became permanent and was expanded to include the Fish and Wildlife Service and National Park Service. In addition to pursuing specific opportunities, the Department intends to expand Service First partnership authority to all Interior bureaus and offices to more broadly empower field and regional resource sharing and co-location.

In 2012, Interior started efforts to expand the Service First approach to help address shared improvements in service delivery across all bureaus and offices. In an initial effort, Interior examined its Wildland Fire Management Program to identify ways to improve the effectiveness and efficiency of the program and direct resources from duplicative or redundant operations to on-the-ground Wildland Fire Management services.

In 2013, Interior is performing a comprehensive review to identify and prioritize short- and long-term opportunities that achieve cost savings or avoidance, rationalize regional locations, decrease leased space, decrease fleet size, and decrease acquisition costs while improving landscape-based management and fostering seamless interaction with partners. Interior is also pursuing additional pilot projects to assess existing administrative functions, future needs, and cost effectiveness of service providers. The Department will also explore opportunities to optimize revenue and fee collection systems and related processes Interior-wide.

The 2014 President's budget requests for the Working Capital Fund appropriation includes $2.0 million to implement high-priority short-term opportunities. Further planning on longer-term initiatives also will be conducted.

Financial Accountability – In 2012, Interior received the 16th consecutive favorable financial audit opinion from KPMG LLP, an independent certified public accounting firm and the Department's external auditor. In addition, the fiscal year 2012 audit noted the removal of the fiscal year 2011 material weakness relating to contingent liabilities, and only three significant deficiencies remain. Efforts are currently underway to mitigate, if not eliminate, the three significant deficiencies. Other efforts are underway to improve financial management including:

- In 2012, Interior implemented accelerated contractor payments as required by the Office of Management and Budget's memorandum M-12-16. All contractor payments by Interior are made within 15 days of invoice approval.

- Interior successfully used financial information to identify parties that should not receive Federal payments as part of the Do Not Pay initiative.

- Interior also received a positive report from the OIG about its compliance with the Improper Payments Elimination and Recovery Improvement Act of 2012.

Financial and Business Management System – The Financial and Business Management System will be deployed to the Bureau of Reclamation in November, 2013, completing bureau deployments. The FBMS will then be delivering a modernized, integrated, secure system that supports and facilitates improved management, accountability, and transparency in budget execution, financial management, acquisition and financial assistance, fleet and facilities management, and property management to all Interior bureaus. The most recent deployment migrated the National Park Service, Bureau of Indian Affairs, and Bureau of Indian Education in the fall of 2012.

The system has delivered on promised improvements in functionality, consistency in reporting, standardized internal controls and processes, and improved data availability. These advances provide the tools necessary for the Department to actively manage its fiscal resources and promote efficient spending to support operations and cut waste. The system has successfully supported the Department's clean financial audits, allowed bureaus and offices to conduct quarterly closings and reconciliations, and allowed Interior to terminate the operation of numerous legacy systems.

During 2014, Interior will deploy a standardized and integrated Department level budget formulation and performance management tool, utilizing a Federal government shared service provider, to improve data quality and consistency across the Department while decreasing manual processes.

Main Interior Modernization – The modernization of five out of six wings within the Main Interior Building has been completed. The modernization project has installed new heating and cooling systems, upgraded fire alarm and sprinkler systems, installed fire rated stairwells and building egress routes, upgraded wiring and cabling for communications and information technology, replaced outdated lighting, installed a green roof, renovated rest rooms, constructed a new cafeteria and child care center, upgraded elevators, and improved energy efficiency and sustainability.

With the challenges facing the Federal Building Fund, the modernization of the final wing of the Main Interior Building has been delayed by almost two years. Funding to support the completion of modernization of the Main Interior Building is included in the budget of the General Services Administration. To reduce costs and improve building utilization, the decision has been made not to reopen the Interior building museum, a feature of the building since it was dedicated in 1936. Although there will be no museum, efforts will continue to inventory, catalog, and restore items in the Interior collections and evaluate the feasibility of making the collection available to scholars and for exhibit. The area previously allocated for museum space is being pursued as potential office space to consolidate Interior bureaus and offices and reduce the need for leased properties elsewhere in Washington, D.C.

Cultural and Scientific Collections – The budget requests an increase of $2.0 million for the Cultural and Scientific Collections program, which will be funded through the Working Capital Fund appropriation. The proposed increase will implement a multi-year corrective action plan to address recommendations included in an assessment published by the Department's OIG in December 2009, regarding Interior's accountability for its cultural and scientific museum holdings.

The OIG developed a list of 13 recommendations to mitigate the problems identified in the audit, including developing and implementing policy, strengthening Departmental oversight and bureau management practices, eliminating the accessioning and cataloging backlogs, and consolidating curatorial facilities. The OIG followed this report in January 2010 with reports on specific preservation and protection issues concerning collections maintained by BLM, Reclamation, FWS, NPS, and BIA.

The 2014 proposal has three components: reduce the museum collections' accessioning and cataloging backlog; identify and assess collections housed at non-Federal locations by a qualified contractor; and correct identified deficiencies in accountability, preservation, and protection of Interior cultural and scientific collections, which includes identifying and acting on opportunities for collections consolidation.

Office of Natural Resources Revenue – The ONRR is entrusted with an important fiduciary role as it collects, accounts for, analyzes, audits, and disburses an average of $10.0 billion in annual revenues from energy and mineral leases and other monies owed for the utilization of public natural resources on the Outer Continental Shelf and onshore Federal and American Indian lands. The ONRR also serves as a trustee of the royalty asset from Indian trust properties and as an advocate for the interests of Indian mineral owners.

As the result of an agency-wide strategic review, ONRR has identified the following Strategic Goals for 2013 and beyond:

- *Overarching Policy* – Strengthening holistic management of oil, gas, and other natural resources by developing policies on Department-wide collaboration and communication, focused on joint strategies and procedures for natural resource revenue collection and risk mitigation.

- *Revenue Collection Road Map* – Inventorying and analyzing the Department's technology systems and statutory requirements related to revenue collection, and developing a strategy to efficiently and effectively align Interior's revenue collection, disbursement, and verification efforts.

- *Royalty Reform* – Improving return to taxpayers by finalizing key reforms, including clarification and simplification of regulations governing valuation of oil and gas on Federal land and coal on Federal and Indian lands, and other strategic initiatives.

- *Data and Information Sharing across Interior* – Providing more efficient exchange of production, well, lease, and revenue data across the Department.

- *Production Measurement Verification* – Leveraging ONRR's expertise to improve Interior's production measurement inspection program to ensure accurate measurement of production volumes and assure that the Department is collecting every dollar due.

- *Revenue Transparency* – Increased focus on making ONRR's data more accessible to the general public, including ONRR's lead role in supporting Interior's implementation of the Extractive Industries Transparency Initiative in consultation with other key stakeholders.

Extractive Industries Transparency Initiative – In September 2011, President Obama announced the United States' intention to implement the Extractive Industries Transparency Initiative, and in October 2011, named Secretary Salazar as the U.S. Senior Official responsible for implementing EITI. In response, Secretary Salazar committed to working with industry and civil societies and designated the Assistant Secretary for Policy, Management and Budget to lead the implementation effort.

The EITI offers a voluntary framework for governments to disclose revenues received from oil, gas, and mining assets belonging to the country, with parallel disclosure by companies of what they have paid the government in royalties, rents, bonuses, taxes, and other payments.

The design of each EITI framework is country-specific and developed through a collaborative process by a multi-stakeholder group comprised of government, industry, and civil societies representatives. The EITI principles align with the Obama Administration's Open Government Initiative and its pledge of a more transparent, participatory, and collaborative government.

The Office of Natural Resources Revenue provides expertise to support the implementation of EITI in the United States. As a member of Interior's Implementation Team, ONRR led efforts to establish the Multi-Stakeholder Group that was convened as a Federal Advisory Committee. In December 2012, Secretary Salazar announced the membership of the Stakeholder Group, which consists of 21 members and 20 alternates representing government, industry, and civil society. The Stakeholder Group held its first meeting in February 2013, and will meet routinely to develop a fully-costed work plan, apply

for EITI candidate country status, and obtain EITI compliant status.

The implementation of the United States EITI provides additional oversight of the collection and disbursement of the Nation's mineral resources revenues and helps ensure the full and fair return to the American people for the utilization of these public resources. Supporting EITI advances the revenue reform efforts underway in ONRR and strengthens the public's trust in ONRR's stewardship through enhanced public participation, transparency, and accountability.

Sustainability and Adaptation Planning – In October 2009, President Obama signed Executive Order 13514 on *Federal Leadership in Environmental, Energy, and Economic Performance,* setting aggressive targets for reducing waste and pollution in Federal operations by 2020. Interior is on track to achieve targets for reducing greenhouse gas emissions from building energy use, fleet fuel use, and other sources. Interior bureaus and offices decreased direct and indirect greenhouse gas emissions in 2012 from the 2008 baseline and remain on track to achieve potable water intensity reduction targets by 2020. New appendices in the 2012 Strategic Sustainability Performance Plan include a Fleet Management Plan and Bio-based Purchasing Strategy that will continue to drive the Department toward its sustainability goals.

Interior's plan also includes the Climate Change Adaptation Plan for 2013, which outlines initiatives to reduce the vulnerability of Interior's programs, assets, and investments to address the impacts of climate change. This plan facilitates the Department's internal efforts to adapt natural and cultural resource management activities to changing conditions, avoiding or minimizing impacts to people and built assets, working with Tribes in adaptation efforts, and providing scientific information and tools to support a range of activities and programs in the face of climate change. Interior's plan is consistent with a new Department-wide climate change adaptation policy finalized in December 2012, which provides guidance to ensure accountability, engender a consistent approach, foster internal and external coordination, and allow for monitoring and evaluation of climate change adaptation efforts.

Evidence-based and Program Evaluations – The budget also funds four independent evaluations to increase the use of evidence and analysis to promote rigor, transparency, and independence in decisionmaking at the Department of the Interior. The Bureau of Indian Education will commission an independent evaluation to examine the role of BIE and guide future reforms to improve educational opportunities for Native American children. Interior will also conduct a comprehensive evaluation of Federal policy and engagement on Indian water rights issues that analyzes options to improve policies, programs, and budgetary coordination. This evaluation will help to strengthen the oversight, management, and analytical capabilities of the Indian Water Rights Office and other bureaus and offices that work on these issues. The budget also supports the Bureau of Reclamation's in-house analytical capabilities to allow for more rigorous economic and evidence-based evaluation of Reclamation's programs, projects, and operations. Finally, the Department will investigate the commission of an independent public evaluation of the Payments in Lieu of Taxes program, which expires at the end of 2013 and is proposed for a one-year extension. The proposed evaluation would review the PILT program–in both concept and practice–with a goal of developing options to put the program on a sustainable long-term funding path.

BUREAU HIGHLIGHTS

BUREAU HIGHLIGHTS

This section summarizes the budget requests of the bureaus and offices of the Department, comparing the 2014 request to the 2012 enacted level. The graph below and the tables on the following pages show the allocation of the proposed 2014 budget authority to the bureaus and offices. Additional details on the Department's budget authority can be found in Appendix A.

FISCAL YEAR 2014
CURRENT APPROPRIATIONS

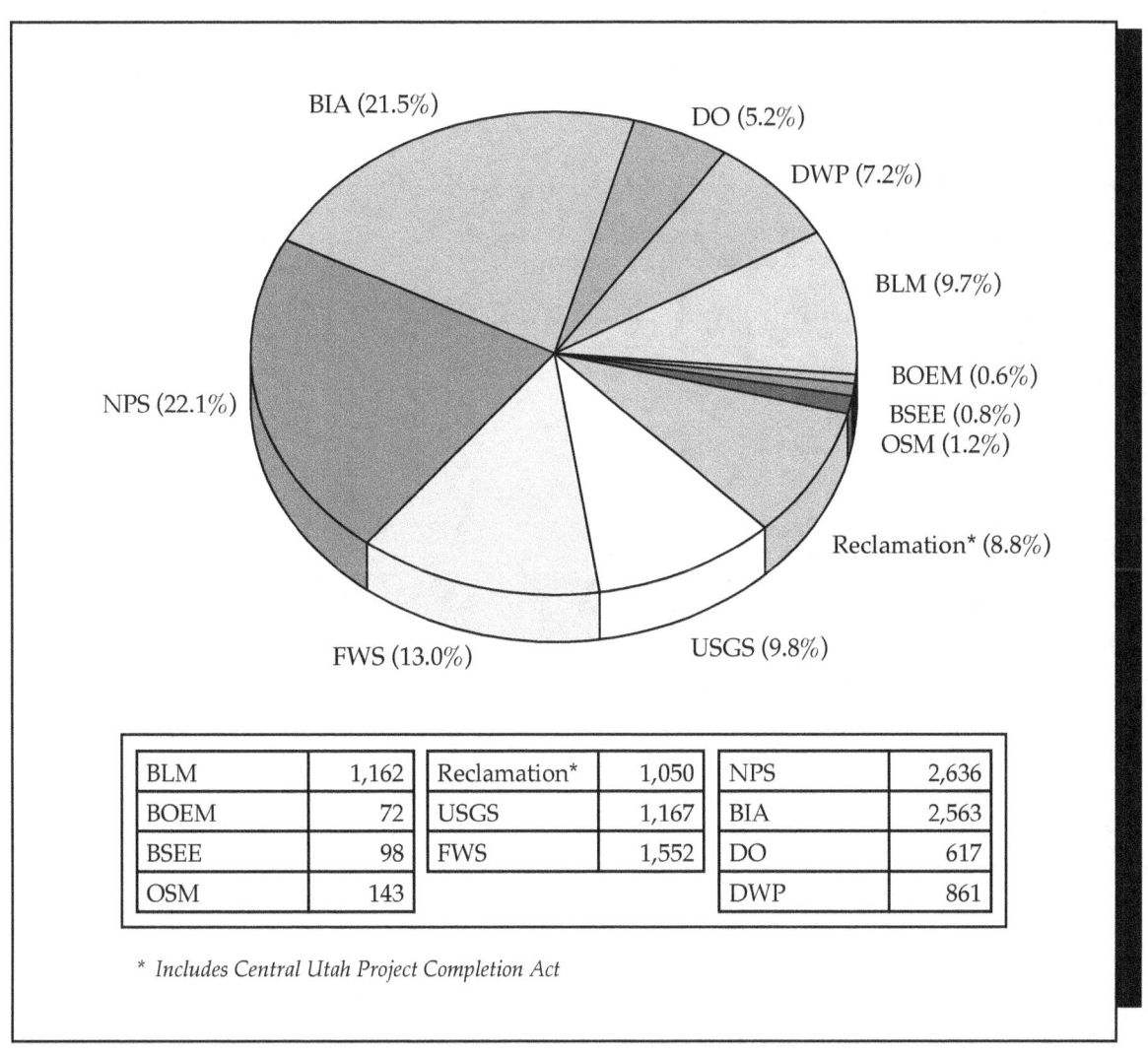

BIA (21.5%)   DO (5.2%)   DWP (7.2%)   BLM (9.7%)   BOEM (0.6%)   BSEE (0.8%)   OSM (1.2%)   Reclamation* (8.8%)   USGS (9.8%)   FWS (13.0%)   NPS (22.1%)

BLM	1,162	Reclamation*	1,050	NPS	2,636
BOEM	72	USGS	1,167	BIA	2,563
BSEE	98	FWS	1,552	DO	617
OSM	143			DWP	861

* Includes Central Utah Project Completion Act

BUDGET AUTHORITY BY BUREAU
(in millions of dollars)

Bureau	2012 Enacted	2012 Actual	2013 Full Year CR	2014 Request
Current Budget Authority				
Bureau of Land Management	1,129	1,129	1,138	1,162
Bureau of Ocean Energy Management	60	60	60	72
Bureau of Safety and Environmental Enforcement	76	76	80	98
Office of Surface Mining Reclamation and Enforcement	150	150	151	143
U.S. Geological Survey	1,068	1,069	1,075	1,167
Fish and Wildlife Service	1,476	1,485	1,553	1,552
National Park Service	2,580	2,564	3,009	2,636
Indian Affairs	2,531	2,531	2,547	2,563
Departmental Offices				
Office of the Secretary - Salaries and Expenses	262	263	624	269
Insular Affairs	104	104	105	92
Office of the Solicitor	66	66	67	66
Office of Inspector General	49	49	50	51
Office of the Special Trustee for American Indians	152	152	153	140
Subtotal, Departmental Offices	*634*	*635*	*998*	*617*
Department-wide Programs				
Central Hazardous Materials	10	10	10	10
Wildland Fire Management	484	677	734	685
FLAME Wildfire Suppression Reserve Account	92	0	92	92
Natural Resource Damage Assessment & Restoration	6	6	6	13
Working Capital Fund	62	62	62	62
Subtotal, Department-wide Programs	*654*	*755*	*905*	*861*
Bureau of Reclamation	1,048	1,048	1,054	1,050
Central Utah Project Completion Act	29	29	29	0
Total Current Budget Authority	**11,434**	**11,531**	**12,598**	**11,920**
Adjustments for M-Savers	-42	0	-40	-42
Adjustments for Mandatory Current Accounts	-58	-58	-61	-61
Adjustment for Discretionary Receipts Offsets	-67	-79	-56	-76
Total Net Discretionary	**11,266**	**11,393**	**12,441**	**11,741**
NPS Contract Authority Rescission	0	30	0	0
Palau Compact Extension	0	-13	0	0
Wildland Fire FLAME Unobligated Balance Transfers	0	-85	0	0
Total Net Discretionary Budget Authority [OMB/MAX]	**11,266**	**11,324**	**12,441**	**11,741**

BUDGET AUTHORITY BY BUREAU
(in millions of dollars)

Bureau	2012 Enacted	2012 Actual	2013 Full Year CR	2014 Request
Total Budget Authority				
Bureau of Land Management..	1,278	1,233	1,251	1,245
Bureau of Ocean Energy Management	60	60	60	72
Bureau of Safety and Environmental Enforcement.....................	76	76	80	98
Office of Surface Mining Reclamation and Enforcement...........	890	890	686	612
U.S. Geological Survey	1,069	1,070	1,076	1,168
Fish and Wildlife Service	2,429	2,445	2,722	2,795
National Park Service	2,984	2,998	3,429	3,115
Indian Affairs...	2,745	2,746	2,654	2,671
Departmental Offices				
Office of the Secretary - Salaries and Expenses	2,371	2,357	4,707	2,525
Insular Affairs...	571	619	649	688
Office of the Solicitor	66	66	67	66
Office of Inspector General..	49	49	50	51
Office of the Special Trustee for American Indians	581	564	566	568
Subtotal, Departmental Offices	*3,638*	*3,655*	*6,039*	*3,897*
National Indian Gaming Commission...	17	19	19	19
Department-wide Programs				
Payment in Lieu of Taxes...	387	393	401	410
Central Hazardous Materials...	10	10	10	10
Wildland Fire Management...	484	677	734	685
FLAME Wildfire Suppression Reserve Account	92	0	92	92
Natural Resource Damage Assessment & Restoration	70	124	88	85
Working Capital Fund..	62	62	62	62
Subtotal, Department-wide Programs	*1,104*	*1,267*	*1,388*	*1,344*
Bureau of Reclamation	1,247	1,219	1,229	1,230
Central Utah Project Completion Act	29	32	29	0
Total Budget Authority	**17,566**	**17,710**	**20,661**	**18,265**

Note: Includes current and permanent authority. Includes enacted transfers.

BUREAU OF LAND MANAGEMENT

Mission – The Bureau of Land Management's mission is to sustain the health, diversity, and productivity of the public lands for the use and enjoyment of present and future generations.

Budget Overview – The 2014 BLM budget request is $1.2 billion, an increase of $32.6 million over the 2012 enacted level. The budget proposes $980.2 million for the Management of Lands and Resources appropriation and $115.5 million for the Oregon and California Grant Lands appropriation, BLM's two operating accounts. This represents a total increase of $23.5 million over the 2012 enacted level. The 2014 budget continues to provide strong support for high priority Administration and Secretarial initiatives, which include America's Great Outdoors, New Energy Frontier, Youth in the Great Outdoors, sage grouse habitat conservation, the Secretary's Western Oregon Strategy, and improved wild horse and burro management.

America's Great Outdoors – The BLM plays a critical role in advancing the President's conservation initiative to reconnect Americans to the outdoors. The 2014 budget includes $8.0 million in programmatic increases in Recreation Resources Management and the National Landscape Conservation System to expand and improve opportunities for recreation, education, and scientific activities while enhancing the conservation and protection of BLM-managed lands and resources. A $2.0 million program increase is proposed in the Recreation Resources Management program to strengthen the scientific analysis underpinning recreation management practices and policies. A $6.0 million program increase in the National Monuments and National Conservation Areas program will allow BLM to increase a variety of activities, including strengthening law enforcement, enhancing visitor safety and experiences, increasing habitat conservation and restoration, and expanding interpretation programs and products.

In 2014, BLM, along with other Department of the Interior bureaus, will participate in interagency AGO projects to demonstrate ecosystem and landscape-scale conservation. The BLM budget request includes an increase of $1.1

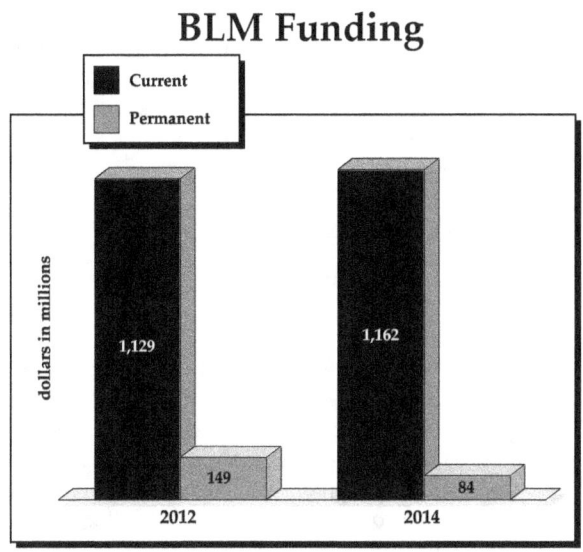

BLM Funding

million for BLM to collaborate with other AGO partners to advance community-based landscape-scale conservation in the Southwest Deserts landscape, the Crown of the Continent landscape, and the Grasslands of the Northern Great Plains landscape. In the Southwest Deserts landscape, BLM will focus on restoring the Aravaipa Creek watershed. For the Crown of the Continent landscape, BLM will support the work of the Crown Management Partnership to control invasive weeds. In the Grasslands of the Northern Great Plains landscape, BLM will work with partners to initiate projects to improve wildlife habitat, such as crested wheatgrass fields.

The 2014 budget also includes increases for programs funded through the Land and Water Conservation Fund, a vital component of the America's Great Outdoors initiative. The 2014 budget proposal includes a total of $48.9 million for BLM Federal land acquisition, including $32.6 million in requested current appropriations and $16.3 million in permanent funding. The 2014 total represents an increase of $26.6 million over the 2012 enacted level, and the current request represents an increase of $10.3 million over 2012. The 2014 Federal Land Acquisition program builds on efforts started in 2011 and 2012 to strategically invest in interagency landscape-scale conservation projects while continuing to meet agency-specific programmatic needs. The Department of the Interior and the U.S. Forest Service collaborated extensively to develop a process to more effectively coordinate land acquisitions with government and local community partners to achieve the highest priority shared conservation goals. The 2014 request includes $29.3 million, in current and permanent appropriations, for collaborative projects, including $21.0 million for projects that are part of Collaborative Landscape Planning in the Southwest Deserts landscape, $5.7 million for projects that are part of Collaborative Landscape Planning for the National Historic-National Scenic Trails landscape, and $2.6 million for projects that are part of Collaborative Landscape Planning for the Crown of the Continent-Northern Rockies landscape.

New Energy Frontier Initiative–The 2014 budget request includes a total of $29.1 million for BLM's Renewable Energy program, a $9.1 million programmatic increase over the 2012 enacted level, reflecting $7.1 million in new program funds and a $2.0 million transfer of geothermal funds previously included within the Oil and Gas Management program. The $7.1 million in new funds will enhance BLM's role in promoting and facilitating the development of renewable energy on public lands and will support additional environmental studies and planning to accelerate the identification of additional prime areas for utility-scale renewable energy project development. With the completion of the Solar Programmatic Environmental Impact Statement in early 2013 and the solar and wind competitive rulemaking process in late 2013, the proposed funding in 2014 will allow BLM to prepare and offer the first competitive lease sales for solar energy development within Solar Energy Zones designated by the Solar Programmatic EIS. Funding

will also be used to implement renewable energy plans scheduled to be completed for Arizona, California, and Nevada. The 2014 request will also enable BLM to continue ongoing program management responsibilities associated with geothermal energy development by replacing now-expired permanent funding, which was previously provided for this purpose through the Geothermal Steam Act Implementation Fund.

The budget request enhances BLM's ability to support oil and gas development on Federal lands. The request for Oil and Gas Management represents a total program increase of $23.0 million over the 2012 enacted level. This includes a $10.0 million increase to fully implement the leasing reforms instituted in May 2010, of which $5.0 million restores a 2012 funding reduction that impeded BLM's ability to implement these reforms and diminished BLM's general oil and gas oversight capabilities. The additional $5.0 million increase in 2014 will allow BLM to more fully achieve the goal of the leasing reforms without sacrificing other program goals, such as providing industry with timely access to Federal oil and gas resources. The increased opportunity for public participation and a more thorough environmental review process and documentation required by BLM's leasing reforms have increased BLM's costs. The additional funds will enable BLM to conduct defensible and timely lease parcel environmental analyses. The 2014 request includes an additional $3.0 million increase for large, regional-scale studies and environmental impact statements for conventional energy issues.

The 2014 budget request also proposes to expand and strengthen BLM's oil and gas inspections and oversight capability through new fees on industry that are comparable to those now assessed for offshore inspections. The fee schedule included in the budget is estimated to generate $48.0 million in collections, which would offset a proposed reduction of $38.0 million in appropriated funds and provide for a net increase of $10.0 million in funds available for this critical BLM management responsibility. Increased funding is aimed at correcting deficiencies identified by the Government Accountability Office in its February 2011 report, which designated Federal management of oil and gas resources, including production and revenue collection as high risk. It will help BLM to more fully implement its new risk-based inspection strategy to improve production accountability, safety, and environmental protection of oil and gas operations.

The budget proposes to continue charging fees for processing Applications for Permits to Drill through appropriations language, generating $32.5 million in 2014. In addition to the current appropriations noted above, the BLM budget request assumes $18.7 million in permanent funding will continue to be available in 2014 for the oil and gas program from the Permit Processing Improvement Fund. Consistent with prior requests, the budget request includes a permanent proposal to terminate this permanent funding in fiscal year 2015.

The Secretary's New Energy Frontier initiative is not only about facilitating the development of renewable and conventional energy resources on public lands, it is also about facilitating the efficient delivery of energy to markets where it is needed to meet growing demand. The aging electrical infrastructure in the West is an impediment to efficient energy transmission and maximizing renewable energy development. Upgrades are needed to improve reliability and increase capacity. The BLM has a critical role to play in expanding electric transmission infrastructure through the issuance of rights-of-way across the vast public lands in the West. To support BLM's role in this important endeavor, the budget includes a $6.0 million increase in the Lands and Realty Management program to enhance BLM's ability to identify and designate energy corridors in low conflict areas and site high voltage transmission lines, substations, and related infrastructure in an environmentally sensitive manner.

Sage Grouse Conservation – The budget includes a $15.0 million increase over the 2012 enacted level to allow BLM to continue implementing sage grouse conservation and restoration measures to help prevent the future listing of the species for protection under the Endangered Species Act. In its March 2010 ruling that listing was "warranted but precluded," the Fish and Wildlife Service said that BLM was not "fully implementing the regulatory mechanisms available" to ensure species conservation. The BLM is addressing the FWS concerns through a planning

process formally initiated in late 2011. The 2014 funding increase, also included in 2013, will enable BLM to ramp up and implement the process, and take other actions before the 2015 deadline when FWS will make a final decision on whether or not to list the sage grouse.

At the 2014 request level, BLM will continue incorporating necessary regulatory mechanisms into BLM's land use plans to address conservation of the sage grouse. As many as 98 BLM resource management plans, in 68 planning areas, will address sage grouse in California, Colorado, Idaho, Montana, Nevada, North Dakota, Oregon, South Dakota, Utah, and Wyoming.

As the planning effort is completed, funding will be directed toward habitat restoration and monitoring efforts. These activities include fence removal or marking to reduce collision mortality, removal of conifers encroaching on sage habitats, seeding of disturbed sites to re-establish native sage plant communities, wet meadow and spring protection, and providing a portion of the funding needed to establish a working capital fund to purchase adequate native seed supplies for sage community restoration. Of the $15.0 million increase, $2.5 million would be transferred to the Natural Resources Conservation Service to continue broad-scale sage-grouse habitat monitoring activities to ascertain the effectiveness of habitat management and the effect of land use authorizations.

The BLM will also continue inventory, monitoring, and mapping efforts to delineate areas of highest priority habitat across the range of sage grouse. As BLM completes range-wide priority habitat maps and inventory work, the bureau is working in coordination with the respective State fish and wildlife agencies through the planning process to identify specific management actions on a landscape level to be undertaken both inside and outside of identified priority habitat to maintain sustainable sage grouse populations.

Youth in the Great Outdoors – The 2014 budget request expands BLM's youth programs and partnerships to accomplish high priority projects, and promote quality participant experiences and pathways to careers. The request includes a $1.3 million increase in Soil, Water, and Air Management for the 21st Century Conservation Service Corps to put more young Americans to work protecting and restoring public lands, as well as cultural and historical resources and treasures. A $1.5 million increase in the Wildlife Management program will be provided to the National Fish and Wildlife Foundation to provide more outdoor work experience to youth while implementing wildlife habitat restoration and improvement projects on public lands. This increase is in addition to $1.0 million in BLM's base NFWF budget currently dedicated to advancing the Secretary's Youth Initiative.

Cooperative Landscape Conservation – The 2014 BLM budget includes a $2.5 million program increase as part of an integrated multi-bureau proposal to effectively plan for and respond to the impacts of climate change. The BLM will use $500,000 for vegetation inventory work, as incomplete coverage of vegetation inventories has been identified as a major gap for adaptation planning. The BLM will coordinate with the Natural Resources Conservation Service, U.S. Forest Service, and U.S. Geological Survey to develop a plan to extend existing vegetation surveys to cover all lands in the lower 48 States, synthesize data from the major surveys to support preparation of regional analyses, and to use the data to enhance the accuracy of LANDFIRE. Data products provided by LANDFIRE or the Landscape Fire and Resource Management Planning Tools are used in many aspects of natural and environmental resource management, including vegetation management, wildlife management, and carbon-climate assessments. The BLM will use $1.0 million to conduct a coordination pilot in the Great Basin to turn information and strategy into coordinated, effective management actions that build resilience to changing conditions. This work will build upon existing collaborations in the Basin regarding sage grouse habitat, the Great Basin Landscape Conservation Cooperative, the Northwest and Southwest Climate Science Centers, and the National Oceanic and Atmospheric Administration. An additional $500,000 will allow BLM to work with FWS, the National Invasive Species Council, and other partners to conduct a pilot project in the Great Basin to develop innovative approaches and tools for early detection of and rapid response to invasive species. The remaining $500,000 will support the design and development of tools to help predict the spread of invasive species and the outcomes of management actions. Other investments in support of the Cooperative Landscape Conservation initiative include an increase of $776,000 in Soil, Water, and Air Management to implement programs that improve the utilization of Rapid Ecoregional Assessments in land use decisions.

Secretary's Western Oregon Strategy – The 2014 budget request includes a program increase of $1.8 million in the Oregon and California Forest Management program to increase the volume of timber offered for sale; support key resource management planning objectives; increase surveying for rare, uncommon, or endangered species; provide for landscape-level timber sale project environmental analyses; and facilitate joint development and implementation of a revised recovery plan for the northern spotted owl. The request also includes an increase of

$1.7 million in O&C Resource Management Planning to support the preparation of six new resource management plans in western Oregon to replace the Western Oregon Plan Revisions previously withdrawn by the Secretary.

Wild Horse and Burro Management Strategy – The budget includes a program increase of $2.0 million for the Secretary's Wild Horse and Burro Management Strategy to implement recommendations of the forthcoming National Academy of Sciences study of the Wild Horse and Burro program. This maintains the 2013 Operating Plan level for the Wild Horse and Burro Management program, in which BLM used a $2.0 million increase above 2012 enacted for research and development on population control. The long-term goal for effective fertility control is to slow the annual population growth rate for wild-horses, while decreasing or eliminating the need to remove excess animals. Reducing gathers will decrease holding costs, the largest single cost-driver in the program.

Other Program Increases – A $4.0 million program increase in the Resource Management Planning program will support high priority planning efforts, including the initiation of new plan revisions in 2014. Resource management plans provide the basis for every BLM management action. Keeping these plans current in an era of rapidly changing resource use patterns, climatic and land health conditions, population growth, and public recreation on the public lands is critical to effective resource management and protection. The budget includes an increase of $2.5 million in the Soil, Water, and Air Management program for applied science projects and information aimed at improving BLM's understanding and management of public lands, which will help BLM address complex resource management challenges, such as implementation of the Sage Grouse Conservation Strategy. The request for Soil, Water, and Air Management includes an additional program increase of $500,000 for activities related to the Klamath Agreements authorized under existing law. Activities will include any additional follow up regarding the evaluation of whether removal of four dams on the Klamath River is in the public interest, any related mitigation, and subsequent ecologic restoration. The budget includes a program increase of $1.0 million in Riparian Management to provide increased science support to improve the effectiveness of riparian habitat conservation and restoration projects.

The budget request also includes program increases of $2.4 million and $2.0 million, respectively, in the Coal Management and Other Mineral Resources Management programs. The BLM will continue to study opportunities to institute cost recovery fees within these programs, but the budget recognizes these fees may not be in place by the start of 2014. An $8.2 million program increase is requested in the Bureau-wide Fixed Cost program to cover costs previously funded through program assessments. The requested increase will properly align these costs with the appropriate budget subactivity. The BLM will use an increase of $1.3 million in Deferred Maintenance to improve management of BLM's Land Mobile Radio facilities, including modernizing and consolidating facilities and infrastructure. The BLM will use a $1.0 million increase in Administrative Support to fund the start up costs for a new congressionally-chartered charitable, non-profit foundation. A legislative proposal to establish the National BLM Foundation is being submitted with the President's Budget. The Foundation will help leverage private funding to support and supplement BLM management of public lands.

Program Reductions – Difficult choices were made during the formulation of the 2014 President's budget request to support the initiatives and priorities described above. A $14.1 million program decrease is proposed in the Rangeland Management program for grazing administration. However, the impact of this funding decrease will be mitigated by a new grazing administration fee of $1 per animal unit month that BLM proposes to implement on a pilot basis, estimated to generate $6.5 million in 2014 for processing grazing permits. The budget includes a program reduction of $12.3 million in the Alaska Conveyance program. Interior will explore opportunities to further streamline the conveyance process and reduce costs. The impact of this funding reduction will be further mitigated by a legislative proposal to use a portion of oil and gas revenues from the National Petroleum Reserve-Alaska to also fund land transfers in support of the Alaska Conveyance program. The 2014 budget request also includes a reduction of $2.1 million in Information Technology Management.

Construction – The budget eliminates the Construction appropriation account with a proposed reduction of $3.6 million. Beginning in 2014, construction projects will be funded in the Deferred Maintenance and Capital Improvements program in the Management of Lands and Resources appropriation.

Land Acquisition – The budget proposes $48.9 million for BLM Land Acquisition, including $32.6 million in requested current appropriations and $16.3 million in permanent funding. The 2014 total represents an increase of $26.6 million over the 2012 enacted level and the current request represents an increase of $10.3 million over 2012. The current request for line-item acquisition projects is $29.1 million, which will fund core projects in four States. Emergencies and Hardships are funded at $1.6 million. A total of $1.9 million is requested for Acquisition

Management. The $16.3 million in permanent funding, which will be allocated to BLM from a proposed new permanent LWCF account in the Office of the Secretary, will fund projects in seven States.

Budget Structure and Technical Changes – Compared to the 2012 enacted budget, the 2014 BLM budget request reflects a few budget structure changes executed in the 2013 Operating Plan. The Operations subactivity and Annual Maintenance subactivity in the Oregon and California Grant Lands appropriation have been combined into a single Annual Maintenance and Operations subactivity. Funding in the Land and Resource Information Systems program and the Information Systems Operations program was consolidated into a new MLR Information Technology Management program. The 2013 Operating Plan also implemented a transfer of $3.0 million from the Land and Resource Information Systems program to the Lands and Realty Management program to directly align land and realty information systems funding with the benefiting program. In 2014, BLM proposes to shift the base funding in the O&C appropriation's Deferred Maintenance program into the newly named Deferred Maintenance and Capital Improvements program in the MLR appropriation. All deferred maintenance and capital improvement projects on public lands and Western Oregon lands will be funded in the MLR appropriation in 2014.

LEGISLATIVE PROPOSALS

Oil and Gas Management Reforms – The Administration proposes a package of legislative and administrative proposals to reform the management of Interior's onshore and offshore oil and gas programs, with a key focus on improving the return to taxpayers from the sale of these Federal resources and on improving transparency and oversight. Proposed changes fall into three general categories: advancing royalty reforms; encouraging diligent development of oil and gas leases; and improving revenue collection processes.

Royalty reforms include evaluating minimum royalty rates for oil, gas, and similar products; adjusting onshore royalty rates; analyzing a price-based tiered royalty rate; and repealing legislatively-mandated royalty relief. Diligent development requirements include shorter primary lease terms, stricter enforcement of lease terms, and monetary incentives to get leases into production e.g., a new per-acre fee on nonproducing leases. Revenue collection improvements include simplification of the royalty valuation process, elimination of interest accruals on company overpayments of royalties, and permanent repeal of Interior's authority to accept in-kind royalty payments. Collectively, these reforms will generate roughly $2.5 billion in net revenue to the Treasury over ten years, of which an estimated $1.76 billion will result from statutory changes. Many States will also benefit from higher Federal revenue sharing payments as a result of these reforms. In addition, the Department will continue to evaluate the use of internet-based oil and gas lease auctions.

The budget also proposes to extend and revamp the oil and gas permitting pilot office authority established under the Energy Policy Act of 2005. Under the proposal, BLM will have flexibility to relocate pilot offices as needed based on changing permitting demands over time. The Administration continues to seek repeal of the Energy Policy Act's prohibition on BLM establishing cost recovery fees for processing applications for oil and gas permits to drill as well as the diversion of mineral leasing receipts from the Treasury to the permanent BLM Permit Processing Improvement Fund. On repeal of these Energy Policy Act provisions, BLM will promulgate regulations to establish cost recovery fees for applications for permits to drill. These fees would help replace the termination of permanent funds, which would become effective in 2015.

Hardrock Mining Reform – The 2014 budget includes two legislative proposals to reform hardrock mining on public and private lands by addressing abandoned mine land hazards and providing a better return to the taxpayer from hardrock production on Federal lands.

The first component of this reform addresses abandoned hardrock mines across the Country through a new AML fee on hardrock production. Just as the coal industry is held responsible for abandoned coal sites, the Administration proposes to hold the hardrock mining industry responsible for abandoned hardrock mines. The legislative proposal will levy an AML fee on uranium and metallic mines on both public and private lands. The proposed AML fee on the production of hardrock minerals will be charged on the volume of material displaced after January 1, 2014. The receipts would be split between Federal and non-Federal lands. The Secretary would disperse the share of non-Federal funds to each State and Tribe based on need. Each State and Tribe would select its own priority projects using established national criteria. The proposed hardrock AML fee and reclamation program will operate in parallel with the coal AML reclamation program as part of a larger effort to ensure the Nation's most dangerous abandoned coal and hardrock AML sites are addressed by the industries that created the problems.

The second legislative proposal institutes a leasing process under the Mineral Leasing Act of 1920 for certain minerals, gold, silver, lead, zinc, copper, uranium, and molybdenum, currently covered by the General Mining Law of 1872. After enactment, mining for these metals on Federal lands would be governed by the new leasing process and subject to annual rental payments and a royalty of not less than five percent of gross proceeds. Half of the receipts would be distributed to the States in which the leases are located and the remaining half would be deposited in the Treasury. Existing mining claims would be exempt from the change to a leasing system, but would be subject to increases in the annual maintenance fees under the General Mining Law of 1872. However, holders of existing mining claims for these minerals could voluntarily convert their claims to leases. The Office of Natural Resources Revenue will collect, account for, and disburse the hardrock royalty receipts.

Reauthorize and Restructure the Helium Program – The 2014 budget includes a legislative proposal to reauthorize BLM's Federal Helium program to facilitate a gradual exit from the helium market, while ensuring the short-term availability of sufficient helium supplies to meet government and industry demand. Under current law, once the helium program debt is retired, the authority for the helium production fund terminates and the program will no longer have the funding resources to continue operations. The Secretary will be making the final repayment on the helium debt at the beginning of 2014.

Alaska Land Conveyance and Remediation of Legacy Wells – The 2014 budget includes a legislative proposal to make permanent funding available for two BLM activities of high priority to the State of Alaska, the Alaska Conveyance program and BLM's efforts to remediate legacy wells on the Alaska North Slope. The proposal will revise the current revenue sharing arrangement for NPR-A revenue to direct 50 percent of the revenue stream to a special Alaska Land Conveyance and Remediation Fund, to be used to supplement current funds in the BLM budget for these two activities. This will enable BLM to accelerate its progress in completing the final transfer of lands to Alaska Native Corporations, individual Alaska Natives, and the State of Alaska and in addressing legacy wells that pose a threat to the fragile North Slope environment. The regular 50/50 revenue sharing arrangement will resume once the work on these two activities is complete.

Reauthorize the Federal Land Transaction Facilitation Act – The 2014 budget proposes to reauthorize the Act, which expired in July 2011, and allow lands identified as suitable for disposal in recent land use plans to be sold using the FLTFA authority. The FLTFA sales revenues would continue to be used to fund the acquisition of environmentally sensitive lands and to cover the administrative costs associated with conducting sales.

Fixed Costs - Fixed costs of $5.3 million are fully funded in the request.

SUMMARY OF BUREAU APPROPRIATIONS
(all dollar amounts in thousands)

Comparison of 2014 Request with 2012 Enacted

	2012 Enacted		2014 Request		Change	
	FTE	Amount	FTE	Amount	FTE	Amount
Current						
Management of Lands and Resources	5,619	960,361	5,639	980,228	+20	+19,867
Construction	8	3,570	0	0	-8	-3,570
Land Acquisition	11	22,344	11	32,618	0	+10,274
Oregon and California Grant Lands	832	111,864	782	115,543	-50	+3,679
Range Improvements	47	10,000	42	10,000	-5	0
Service Charges, Deposits and Forfeitures *(Indefinite)*	208	32,448	208	32,465	0	+17
Minus SCDF Offset	0	-32,448	0	-32,465	0	-17
Miscellaneous Trust Funds *(Indefinite)*	97	20,815	97	23,125	0	+2,310
Subtotal, Current	6,822	1,128,954	6,779	1,161,514	-43	+32,560

Comparison of 2014 Estimates with 2013 Estimates

	2013 Estimate		2014 Estimate		Change	
	FTE	Amount	FTE	Amount	FTE	Amount
Permanent and Trust						
Miscellaneous Trust Funds	13	1,800	11	1,800	-2	0
Miscellaneous Permanent Payments	9	45,729	0	4,369	-9	-41,360
Land Acquisition	0	0	0	16,308	0	+16,308
Permanent Operating Funds						
Operations and Maintenance of Quarters	1	600	2	600	+1	0
Recreation Fee Demonstration	125	18,000	123	18,500	-2	+500
Forest Ecosystems Health and Recovery	78	6,043	56	4,576	-22	-1,467
Expenses, Road Maintenance Deposits	6	2,000	5	2,000	-1	0
Timber Sale Pipeline Restoration Fund	31	3,824	35	1,810	+4	-2,014
Southern Nevada Land Sales	55	12,727	55	4,511	0	-8,216
Southern Nevada Earnings on Investments	0	1,000	0	1,000	0	0
Lincoln County Land Sales	8	22	5	311	-3	+289
Interest, Lincoln County Land Sales Act	0	0	0	220	0	+220
Owyhee Land Acquisition Account	0	0	0	768	0	+768
Silver Saddle Endowment	0	0	0	0	0	0
Carson City Special Account	0	208	0	0	0	-208
Stewardship Contract, Excess Receipts	0	20	0	20	0	0
Naval Petroleum Reserve #2 Lease Revenues	0	29	0	53	0	+24
Geothermal Lease and Use Auth. Fund	25	0	5	0	-20	0
Oil and Gas Permit Processing Imp. Fund	192	20,698	165	18,726	-27	-1,972
Federal Land Disposal Account	0	0	2	4,800	+2	+4,800
White Pine (85 percent special account)	0	171	0	175	0	+4
Washington County, Utah						
Land Acquisition Account	0	0	0	96	0	+96
Alaska Programs	0	0	1	3,010	+1	+3,010
Subtotal, Permanent Operating Funds	521	65,342	454	61,176	-67	-4,166
Helium Fund	49	212,000	49	24,963	0	-187,037
Offsetting Collections	0	-212,000	0	-24,963	0	+187,037
Working Capital Fund	24	64,000	24	64,000	0	0
Offsetting Collections	0	-64,000	0	-64,000	0	0
Subtotal, Permanent and Trust	616	112,871	538	83,653	-78	-29,218
Reimbursable and Other FTE	3,080	0	2,974	0	-106	0

APPROPRIATION: Management of Lands and Resources

	2013 Full Year CR	2012 Enacted	2014 Request	Change from 2012
Land Resources				
Soil, Water, and Air Management.........	44,477	46,229	54,822	+8,593
Rangeland Management.........................	81,490	87,392	75,102	-12,290
Grazing Permit Admin. Fees.............	0	0	6,500	+6,500
Grazing Permit Admin. Offset..........	0	0	-6,500	-6,500
Public Domain Forest Management.....	6,318	9,714	9,838	+124
Riparian Management............................	22,874	22,682	24,009	+1,327
Cultural Resources Management..........	16,234	16,105	16,329	+224
Wild Horse and Burro Management....	77,072	74,888	77,245	+2,357
Subtotal, Land Resources..................	248,465	257,010	257,345	+335
Wildlife and Fisheries Management				
Wildlife Management.............................	52,149	36,914	53,838	+16,924
Fisheries Management............................	13,442	13,333	13,519	+186
Subtotal, Wildlife/Fisheries Mgmt...	65,591	50,247	67,357	+17,110
Threatened/Endangered Species Mgmt..	21,807	21,633	21,942	+309
Recreation Management				
Wilderness Management.........................	18,561	18,392	18,687	+295
Recreation Resources Management......	49,490	49,074	51,819	+2,745
Subtotal, Recreation Management....	68,051	67,466	70,506	+3,040
Energy and Minerals Management				
Oil and Gas Management	76,042	72,466	46,699	-25,767
Permit Processing Fees.......................	32,500	32,500	32,500	0
Offsetting Collections (Fees)	-32,500	-32,500	-32,500	0
Inspection Fees	0	0	47,950	+47,950
Offsetting Collections (Inspection Fees)	0	0	-47,950	-47,950
Coal Management..................................	8,103	7,043	9,595	+2,552
Other Mineral Resources Mgmt...........	9,478	8,402	10,586	+2,184
Renewable Energy	22,826	19,703	29,061	+9,358
Subtotal, Energy/Minerals Mgmt	116,449	107,614	95,941	-11,673
Realty and Ownership Management				
Alaska Conveyance and Lands.............	18,741	29,061	16,976	-12,085
Cadastral Survey....................................	12,098	11,996	12,177	+181
Land/Realty Management	35,923	32,605	42,162	+9,557
Subtotal, Realty/Ownership Mgmt .	66,762	73,662	71,315	-2,347
Resource Protection and Maintenance				
Resource Management Planning..........	39,830	38,060	42,504	+4,444
Abandoned Mine Lands	17,903	19,819	19,947	+128
Resource Protection/Law Enfrcmt.......	27,170	27,024	27,283	+259
Hazardous Materials Management......	16,749	16,641	16,823	+182
Subtotal, Resource Protection............	101,652	101,544	106,557	+5,013
Transportation/Facilities Maintenance				
Deferred Maintenance............................	30,037	29,960	32,369	+2,409
Annual Maintenance and Ops Costs....	41,453	41,160	41,692	+532
Subtotal, Trans/Facilities Main.........	71,490	71,120	74,061	+2,941

	2013 Full Year CR	2012 Enacted	2014 Request	Change from 2012
Land/Resource Information System........	0	15,827	0	-15,827
Mining Law Administration				
Administration	39,696	39,696	39,696	0
Offsetting Fees	-39,696	-39,696	-39,696	0
Subtotal, Mining Law Admin............	0	0	0	0
Workforce and Organizational Support				
Information Systems Operations..........	0	14,673	0	-14,673
Information Technology Mgmt.............	27,638	0	25,696	+25,696
Administrative Support	49,488	49,130	50,778	+1,648
Bureau-wide Fixed Costs	94,169	91,161	92,901	+1,740
Subtotal, Support	171,295	154,964	169,375	+14,411
Communications Site Management				
Communications Site Management	2,000	2,000	2,000	0
Offsetting Fees	-2,000	-2,000	-2,000	0
Subtotal, Comm. Site Mgmt	0	0	0	0
Challenge Cost Share...............................	2,588	7,455	7,477	+22
National Landscape Conservation System National Monuments and				
National Conservation Areas	32,088	31,819	38,352	+6,533
TOTAL APPROPRIATION	966,238	960,361	980,228	+19,867

Detail of Budget Changes

	2014 Change from 2012 Enacted		2014 Change from 2012 Enacted
TOTAL APPROPRIATION	+19,867		
Land Resources...	+335	Riparian Management...	+1,327
Soil, Water, and Air Management	+8,593	Applied Science	+1,000
Youth Partnerships.....................................	+1,250	Fixed Costs	+327
Applied Science	+2,500	Cultural Resources Management............................	+224
Klamath Basin Restoration Agreement	+500	Fixed Costs	+224
Cooperative Landscape Conservation/REAs ...	+776	Wild Horse and Burro Management	+2,357
Climate Adaptation - Vegetation Survey	+500	Implementation of NAS Recommendations......	+2,032
Climate Adaptation - Landscape Decision Tool	+500	Fixed Costs	+325
Climate Adaptation - Coordination		Wildlife and Fisheries Management...........................	+17,110
Pilot/Sage Grouse	+1,000	Wildlife Management	+16,924
America's Great Outdoors		National Fish and Wildlife	
Demonstration Landscapes............................	+1,100	Foundation/Youth Initiative..........................	+1,500
Fixed Costs	+467	Sage Grouse Conservation Activities	+15,000
Rangeland Management	-12,290	Fixed Costs	+424
Grazing Permit Renewal and Monitoring	-14,065	Fisheries Management..	+186
Climate Adaptation - Invasive Species..............	+500	Fixed Costs	+186
Grazing Permit Administration Fees.................	+6,500	Threatened and Endangered Species Management	+309
Grazing Permit Administration Offset..............	-6,500	Fixed Costs	+309
Fixed Costs	+1,275	Recreation Management	+3,040
Public Domain Forest Management	+124	Wilderness Management...	+295
Fixed Costs	+124	Fixed Costs	+295

	2014 Change from 2012 Enacted
Recreation Resources Management	+2,745
Applied Science	+2,000
Fixed Costs	+745
Energy and Minerals Management	-11,673
Oil and Gas Management	-25,767
Transfer Geothermal Funds to	
Renewable Energy Subactivity	-2,000
General Program Increase	+8,000
Leasing Reform	+5,000
Decrease Base Funding for	
Inspections/Shift Cost to Fees	-37,950
Inspection Fees	+47,950
Offsetting Collections (Inspection Fees)	-47,950
Fixed Costs	+1,183
Coal Management	+2,552
Inspections and Enforcement	+2,421
Fixed Costs	+131
Other Mineral Resources	+2,184
Inspections and Enforcement	+2,025
Fixed Costs	+159
Renewable Energy	+9,358
Transfer Geothermal Funds	
from Oil and Gas Management	+2,000
Environmental Studies and	
Geothermal Management	+7,121
Fixed Costs	+237
Realty and Ownership Management	-2,347
Alaska Conveyance and Lands	-12,085
General Program Decrease	-12,320
Fixed Costs	+235
Cadastral Survey	+181
Fixed Costs	+181
Lands and Realty Management	+9,557
Transfer Base Funding from	
Land and Resources Information System	+3,000
Transmission Corridors	+6,000
Fixed Costs	+557
Resource Protection and Maintenance	+5,013
Resource Management Planning	+4,444
High Priority Planning Efforts	+4,000
Fixed Costs	+444
Abandoned Mine Lands	+128
Fixed Costs	+128
Resource Protection and Law Enforcement	+259
Fixed Costs	+259

	2014 Change from 2012 Enacted
Hazardous Materials Management	+182
Fixed Costs	+182
Transportation and Facilities Maintenance	+2,941
Deferred Maintenance	+2,409
Transfer from O&C Account	+1,039
Land Mobile Radio	+1,250
Fixed Costs	+120
Annual Maintenance and Operation Costs	+532
Fixed Costs	+532
Land and Resource Information Systems	-15,827
Transfer Base Funding to Information	
Technology Management and Land and	
Realty Management	-15,827
Workforce and Organizational Support	+14,411
Information Systems Operations	-14,673
Transfer Base Funding to	
Information Technology Management	-14,673
Information Technology Management	+25,696
Transfer Base Funding from	
Information Systems Operation	+14,673
Transfer Base Funding from Land	
and Resources Information System	+12,827
Reduce Base Funding	-2,072
Fixed Costs	+268
Administrative Support	+1,648
National BLM Foundation	+1,000
Fixed Costs	+648
Bureau-wide Fixed Costs	+1,740
Realign Base Funding	+8,164
Fixed Costs	-6,424
Challenge Cost Share	+22
Fixed Costs	+22
National Monuments and	
National Conservation Areas	+6,533
General Program Increase -	
America's Great Outdoors	+6,044
Fixed Costs	+489
Subtotals for Changes Across Multiple Subactivities	
Applied Science	[+5,500]
Climate Adapt/Coop Landscape Conservation	[+3,276]
Fixed Costs	[+4,052]

APPROPRIATION: Construction

	2013 Full Year CR	2012 Enacted	2014 Request	Change from 2012
TOTAL APPROPRIATION	3,592	3,570	0	-3,570

Detail of Budget Changes

	2014 Change from 2012 Enacted
TOTAL APPROPRIATION	-3,570
Eliminate Program	-3,570

APPROPRIATION: Land Acquisition

	2013 Full Year CR	2012 Enacted	2014 Request	Change from 2012
Acquisitions	19,083	18,969	29,104	+10,135
Emergencies and Hardships	1,506	1,498	1,616	+118
Acquisition Management	1,892	1,877	1,898	+21
TOTAL APPROPRIATION	22,481	22,344	32,618	+10,274

See Appendix F for proposed 2014 land acquisition projects.

Detail of Budget Changes

	2014 Change from 2012 Enacted
TOTAL APPROPRIATION	+10,274
Acquisitions	+10,135
Collaborative Landscape Acquisition Projects	+23,318
Core Projects	-13,183
Emergencies and Hardships	+118
Acquisition Management	
Fixed Costs	+21

APPROPRIATION: Oregon and California Grant Lands

	2013 Full Year CR	2012 Enacted	2014 Request	Change from 2012
W. Oregon Resources Management	98,634	97,899	102,464	+4,565
W. Oregon Info/Resources Data Sys........	1,937	1,923	1,940	+17
W. Oregon Transp and Facilities Maint....	10,908	10,984	10,063	-921
W. Oregon Construction/Acquisition......	313	310	315	+5
W. Oregon NLCS..	757	748	761	+13
TOTAL APPROPRIATION	112,549	111,864	115,543	+3,679

Detail of Budget Changes

2014 Change from
2012 Enacted

TOTAL APPROPRIATION	+3,679
Western Oregon Resources Management..................	+4,565
Forest Management...	+2,245
Secretary's Western Oregon Strategy.................	+1,801
Fixed Costs	+444
Reforestation and Forest Development.................	+229
Fixed Costs	+229
Other Forest Resources Management....................	+369
Fixed Costs	+369
Resource Management Planning	+1,722
Secretary's Western Oregon Strategy.................	+1,670
Fixed Costs	+52
Western Oregon Info/Resources Data System	+17
Fixed Costs	+17
Western Oregon Transportation/Facilities Mgmt....	-921
Operations..	-2,081
Create New Operations and Annual Maintenance Subactivity..................	-2,081
Annual Maintenance..	-7,864
Create New Operations and Annual Maintenance Subactivity..................	-7,864
Deferred Maintenance	-1,039
Transfer to MLR Account	-1,039
Operations and Annual Maintenance	+10,063
Create New Operations and Annual Maintenance Subactivity..................	+9,945
Fixed Costs	+118
Western Oregon Construction/Acquisition.............	+5
Fixed Costs	+5
Western Oregon National Monuments and National Conservation Areas	+13
Fixed Costs	+13
Subtotals for Changes Across Multiple Subactivities Fixed Costs	[+1,247]

APPROPRIATION: Range Improvements

	2013 Full Year CR	2012 Enacted	2014 Request	Change from 2012
Improvements to Public Lands	7,873	7,873	7,873	0
Farm Tenant Act Lands	1,527	1,527	1,527	0
Administrative Expenses	600	600	600	0
TOTAL APPROPRIATION	10,000	10,000	10,000	0

APPROPRIATION: Service Charges, Deposit, and Forfeitures

	2013 Full Year CR	2012 Enacted	2014 Request	Change from 2012
Rights-of-Way Processing	16,900	16,847	16,900	+53
Energy and Minerals Cost Recovery	3,320	3,292	3,320	+28
Recreation Cost Recovery	1,500	1,890	2,000	+110
Adopt-a-Horse Program	450	455	450	-5
Repair of Damaged Lands	3,550	3,890	3,550	-340
Cost Recoverable Realty Cases	900	814	900	+86
Timber Purchaser Expenses	20	67	20	-47
Commercial Film and Photography Fees	225	224	225	+1
Copy Fees	1,100	1,103	1,100	-3
Trans Alaska Pipeline	4,000	3,866	4,000	+134
TOTAL APPROPRIATION	31,965	32,448	32,465	+17
Offsets	-31,965	-32,448	-32,465	-17
TOTAL APPROPRIATION	0	0	0	0

APPROPRIATION: Miscellaneous Trust Funds

	2013 Full Year CR	2012 Enacted	2014 Request	Change from 2012
TOTAL APPROPRIATION	23,125	20,815	23,125	+2,310

BUREAU OF OCEAN ENERGY MANAGEMENT

Mission – The Bureau of Ocean Energy Management manages the development of the Nation's offshore energy and mineral resources in an environmentally and economically responsible way.

Budget Overview – The 2014 budget request for BOEM is $169.4 million, including $71.5 million in current appropriations and $97.9 million in offsetting collections from rental receipts and cost recoveries. The BOEM estimates staffing will equal 580 full time equivalents in 2014. The 2014 gross budget request for the total program is an $8.7 million increase above the 2012 enacted level. The net request of $71.5 million in appropriated funds is an increase of $11.9 million above the 2012 level.

The total 2014 estimate of $97.9 million for offsetting collections assumes a decrease of $3.8 million below the 2012 estimate for rental receipts and a slight increase of $640,000 above the 2012 estimate for cost recoveries. The net result is a decrease of $3.2 million from the 2012 estimate. Within cost recoveries, the 2014 budget also proposes to establish an offsetting fee in the Marine Minerals program to recover costs associated with processing offshore sand and gravel mining permits. The fees are estimated to generate approximately $470,000 in revenue in 2014, and would be implemented through existing regulatory authority under the Outer Continental Shelf Lands Act.

Progress through Reform – Interior Secretary Ken Salazar issued a Secretarial Order in 2010 to reorganize the former Minerals Management Service into three independent entities to institute strong internal controls over the development, regulation, and revenue collection activities in the Federal offshore energy regulatory system. The three agencies, the Bureau of Ocean Energy Management, Bureau of Safety and Environmental Enforcement, and Office of Natural Resources Revenue within the Office of the Secretary, were subsequently established to correct prior oversight weaknesses in the Federal offshore energy regulatory system. The reorganization was implemented on October 1, 2011. The BOEM is responsible for managing the development of the Nation's offshore energy

BOEM Funding

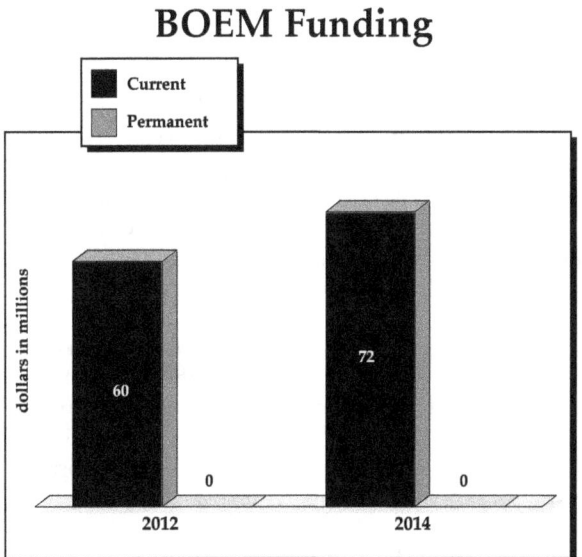

resources through offshore leasing, resource evaluation, review and administration of oil and gas exploration and development plans, renewable energy development, economic analysis, National Environmental Policy Act analysis, and environmental studies. The BOEM also is committed to applying science to decisionmaking through research and rigorous analytical standards, balanced decisionmaking regarding the development of domestic offshore, conventional, and renewable energy resources, and ensuring that appropriate consideration of the environment is given in every case.

Under the reorganization, BOEM's responsibilities are grouped into three primary functions, Conventional Energy, Renewable Energy, and Environmental Assessment and Studies, which are carried out among the headquarters office in Washington, DC, and three regional offices in New Orleans, Louisiana; Camarillo, California; and Anchorage, Alaska. The regional offices are integral to oil and gas resource evaluations, environmental studies and assessments, leasing activities, review of exploration and development plans, fair market value determinations, and geological and geophysical permitting.

Ocean Energy Management – The 2014 budget request includes $169.4 million for offshore ocean energy activities, including renewable, conventional, and environmental activities, an increase of $8.7 million from the 2012 enacted level. This budget request funds the leasing and management of the Nation's offshore energy resources.

The budget requests $24.1 million for renewable energy activities, an increase of $1.4 million above the 2012 enacted level. Renewable energy development activities include the siting and construction of offshore wind farms on the Outer Continental Shelf, as well as other forms of renewable energy such as wave and current. The Energy Policy Act of 2005 authorizes the Secretary, who has delegated to BOEM, the authority to grant leases, easements, or rights-of-way for activities on the OCS that produce or support production, transportation, or transmission of energy from renewable sources. Under this authority, in October 2010, Secretary Salazar signed the Nation's first commercial lease for wind energy development on the OCS for the Cape Wind energy project.

The Department and BOEM have continued to advance renewable energy efforts. On October 23, 2012, BOEM reached agreement on a lease for commercial wind energy development in Federal waters that covers 96,430 acres, nearly 11 nautical miles off the coast of Delaware as a part of Interior's Smart from the Start approach. The Smart from the Start initiative facilitates environmentally responsible offshore wind development along the OCS by identifying wind energy areas in a coordinated, focused approach with extensive environmental analysis, public review, and large-scale planning.

In 2012, the Department issued proposed sale notices for the sale of commercial wind energy leases in the Virginia and Rhode Island/Massachusetts offshore wind energy areas. The lease sales, to be held during 2013, hold the potential to produce more than 4,000 megawatts of energy, enough to power about 1.4 million homes, and serve as a major milestone in the Department's Atlantic Smart from the Start wind energy initiative.

In another milestone for renewable energy development, BOEM issued a Determination of No Competitive Interest for the proposed first-of-its-kind Mid-Atlantic offshore wind energy transmission line, clearing the way for the project to move forward with the environmental review necessary to grant the project proponent a right-of-way to build a backbone transmission line that would enable up to 7,000 megawatts of wind turbine capacity to be integrated with the electric grid. The proposed project is a high voltage, direct current subsea transmission system that would collect power generated by wind turbine facilities off the Atlantic coasts of New York, New Jersey, Delaware, Maryland, and Virginia, and is the first such offshore infrastructure proposed in the United States. The determination that no other developers were interested in constructing transmission facilities in the same area and following a public solicitation and comment process is a necessary step in advancing the proposed transmission line.

The 2014 budget provides $50.9 million for conventional energy development, an increase of $3.7 million above 2012. These increases support high priority offshore oil and gas development activities, particularly those outlined in BOEM's Five Year OCS Oil and Gas Leasing Program for 2012-2017, finalized on August 27, 2012. The 2012-2017 program makes areas containing an estimated 75 percent of the technically recoverable oil and gas resources estimated to be in the OCS available for exploration and development, and it advances a regionally targeted approach that accounts for the distinct needs of different offshore areas. The program includes 12 potential lease sales in the Gulf of Mexico, and three off the coast of Alaska. The first sale in the new program was held in November 2012; this sale and the two lease sales held in 2012 combined to raise over $2.1 billion in bonuses paid to the Treasury. The second sale, held in March 2013, generated more than $1.2 billion in high bids.

To begin preparation for future leasing decisions, which could include the Atlantic Ocean, BOEM released a draft Environmental Impact Statement regarding proposed geological and geophysical activities in the Mid- and South Atlantic in the spring of 2012. Once completed, this environmental review could support approval of new seismic and other survey activities in these areas in 2013. An increase of $700,000 will allow BOEM to acquire and analyze data gathered under these new activities to improve its knowledge of a region's resource potential and support future decisions regarding oil and gas activity in the Atlantic. Recognizing the diverse interests that may exist in this region, BOEM continues to work with the Department of Defense and others to identify and resolve potential conflicts.

The 2014 budget also includes increases for conventional energy activities that will support offshore leasing and planning activities in all regions: $1.5 million for the development of an electronic, web-based tool called ePlans to facilitate efficient and expeditious plan submission and review; and $1.5 million to conduct marine mineral activities that will support beach replenishment and restoration along U.S. coastlines. The new offsetting Marine Minerals program fee generated from processing sand and gravel permits will further enhance BOEM's capability to meet its statutory responsibility for approving marine mineral resource development. The budget also includes an increase of $800,000 to review Alaska exploration and development plans.

Paramount to BOEM's renewable and conventional energy efforts are its environmental assessments and studies, for which the 2014 budget provides $63.8 million, an increase of $1.8 million above 2012. The reorganization established a Chief Environmental Officer to ensure the integration of applied scientific research and information with the environmental analyses that BOEM conducts in support of programmatic decisions. Through its environmental assessment and studies activity, BOEM facilitates top quality research by talented scientists from a range of disciplines, as well as targeted scientific study to support policy needs and priorities. Through these efforts, BOEM continues to ensure that science-based decisionmaking is transparent and accessible.

As part of the Consolidated Appropriations Act, 2012, Congress increased the scope of BOEM's jurisdiction for air pollution to include the Beaufort Sea and Chukchi Sea OCS Planning Areas. With this statutory change in place, the Department, through BOEM, now has responsibility for thoroughly reviewing the potential air quality effects of new offshore operations in these arctic areas, in addition to areas of the Western and Central Gulf of Mexico where BOEM already has jurisdiction. Within the

increase for Environmental Assessments is $1.1 million to support activities surrounding this newly expanded authority, including air quality research, NEPA studies, legal expertise, program expertise, and data management.

Within the amounts identified previously, the request includes $14.3 million for General Support activities and $16.3 million for Executive Direction. These activities support executive leadership, bureau-level coordination and policy, as well as administrative functions such as finance, human resources, information management, procurement, facilities management, and similar support services.

LEGISLATIVE PROPOSALS

Federal Oil and Gas Reforms – The 2014 budget includes a proposed package of legislative and administrative proposals to reform the management of Interior's onshore and offshore oil and gas programs, with a key focus on improving the return to taxpayers from the sale of these Federal resources and on improving transparency and oversight. Proposed changes fall into three general categories: advancing royalty reforms; encouraging diligent development of oil and gas leases; and improving revenue collection processes.

Royalty reforms include evaluating minimum royalty rates for oil, gas, and similar products; adjusting the onshore oil and gas royalty rate; analyzing a price-based tiered royalty rate; and repealing legislatively mandated royalty relief. Diligent development requirements include shorter primary lease terms, stricter enforcement of lease terms, and monetary incentives to get leases into production, e.g., a new per-acre fee on nonproducing leases. Revenue collection improvements include simplification of the royalty valuation process, elimination of interest accruals on company overpayments of royalties, and permanent repeal of Interior's authority to accept in-kind royalty payments. Collectively, these reforms will generate roughly $2.5 billion in net revenue to the Treasury over ten years, of which nearly $1.7 billion would result from statutory changes. Many States will also benefit from higher Federal revenue sharing payments as a result of these reforms.

Transboundary Gulf of Mexico Agreement – The 2014 budget includes a legislative proposal to enact the recently completed U.S.-Mexico Transboundary Agreement. Under this Agreement, which the Departments of the Interior and State reached with the government of Mexico, a framework is established through which U.S. oil companies and Mexico's national oil company may jointly develop transboundary oil and natural gas reservoirs beneath the delimited U.S.-Mexico maritime boundary in the Gulf of Mexico. This Agreement, if approved by Congress, removes uncertainties regarding development of transboundary resources in the resource-rich Gulf. As a result of this Agreement, nearly 1.5 million acres of the U.S. Outer Continental Shelf, containing as much as 172 million barrels of oil and 304 billion cubic feet of natural gas, will be made more accessible for exploration and production activities.

Fixed Costs – Fixed costs of $2.9 million are fully funded.

SUMMARY OF BUREAU APPROPRIATIONS
(all dollar amounts in thousands)

Comparison of 2014 Request with 2012 Enacted

	2012 Enacted		2014 Request		Change	
	FTE	Amount	FTE	Amount	FTE	Amount
Current						
Ocean Energy Management	572	59,696	580	71,549	+8	+11,853
Subtotal, Current..	572	59,696	580	71,549	+8	+11,853
Offsetting Collections	0	101,082	0	97,891	0	-3,191
TOTAL, BUREAU OF OCEAN ENERGY MGMT.						
(w/ offsetting collections)	572	160,778	580	169,440	+8	+8,662

APPROPRIATION: Ocean Energy Management

	2013 Full Year CR	2012 Enacted	2014 Request	Change from 2012
Renewable Energy				
Appropriation......................................	8,684	7,454	11,325	+3,871
Offsetting Collections............................	14,047	15,231	12,771	-2,460
Subtotal, Renewable Energy..............	22,731	22,685	24,096	+1,411
Conventional Energy				
Appropriation......................................	24,541	24,301	28,527	+4,226
Offsetting Collections............................	22,853	22,944	22,414	-530
Subtotal, Conventional Energy	47,394	47,245	50,941	+3,696
Environmental Assessment and Studies				
Appropriation......................................	13,906	15,403	15,321	-82
Offsetting Collections............................	48,204	46,613	48,506	+1,893
Subtotal, Environ Assess/Studies.....	62,110	62,016	63,827	+1,811
General Support Services				
Appropriation......................................	3,330	3,476	4,834	+1,358
Offsetting Collections............................	9,476	9,309	9,486	+177
Subtotal, General Support Services ..	12,806	12,785	14,320	+1,535
Executive Direction				
Appropriation......................................	9,600	9,062	11,542	+2,480
Offsetting Collections............................	6,502	6,985	4,714	-2,271
Subtotal, Executive Direction............	16,102	16,047	16,256	+209
Total Appropriation	60,061	59,696	71,549	+11,853
Total Offsetting Collections	101,082	101,082	97,891	-3,191
TOTAL APPROPRIATION	161,143	160,778	169,440	+8,662

Detail of Budget Changes

	2014 Change from 2012 Enacted		2014 Change from 2012 Enacted
TOTAL APPROPRIATION	+8,662		
Renewable Energy	+1,411	Environmental Assessment and Studies...................	+1,811
Auction Support Services (2013)............................	+1,296	Environmental Studies (2013)................................	+700
Fixed Costs	+115	Air Quality Review	+1,100
		Base Program Adjustment	-386
Conventional Energy...	+3,696	Fixed Costs	+397
Development of ePlans Portal...............................	+1,500		
Atlantic G and G Data Acquisition and Mgmt	+655	General Support Services..	+1,535
Alaska Plans Review...	+800	Fixed Costs	+1,535
Marine Minerals Program......................................	+1,470		
Base Program Adjustment	-1,383	Executive Direction..	+209
Fixed Costs	+654	Fixed Costs	+209
		Subtotals for Changes Across Multiple Activities	
		Fixed Costs	[+2,910]

BUREAU OF SAFETY AND ENVIRONMENTAL ENFORCEMENT

Mission – The Bureau of Safety and Environmental Enforcement works to promote safety, protect the environment, and conserve resources offshore through vigorous regulatory oversight and enforcement.

Budget Overview – The 2014 budget request for the Bureau of Safety and Environmental Enforcement is $222.1 million, including $98.2 million in current appropriations and $124.0 million in offsetting collections from rental receipts, cost recoveries, and inspection fees. The BSEE estimates staffing will equal 763 full time equivalents in 2014. The 2014 budget request is a $24.8 million increase above the 2012 enacted level, including an increase of $21.9 million in current appropriations. All increases support the New Energy Frontier initiative.

The total 2014 estimate of $124.0 million in offsetting collections assumes a decrease of $2.0 million from the 2012 estimate for rental receipts, an increase of $1.9 million from the 2012 estimate for cost recoveries, and an increase of $3.0 million for inspection fee collections. The net result is additional revenue of $2.9 million from the 2012 estimate.

Progress through Reform – Secretary Ken Salazar issued a Secretarial Order in 2010 to reorganize the former Minerals Management Service into three independent entities to institute strong internal controls over the development, regulation, and revenue collection activities in the Federal offshore energy regulatory system. The three agencies, the Bureau of Ocean Energy Management, Bureau of Safety and Environmental Enforcement, and Office of Natural Resources Revenue within the Office of the Secretary, were subsequently established to correct prior oversight weaknesses in the Federal offshore energy regulatory system. The reorganization was implemented on October 1, 2011. The Bureau is responsible for oil and gas permitting, facility inspections, regulations and standards development, safety research, field operations, environmental compliance and enforcement, review of operator oil spill response plans, production and development oversight, and resource conservation efforts. The BSEE promotes safety at all levels, at all times.

BSEE Funding

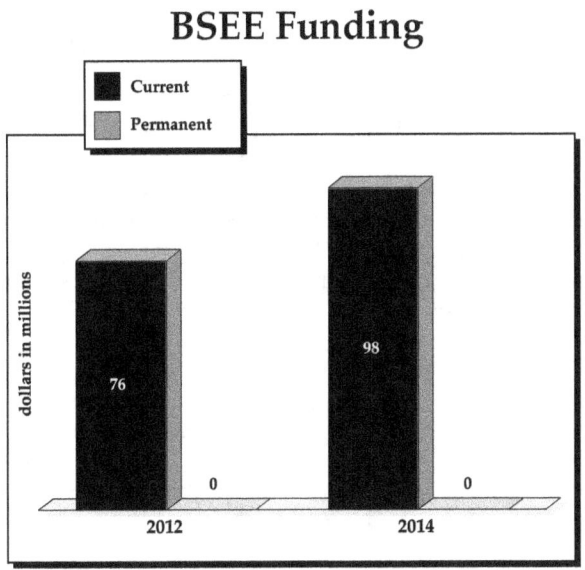

Building on recent progress, BSEE continues to recruit professionals into the workforce and train all personnel to better compare, assess, and identify risks and mitigation strategies to promote safety, protect the environment, and conserve resources offshore through vigorous regulatory oversight and enforcement. These professionals review permits and response plans, and conduct inspections, investigations, and enforcement activities to properly define, assess, and mitigate risks. The BSEE training activities will provide newly hired technical staff with a base-level competency that they will use and build on throughout their careers. All BSEE technical personnel will continue to engage in formal classroom training, on-the-job training and mentoring, and field-based classes when applicable to ensure they are current on the latest offshore oil and gas technologies and practices.

In 2012, BSEE continued working to refine internal controls and processes and expand the use of information and data management systems to enhance continuous offshore safety and an environmental enforcement presence. The Bureau is further advancing new protocols that emphasize risk-based inspections with the intent of identifying and focusing inspections on the highest risk

- **Established October 1, 2011.**
- **Conducts more than 21,000 inspections per year to ensure the safe and environmentally responsible operation of nearly 3,400 offshore oil and gas drilling and production facilities and pipelines.**
- **Operates the largest facility in the United States that can test oil spill response equipment with a variety of crude oils and refined petroleum products under reproducible marine conditions.**
- **Conducts studies to continuously improve operational safety and pollution prevention related to offshore oil and natural gas exploration and development and renewable energy facilities, including Best Available and Safest Technologies.**

activities and facilities. The BSEE is currently working to implement a real time monitoring program to improve and increase the regulatory oversight of critical offshore operations and equipment. The BSEE is also strengthening the Inspection and Enforcement program through the development of new enforcement and investigative tools and the enhancement of existing capabilities.

New Energy Frontier Initiative – In March 2011, President Obama released his Blueprint for a Secure Energy Future that includes a three-part strategy to produce more energy with domestic resources, reduce reliance on foreign energy sources, lead the development of clean alternative fuels, and improve efficiency.

The 2014 BSEE budget fully supports the President's Blueprint by ensuring development of the Nation's vast offshore energy resources is conducted in a safe and environmentally responsible manner. Funds will be used to recruit expert engineers, scientists, and oil spill response specialists to support the development of strong scientific information and the timely and thorough review of permits. The 2014 budget request includes increases of $2.5 million to support growth in the Alaska Region for activities such as oversight of exploration, development, and production activities, and $1.0 million for development of a modern ePermitting electronic system that will increase efficiency and effectiveness of the permitting process.

Offshore Safety and Environmental Enforcement – The 2014 budget request includes $207.2 million for offshore safety and environmental enforcement programs, primarily for conventional energy activities, an increase of $24.8 million over the 2012 level.

The request increases programmatic funding for Operational Safety and Regulation by $14.2 million. This will strengthen regulatory and oversight capability on the U.S. Outer Continental Shelf and increase the capacity in multiple disciplines to adequately staff regulatory,

safety management, structural and technical support, and oil spill response programs. Continued outreach and dialogue with stakeholders from academia, industry, non-governmental organizations, and other governmental agencies will enhance the knowledge base of technical personnel related to innovative technologies, regulatory gaps, real-time monitoring capabilities, and risk-based decisionmaking for safety and environmental enforcement.

Specific program increases of $1.4 million are proposed to support research requirements for well structure integrity and $2.0 million for offshore safety systems and operations. An increase of $3.7 million for inspection activities will be used to support the National Offshore Training program to provide contemporary learning and development opportunities for BSEE's inspectors and engineers. Courses are designed to enhance safety and environmental stewardship using the best science and technology to evaluate, protect, and preserve the human, marine, and coastal environments. An additional request of $4.5 million will support ongoing reorganization efforts identified as critical to the success of BSEE in strengthening post Deepwater Horizon regulatory and oversight capabilities. This increase supports a cross section of staffing for newly identified efforts and increased activities such as development of regulations, safety management, structural and technical support, and oil spill response.

An increase of $2.5 million will support the growth in exploration, development, and production activities on the Alaska OCS, including building dependable inspection capabilities for significantly expanded drilling activity, providing basic engineering support for platform and pipeline functions, and building basic engineering and geoscience support for unitization, reservoir, and resource conservation functions. As the Bureau continues to implement reforms to increase efficiency and demonstrate effectiveness, a program increase of $1.0 million will be used to streamline the permitting process to support the development of a modern electronic system to manage the permitting process. These funds will be used to improve the availability and reliability of information needed to make management decisions to ensure compliance with safety and environmental regulations.

The Environmental Enforcement program fosters environmental compliance, inspection, investigation, and enforcement programs to maintain the highest level of environmental standards for all offshore energy activities. The 2014 budget request will provide $4.2 million for the further development of this important function and be used to hire, train, equip, and support personnel to conduct environmental inspections and investigations; take enforcement actions; and evaluate the effectiveness of environmental mitigation activities.

Each of these functions and the Bureau's existing activities will be supported by a program increase of $4.0 million for administrative support for new engineers, inspectors, scientists, and other professionals in the reorganized and expanded program. Savings from management efficiencies of $2.8 million have been identified across all BSEE programs. This reduction will be achieved through leveraging efficiencies across programs, cost savings, and administrative adjustments.

Oil Spill Research – This program supports oil pollution research and other activities related to oil spill prevention, as authorized by the Oil Pollution Act of 1990. The Oil Spill Research program plays a pivotal role in initiating applied research used to support decisionmaking pertaining to offshore energy development. This is especially true regarding the program's long history of research in oil spill containment and response in the field, as well as training at its large test tank facility, Ohmsett, located in Leonardo, New Jersey. The test facility is the only one of its type in the world providing full-scale equipment and methodology testing for offshore spills in a safe, controlled environment.

The 2014 budget proposes $14.9 million for Oil Spill Research, equal to the 2012 enacted level. The request will address key knowledge and technology gaps in oil spill response, focusing on deepwater and arctic environments. The studies will leverage other funds through cooperative efforts with the National Oceanic and Atmospheric Administration, Department of the Navy, and U.S. Coast Guard.

Fixed Costs – Fixed costs of $4.3 million are fully funded.

SUMMARY OF BUREAU APPROPRIATIONS
(all dollar amounts in thousands)

Comparison of 2014 Request with 2012 Enacted

	2012 Enacted		2014 Request		Change	
	FTE	Amount	FTE	Amount	FTE	Amount
Current						
Offshore Safety / Environmental Enforcement........	617	61,375	675	83,263	+58	+21,888
Oil Spill Research	20	14,899	22	14,899	+2	0
Subtotal, Current...	637	76,274	697	98,162	+60	+21,888
Offsetting Collections	66	121,081	66	123,970	0	+2,889
TOTAL, BUREAU OF SAFETY AND ENVIRONMENTAL ENFORCEMENT *(w/ OC)*	**703**	**197,355**	**763**	**222,132**	**+60**	**+24,777**

APPROPRIATION: Offshore Safety and Environmental Enforcement

	2013 Full Year CR	2012 Enacted	2014 Request	Change from 2012
Environmental Enforcement				
Appropriation......................................	1,507	1,498	5,586	+4,088
Offsetting Collections............................	2,610	2,610	2,728	+118
Subtotal, Environmental Enforce......	4,117	4,108	8,314	+4,206
Operations, Safety and Regulation				
Appropriation......................................	37,140	36,913	49,842	+12,929
Offsetting Collections............................	95,166	95,166	97,440	+2,274
Subtotal, Ops, Safety, Regulation......	132,306	132,079	147,282	+15,203
Administrative Operations				
Appropriation......................................	5,023	4,992	8,820	+3,828
Offsetting Collections............................	10,553	10,553	10,785	+232
Subtotal, Administrative Operations	15,576	15,545	19,605	+4,060
General Support Services				
Appropriation......................................	4,018	3,994	5,109	+1,115
Offsetting Collections............................	8,613	8,613	8,802	+189
Subtotal, General Support Services..	12,631	12,607	13,911	+1,304
Executive Direction				
Appropriation......................................	14,063	13,978	13,906	-72
Offsetting Collections............................	4,139	4,139	4,215	+76
Subtotal, Executive Direction............	18,202	18,117	18,121	+4
Total Appropriation	61,751	61,375	83,263	+21,888
Total Offsetting Collections	121,081	121,081	123,970	+2,889
TOTAL APPROPRIATION	182,832	182,456	207,233	+24,777

Detail of Budget Changes

	2014 Change from 2012 Enacted
TOTAL APPROPRIATION	+24,777

	2014 Change from 2012 Enacted			2014 Change from 2012 Enacted
Environmental Enforcement......................................	+4,206		Administrative Operations...	+4,060
Environmental Enforcement Program	+4,177		Sustain Administrative Operations	+4,045
Management Efficiencies......................................	-21		Management Efficiencies......................................	-456
Fixed Costs	+50		Fixed Costs	+471
Operations, Safety and Regulation............................	+15,203		General Support Services..	+1,304
R&D for Offshore Drilling....................................	+2,000		Management Efficiencies......................................	-1,386
Operational Safety..	+4,495		Fixed Costs	+2,690
National Offshore Training Program......................	+3,685			
Wellbore Integrity..	+1,395		Executive Direction...	+4
Alaska Program Growth	+2,500		Management Efficiencies......................................	-114
ePermit for Regulatory Enforcement.....................	+1,000		Fixed Costs	+118
Management Efficiencies......................................	-838			
Fixed Costs	+966		Subtotals for Changes Across Multiple Subactivities	
			Management Efficiencies..	[-2,815]
			Fixed Costs	[+4,295]

APPROPRIATION: Oil Spill Research

	2013 Full Year CR	2012 Enacted	2014 Request	Change from 2012
TOTAL APPROPRIATION	14,990	14,899	14,899	0
Supplemental...	+3,000	0	0	0
TOTAL APPROPRIATION *(w/ supp)*..........	17,990	14,899	14,899	0

OFFICE OF SURFACE MINING RECLAMATION AND ENFORCEMENT

Mission – The mission of the Office of Surface Mining Reclamation and Enforcement is to ensure that through a nationwide regulatory program, coal mining is conducted in a manner that protects communities and the environment during mining, restores the land to beneficial use following mining, and mitigates the effects of past mining by aggressively pursuing reclamation of abandoned mine lands.

Budget Overview – The 2014 budget request for OSM is $143.1 million in discretionary appropriations, $7.1 million below the 2012 enacted level. The OSM estimates that staffing will equal 522 full time equivalents in 2014.

Regulation and Technology – The 2014 budget for Regulation and Technology is $115.1 million, a decrease of $7.8 million below the 2012 level. The request includes $12.6 million, an increase of $4.0 million above 2012, to improve implementation of existing laws and support States and Tribes. State and tribal regulatory grants are funded at $57.7 million in 2014, a decrease of $10.9 million below 2012. States are encouraged to recover more of their regulatory costs from the coal industry through user fees. In addition, the budget proposes to recover the cost of reviewing, administering, and enforcing permits for surface coal mining and reclamation in Federal programs and on Indian Lands where OSM is the regulatory authority. The OSM expects to collect $2.4 million in permit fees in 2014. The budget includes $1.2 million for applied science to conduct studies that would advance technologies and practices specific to coal mined sites for more comprehensive ecosystem restoration, including reforestation and reclamation using native vegetation and plant habitat.

Abandoned Mine Reclamation Fund – The total discretionary funding requested for this account is $28.0 million, an increase of $614,000 above 2012. The Surface Mining Control and Reclamation Act established the Abandoned Mine Reclamation Fund to receive the Abandoned Mine Land fees and finance reclamation of coal AML sites. The increase includes $400,000 for applied science studies pertaining to abandoned mines.

OSM Funding

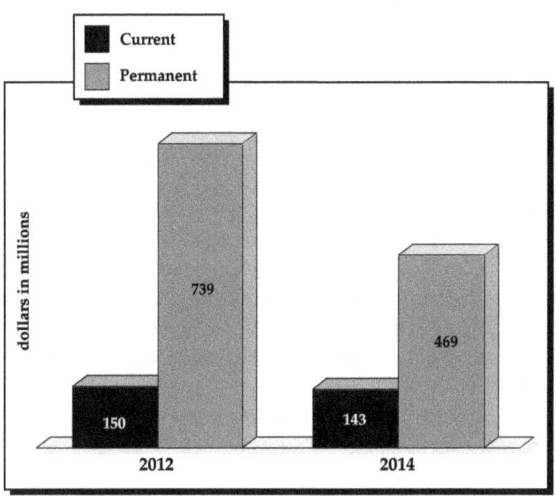

Legislative Proposals – In 2014, OSM will distribute an estimated $468.5 million in permanent appropriations. This includes $273.5 million to non-certified States and Tribes in reclamation grants and $195.0 million in payments to the United Mine Workers of America retiree health plans. The Administration proposes to focus reclamation grant funds on the highest priority AML sites. The budget proposes to end permanent payments to States and Tribes that have finished restoring their abandoned coal mines, saving the taxpayer $32.0 million in 2014 and $327.0 million over the next ten years. These payments currently can be used for any purpose and therefore may not contribute to the goal of addressing abandoned mine hazards.

The budget proposes to return coal fees to the level prior to 2006, when an amendment to the Surface Mining Control and Reclamation Act reduced the fees. The proposal to return the fees to their historic levels will generate an additional $53.0 million in 2014 that will be used to reclaim priority abandoned mine sites and reduce some of the $3.9 billion in remaining dangerous AML sites nationwide.

The budget also includes a legislative proposal to establish a new fee on hardrock mineral production to fund the reclamation of abandoned hardrock mines across the Country. Just as the coal industry is held responsible for the actions of its predecessors, the Administration proposes to hold the hardrock mining industry responsible for abandoned hardrock mines. The legislative proposal will levy an AML fee on uranium and metallic mines on both public and private lands. The proposed AML fee on the production of hardrock minerals will be based on the volume of material displaced after January 1, 2014. The fee will be collected by OSM. The receipts will be distributed through a set allocation of funds between Federal and non-Federal lands. Based on need, the Secretary would disperse the non-Federal share to States and Tribes who would select their own priority restoration projects, using national criteria. The proposed hardrock AML fee and reclamation program would operate in parallel to the coal AML reclamation program, as two parts of a larger proposal to ensure the Nation's most dangerous coal and hardrock AML sites are addressed by the industries that created the problems. This proposal is expected to generate $1.8 billion over ten years for the reclamation of abandoned mine lands.

Fixed Costs – Fixed costs of $925,000 are fully funded.

SUMMARY OF BUREAU APPROPRIATIONS
(all dollar amounts in thousands)

Comparison of 2014 Request with 2012 Enacted

	2012 Enacted		2014 Request		Change	
	FTE	Amount	FTE	Amount	FTE	Amount
Current						
Regulation and Technology	344	122,813	363	115,055	+19	-7,758
Abandoned Mine Reclamation Fund	159	27,399	159	28,013	0	+614
Subtotal, Current *(w/o offsetting collections)*	503	150,212	522	143,068	+19	-7,144
Offsetting Collections	0	40	0	2,400	0	+2,360
Subtotal, Current *(w/ offsetting collections)*	503	150,252	522	145,468	+19	-4,784

Comparison of 2014 Estimate with 2013 Estimate

	2013 Estimate		2014 Estimate		Change	
	FTE	Amount	FTE	Amount	FTE	Amount
Permanent						
Payments to UMWA Health Plans (AML)	0	54,789	0	15,000	0	-39,789
Payments to UMWA Health Plans (Treasury Funds) ...	0	140,663	0	180,000	0	+39,337
Payments to States in Lieu of						
Coal Fee Receipts (Treasury Funds)	0	129,301	0	85,300	0	-44,001
Mandatory Grants to States and Tribes (AML)	0	210,145	0	188,200	0	-21,945
Subtotal, Permanent	0	534,898	0	468,500	0	-66,398

APPROPRIATION: Regulation and Technology

	2013 Full Year CR	2012 Enacted	2014 Request	Change from 2012
Environmental Protection	92,394	91,832	82,795	-9,037
Permitting Fees	40	40	2,400	+2,360
Offsetting Collections	-40	-40	-2,400	-2,360
Technology Development and Transfer	14,543	14,455	15,872	+1,417
Financial Management	508	505	513	+8
Executive Direction/Administration	16,019	15,921	15,775	-146
TOTAL APPROPRIATION *(w/o civil penalties)*	123,464	122,713	114,955	-7,758
Civil Penalties	100	100	100	0
TOTAL APPROPRIATION *(w/ civil penalties)*	123,564	122,813	115,055	-7,758

Detail of Budget Changes

	2014 Change from 2012 Enacted
TOTAL APPROPRIATION	-7,758
Environmental Protection	-9,037
Reduce State and Tribal Regulatory Grants	-10,916
Improve Implementation and Support to States/Tribes	+3,734
Federal Programs	-1,652
Indian Lands	-708
Fixed Costs	+505
Technology Development and Transfer	+1,417
Applied Science	+1,199
Fixed Costs	+218
Financial Management	+8
Fixed Costs	+8
Executive Direction	-146
Fixed Costs	-146
Subtotals for Changes Across Multiple Subactivities	
Fixed Costs	[+585]

APPROPRIATION: Abandoned Mine Reclamation Fund

	2013 Full Year CR	2012 Enacted	2014 Request	Change from 2012
Environmental Restoration.........................	9,538	9,480	9,510	+30
Technology Development and Transfer...	3,566	3,544	3,994	+450
Financial Management..............................	6,435	6,396	6,490	+94
Executive Direction and Administration.	8,028	7,979	8,019	+40
TOTAL APPROPRIATION	27,567	27,399	28,013	+614

Detail of Budget Changes

	2014 Change from 2012 Enacted
TOTAL APPROPRIATION	+614
Environmental Restoration...	+30
Project Monitoring	+209
Reduce Watershed Cooperative Agreements........	-335
Fixed Costs	+156
Technology Development and Transfer.....................	+450
Applied Science..	+400
Fixed Costs	+50
Financial Management..	+94
Fixed Costs	+94
Executive Direction..	+40
Fixed Costs	+40
Subtotals for Changes Across Multiple Subactivities	
Fixed Costs	[+340]

BUREAU OF RECLAMATION

Mission – The Bureau of Reclamation's mission is to manage, develop, and protect water and related resources in an environmentally and economically sound manner in the interest of the American public.

Budget Overview – Reclamation's 2014 budget, including the Central Utah Project Completion Act, is $1.0 billion. These expenditures are offset by current receipts in the Central Valley Project Restoration Fund, estimated to be $53.3 million. The budget proposal for permanent appropriations totals $180.6 million. The budget also proposes the establishment of a new Indian Water Rights Settlement account and a current appropriation within the San Joaquin Restoration Fund. Further, the budget proposes to transition CUPCA to within Reclamation, while maintaining a separate account. This consolidation is part of broader Administration efforts to implement good government solutions, to consolidate activities when possible, and reduce duplication and overlap.

As the largest supplier and manager of water in the 17 western States and the Nation's second largest producer of hydroelectric power, Reclamation's projects and programs are critical to driving and maintaining economic growth in the western States. Reclamation manages water for agricultural, municipal and industrial use, and provides flood risk reduction and recreation for millions of people. According to *The Department of the Interior's Economic Contributions Fiscal Year 2011*, July 9, 2012, Reclamation's activities, including recreation, have an economic contribution of $46.0 billion, and support nearly 312,000 jobs. Reclamation's 58 hydroelectric power plants generate more than 40 billion kilowatt hours of electricity to meet the annual needs of over 3.5 million households and generate over $1 billion in gross revenues for the Federal government. Of the 58 power plants owned by Reclamation, five are operated by other entities though the power is marketed through a Federal power marketing administration. It would take more than 23.5 million barrels of crude oil or about 6.8 million tons of coal to produce an equal amount of energy with fossil fuels. As a result, Reclamation's facilities eliminate the production of over 27 million tons of carbon dioxide that would have been produced by fossil fuel power plants.

Reclamation Funding

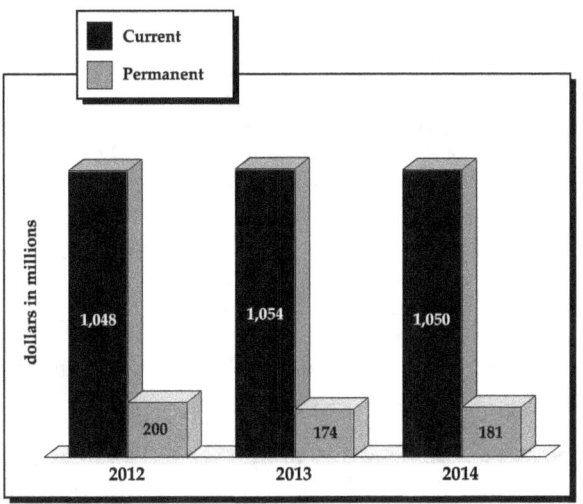

The 2014 budget allocates funds to projects and programs based on objective, performance-based criteria to most effectively implement Reclamation's programs and its management responsibilities for water and power infrastructure in the West. The 2014 budget emphasizes the following principles:

- *Shared Responsibility* – Securing non-Federal cost-share partners to meet project or program funding needs, and leveraging funding through these collaborative partnerships.

- *Merit-Based Funding* – Utilizing competitive processes for the awarding of grants, contracts, or other services based on criteria that reflect Interior priorities.

- *Regional Equity* – Conducting the management of Reclamation's water infrastructure and programs by setting priorities on a West-wide basis.

Water and Related Resources – The 2014 budget for Water and Related Resources, Reclamation's principal operating

- Established in 1902.
- Manages, develops, and protects water resources in an environmentally and economically sound manner.
- Largest supplier and manager of water in the 17 western States.
- Manages 476 dams and 337 reservoirs with the capacity to store 245 million acre-feet of water.
- Delivers water to one in every five western farmers for about 10 million acres of irrigated land, and provides water to over 31 million people for municipal, rural, and industrial uses.
- Is the Nation's second largest producer of hydroelectric power, generating 40 billion kilowatt hours of energy per year from 58 power plants.

account, is $791.1 million, a decrease of $109.3 million from the 2013 Full Year Continuing Resolution, P.L. 112-175. This decrease is due, in part, to shifts in funding of $78.7 million for the establishment of the Indian Water Rights Settlement Account and $26.0 million for a current appropriation within the San Joaquin Restoration Fund. Other significant changes include a decrease of $23.2 million for the completion of the Mni Wiconi Project, an increase of $22.6 million in the Central Valley Project for court ordered drainage requirements, and reductions of $20.5 million in the WaterSMART program, aligning the program closer to the 2012 enacted level.

The 2014 budget includes a total of $373.3 million at the project/program level for water, energy, land, and fish and wildlife resource management and development activities. Funding in these activities provides for planning, construction, water sustainability activities, management of Reclamation lands, including recreation areas, and actions to address the impacts of Reclamation projects on fish and wildlife.

The budget also provides a total of $417.8 million at the project level for water and power facility operations, maintenance, and rehabilitation activities. Reclamation emphasizes safe, efficient, economic, and reliable operation of facilities, ensuring systems and safety measures are in place to protect the facilities and the public. Providing adequate funding for these activities continues to be one of Reclamation's highest priorities.

Water Challenges – Interior's Water Challenges initiative is accomplished through the WaterSMART program – Sustain and Manage America's Resources for Tomorrow. WaterSMART is one method Reclamation employs to stretch water supplies in the West and prepare for ongoing challenges such as drought and climate change. The programs included in WaterSMART are collaborative in nature and work across jurisdictional boundaries to effectively achieve sustainable water management.

WaterSMART Grants, Title XVI Water Reclamation and Reuse, and the Water Conservation Field Services program, along with other Reclamation activities, support the Department's Priority Goal for Water Conservation.

In the 2014 budget, Reclamation proposes to fund WaterSMART at $35.4 million, in recognition of the constrained fiscal environment. The WaterSMART components include: WaterSMART Grants funded at $12.0 million; the Basin Studies program funded at $4.7 million; the Title XVI Water Reclamation and Reuse Program funded at $14.0 million; a new external water resources grants program called the Shared Investment Water Innovation Program funded at $1.0 million; Water Conservation Field Services program, funded at $3.4 million; and the Cooperative Watershed Management program, funded at $250,000.

Climate Change Adaptation – Reclamation is actively engaged in developing and implementing approaches to understand, and effectively adapt to, the risks and impacts of a changing environment on western water management. The Basin Studies program represents a coordinated approach to assessing these risks and impacts, developing landscape-level science; communicating information and science to other entities and agencies; and working with stakeholders to develop adaptation strategies to cope with water supply and demand imbalances on a collaborative basis. Additionally, within Reclamation's Science and Technology program is water resources research targeting improved capability for managing water resources under multiple drivers, including a changing climate. This research agenda will be collaborated and leveraged with capabilities of the Interior Climate Science Centers. Reclamation's WaterSMART grants, Field Services, and Title XVI programs are also enabling the West to better adapt to the impacts of a changing environment by helping to conserve tens of thousands of acre-feet of water each year in urban and rural settings, and on both large and small scales.

In 2014, Reclamation will: 1) continue to implement the West-wide Climate Risk Assessments, which provide consistent projections of risks to water supplies and demands, as well as impacts to Reclamation's operations; 2) continue work with stakeholders to identify strategies to adapt to current or future water supply and demand imbalances; and 3) through the Desert and Southern Rockies Landscape Conservation Cooperatives, continue to identify and implement potential new adaptation strategies, facilitate data sharing, develop and implement adaptive management techniques and monitoring plans, and build and expand on existing applied science tools and capabilities to identify gaps that can be addressed through the Department's Climate Science Centers, universities, and other sources to address climate change impacts.

Supporting the New Energy Frontier – To support the New Energy Frontier initiative and the Renewable Energy priority goal, the 2014 Reclamation budget allocates $1.1 million for a pilot initiative to increase renewable generation by exploring how renewable energy technologies, including solar, small hydropower, and hydrokinetics, can be integrated into Reclamation projects. Reclamation will continue efforts to: optimize its hydropower projects to produce more energy with the same amount of water; investigate hydro pump-storage projects that can help integrate large amounts of different renewable resources such as wind and solar into the electric grid; and work with Tribes to assist them in developing renewable energy sources. These important projects will assist in the production of cleaner, more efficient renewable energy.

Tribal Nations – The 2014 Reclamation budget supports the Tribal Nations initiative through a number of activities and projects. For example, the budget includes $7.4 million in support of Reclamation's activities with Tribes, including technical assistance, Indian Water Rights Settlement negotiations, implementation of enacted settlements, and outreach to Tribes; and $12.4 million to continue the operation and maintenance associated with the delivery of 89,500 acre-feet of water to the Ak-Chin community. Ongoing authorized rural water projects also benefit both tribal and non-tribal communities. The projects benefiting Tribes include the rural water component of the Pick-Sloan Missouri Basin Program, Garrison Diversion Unit; Fort Peck Reservation/Dry Prairie; and Rocky Boy's/North Central Montana. Numerous other projects and programs, such as the Columbia/Snake River Salmon Recovery, Klamath, and the Yakima River Basin Water Enhancement Project also benefit Tribes. In 2014, funding for Indian Water Rights Settlements construction is being proposed in a new separate account.

Rural Water Projects – Congress has specifically authorized Reclamation to undertake the design and construction of seven projects intended to deliver potable water supplies to specific rural communities and Tribes located in the 17 western States — primarily in Montana, New Mexico, North Dakota, and South Dakota. The 2014 Reclamation budget includes $40.0 million for rural water projects, $29.5 million below the 2013 Full Year Continuing Resolution partially due to the scheduled completion of the Mni Wiconi Project in 2013.

Ecosystem Restoration – In order to meet Reclamation's mission goals of securing America's energy resources and managing water in a sustainable manner for the 21st century, one focus of its programs must be the protection and restoration of the aquatic and riparian environments influenced by its operations. Ecosystem restoration involves a large number of activities, including Reclamation's Endangered Species Act recovery programs, which directly address the environmental aspects of the Reclamation mission.

In 2014, additional river restoration programs within Reclamation are included in the America's Great Outdoors Program. A total of $120.2 million in Reclamation's 2014 budget directly support the goals of the AGO program, through local and basin-wide collaboration in watershed partnerships. Reclamation's river restoration helps reduce environmental conflicts and litigation, as evidenced by the San Joaquin River Restoration Program, where 18 years of litigation was settled providing restored water flows and reintroduction of salmon to the River, as well as certainty on water and power delivery to customers. Restoration programs support tribal needs in restoring fisheries affected by water and power operations as demonstrated by the Trinity River Restoration program which is re-establishing the physical process and rescaling the Trinity River as a foundation for fishery recovery. Restoration programs also develop valuable conservation skills for young people working on projects, as seen on the Lower Colorado River Multi-Species Conservation program among others.

The 2014 budget provides $152.5 million to operate, manage, and improve California's Central Valley Project. Within this total, $14.0 million and an additional $2.0 million in the Central Valley Project Restoration Fund is for the Trinity River Restoration program, and $38.2 million continues actions required for drainage services in the West San Joaquin Division, San Luis Unit.

The budget provides $27.8 million for Lower Colorado River Operations to fulfill the role of the Secretary as Water Master for the Lower Colorado River. This amount includes $18.2 million for the multi-species conservation program which provides long-term Endangered Species Act compliance for the river operations.

The budget includes $39.2 million for Endangered Species Act Recovery Implementation programs that includes $10.1 million in the Great Plains Region for the Platte River Endangered Species Recovery Implementation program, which provides measures to help recover four endangered or threatened species, thereby enabling existing water projects in the Platte River Basin to continue operations, as well as allowing new water projects to be developed in compliance with the Endangered Species Act. This program also provides $8.5 million for the Upper Colorado and San Juan River Endangered Fish Recovery programs. This funding will continue construction of a system that automates canal operations to conserve water by matching river diversions with actual consumptive use demands and redirecting the conserved water to improve instream flows. The budget also provides $18.0 million for the Columbia/Snake River Salmon Recovery program. This funding will be used to implement the required Biological Opinion actions which include extensive hydro actions that vary downstream flow regimes and tributary habitat and hatchery improvements as offsets for the impacts of the Federal Columbia River Power System operations.

The 2014 budget includes $18.0 million for the Klamath project, which supports studies and initiatives to improve water supplies to meet the competing demands of agricultural, tribal, wildlife refuge, and environmental needs along with facilities operations and maintenance activities. Within that amount, $4.3 million will continue actions that address water supply enhancement and restoration of natural resources that support the Klamath Basin Restoration Agreement and are authorized under existing law.

The 2014 budget includes $25.9 million for the Middle Rio Grande project, of which $10.2 million will continue funding endangered species activities and Reclamation's participation in the Middle Rio Grande Endangered Species Act Collaborative Program. Funds support the acquisition of supplemental non-Federal water for Endangered Species Act efforts including low flow conveyance channel pumping into the Rio Grande during the irrigation season. Further, funding will be used for recurring river maintenance necessary to ensure uninterrupted and efficient water delivery to Elephant Butte Reservoir, reduce the risk of flooding, as well as meeting water delivery obligations to Mexico.

A total of $15.4 million is provided for the Yakima River Basin. This includes $7.4 million to operate and maintain existing project facilities and $8.0 million for the Yakima River Basin Water Enhancement project, which will continue funding grants to implement conservation measures and monitor the effects of those measures on the river diversions.

Dam Safety Program - A total of $88.1 million is provided for Reclamation's Safety of Dams program, which includes $66.5 million directed to dam safety modifications to correct identified safety issues. Of that amount, $24.6 million is for work at Folsom Dam. Funding also includes $20.3 million for safety evaluations of existing dams and $1.3 million to oversee the Interior Department's Safety of Dams program.

Site Security - A total of $27.8 million is provided for Site Security to ensure the safety and security of the public, Reclamation's employees, and key facilities. This funding includes $6.4 million for physical security upgrades at high risk critical assets and $21.4 million to continue all aspects of Bureau-wide security efforts including law enforcement, risk and threat analysis, personnel security, information security, risk assessments and security-related studies, and guards and patrols.

Central Utah Project Completion Act – Interior's 2014 budget proposes to consolidate the CUPCA project within Reclamation while maintaining a separate account for CUPCA. This consolidation is part of broader Administration efforts to implement good government solutions, to consolidate activities when possible, and reduce duplication and overlap. The 2014 CUPCA budget is $3.5 million, a decrease of $25.4 million from the 2013 Full Year Continuing Resolution. Of this amount, $1.0 million will be transferred to the Utah Reclamation Mitigation and Conservation Account for use by the Mitigation Commission. The 2014 funding will be used to provide program oversight for on-going construction, the Ute Tribal settlement, fish and wildlife development, and Endangered Species Act recovery. In recognition of the constrained fiscal environment, no new construction funding is included.

Central Valley Project Restoration Fund – The 2014 budget includes a total of $53.3 million for the CVPRF. This amount is indexed to 1992 price levels and determined on the basis of a three-year rolling average not to exceed $50.0 million per year. These expenditures are offset by collections estimated at $53.3 million from mitigation and restoration charges authorized by the Central Valley Project Improvement Act. The San Joaquin Restoration Fund section below describes the impact the San Joaquin River Restoration Settlement Act has on the CVPRF.

California Bay-Delta Restoration – The 2014 budget provides $37.0 million for California Bay-Delta Restoration, a decrease of $2.9 million from the 2013 Full Year Continuing Resolution. The account focuses on the health of the Bay-Delta ecosystem and improving water management and supplies. The budget will support implementation of the Bay-Delta Conservation Plan, under the following program activities: $1.7 million for a Renewed Federal State Partnership, $9.9 million for Smarter Water Supply and Use, and $25.5 million for Habitat Restoration. These program activities are based on the Interim Federal Action Plan for the California Bay-Delta issued December 22, 2009.

San Joaquin River Restoration Fund – The 2014 budget funds activities consistent with the settlement of *Natural Resources Defense Council* v. *Rodgers* as authorized by the San Joaquin River Restoration Settlement Act. The Act includes a provision to establish the San Joaquin Restoration Fund to implement the provisions of the Settlement. The Settlement's two primary goals are to restore and maintain fish populations, and restore and avoid adverse water impacts. Under the Settlement, the legislation provides for nearly $2.0 million in permanent annual appropriations from the Central Valley Project Restoration Fund for this purpose. Reclamation proposes $26.0 million of current funds for the San Joaquin Restoration Fund account in 2014.

Indian Water Rights Settlements – The total budget for Reclamation's implementation of Indian Water Rights Settlements in 2014 is $99.7 million in current funding. Reclamation is proposing establishment of an Indian Water Rights Settlements account to assure continuity in the construction of the authorized projects and to highlight and enhance transparency in handling these funds.

The budget includes $18.2 million to continue implementation of the four settlements authorized in the Claims Resolution Act of 2010. These settlements will deliver clean water to the Taos Pueblo of New Mexico, the Pueblos of New Mexico named in the Aamodt case, the Crow Tribe of Montana, and the White Mountain Apache Tribe of Arizona. The budget also includes $60.5 million for the ongoing Navajo-Gallup Water Supply project. The $78.7 million for these settlements is proposed in a separate account in order to have major current funding for constructing Reclamation's Indian Water Rights Settlements in a single account. Additionally, $60.0 million in new permanent authority is available in 2014 for the Indian water rights settlements.

The 2014 budget also contains $21.0 million in the Water and Related Resources Account for on-going settlement operation and maintenance functions including the Ak Chin Indian Water Rights Settlement Act, San Carlos Apache Tribe Water Settlement Act, Colorado Ute Settlement Act Animas-La Plata Project, and Nez Perce/Snake River Water Rights Act which is part of the Columbia and Snake River Recovery Project.

Policy and Administration – The 2014 budget for Policy and Administration, the account that finances Reclamation's central and regional management functions, is $60.0 million.

Working Capital Fund – This fund is operated for the purpose of managing financial activities such as acquisition and replacement of capital equipment; recovery of the cost of services provided to others; indirect cost recovery for the Technical Service Center; management services and human resources in regional and area offices; and information technology related costs and services. The fund operates on a self-supporting basis through user charges.

Permanent Appropriations – The total permanent appropriation in 2014 of $180.6 million primarily includes $110.1 million for the Colorado River Dam Fund and $60.0 million for Reclamation's Water Settlements Fund. In 2014, the Utah Reclamation Mitigation and Conservation Commission will be authorized to begin using the interest from the Utah Reclamation Mitigation and Conservation Investment Account, estimated to be $7.2 million.

SUMMARY OF BUREAU APPROPRIATIONS
(all dollar amounts in thousands)

Comparison of 2014 Request with 2013 Full Year Continuing Resolution [1]

	2013 Full Year CR		2014 Request		Change	
	FTE	Amount	FTE	Amount	FTE [2]	Amount
Current						
Water and Related Resources	2,831	900,477	2,831	791,135	0	-109,342
San Joaquin River Restoration Fund [3]	0	[18,000]	0	26,000	0	+26,000
Indian Water Rights Settlement [3]	0	[50,454]	0	78,661	0	+78,661
Subtotal	2,831	900,477	2,831	895,796	0	-4,681
Policy and Administration	296	60,367	296	60,000	0	-367
Central Valley Project Restoration Fund	18	53,393	18	53,288	0	-105
California Bay-Delta Restoration	31	39,894	31	37,000	0	-2,894
Central Utah Project Completion Account [3]	[4]	[26,867]	4	2,500	+4	+2,500
Utah Reclamation Mitigation and Conservation [3]	[10]	[2,012]	10	1,000	+10	+1,000
Working Capital Fund	1,850	0	1,848	0	-2	0
Subtotal, Current	5,026	1,054,131	5,038	1,049,584	+12	-4,547
Adjustment to 2012 Enacted	0	-6,412	0	0	0	+6,412
Subtotal, Current Adjusted	5,026	1,047,719	5,038	1,049,584	+12	+1,865
Central Valley Project Restoration Fund Offset	0	-39,582	0	-53,288	0	-13,706
Adjustment to 2012 Enacted	0	-13,185	0	0	0	+13,185
Subtotal, Central Valley Project Restoration CVPRF Offset Adjusted	0	-52,767	0	-53,288	0	-521
Subtotal Net Current	5,026	1,014,549	5,038	996,296	+12	-18,253
Adjustment to 2012 Enacted	0	-19,597	0	0	0	+19,597
Subtotal, Net Current Adjusted	5,026	994,952	5,038	996,296	+12	+1,344

Comparison of 2014 Estimates with 2013 Estimates

	2013 Estimate		2014 Request		Change	
	FTE	Amount	FTE	Amount	FTE [2]	Amount
Permanent						
Colorado River Dam Fund, Boulder Canyon Project	218	111,098	218	110,053	0	-1,045
Basin Funds	117	0	119	0	+2	0
Loan Program Liquidating Account	0	-853	0	-869	0	-16
Miscellaneous Permanents	0	515	0	515	0	0
Reclamation Trust Funds	1	3,000	1	3,000	0	0
Federal Lands Recreation Enhancement Act	0	685	0	685	0	0
San Joaquin River Restoration Fund	22	0	22	0	0	0
Reclamation Water Settlements Fund	0	60,000	0	60,000	0	0
Utah Reclamation Mitigation and Conservation	0	0	0	7,170	0	+7,170
Subtotal, Permanent and Other	358	174,445	360	180,554	+2	+6,109

[1] *Reclamation account details for the 2014 request are compared to the 2013 Full Year CR, P.L. 112-175 level to more accurately reflect annual schedule changes in construction, restoration or rehabilitation projects.*

[2] *Net change in FTE for the Bureau of Reclamation is +14, which is primarily a result of incorporating 14 FTEs from the Central Utah project.*

[3] *The amounts displayed in brackets are provided for comparative purposes only as these amounts were appropriated in different accounts for 2012 and under the 2013 Full Year CR, P.L. 112-175.*

HIGHLIGHTS OF BUDGET CHANGES
By Appropriation Activity/Subactivity

APPROPRIATION: Water and Related Resources [1]

	2012 Enacted	2013 Full Year CR	2014 Request	Change from 2013
Animas-La Plata Project	12,600	2,334	2,204	-130
Central Arizona Project	6,941	7,892	9,038	+1,146
Central Valley Project	172,762	146,037	152,545	+6,508
Colorado-Big Thompson Project	11,500	13,646	13,134	-512
CO River Basin Salinity Control Program	22,478	23,303	22,938	-365
Colorado River Storage Project	12,128	13,595	12,566	-1,029
Columbia Basin Project	9,382	9,031	9,516	+485
Columbia/Snake River Salmon Recovery	17,616	18,000	18,000	0
Dam Safety Program	83,466	87,450	88,084	+634
Endangered Species Act Recovery Implementation	20,715	22,890	21,207	-1,683
Indian Water Rights Settlements [2] (including Navajo-Gallup)	50,865	50,454	0	-50,454
Klamath Project	18,385	25,734	18,000	-7,734
Lower Colorado River Operations Program	25,668	30,190	27,839	-2,351
Middle Rio Grande Project	24,289	22,537	25,934	+3,397
Native American Affairs Program	6,868	6,493	7,412	+919
Pick-Sloan Missouri Basin Program (excluding Garrison)	43,063	42,412	40,967	-1,445
Garrison Diversion Unit (Non-Rural Water)	8,965	9,619	9,623	+4
Subtotal, Pick-Sloan Missouri Basin	52,028	52,031	50,590	-1,441
Rural Water Supply Projects				
Eastern NM Rural Water System	1,000	1,978	649	-1,329
Fort Peck Reservation/Dry Prairie Rural Water System	9,487	7,500	4,300	-3,200
Jicarilla Apache Rural Water System	690	500	0	-500
Lewis and Clark Rural Water System	5,487	4,500	3,200	-1,300
Mni Wiconi Project	26,012	35,200	12,000	-23,200
P-SMBP, Garrison Diversion Unit	18,077	15,900	14,492	-1,408
Rocky Boy's/North Central Montana Rural Water System	4,387	4,000	5,400	+1,400
Subtotal, Rural Water Projects	65,140	69,578	40,041	-29,537
Research and Development	12,048	13,048	16,566	+3,518
Site Security	25,631	26,900	27,800	+900
WaterSMART Program				
Basin Studies	4,928	6,000	4,734	-1,266
Cooperative Watershed Management	247	250	250	0
Shared Investment Water Innovation Program	0	0	1,000	+1,000
Title XVI Water Reclamation and Reuse Projects	24,653	20,271	14,000	-6,271
WaterSMART Grants	12,233	24,500	12,000	-12,500
Water Conservation Field Services Program	5,047	4,886	3,437	-1,449
Subtotal, WaterSMART Program	47,108	55,907	35,421	-20,486

APPROPRIATION: Water and Related Resources [1]

	2012 Enacted	2013 Full Year CR	2014 Request	Change from 2013
Yakima Project and Yakima River Basin Water Enhancement Project..................	17,288	18,318	15,436	-2,882
Yuma Area Projects.....................................	22,302	22,015	23,842	+1,827
Other Project/Programs............................	157,792	163,094	153,022	-10,072
TOTAL APPROPRIATION	895,000	900,477	791,135	-109,342
Adjustment to 2012 Enacted..................	0	-5,477	0	+5,477
TOTAL APPROPRIATION *(compared to 2012)*...	895,000	895,000	791,135	-103,865

[1] *Reclamation project details for the 2014 request are compared to the 2013 Full Year CR, P.L. 112-175 level to more accurately reflect annual schedule changes in construction, restoration or rehabilitation projects.*
[2] *A new separate Indian Water Rights Settlements Appropriation Account is requested to be established in 2014.*

Program Highlights
Water and Related Resources

The 2014 budget includes funds for the following projects and programs.

Animas-La Plata Project

> In 2014, funds are provided for continued oversight and administration of required repayments, water service contracts, water quality monitoring, land use management, cultural resources management, law enforcement contracting, recreation facilities management, fish and wildlife monitoring, and facility operations and maintenance activities.

Central Arizona Project

> Funds are for continued work activities to include fulfilling native fish protection requirements through fish barrier projects, continued planning work on the New Mexico Unit, and work with Tucson area municipal entities on preconstruction activities for the Tucson Northwest Reservoir. The increase will 'fast track' the implementation process for the design and construction of recharge and recovery facilities for the Tohono O'odham Nation's San Xavier and Schuk Toak Districts.

Central Valley Project

> Funds are provided for continued facility operations, maintenance, and rehabilitation, numerous management and development efforts, and water conservation. In response to a Federal Court Order, funding continues to support implementation of the San Luis drainage management plan that addresses groundwater pumping, drainage reuse, drainage treatment, and salt disposal. Funding also provides for the Trinity River restoration program and related activities that will be funded by the CVP Restoration Fund and California Bay-Delta appropriation.

Colorado-Big Thompson Project

> The Colorado-Big Thompson project diverts approximately 260,000 acre-feet of water annually from the Colorado River headwaters on the western slope of the Rocky Mountains for distribution to eastern slope project lands. Funding is provided for project operations and continued coordination of activities associated with conservation, enhancement, development, and restoration of fish and wildlife populations and their habitats.

Colorado River Basin Salinity Control Program

> Funds are provided for operation, maintenance and rehabilitation of completed projects in the Upper Colorado River Basin and for a basin-wide program to identify and implement cost-effective salinity control options based on proposals from non-Federal interests. The funds will be used to meet United States obligations under the 1944 Water Treaty with Mexico and subsequent Minutes to the Treaty, which clarify and resolve Treaty issues. To help meet the Treaty requirements, Reclamation continues maintenance of the U.S. and Mexico bypass drains, wellfields, and conveyance systems, continues operations and delivery of Colorado River water to Mexico, and the management of water quality. Reclamation works to identify and evaluate the options for replacing or recovering bypass flows to Mexico, as it relates to the Yuma Desalting Plant. The increase is primarily due to more frequent and extensive repairs necessary for aging groundwater wells and conveyances.

Colorado River Storage Project

Funds are included for the Federal share of the costs of facility operations, maintenance, and rehabilitation, including the rehabilitation of recreation facilities at Reclamation constructed reservoirs. Implementation of mitigation measures continues.

Columbia Basin Project

The Bonneville Power Administration, through a memorandum of agreement, directly funds power operation and maintenance costs. In addition, BPA directly funds through subagreements, major power replacements, additions, and improvements. Funds are provided for the day-to-day operation of two storage dams and reservoirs, three Grand Coulee power plants, one pump and generating plant, associated switchyards and transmission lines, the feeder canal at Grand Coulee, and the distribution canal systems for the irrigation reserved works.

Columbia/Snake River Salmon Recovery

This program implements actions required by the Endangered Species Act and the 2008 and 2010 supplemental Biological Opinions issued by the National Oceanic and Atmospheric Administration of the National Marine Fisheries Service. A separate 2000 Biological Opinion issued by the Fish and Wildlife Service is still in effect as well. These Biological Opinions require extensive collaboration with States and Tribes in the Columbia River Basin to ensure that operation of the Federal Columbia River Power System by the agencies is not likely to jeopardize the continued existence of endangered or threatened species, or to adversely modify or destroy their designated critical habitats. Reclamation actions include modifications to hydrosystem operations and specific actions to improve tributary habitat and hatcheries for salmon and steelhead.

Dam Safety Program

This program provides funding for the Safety of Dams Evaluation and Modification program, which identifies and evaluates safety issues at Reclamation dams, and implements modifications to reduce associated risks to the public. The budget continues dam safety risk management and risk reduction activities throughout Reclamation's inventory of high and significant hazard dams. The program continues planned ongoing dam safety modification activities at Folsom and Stampede Dams, California; Red Willow Dam, Nebraska; Nelson Dikes, Montana; Echo Dam, Utah; and Glendo/Guernsey Dams, Wyoming. Pre-construction and project formulation activities are planned for several other dams. Funds are also provided to oversee the broader Dam Safety Program managed by the Department of the Interior.

Endangered Species Act Recovery Implementation

This program provides for the development and implementation of measures for the preservation, conservation, and recovery of native and endangered, threatened, proposed, and candidate species that are resident in, or migratory to, habitats affected by the operation of Reclamation projects. Ongoing efforts funded by this program involve the Colorado, San Juan, and Platte River Basins, as well as watersheds in the Pacific Northwest and areas impacted by the Central Valley Project.

Indian Water Rights Settlements (including Navajo-Gallup Water Supply)

In 2014, Reclamation is proposing establishment of an Indian Water Rights Settlements account to assure continuity in the construction of the authorized projects and to highlight and enhance transparency in handling the four new water settlements identified in the Claims Resolution Act of 2010. In establishing this account, Reclamation is also proposing to include the ongoing Navajo-Gallup Water Supply project (Title X of Public Law 111-11) to have all major current funding for constructing Reclamation's Indian Water Rights Settlement projects in a single account. Funding will provide for ongoing pre-construction and construction activities of the White Mountain Apache, Crow, Aamodt, and Navajo-Gallup Settlements and the planning and design of the mutual benefit projects for the Taos Settlement.

Klamath Project

The budget includes funds for projects and initiatives related to improving water supplies to meet the competing demands of agricultural, tribal, wildlife refuge, and environmental needs in the Klamath River Basin along with facilities operation and maintenance. Key areas of focus include continuing a water user mitigation program, making improvements in fish passage and habitat, taking actions to improve water quality, developing a basin-wide recovery plan, and increasing surface and groundwater supplies.

Lower Colorado River Operations Program

This program funds work necessary to carry out the Secretary's responsibilities as Water Master of the lower Colorado River, including the administration of the Colorado River interim guidelines and reservoir management strategies during low reservoir conditions. This program funds activities under the Lower Colorado River Multi-Species Conservation Program to provide long-term Endangered Species Act compliance for lower Colorado River operations for both Federal and non-Federal purposes. The MSCP provides a cost-share benefit in which non-Federal partners match Federal funding on a 50/50 basis.

Middle Rio Grande Project

Funds are included for operations, maintenance, and rehabilitation of project facilities, river maintenance, and for efforts focused on the protection and recovery of the Rio Grande silvery minnow and southwestern willow flycatcher. Project partnerships, through the Middle Rio Grande Endangered Species Act Collaborative Program, provide an alternative to litigation and preserve, protect, and improve the status of endangered species. River maintenance directly benefits water salvage and effective water delivery to Elephant Butte Reservoir, nine Tribes and Pueblos along the river, and a national wildlife refuge. It also reduces flood risks and protects life, critical riverside facilities and property. The project provides for collection of mission essential lifecycle hydrologic data in the Middle Rio Grande system and maintenance of the surface water hydrologic computer model required for efficient and effective water delivery. The increase supports expected tasks related to the new Biological Opinion.

Native American Affairs Program

This program provides funding to promote the successful application of Reclamation's programs for Indian issues and needs. The program supports Indian water rights negotiations and the implementation of enacted settlements and assists Tribes in their efforts to become self-sufficient in the management and development of their water resources. The increase supports Federal negotiations in developing the most cost effective options for reaching settlement and meeting tribal trust responsibilities.

Pick-Sloan Missouri Basin Program

Funds are provided for the Federal share of the costs of operations, maintenance, and rehabilitation of facilities on 32 units of the Pick-Sloan Missouri Basin program. The rural water portion of the P-SMBP, Garrison Diversion Unit, is described under Rural Water Supply projects.

Rural Water Supply Projects

Congress has specifically authorized Reclamation to undertake the design and construction of seven projects intended to deliver potable water supplies to specific rural communities and Tribes located primarily in Montana, New Mexico, North Dakota, and South Dakota. In addition to funding for rural water project construction, the budget includes funds for the operation and maintenance of tribal features of the Mni Wiconi project and the Pick-Sloan Missouri Basin Program, Garrison Diversion Unit. The reduction is due primarily to the anticipated 2013 completion of the Federal portion of the Mni Wiconi construction.

Eastern New Mexico Rural Water System

Funds are provided to extend the main transmission line to the north to Canon Air Force Base toward the Ute reservoir.

Fort Peck Reservation/Dry Prairie Rural Water System

Funds are provided for completion of a waterline and continued planning, designing, and construction of pipeline branch lines.

Jicarilla Apache Reservation Rural Water System

No funds are proposed in 2014 as the Jicarilla Apache Nation has not obligated funds already appropriated for the project.

Lewis and Clark Rural Water System

Funds are provided for the construction of a meter building, including booster pumps, required for the Rock Rapids connection and a portion of the TWP MN-1A pipeline.

Mni Wiconi Project

Funds are provided for operation and maintenance of new and existing facilities on the Indian reservations. Construction of the Federal portion of the Mni Wiconi Project is projected to be completed in 2013.

Pick-Sloan Missouri Basin Program, Garrison Diversion Unit

Funds are provided for continued oversight of preconstruction and construction activities on approved State, municipal, rural, and industrial systems, including the continued construction of the Northwest Area Water Supply System. Funding also provides for operation and maintenance of completed project facilities.

Rocky Boy's/North Central Montana Rural Water System

Funds are provided for the Tribes and the non-Federal sponsor, North Central Authority, to perform construction of the Core system pipeline, as well as design of the water treatment plant and build-out of non-core pipeline distribution systems.

Research and Technology – Science and Technology Program

Funds are included for the development of new solutions and technologies that respond to the Bureau of Reclamation's mission-related needs, which provide for innovative management, development, and protection of water and related resources. Additionally, this program supports Interior's integrated strategy for responding to changing climate impacts on the resources managed by the Department. The increase is primarily for testing technology to prevent invasive mussel settlement and to initiate a Water Solutions Technology Challenge Program, initially focused on water purification technologies.

Site Security

Funds are provided to continue Reclamation's ongoing site security efforts including physical security upgrades at high risk critical assets, law enforcement, risk and threat analysis, personnel security, information security, security risk assessments, security related studies, and guards and patrol of facilities.

WaterSMART Program

Funds support the Department's WaterSMART program, which concentrates on implementing sustainable water management strategies and expanding and stretching limited water supplies in the West to address current and future water shortages, increased demands for water and energy from growing populations, amplified recognition of environmental water requirements, and the potential for decreased water supply availability due to drought and climate change.

The WaterSMART program includes Reclamation's Basin Studies program, Shared Investment Water Innovation program, Title XVI Water Reclamation and Reuse program, Water Conservation Fields Services program, WaterSMART Grants, and participation in the Cooperative Watershed Management program. Through these programs, Reclamation will continue to provide competitive cost-shared financial assistance for water and energy efficiency improvements, as well as other activities that enhance water management. The program also conducts basin-wide activities under the SECURE Water Act that support Landscape Conservation Cooperatives and the Department of the Interior's integrated strategy for responding to new weather patterns in a changing environment; continues funding of water reclamation and reuse projects through its Title XVI program; continues funding of smaller scale water conservation improvements and planning efforts through the Water Conservation Field Services program; and assists the Department in implementing collaborative conservation efforts in the management of local watersheds through the Cooperative Watershed Management program. The WaterSMART program also supports the Department's Priority Goals for water conservation and climate change. The decrease is in recognition of the constrained fiscal environment.

Yakima Project/Yakima River Basin Water Enhancement Project

Funds are provided for addressing water supply shortages for fish and wildlife and dry-year irrigation and municipal water supplies to include hydraulic modeling, cultural surveys, and designs data collection for the Cle Elum Fish Passage which will open upstream for fish habitat. Additionally, funding would enable continued implementation of specific environmental compliance related to inactive storage in the reservoir on the Kachess Inactive Storage.

Yuma Area Projects

The budget funds infrastructure maintenance along the lower Colorado River necessary to ensure uninterrupted water delivery to both urban and agricultural users in Arizona, California, Nevada, and Mexico. Funding also supports river management, well inventory, drainage control, protection of endangered species and their habitats, and land use management activities. The increase is primarily for necessary maintenance and upgrades on aging well fields, drainage, and conveyance systems.

Other Projects and Programs

The 2014 budget also includes funds for numerous smaller projects and programs that further the mission of Reclamation throughout the 17 western States. Though each of these projects may constitute a relatively small portion of Reclamation's budget, together they amount to $153.0 million and provide critical services to thousands of individuals, farmers, municipalities, and industries throughout the arid West.

APPROPRIATION: San Joaquin River Restoration Fund [1/]

	2012 Enacted	2013 Full Year CR	2014 Request	Change from 2013
TOTAL APPROPRIATION	[8,892]	[18,000]	26,000	+26,000
Adjustment to 2012 Enacted.................	0	[-9,108]	0	0
TOTAL APPROPRIATION	[8,892]	[8,892]	26,000	+26,000

Program Highlights

San Joaquin Restoration Fund

Reclamation proposes $26.0 million of current funds, an $8.0 million increase over the 2013 Full Year Continuing Resolution, for the San Joaquin Restoration Fund in 2014. Funding in 2013 and prior years has been in the Water and Related Resources account under the Central Valley Project, Friant Division. Providing the funds in the San Joaquin Restoration Fund will highlight and enhance transparency in handling these funds. The increase will primarily be used for the Mendota Pool Bypass and Reach 2B Channel and Structural Improvements Project which implements two of the highest priority projects identified in the Settlement. This project is also a key component of the San Joaquin River Restoration Program's America's Great Outdoors activities.

APPROPRIATION: Indian Water Rights Settlements [1/]

	2012 Enacted	2013 Full Year CR	2014 Request	Change from 2013
White Mountain Apache Tribe				
Water Rights Quantification Act	[4,891]	[2,500]	2,000	+2,000
Crow Tribe Rights Settlement Act	[8,236]	[10,000]	7,500	+7,500
Taos Pueblo Indian Water Rights				
Settlement Act..	[3,952]	[4,000]	4,000	+4,000
Aamodt Litigation Settlement Act............	[9,287]	[5,000]	4,664	+4,664
Navajo-Gallup Water Supply	[24,499]	[28,954]	60,497	+60,497
TOTAL APPROPRIATION	[50,865]	[50,454]	78,661	+78,661
Adjustment to 2012 Enacted.................	0	[411]	0	0
TOTAL APPROPRIATION	[50,865]	[50,865]	78,661	+78,661

Program Highlights

Indian Water Rights Settlements

In 2014, Reclamation is proposing establishment of an Indian Water Rights Settlements account to assure continuity in the construction of the authorized projects and to highlight and enhance transparency in handling the construction funds.

White Mountain Apache Tribe Water Rights Quantification Act

Funds will be used for pre-construction activities under the Public Law 93-638 cooperative agreement with the White Mountain Apache Tribe to perform the planning, engineering, design, and environmental compliance for the Miner Flat Project.

Crow Tribe Rights Settlement Act

Reclamation will serve as the lead agency to implement the two major components of the Crow Tribe Water Rights Settlement Act. Reclamation will rehabilitate and improve the Crow Irrigation Project under which Reclamation will carry out such activities as are necessary to rehabilitate and improve the water diversion and delivery features of the CIP. Reclamation will also design and construct a municipal, rural, and industrial system under which Reclamation will plan, design, and construct the water diversion and delivery features of the municipal, industrial and rural water system, in accordance with one or more agreements between the Secretary and the Tribe.

[1/] *The amounts displayed in brackets are provided for comparative purposes only, as these amounts were appropriated in different accounts for 2012 and 2013.*

Taos Pueblo Indian Water Rights Settlement Act

Funds are provided to begin the planning and design of potential mutual benefit projects and then to provide grants to non-tribal entities to minimize adverse impacts on the Pueblo's water resources by pumping future non-Indian groundwater away from the Pueblo's Buffalo Pasture; and implement the resolution of a dispute over the allocation of certain surface water flows between the Pueblo and non-Indian irrigation water rights owners in the community of Arroyo Seco Arriba.

Aamodt Litigation Settlement Act

Funds are provided to plan, design, and construct a regional water system, in accordance with the Settlement Agreement. The system will divert and distribute water to the Pueblos of Nambe, Pojoaque, Tesuque, and San Ildefonso, and the Santa Fe County water utility; and include treatment, transmission, storage and distribution facilities, and well fields to meet water delivery requirements.

Navajo-Gallup Water Supply Project

Funds will be used to continue oversight, management, coordination, and construction on several reaches on both the San Juan Lateral and the Cutter Lateral. Funding will also provide for design data collection, design, rights-of-way acquisition, and environmental and cultural resources compliance activities for remaining project features.

APPROPRIATION: Policy and Administration

	2012 Enacted	2013 Full Year CR	2014 Request	Change from 2013
TOTAL APPROPRIATION	60,000	60,367	60,000	-367
Adjustment to 2012 Enacted	0	-367	0	+367
TOTAL APPROPRIATION	60,000	60,000	60,000	0

APPROPRIATION: Central Valley Project Restoration Fund

	2012 Enacted	2013 Full Year CR	2014 Request	Change from 2013
Fish and Wildlife Resources Habitat	39,744	36,860	41,113	+4,253
Fish and Wildlife Resources Mgmt	13,324	16,533	12,175	-4,358
TOTAL APPROPRIATION	53,068	53,393	53,288	-105
Adjustment to 2012 Enacted	0	-325	0	+325
TOTAL APPROPRIATION	53,068	53,068	53,288	+220

Program Highlights

Central Valley Project Restoration Fund

The 2014 budget includes Fish and Wildlife Resources Habitat at $41.1 million, an increase of $4.3 million, and Fish and Wildlife Resources Management at $12.2 million, a decrease of $4.4 million.

APPROPRIATION: California Bay-Delta Restoration

	2012 Enacted	2013 Full Year CR	2014 Request	Change from 2013
TOTAL APPROPRIATION	39,651	39,894	37,000	-2,894
Adjustment to 2012 Enacted	0	-243	0	+243
TOTAL APPROPRIATION	39,651	39,651	37,000	-2,651

Program Highlights

California Bay-Delta Restoration
> Funds are provided for the following program activities: $1.7 million for Renewed Federal-State Partnership; $9.9 million for Smarter Water Supply and Use; and $25.5 million for Habitat Restoration. The $2.9 million decrease from the 2013 Full Year Continuing Resolution is composed of decreases of $5.2 million in Habitat Restoration and Renewed Federal State Partnership, offset by an increase of $2.3 million in Smarter Water Supply and Use. These program activities are based on the Interim Federal Action Plan for the California Bay-Delta issued December 22, 2009.

APPROPRIATION: Central Utah Project Completion Account [1/]

	2012 Enacted	2013 Full Year CR	2014 Request	Change from 2013
Central Utah Project Construction	[24,000]	[24,367]	0	0
Fish and Wildlife Conservation	[1,154]	[1,200]	1,200	+1,200
Program Administration	[1,550]	[1,300]	1,300	+1,300
TOTAL APPROPRIATION	[26,704]	[26,867]	2,500	+2,500
Adjustment to 2012 Enacted	0	[-163]	0	0
TOTAL APPROPRIATION	[26,704]	[26,704]	2,500	+2,500

Program Highlights

Central Utah Project Completion Act
> Interior's 2014 budget proposes to consolidate the CUPCA Project within Reclamation. In 2014, funding provides program oversight for ongoing construction, Ute Tribal Settlement, fish and wildlife development and Endangered Species Act recovery. The decrease is in recognition of the constrained fiscal environment and the difficult choices it necessitates; therefore, no construction funding is included.

APPROPRIATION: Utah Reclamation Mitigation and Conservation Account [1/]

	2012 Enacted	2013 Full Year CR	2014 Request	Change from 2013
TOTAL APPROPRIATION	[2,000]	[2,012]	1,000	+1,000
Adjustment to 2012 Enacted	0	[-12]	0	0
TOTAL APPROPRIATION	[2,000]	[2,000]	1,000	+1,000

Program Highlights

Utah Reclamation Mitigation and Conservation Commission
> Interior's 2014 budget proposes to consolidate the CUPCA Project within Reclamation. The budget funds, at a reduced level, implementation of the fish, wildlife, and recreation mitigation and conservation projects authorized in Title III of the Act and continues mitigation measures committed to in pre-1992 Reclamation planning documents.

[1/] *The amounts displayed in brackets are provided for comparative purposes only, as these amounts were appropriated in different accounts for 2012 and 2013.*

U.S. GEOLOGICAL SURVEY

Mission – The mission of the U.S. Geological Survey is to provide reliable scientific information to describe and understand the Earth, minimize loss of life and property from natural disasters, manage water, biological, energy, and mineral resources, and enhance and protect the quality of life.

Budget Overview – The 2014 USGS budget request is $1.2 billion, which is $98.8 million above the 2012 enacted level. The USGS estimates staffing will equal 8,646 full time equivalents in 2014. The 2014 budget reflects the Administration's commitment to investing in research and development to support sound decisionmaking and sustainable stewardship of natural resources in support of a robust economy and resilient Nation. This funding level will enable USGS to continue to provide world-class science and priorities outlined in the USGS Science Strategy. The budget prioritizes programs that are unique to USGS, have national impacts, and provide monitoring, research, and tools to make science immediately usable by decisionmakers, particularly in support of Interior's resource and land management missions and trust responsibilities. To optimize investments in these priorities, some targeted reductions were made. Highlights of the budget include increases for priorities in ecosystem restoration, water resources management, sustainable energy development, climate adaptation, and earth observation systems, such as streamgages and light detection and ranging tools which provide critical data to the Nation. Continuation of a hydraulic fracturing research and development effort with the Department of Energy and the Environmental Protection Agency will support research to better understand and minimize potential environmental, health, and safety impacts of energy development through hydraulic fracturing.

New Energy Frontier – The 2014 budget provides $49.7 million for the Secretary's New Energy Frontier initiative, $18.7 million above the 2012 enacted level. A program increase of $2.0 million is provided for Energy Future and Wildlife Sustainability and an additional $2.0 million is provided to support agencies responsible for alternative energy permitting on Federal lands. These funds will be used to study geothermal resources as a potential energy

USGS Funding

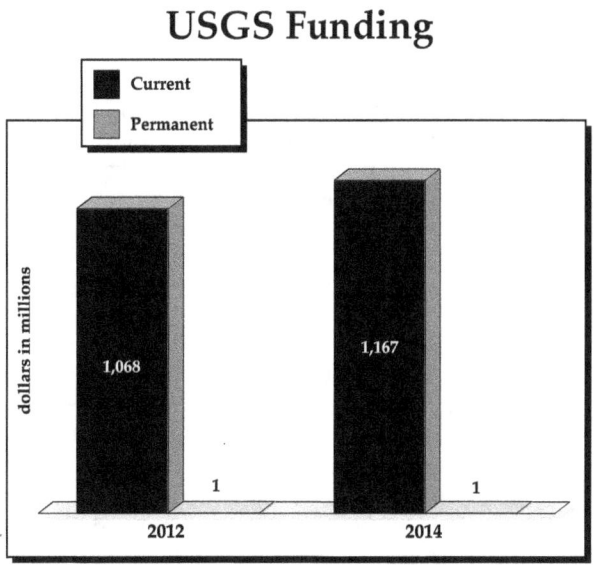

source and build on current USGS efforts to develop an assessment methodology for wind energy impacts. Included in the request is $18.6 million, $13.0 million over 2012, to support the interagency effort to better understand potential impacts of hydraulic fracturing. Funding for other conventional energy programs, including oil, gas, and coal assessments, totals $21.2 million.

Water Challenges – The 2014 budget provides $22.5 million for USGS activities in support of the Water Challenges initiative, an increase of $14.5 million above the 2012 enacted level. The increase will enhance implementation of the WaterSMART Availability and Use Assessment through development of regional water availability models, integration and dissemination of data through online science platforms and databases, and support for the National Groundwater Monitoring Network. In 2014, USGS will begin development of an ecological flows model that integrates hydrological and biological variables, to better understand hydrological needs of ecosystems when making decisions.

Ecosystems – The 2014 budget includes $180.8 million for the Ecosystems activity, $22.5 million above the 2012

U.S. GEOLOGICAL SURVEY
FACTS

- Founded by an Act of Congress in 1879.
- The Nation's largest water, earth, and biological science and civilian mapping agency.
- Employs over 8,500 scientists, technicians, and support staff working in more than 400 locations throughout the United States.
- With over 2,000 strategic partnerships, USGS is a primary Federal source of science-based information on ecosystem science, climate and land use change, energy and mineral resources, environmental impacts, natural hazards, water resource use and availability, and updated maps and images for the Earth's features available to the public.
- Generates and maintains data from over 8,000 streamgages and over 2,100 earthquake sensors that are available to the public.
- Provides direct access to 3.7 million Landsat images spanning the globe from 1972 to present; archives contain 7.6 million air photos dating to 1939 and over 100 other satellite, cartographic, and topographic datasets characterizing the Earth's surface; and available data is provided at no cost to the user.

enacted level. Through this activity, USGS conducts research and monitoring to better understand how ecosystems are structured and function. Information generated by the Ecosystems activity helps improve management of the Nation's natural resources and address hazards that threaten land, coastlines, and population. The budget includes a program increase of $3.0 million for research on new methods to eradicate, control, and manage Asian carp in the Upper Mississippi River Basin and prevent entry into the Great Lakes. Program increases are also provided for the following priority ecosystem restoration initiatives: $1.0 million for the California Bay-Delta, $901,000 to support fish health and water quality studies for the Klamath Basin Restoration Agreement, and $1.0 million for research to control and manage invasive species in the Everglades, particularly the Burmese python. Additional program increases totaling $4.6 million are provided to address brown tree snakes, the white-nose syndrome in bats, coral reef health, new and emerging invasive species of national concern, and ecosystem restoration in the Puget Sound, Columbia River, and Chesapeake Bay. A program increase of $3.0 million will support efforts to further the science and integration of ecosystems services frameworks into decisionmaking and implementation of efforts to assess and sustain the Nation's environmental capital. Increases are also provided for hydraulic fracturing, WaterSMART, and a $2.4 million transfer from the Climate and Land Use Change mission area for science support for the Department's bureaus.

Climate and Land Use Change – The 2014 budget provides a total of $156.0 million for Climate and Land Use Change. This activity provides practical scientific information to inform resilient and adaptive natural resource and land management on a landscape scale. The proposed budget for the Climate Variability subactivity

is $71.7 million, an increase of $13.6 million above the 2012 enacted level. The National Climate Change and Wildlife Science Center and the eight Department of the Interior Climate Science Centers are funded at $35.3 million. This includes a program increase of $3.5 million for CSC grants, focused on providing translational and applied science needed for decisionmaking, particularly in resource management and biological sequestration. To further collaboration, better leverage resources, and reduce potential for duplication, a program increase of $3.2 million will support coordination efforts with other Federal climate science entities and ensure that scientific results and products are made available to the public in a centralized, web-accessible format. Also included are program increases of $2.5 million for applied science and capacity-building in support of tribal climate adaptation needs in each CSC region and $800,000 for climate adaptation and resiliency research leading to a Vulnerability Assessment Database and Field Guide.

The budget includes a $3.2 million program increase in the Climate Research and Development program to support climate science priorities such as the identification of long term patterns of drought, improving estimates of potential sea level rise magnitudes and ranges, and ecosystem response to sea level changes. A program increase of $3.0 million is included to support completion of the national biological carbon sequestration assessment and to develop tools in collaboration with other agencies, to support biological sequestration activities on public lands.

The 2014 request for the Land Use Change subactivity is $84.3 million, $1.0 million above the 2012 enacted level. This subactivity ensures Earth observation imagery collected via satellite is available and accessible to users and provides analyses of these data to quantify rates of land use change, identify key driving forces, and forecast future trends of landscape change. The Landsat program in this subactivity is funded at $53.3 million, level with 2012, and includes funding for ground systems, satellite operations, and advancement of the science, usability, and centralized sharing of Landsat data, applications, and software. In 2014, USGS will work with the National Aeronautics and Space Administration to analyze user requirements and develop a successor mission to Landsat 8, formerly known as the Landsat Data Continuity Mission. Funding to begin work on the successor mission is provided in the 2014 budget for NASA, which will be responsible for development of Landsat-class land imaging satellites going forward. The USGS will continue its operational role in managing the collection, archiving, and dissemination of Landsat data to users. In addition to an increase for WaterSMART, the budget also includes a program increase of $757,000 within the Land Change Science program to support rapid disaster response efforts and a program increase of $1.5 million to support land use science and Chesapeake Bay ecosystem restoration. Increases are partially offset by reductions in several activities within the CLU Mission Area.

Energy, Minerals, and Environmental Health – The 2014 budget includes $107.4 million for Energy, Minerals, and Environmental Health, $11.4 million above the 2012 enacted level. This activity includes programs that conduct research and assessments on the location, quantity, and quality of the Nation's mineral and energy resources. The activity also conducts research on the impacts of human activities that introduce chemical and pathogenic contaminants into the environment and threaten human, animal, and ecological health. The 2014 budget includes program increases of $2.6 million to address emerging contaminants and pathogens, $3.0 million to study the environmental impacts of uranium mining, and $400,000 for Chesapeake Bay and Columbia River ecosystem restoration efforts. In addition to program increases for WaterSMART and research related to wind energy and hydraulic fracturing, the budget also includes a program increase of $2.1 million to support research on high priority minerals, such as rare earth elements, that are critical to American manufacturing. A net reduction of $2.4 million in the Minerals Resources Program is included as the program evaluates options to modernize and realign in an era of rapidly changing minerals information and science needs.

Natural Hazards – The 2014 budget provides $142.6 million for Natural Hazards, $11.4 million above the 2012 enacted level. This activity provides scientific information and tools to reduce potential fatalities, injuries, and economic loss from volcanoes, earthquakes, tsunamis, and landslides, among others. In addition to program increases to support research related to hydraulic frac-

turing, the budget includes program increases of $1.8 million to improve rapid disaster response, $1.2 million for earthquake hazards research and monitoring in the eastern United States, and $108,000 for enhanced geomagnetism monitoring. The 2014 budget also includes a program increase of $6.6 million for Coastal and Marine Geology to support marine and coastal science, ecosystem restoration and management, resource and vulnerability assessments, climate adaptation, and enhanced information about and response to coastal storms. A program increase of $2.0 million is included for the collection of coastal LIDAR data, to be planned and collected in partnership with the 3-D Elevation Program and coordinated with other agencies to implement a national LIDAR program. Increases are offset by reductions in research activities that are of lower national priority.

Water Resources – The 2014 budget includes $222.9 million for Water Resources, $13.3 million above the 2012 enacted level. This activity includes programs that collect, manage, and disseminate hydrologic data, model and analyze hydrologic systems, and conduct research and development leading to new understandings of and methods for gathering data. The activities are supported by a national network of streamgages, wells, and monitoring sites, which are leveraged by funds from State, tribal, and local partners. In addition to program increases for activities related to WaterSMART and hydraulic fracturing, a program increase of $7.2 million for streamgages will fund more than 400 streamgages, strengthening the Federal backbone at high priority sites sensitive to drought, flooding, and the potential effects of climate change. The 2014 budget includes program increases of $1.0 million for streamgage research and development to lower the costs of next generation streamgage technologies and $1.0 million to enhance water quality studies. A $1.0 million program increase is included in the budget to provide water science and technical support to Tribes, in coordination with other relevant Interior offices and in support of tribal trust responsibilities. The budget also includes program increases totaling $2.9 million for ecosystem restoration efforts in the Chesapeake Bay, California Bay-Delta, Puget Sound, and Upper Mississippi River. These increases are offset by refocusing lower priority work toward these higher priority efforts.

Core Science Systems – The 2014 budget provides $137.2 million for Core Science Systems, $22.9 million above the 2012 enacted level. This activity provides the Nation with access to science, information, and geospatial frameworks used to manage natural resources and plan for and respond to natural hazards. Biologic and geologic data archives and geospatial data in The National Map provide critical data about the Earth, its complex processes and natural resources. The budget includes a program increase of $9.0 million to coordinate and implement the Big Earth Data Initiative for the Department of the Interior. This interagency initiative will improve access to and use of data from the satellite, airborne, terrestrial, and ocean-based Earth observing systems that the Department, and particularly the USGS, invest millions of dollars in every year. These investments in data will provide wide-ranging benefits in natural resource management and hazard mitigation, by providing access to information critical for decisionmaking, scientific discovery, and technological innovation.

The USGS also will work with other mission areas to centralize and consolidate data sets, software applications, models, and other tools into a streamlined online format to promote greater accessibility, collaboration, and a reduction in duplication. The 2014 budget includes a program increase of $9.0 million for the 3-D Elevation Program to collect LIDAR data, which are used for a wide range of critical applications including mapping, agriculture, flood inundation prediction, and ecosystem restoration. Data collection will be coordinated with other agencies to implement a national LIDAR program. In conjunction with this effort, a program increase of $1.0 million will enhance LIDAR data collection and mapping in Alaska. In addition to increases for WaterSMART and hydraulic fracturing, the budget also includes program increases totaling $2.3 million for data preservation activities, ecosystem informatics, coastal and ocean science, and ecosystem restoration activities in the Columbia River and Puget Sound. These increases are partially offset by a reduction in lower priority activities.

Administration and Enterprise Information – The 2014 budget includes $115.6 million for Administration and Enterprise Information, a $1.3 million decrease below the 2012 enacted level. This activity funds the executive, managerial, and accounting activities, information technology, and bureau support services of USGS. The budget includes a program increase of $1.0 million to put young Americans to work providing science to support the protection, restoration, and enhancement of public and tribal lands and waters. The AEI activity includes a reduction of $3.1 million in administrative services within the USGS.

Facilities – The 2014 President's budget request provides $104.5 million for Facilities, $4.1 million above the 2012 enacted level. This activity provides safe, functional workspace, laboratories, and other facilities needed to accomplish the USGS scientific mission. The increase will be used to reduce the facilities footprint nationwide by consolidating and improving the efficiency of space and real property.

Fixed Costs – Fixed costs of $10.4 million are fully funded in the budget.

SUMMARY OF BUREAU APPROPRIATIONS
(all dollar amounts in thousands)

Comparison of 2014 Request with 2012 Enacted

	2012 Enacted		2014 Request		Change	
	FTE	Amount	FTE	Amount	FTE	Amount
Current						
Surveys, Investigations, and Research	5,466	1,068,032	5,531	1,166,855	+65	+98,823
Subtotal, Current	5,466	1,068,032	5,531	1,166,855	+65	+98,823

Comparison of 2014 Estimates with 2013 Estimates

	2013 Estimates		2014 Estimates		Change	
	FTE	Amount	FTE	Amount	FTE	Amount
Permanent						
Operations and Maintenance of Quarters	0	40	0	42	0	+2
Contributed Funds	11	1,122	6	1,081	-5	-41
Subtotal, Permanent	11	1,162	6	1,123	-5	-39
Reimbursable, Allocation, and Other						
Reimbursements	2,823	0	2,838	0	+15	0
Allocation	14	0	27	0	+13	0
Working Capital Fund	204	0	244	0	+40	0
Subtotal, Reimbursable, Allocation, Other	3,041	0	3,109	0	+68	0

HIGHLIGHTS OF BUDGET CHANGES
By Appropriation Activity/Subactivity

APPROPRIATION: Surveys, Investigations, and Research

	2013 Full Year CR	2012 Enacted	2014 Request	Change from 2012
Ecosystems				
Status and Trends	21,733	21,733	21,871	+138
Fisheries	22,172	22,172	26,827	+4,655
Wildlife	47,978	46,978	50,785	+3,807
Environments	36,620	36,120	44,473	+8,353
Invasive Species	13,824	12,824	18,250	+5,426
Cooperative Research Units	18,441	18,441	18,566	+125
Subtotal, Ecosystems	160,768	158,268	180,772	+22,504
Climate and Land Use Change				
Climate Variability	58,189	58,189	71,741	+13,552
Land Use Change	83,350	83,214	84,251	+1,037
Subtotal, Climate/Land Use Change	141,539	141,403	155,992	+14,589
Energy, Minerals, and Envirnmtl Health				
Mineral Resources	48,760	48,760	46,357	-2,403
Energy Resources	28,820	27,570	31,001	+3,431
Contaminant Biology	9,180	9,180	13,955	+4,775
Toxic Substances Hydrology	10,580	10,580	16,134	+5,554
Subtotal, Energy, Minerals, and Environmental Health	97,340	96,090	107,447	+11,357
Natural Hazards				
Earthquake Hazards	54,379	53,879	57,924	+4,045
Volcano Hazards	24,122	24,122	24,698	+576
Landslide Hazards	3,168	3,168	3,693	+525
Global Seismographic Network	5,151	5,151	5,166	+15
Geomagnetism	2,004	2,004	2,127	+123
Coastal and Marine Geology	42,221	42,821	48,954	+6,133
Subtotal, Natural Hazards	131,045	131,145	142,562	+11,417
Water Resources				
Groundwater Resources	8,731	8,731	12,722	+3,991
National Water Quality Assessment	61,570	61,570	62,043	+473
National Streamflow Info Program	28,977	28,977	36,245	+7,268
Hydrologic Research/Development	12,667	11,417	16,365	+4,948
Hydrologic Networks and Analysis	30,597	29,797	31,480	+1,683
Cooperative Water Program	62,632	62,632	63,014	+382
Water Resources Research Act Prog	6,490	6,490	1,000	-5,490
Subtotal, Water Resources	211,664	209,614	222,869	+13,255
Core Science Systems				
Science Synthesis, Analysis, and Research	25,888	25,388	36,143	+10,755
Natl Cooperative Geologic Mapping	25,901	25,901	28,259	+2,358
National Geospatial Program	63,188	62,988	72,772	+9,784
Subtotal, Core Science Systems	114,977	114,277	137,174	+22,897

	2013 Full Year CR	2012 Enacted	2014 Request	Change from 2012
Administration and Enterprise Information				
Science Support	91,786	91,786	91,010	-776
Security and Technology	25,028	25,028	24,548	-480
Subtotal, Administration and Enterprise Information	116,814	116,814	115,558	-1,256
Facilities				
Rental Payments and Operations and Maintenance	93,141	93,141	97,201	+4,060
Deferred Maintenance and Capital Improvement	7,280	7,280	7,280	0
Subtotal, Facilities	100,421	100,421	104,481	+4,060
TOTAL APPROPRIATION _(w/o transfers)_	1,074,568	1,068,032	1,166,855	+98,823
Transfers	0	806	0	-806
TOTAL APPROPRIATION _(w/ transfers)_	1,074,568	1,068,838	1,166,855	+98,017

Detail of Budget Changes

	2014 Change from 2012 Enacted		2014 Change from 2012 Enacted
TOTAL APPROPRIATION	+98,823		
Ecosystems	+22,504	Ecosystem Priority	
Status and Trends	+138	Everglades	+1,000
General Program Reduction	-145	Great Lakes Restoration Initiative	
Fixed Costs	+283	Asian Carp Control Framework	+2,000
Fisheries Program	+4,655	Upper Mississppi River	
Ecosystem Priority		Asian Carp Control	+1,000
Klamath Basin Restoration Agreement	+901	New and Emerging Invasives of	
Hydraulic Fracturing	+2,200	National Concern	+874
WaterSMART Water Quality Enhancement	+1,386	General Program Reduction	-59
General Program Reduction	-172	Fixed Costs	+111
Fixed Costs	+340	Cooperative Research Units	+125
Wildlife Program	+3,807	General Program Reduction	-132
Energy Future and Wildlife Sustainability	+2,000	Fixed Costs	+257
White-nose Syndrome	+1,505	Climate and Land Use Change	+14,589
General Program Reduction	-320	Climate Variability	+13,552
Fixed Costs	+622	Climate Adaptation and Resiliency	
Environments Program	+8,353	Vulnerability Assessment Database	
Coral Reef Health	+442	Field Guide	+800
Ecosystem Priority		Interagency Coordination	+3,223
California Bay Delta	+1,000	Tribal Climate Science Partnerships	+2,500
Chesapeake Bay	+615	Translational Science Grants	+3,500
Columbia River	+300	Emerging Science Needs	+3,172
Puget Sound	+369	Biologic Carbon Sequestration	+2,958
Sustaining Environmental Capital	+2,000	Geologic Carbon Sequestration	-532
National Ecosystems Services Framework	+1,000	General Program Reduction	-300
General Program Reduction	-283	Science Support for Interior Bureaus	
Science Support for Interior Bureaus		Internal Transfer	-2,358
Internal Transfer	+2,358	Fixed Costs	+589
Fixed Costs	+552	Land Use Change	+1,037
Invasive Species	+5,426	Ecosystem Priority	
Brown Tree Snake	+500	Chesapeake Bay	+500
		Land Use Science	+1,000

	2014 Change from 2012 Enacted
Rapid Disaster Response	
Scenarios and Crisis Response	+757
WaterSMART	+136
National Civil Applications Program	
Civil Applications Committee	-576
North America Data Buy	-1,000
General Program Reduction	-236
Fixed Costs	+456
Energy, Minerals, and Environmental Health	+11,357
Mineral Resources	-2,403
Rare Earth Elements Research	+1,000
High Priority Research on Critical Minerals	+1,130
Minerals Resources	-1,000
Minerals Information	-1,157
Research and Assessment	-2,803
General Program Reduction	-439
Fixed Costs	+866
Energy Resources	+3,431
Alternative Energy Permitting	
on Federal Lands	+2,000
Hydraulic Fracturing	+1,250
General Program Reduction	-189
Fixed Costs	+370
Contaminant Biology	+4,775
Ecosystem Priority	
Chesapeake Bay	+100
Columbia River	+100
Hydraulic Fracturing	+1,400
WaterSMART	
Water Quality Enhancement	+1,000
Emerging Contaminants/Chemical Mixtures	+1,000
Pathogens and Contaminants	+611
Environmental Impacts of Uranium Mining	+500
General Program Reduction	-67
Fixed Costs	+131
Toxic Substances Hydrology	+5,554
Ecosystem Priority	
Chesapeake Bay	+100
Columbia River	+100
WaterSMART	
Water Quality Enhancement	+1,800
Emerging Contaminants/Chemical Mixtures	+1,000
Environmental Impacts of Uranium Mining	+2,500
General Program Reduction	-57
Fixed Costs	+111
Natural Hazards	+11,417
Earthquake Hazards	+4,045
Hydraulic Fracturing	+1,700
Rapid Disaster Response	
Robust Monitoring Networks	+850
Eastern U.S. Earthquake Research and	
Assessment/Transportable Array in	
Central and Eastern U.S.	+1,200
General Program Reduction	-312
Fixed Costs	+607

	2014 Change from 2012 Enacted
Volcano Hazards	+576
Rapid Disaster Response	
Early Warning Networks	+400
General Program Reduction	-188
Fixed Costs	+364
Landslide Hazards	+525
Rapid Disaster Response	
Early Warning Networks	+500
General Program Reduction	-27
Fixed Costs	+52
Global Seismographic Network	+15
General Program Reduction	-17
Fixed Costs	+32
Geomagnetism	+123
Enhanced Monitoring	+108
General Program Reduction	-17
Fixed Costs	+32
Coastal and Marine Geology	+6,133
Science for Coastal and Ocean Stewardship	+5,750
Enhanced Coastal Storm Response Capability	+850
3-D Elevation Program	
Enhanced Elevation for the Nation	
Coastal LIDAR	+2,000
Great Lakes Beach Health Study	-600
Management-Supporting	
Habitat and Service Mapping	-2,150
General Program Reduction	-300
Fixed Costs	+583
Water Resources	+13,255
Groundwater Resources	+3,991
Hydraulic Fracturing	+2,100
WaterSMART	
Groundwater Network	+627
Baseflow, Recharge, and Regional	
Availability	+1,200
General Program Reduction	-69
Fixed Costs	+133
National Water Quality Assessment	+473
Ecosystem Priority	
California Bay Delta	+1,000
Chesapeake Bay	+500
Upper Mississippi River	+200
WaterSMART	
National/Regional Synopsis and Surveys	+500
Predictive Models	+500
Program and Information Management	+500
Water Quality Enhancement	+1,800
Methods Development and Assessments	-5,000
General Program Reduction	-500
Fixed Costs	+973
National Streamflow Information Program	+7,268
Streamgages	+7,161
General Program Reduction	-114
Fixed Costs	+221
Hydrologic Research and Development	+4,948

	2014 Change from 2012 Enacted
Ecosystem Priority	
California Bay Delta	+982
Puget Sound	+200
Hydraulic Fracturing	+2,200
WaterSMART	
Streamflow and Stressors to Hydrology	+300
Streamgage Research and Development	+1,000
General Program Reduction	-280
Fixed Costs	+546
Hydrologic Networks and Analysis	+1,683
WaterSMART	
Ecological Flows	+746
Ecological Water Science	+100
Estimating Water Budget	+100
Program and Information Management	+1,400
Data Collection and Research	-867
General Program Reduction	-219
Fixed Costs	+423
Cooperative Water Program	+382
WaterSMART	
Water Use Research	+1,500
Streamflow Estimation	+500
NAQWA Related Studies	+1,000
Tribes	+1,000
Interpretive Studies/Assessments	-4,000
General Program Reduction	-403
Fixed Costs	+785
Water Resources Research Act Program	-5,490
Water Resources Research Act Program	-5,490
General Program Reduction	-4
Fixed Costs	+4
Core Science Systems	+22,897
Science Synthesis, Analysis and	
Research Program	+10,755
Ecosystem Priority Eco Informa	+800
Hydraulic Fracturing	+185
Geological/Geophysical Data Preservation	+400
Science for Coastal and Ocean Stewardship	+300
Earth and Environmental Observations	
Innovation and Applications-	
Big Earth Data Initiative	+9,000
General Program Reduction	-100
Fixed Costs	+170

	2014 Change from 2012 Enacted
National Cooperative Geologic Mapping	+2,358
Hydraulic Fracturing	+2,000
WaterSMART	
Information Management	+200
General Program Reduction	-165
Fixed Costs	+323
National Geospatial Program	+9,784
Ecosystem Priority	
Columbia River	+354
Puget Sound	+450
WaterSMART	
Information Management	+200
3-D Elevation Program	
Enhanced Elevation for the Nation - LIDAR	+9,000
Alaska Mapping	+1,044
Federal Geographic Data Committee	-1,697
General Program Reduction	-460
Fixed Costs	+893
Administration and Enterprise Information	-1,256
Science Support	-776
Earth Scientists for Tomorrow -	
Youth in the Great Outdoors	+1,000
Reduction to Administrative Services	-1,906
General Program Reduction	-22
Fixed Costs	+152
Security and Technology	-480
Reduction to Administrative Services	-1,229
General Program Reduction	-165
Fixed Costs	+437
Fixed Costs IT Transformation	+477
Facilities	+4,060
Rental Payments and Operations and Maintenance	+4,060
Operations and Maintenance Efficiencies to Reduce Facilities Footprint	+6,385
General Program Reduction	-868
Fixed Costs Including Rent	-1,457

Subtotals for Changes Across Multiple Subactivities	
Fixed Costs	[+10,438]

FISH AND WILDLIFE SERVICE

Mission – The mission of the Fish and Wildlife Service is to work with others to conserve, protect, and enhance fish, wildlife, plants, and their habitats for the continuing benefit of the American people.

Budget Overview – The 2014 President's budget request for current appropriations totals $1.6 billion, an increase of $76.4 million compared to the 2012 level. The budget also includes $1.2 billion available under permanent appropriations, most of which will be provided directly to States for fish and wildlife restoration and conservation. The FWS estimates staffing will equal 9,518 full time equivalents in 2014, an increase of 150 FTE from the 2012 level.

America's Great Outdoors Initiative – In 2014, a total of $1.6 billion is proposed for FWS as part of the Administration's initiative to reconnect Americans to the outdoors. This includes $1.3 billion for FWS operations, an increase of $68.9 million over the 2012 level. A critical component of America's Great Outdoors is the national wildlife refuge system, which has unique authorities and flexible programs that deliver landscape level conservation, while providing compatible outdoor recreation. The FWS Endangered Species program, working in partnership with States, Tribes, conservation groups, and others, has successfully encouraged private landowners to protect and restore habitat for listed and candidate species under the Endangered Species Act. The Fisheries program carries out its aquatic resources conservation work through a nationwide network of over 150 facilities that includes national fish hatcheries, fish and wildlife conservation offices, fish health centers, and fish technology centers. These facilities are neighbors to communities across the Nation, providing significant contributions to Americans by hosting a variety of annual outdoor and classroom events that reconnect youth and their families to the Nation's natural resource heritage.

In 2014, FWS will extend a landscape level conservation approach to river systems throughout the Country under the Administration's National Blueways System. Rivers play a vital role in connecting Americans with the lands and waters that provide economic, recreational, social, cultural, and ecological value to their communities.

FWS Funding

The National Blueways System, established by Secretary Salazar in May, 2012, provides a new emphasis on the unique value and significance of a comprehensive "headwaters to mouth" approach to river management and creates a mechanism to encourage stakeholders to integrate their land and water stewardship efforts. The budget request includes a programmatic increase of $3.3 million for FWS to lead Department-wide implementation of this collaborative program. Funds will be available to Interior bureaus including BLM, Reclamation, FWS, and NPS as grants and cooperative agreements. Projects will be selected via a joint decision-making process of the National Blueways Committee, consisting of members from these bureaus.

The 2014 budget includes increases for programs funded through the Land and Water Conservation Fund, a vital component of the America's Great Outdoors initiative. The 2014 budget includes $106.3 million for Federal land acquisition, which includes $70.8 million in current funding and $35.5 million in permanent funding, an increase of $51.7 million above the 2012 level. The 2014 Federal Land Acquisition program builds on efforts started in 2011 to strategically invest in interagency landscape-scale conservation projects while continuing to meet

FISH AND WILDLIFE SERVICE
FACTS

- Originated in 1871 with the purpose of studying and recommending solutions to a decline in food fish.
- Manages nearly 150 million acres of land and waters in the national wildlife refuge system composed of 561 national wildlife refuges and thousands of small wetlands.
- Operates 73 national fish hatcheries, 65 fishery resource offices, and 80 ecological services field stations nationwide.
- Produces the Federal Duck Stamp, which raises nearly $25 million annually to fund wetland habitat acquisition for the national wildlife refuge system.
- Employs over 10,000 staff nationwide and over 45,000 volunteers contribute in excess of 1.5 million hours annually.

agency-specific programmatic needs. The Department of the Interior and U.S. Forest Service collaborated extensively to more effectively coordinate land acquisitions with government and local community partners to achieve the highest priority shared conservation goals. In addition, the budget proposes an increase above the 2012 level of $36.3 million for the Cooperative Endangered Species Conservation Fund, of which $28.0 million is associated with the LWCF permanent funding proposal.

The budget requests funds for grant programs administered by FWS that support America's Great Outdoors goals. The request proposes an increase of $3.9 million for the North American Wetlands Conservation Fund, supported by sportsmen and conservationists alike. Funding for State fish and wildlife efforts is maintained for the State and Tribal Wildlife Grants at the 2012 level of $61.3 million.

New Energy Frontier – The budget proposes $17.5 million, an increase of $7.4 million, for activities associated with energy development, including program increases of $1.5 million for the Endangered Species Consultation program to support assessments of renewable energy projects, $2.8 million for renewable energy Conservation Planning Assistance, $750,000 to strengthen migratory bird conservation in areas with wind energy development, and $1.0 million to bolster FWS law enforcement activities to help address the impact of new energy development and ongoing energy production on wildlife and wildlife habitat. These increases will enable FWS to participate more fully in priority landscape level planning and assist industry and State fish and wildlife agencies to site renewable energy projects and transmission corridor infrastructure in areas likely to reduce environmental conflict. The request also includes an increase of $1.4 million for scientific research to identify impacts from

energy transmission infrastructure and development in the American West and inform mitigation strategies.

Cooperative Recovery – Nearly 300 species listed as threatened or endangered are found in or around units of the refuge system and 59 wildlife refuges were established for the purpose of recovering threatened and endangered species. Human demands on the environment combined with environmental stressors are creating an urgent need for conservation. Only through cooperative efforts can the Nation successfully recover its most imperiled species: endangered, threatened, and candidate wildlife and plants. The budget request supports the Cooperative Recovery initiative to implement recovery plan actions in and around wildlife refuges. Combining the resources of multiple FWS programs, this national, proposal-driven process identifies and implements the highest priority projects with the likelihood of achieving recovery on-the-ground or preventing extinction. The budget requests a program increase for Cooperative Recovery totaling $9.4 million, including $3.2 million for Refuge Wildlife and Habitat Management, $1.9 million for Endangered Species, $1.5 million for Partners for Fish and Wildlife, $1.5 million for Fisheries Population Assessment, $770,000 for Service Science, and $500,000 for Migratory Birds.

Resource Management – The 2014 request for the principal FWS operating account, Resource Management, is $1.3 billion, an increase of $68.9 million above the 2012 level. The increase includes $17.3 million for fixed costs, $55.0 million in net program increases, and a reduction of $3.4 million to reflect the movement of refuge land protection planning activities to the Land Acquisition appropriation. The 2014 FWS budget proposes a total of $15.9 million across the operating account to introduce children and young adults to the importance of fish and wildlife conservation and encourage careers in natural science through work on conservation projects, habitat management, and visitor services at wildlife refuges.

Endangered Species – The budget includes $185.4 million to administer the Endangered Species Act, an increase of $9.5 million compared with the 2012 level. In addition to programmatic increases provided for renewable energy and cooperative recovery projects, the budget includes a program increase of $1.0 million for science to support pesticide consultations. A net increase of $1.8 million is requested for listing activities.

Habitat Conservation – The budget includes $114.4 million for Habitat Conservation, an increase of $3.8 million compared with the 2012 level. This includes programmatic increases of $2.8 million for renewable energy and $1.5 million for cooperative recovery.

Environmental Contaminants – The budget includes $13.2 million for Environmental Contaminants, an increase of $98,000 compared with the 2012 level. Contaminants funding will be used primarily to increase restoration activities and, to a lesser extent, initiate injury assessment investigations associated with Natural Resource Damage Assessment and Restoration cases. Additionally, this funding will support ongoing NRDAR efforts resulting from the Deepwater Horizon incident and the implementation of the Resources and Ecosystems Sustainability, Tourist Opportunities and Revived Economies of the Gulf Coast States Act.

National Wildlife Refuge System – Funding for the operation and maintenance of the national wildlife refuge system is requested at $499.2 million, an increase of $13.5 million above the 2012 level. In addition to programmatic increases for cooperative recovery activities and the National Blueways System, the request includes programmatic increases of $3.0 million for the refuge inventory and monitoring program to develop baseline scientific data on ecological conditions across the refuge system, $3.6 million for Challenge Cost Share partnerships, and $1.3 million for refuge law enforcement activities to support a multi-bureau initiative to improve and consolidate radio infrastructure. These increases are partially offset by program reductions totaling $4.3 million. The budget also moves $3.4 million from the Resource Management account to the Land Acquisition account for Land Protection Planning program activities.

Migratory Bird Management – The budget request includes $50.1 million for the Migratory Bird Management program, a reduction of $1.4 million from the 2012 level. This request includes program increases of $500,000 for cooperative recovery activities and $750,000 to respond to increasing numbers of permit requests from the energy industry for compliance with the Endangered Species Act, Migratory Bird Treaty Act, and Bald and Golden Eagle Protection Act. To fund higher priority conservation activities, the budget includes program reductions of $250,000 for Junior Duck Stamp activities and $2.2 million for Avian Health and Disease.

Law Enforcement – The budget provides $68.3 million for the law enforcement program to investigate wildlife crimes and enforce the laws that govern the Nation's wildlife trade, an increase of $6.1 million over the 2012 level. The request includes a program increase of $1.0 million to strengthen enforcement of conservation laws such as the Bald and Golden Eagle Protection Act in areas with energy development and a general program increase of $4.2 million for enforcement of the Lacey Act, to address technical challenges in wildlife science forensics and support partnerships with foreign governments to reduce demand for illegal wildlife products.

International Affairs – The budget request includes a total of $13.5 million, an increase of $535,000 over the 2012 level. Increased funding will support conservation activities that target market and consumer demands for illegal products, which are driving a rapid increase in poaching of flagship species such as tigers, elephants, and rhinos.

Science Support – The 2014 request for Science Support is $33.3 million, a programmatic increase of $11.8 million above the 2012 level. This new subactivity was formerly included within the Cooperative Landscape Conservation and Adaptive Science subactivity. In 2014, FWS will separate funding for Cooperative Landscape Conservation from Science Support to enable broader application of science to activities across the FWS and Landscape Conservation Cooperatives. The budget request supports applied science to address high impact questions surrounding threats to fish and wildlife resources to provide the answers needed on-the-ground to manage species to healthy, sustainable, desired levels.

The 2014 request includes a program increase of $770,000 for cooperative recovery and a program increase of $1.5 million to direct, focus, and accelerate the science efforts of partnering universities, cooperative wildlife units, and other institutions to answer some of the remaining questions about how to address and mitigate the threats posed by the white-nose syndrome on bat populations. A program increase of $1.4 million is provided to research the impacts and identify mitigation strategies related to energy transmission corridors in the American West. This energy research will identify impacts to the sage grouse and desert tortoise from energy infrastructure such as overhead transmission lines and solar arrays. Additional science funding of $2.9 million will support ecosystem and landscape scale conservation on demonstration landscapes, climate adaptation implementation, invasive species early detection and rapid response, and biological carbon sequestration.

Fisheries and Aquatic Resource Conservation – The budget request includes a total of $140.9 million for the Fisheries and Aquatic Resource Conservation program, an increase of $5.6 million from the 2012 level. The budget includes program increases of $1.5 million for cooperative recovery, as well as $1.5 million for fish passage improvements, $1.6 million for authorized activities to support the Klamath Basin Restoration Agreement, and $5.9 million to address the invasion of Asian carp in the Great Lakes and priority watersheds including the Missouri, Ohio, and Upper Mississippi River watersheds. These increases are offset by reductions in other program activities, including a $2.3 million program reduction for costs associated with subsistence fishing.

Cooperative Landscape Conservation – The budget request funds Cooperative Landscape Conservation at $17.6 million, an increase of $2.1 million above the 2012 level. The FWS will focus funding and support on those LCCs best able to deliver priority conservation outcomes as defined by LCC partners. Targeted funding will provide for continued development of critical partnerships associated with LCCs and will focus efforts to directly benefit fish, wildlife, plants, and their habitats.

General Operations – The General Operations request totals $159.1 million, an increase of $12.5 million above the 2012 level. The request includes a program increase of $2.5 million for a FWS-wide effort led by the National Conservation Training Center to introduce youth to the outdoors and natural sciences. The request also includes an increase of $1.0 million for the National Fish and Wildlife Foundation for the Landscape Conservation Stewardship Program to build capacity with community partners to strengthen collaborative efforts to conserve large landscapes, and a program increase of $1.0 million to improve tribal consultation associated with expanded landscape conservation. Included in General Operations is a transfer of $4.2 million from other activities within Resource Management to the FWS Office of Diversity and other changes attributable primarily to fixed costs.

Construction – The 2014 Construction budget request totals $15.7 million, a decrease of $7.3 million below the 2012 level. The budget request includes $6.7 million for line-item construction projects, a $5.5 million reduction from 2012. The specific refuge and fish hatchery projects funded within the request are ranked as the top priorities using the FWS merit-based process to identify projects in the five-year construction plan.

Land Acquisition – The 2014 budget proposal includes $106.3 million for Federal land acquisition, composed of $70.8 million in current funding and $35.5 million in proposed permanent funding. The budget provides an overall increase of $51.7 million above the 2012 level to strategically invest in interagency landscape-scale conservation projects while continuing to meet agency-specific programmatic needs. This increase continues the Administration's commitment to protect sensitive areas where land acquisition is needed to conserve important habitat. The Department of the Interior and the U.S. Forest Service collaborated extensively to develop a process to more effectively coordinate land acquisitions with government and local community partners to achieve the highest priority shared conservation goals.

Included in the budget is $37.7 million for high priority line-item acquisition projects, selected using a strategic, merit-based process with a focus on landscape conservation goals, leveraging with non-Federal partners, alignment with other Interior bureau projects, and collaboration with Federal agencies, Tribes, States, and other partners. Interior land acquisition bureaus worked together to align and prioritize projects to optimize landscape conservation goals. In 2014, FWS requests $45.9 million for collaborative projects in the Longleaf Pine, Crown of the Continent, and Desert Southwest landscapes and National Trails.

Funding to administer land acquisition projects totals $22.8 million in 2014. Of this amount, $3.4 million results from the movement of the Land Protection Planning program from the Resource Management account to the Land Acquisition account.

Cooperative Endangered Species Conservation Fund – The budget includes a total of $84.0 million for the Cooperative Endangered Species Conservation Fund to support America's Great Outdoors using current grant authorities. Of the total funding, $56.0 million is requested from current funds while an additional $28.0 million in permanent funding is included as part of the LWCF legislative proposal to be submitted to Congress. The current funds include $12.6 million for conservation grants to States, $7.0 million for Habitat Conservation Planning Assistance grants, $15.5 million to support Species Recovery Land Acquisition, $17.9 million for Habitat Conservation Plans Land Acquisition Grants to States, and $3.0 million for administrative costs.

National Wildlife Refuge Fund – The budget request eliminates the current funding contribution to the National Wildlife Refuge Fund, a reduction of $14.0 million below 2012. Since these payments distributed to counties can be used for any purpose, the current funding contribution does not significantly address conservation goals. The permanent receipts under the program will remain a source of revenue for counties.

North American Wetlands Conservation Fund – The 2014 budget request is $39.4 million for the North American Wetlands Conservation Fund, an increase of $3.9 million over the 2012 level. Funded projects are leveraged by more than one-to-one with partners for wetlands and waterfowl conservation to support conservation and important sportsman activities.

Multinational Species Conservation Fund – The 2014 budget request includes $9.8 million for the Multinational Species Conservation Fund, an increase of $321,000 above the 2012 level. These grants are critical to the protection of African and Asian elephants, rhinoceros, tigers, great apes, and marine turtles and leverage funds from partners to nearly triple the available funding for these important species.

Neotropical Migratory Bird Conservation Fund – The 2014 request includes $3.8 million for the Neotropical Migratory Bird Conservation Fund, maintaining the 2012 level. Grants for the conservation of migratory birds are matched at least three-to-one by partners throughout the western hemisphere.

State and Tribal Wildlife Grants – The State and Tribal Wildlife Grants budget request is $61.3 million, maintaining the 2012 level. These grants support high priority species conservation by States. In addition, the request shifts $7.3 million of the amount directed to States through formula grants to a competitive allocation. This change will help to target grants toward the highest priority conservation challenges and promote multi-State landscape level planning.

Duck Stamp Legislative Proposal – The budget includes a proposal to increase the cost of a Federal Migratory Bird Hunting and Conservation Stamp to $25.00 per year, beginning in 2014, from its current cost of $15.00. With the additional receipts, the Department anticipates acquisition of approximately 7,000 additional acres in fee simple and approximately 10,000 additional conservation easement acres in 2014 to benefit waterfowl habitat. The legislation also proposes the price of a Federal Migratory Bird Hunting and Conservation Stamp can be increased after 2014 by the Secretary with approval of the Migratory Bird Conservation Commission.

Fixed Costs – Fixed costs increases of $17.6 million over the 2012 level are fully funded.

SUMMARY OF BUREAU APPROPRIATIONS
(all dollar amounts in thousands)

Comparison of 2014 Request with 2012 Enacted

	2012 Enacted		2014 Request		Change	
	FTE	Amount	FTE	Amount	FTE	Amount
Current						
Resource Management	7,436	1,226,177	7,560	1,295,085	+124	+68,908
Construction	82	23,051	67	15,722	-15	-7,329
Land Acquisition	86	54,632	106	70,833	+20	+16,201
Cooperative Endangered Species Fund	18	47,681	18	56,000	0	+8,319
National Wildlife Refuge Fund	0	13,958	0	0	0	-13,958
North American Wetlands Conservation Fund	9	35,497	9	39,425	0	+3,928
Multinational Species Conservation Fund	4	9,466	4	9,787	0	+321
Neotropical Migratory Bird Grants	1	3,786	1	3,786	0	0
State and Tribal Wildlife Grants	23	61,323	23	61,323	0	0
Subtotal, Current	7,659	1,475,571	7,788	1,551,961	+129	+76,390

Comparison of 2013 Estimate with 2014 Estimate

	2013 Estimate		2014 Estimate		Change	
	FTE	Amount	FTE	Amount	FTE	Amount
Permanent						
Federal Lands Recreation Enhancement Act	32	5,100	32	5,100	0	0
Land Acquisition	0	0	0	35,497	0	+35,497
Migratory Bird Conservation Account	65	52,000	75	66,000	+10	+14,000
National Wildlife Refuge Fund	11	8,000	11	8,000	0	0
North American Wetlands Conservation Fund	0	500	0	700	0	+200
Sport Fish Restoration Account	60	462,662	60	420,516	0	-42,146
Federal Aid in Wildlife Restoration	53	570,644	53	610,652	0	+40,008
Miscellaneous Permanent Appropriations	5	4,198	5	3,760	0	-438
Contributed Funds	18	3,000	18	3,000	0	0
Cooperative Endangered Species Fund	0	62,636	0	89,524	0	+26,888
Coastal Impact Assistance Program	15	0	15	0	0	0
Subtotal, Permanent	259	1,168,740	269	1,242,749	+10	+74,009
Reimbursement and Transfer						
Reimbursements	871	0	928	0	+57	0
Energy Policy Act	13	0	13	0	0	0
Southern Nevada Public Lands Management Act	21	0	21	0	0	0
Wildland Fire Management	453	0	398	0	-55	0
Natural Resource Damage Assessment	72	0	72	0	0	0
Central Hazardous Materials	7	0	7	0	0	0
Federal Roads (FHWA)	21	0	21	0	0	0
Forest Pest (Agriculture)	1	0	1	0	0	0
Subtotal, Reimbursement and Transfer	1,459	0	1,461	0	+2	0

HIGHLIGHTS OF BUDGET CHANGES
By Appropriation Activity/Subactivity

APPROPRIATION: Resource Management

	2013 Full Year CR	2012 Enacted	2014 Request	Change from 2012
Ecological Services				
Endangered Species				
Candidate Conservation	11,439	11,337	11,530	+193
Listing	20,997	20,869	22,622	+1,753
Consultation	61,673	60,943	64,751	+3,808
Recovery	81,483	82,806	86,543	+3,737
Subtotal, Endangered Species	175,592	175,955	185,446	+9,491
Habitat Conservation	109,052	110,637	114,407	+3,770
Environmental Contaminants	11,495	13,128	13,226	+98
Subtotal, Ecological Services	296,139	299,720	313,079	+13,359
National Wildlife Refuge System				
Wildlife and Habitat Management	225,962	223,439	238,507	+15,068
Visitor Services	74,077	74,225	74,246	+21
Refuge Law Enforcement	38,261	37,373	40,085	+2,712
Conservation Planning [1]	10,034	11,704	6,674	-5,030
Subtotal, Refuge Operations	348,334	346,741	359,512	+12,771
Refuge Maintenance	138,160	138,950	139,680	+730
Subtotal, NWR System	486,494	485,691	499,192	+13,501
Migratory Birds, Law Enforcement				
and International Affairs				
Migratory Bird Management	50,856	51,453	50,062	-1,391
Law Enforcement				
Operations	61,297	61,168	67,300	+6,132
Equipment Replacement	975	975	975	0
Subtotal, Law Enforcement	62,272	62,143	68,275	+6,132
International Affairs	13,037	12,971	13,506	+535
Science Support [2]	0	0	33,276	+33,276
Subtotal, Migratory Birds, Law Enforcement, and Int'l Affairs	126,165	126,567	165,119	+38,552
Fisheries/Aquatic Resources Conservation				
National Fish Hatchery System Ops	46,075	46,075	46,528	+453
Maintenance and Equipment	17,997	18,031	17,997	-34
Aquatic Habitat and Species Conserv	73,910	71,211	76,410	+5,199
Subtotal, Fisheries/Aquatic Resources	137,982	135,317	140,935	+5,618
Cooperative Landscape Conservation and				
Adaptive Science				
Cooperative Landscape Conservation	15,534	15,475	17,615	+2,140
Adaptive Science [2]	21,493	16,723	0	-16,723
Subtotal, Cooperative Landscape Conservation/Adaptive Science	37,027	32,198	17,615	-14,583

APPROPRIATION: Resource Management *(continued)*

	2013 Full Year CR	2012 Enacted	2014 Request	Change from 2012
General Operations				
Central Office Operations	41,846	38,605	43,339	+4,734
Regional Office Operations....................	40,726	40,951	43,146	+2,195
Operational Support..............................	36,207	36,039	37,819	+1,780
Nat'l Conservation Training Center	23,570	23,564	26,316	+2,752
Nat'l Fish and Wildlife Foundation	7,525	7,525	8,525	+1,000
Subtotal, General Operations	149,874	146,684	159,145	+12,461
TOTAL APPROPRIATION *(w/o transfers)*	1,233,681	1,226,177	1,295,085	+68,908
Transfers	0	9,000	0	-9,000
TOTAL APPROPRIATION *(w/ transfers)*	1,233,681	1,235,177	1,295,085	+59,908

1/ *In 2014, the Land Protection Planning program is moved from the Resource Management account to the Land Acquisition account.*

2/ *In 2014, FWS will redistribute funding for Cooperative Landscape Conservation and Adaptive Science to Science Support to enable broader application of funding for scientific activities across the FWS and Landscape Conservation Cooperatives.*

Detail of Budget Changes

	2014 Change from 2012 Enacted
TOTAL APPROPRIATION	+68,908

	2014 Change from 2012 Enacted			2014 Change from 2012 Enacted
Ecological Services...	+13,359	Internal Transfers...	-346
Endangered Species	+9,491	Fixed Costs	+566
Candidate Conservation...................................	+193	Coastal Programs..	+78
Internal Transfers...	-33	General Program Activities.............................	-69
Fixed Costs	+226	Internal Transfers...	-30
Listing...	+1,753	Fixed Costs	+177
Critical Habitat...	-2,945	National Wetlands Inventory............................	+555
Listing...	+4,459	General Program Activities.............................	+521
Internal Transfers...	-55	Internal Transfers...	-8
Fixed Costs	+294	Fixed Costs	+42
Consultation...	+3,808	Environmental Contaminants	+98
Renewable Energy..	+1,500	General Program Activities.............................	+198
Pesticide Consultations.................................	+1,000	Internal Transfers...	-289
Tribal Consultations	+510	Fixed Costs	+189
General Program Activities.............................	+70		
Internal Transfers...	-190	National Wildlife Refuge System.............................	+13,501
Fixed Costs	+918	Wildlife and Habitat Management	+15,068
Recovery	+3,737	Cooperative Watershed Management	+3,250
Wolf Livestock Loss Demonstration	-998	Challenge Cost share Partnerships	+3,600
State of the Birds...	-995	Climate Change Inventory and Monitoring......	+3,000
Cooperative Recovery.....................................	+1,900	Cooperative Recovery......................................	+3,200
General Program Activities.............................	+3,108	Alaska Subsistence	-636
Internal Transfers...	-230	Feral Swine Eradication Pilot Program	-998
Fixed Costs	+952	General Program Activities.............................	+849
Habitat Conservation..	+3,770	Internal Transfers...	-86
Partners for Fish and Wildlife Program	+1,949	Fixed Costs	+2,889
Cooperative Recovery.....................................	+1,483	Visitor Services...	+21
General Program Activities.............................	+38	Youth and Careers in Nature	+128
Internal Transfers...	-112	General Program Activities.............................	-946
Fixed Costs	+540	Internal Transfers...	-288
Conservation Planning Assistance		Fixed Costs	+1,127
Project Planning..	+1,188	Refuge Law Enforcement......................................	+2,712
Renewable Energy..	+2,750	General Program Activities.............................	+1,068
General Program Activities.............................	-1,782	Radio Initiative..	+1,250

	2014 Change from 2012 Enacted
Internal Transfers	-110
Fixed Costs	+504
Refuge Conservation Planning	-5,030
Refuge Planning	-1,667
Move Land Protection Planning to Land Acquisition Account	-3,434
Internal Transfers	-87
Fixed Costs	+158
Refuge Maintenance	+730
Maintenance Support	-32
Deferred Maintenance	+604
Internal Transfers	-790
Fixed Costs	+948
Conservation, Enforcement and Science	+38,552
Migratory Birds	-1,391
Renewable Energy	+750
Cooperative Recovery	+500
Avian Health and Disease	-2,189
Junior Duck Stamp	-250
General Program Activities	-757
General Operations for Permits	+5
Internal Transfers	-111
Fixed Costs	+661
Law Enforcement	+6,132
Renewable Energy	+1,000
Tribal Consultations	+50
General Program Activities	+4,247
Internal Transfers	-121
Fixed Costs	+956
International Affairs	+535
Wildlife Without Borders	+327
Internal Transfers	-28
Fixed Costs	+236
Science Support - New Subactivity Structure	+33,276
Adaptive Science	+15,199
General Program Activities	+1,680
Biological Carbon Sequestration	+500
Internal Transfers	+12,988
Fixed Costs	+31
Service Science	+18,077
General Program Activities	+4,272
Ecosystem and Landscape Conservation	+1,400
Biological Carbon Sequestration	+500
Climate Adaptation: Invasive Species	+500
Energy Transmission Corridors	+1,400

	2014 Change from 2012 Enacted
White-nose Syndrome	+1,500
Internal Transfers	+8,505
Fisheries and Aquatic Resource Conservation	+5,618
National Fish Hatchery Operations	+453
General Program Activities	-172
Internal Transfers	-165
Fixed Costs	+790
Maintenance and Equipment	-34
Internal Transfers	-34
Aquatic Habitat and Species Conservation	+5,199
Fish Passage Improvements	+1,518
Klamath Basin Restoration Agreement	+1,610
Ecosystem Restoration - Chesapeake Bay	+145
Alaska Fisheries Subsistence	-2,254
Cooperative Recovery	+1,500
State Plans - NISA	+132
Control and Management	-507
Tribal Consultation	+180
Asian Carp	+5,903
Prevention	-149
General Program Activities	-3,789
Internal Transfers	-143
Fixed Costs	+1,053
Cooperative Landscape Conservation and Adaptive Science	-14,583
Cooperative Landscape Conservation	+2,140
General Program Activities	+2,007
Internal Transfers	-9
Fixed Costs	+142
Adaptive Science - Revised Budget Structure	-16,723
Adaptive Science - General Prog. Activities	-117
Service Science	+4,000
Cooperative Recovery	+770
Internal Transfers	-21,394
Fixed Costs	+18
General Operations	+12,461
General Program Activities	+5,380
Internal Transfers	+3,166
Fixed Costs	+3,915
Subtotals for Changes Across Multiple Subactivities	
Fixed Costs	[+17,332]

APPROPRIATION: Construction

	2013 Full Year CR	2012 Enacted	2014 Request	Change from 2012
Line Item Construction	12,208	12,129	6,661	-5,468
Dam Safety	1,113	1,113	1,113	0
Bridge Safety	739	739	739	0
Engineering Services	9,132	9,070	7,209	-1,861
TOTAL APPROPRIATION (w/o supplemental)	23,192	23,051	15,722	-7,329
Supplemental	68,200	0	0	0
TOTAL APPROPRIATION (w/ supplemental)	91,392	23,051	15,722	-7,329

See Appendix J for proposed 2014 construction projects.

Detail of Budget Changes

	2014 Change from 2012 Enacted
TOTAL APPROPRIATION	-7,329
Core Engineering Services	-1,984
Construction Projects	-5,468
Fixed Costs	+123

APPROPRIATION: Land Acquisition

	2013 Full Year CR	2012 Enacted	2014 Request	Change from 2012
Acquisition Management	12,658	12,535	12,781	+246
Land Protection Planning *	0	0	3,434	+3,434
Acquisition - Federal Refuge Lands	35,320	35,109	48,071	+12,962
Exchanges	2,496	2,496	1,500	-996
Inholdings, Emergencies, and Hardships	4,492	4,492	5,047	+555
TOTAL APPROPRIATION	54,966	54,632	70,833	+16,201

* In 2014, the Land Protection Planning program is moved from the Resource Management account to the Land Acquisition account.

See Appendix F for proposed 2014 land acquisition projects.

Detail of Budget Changes

	2014 Change from 2012 Enacted
TOTAL APPROPRIATION	+16,201
Acquisition Management	+246
Move Land Protection Planning from Resource Management account	+3,434
Land Acquisition Refuges	+12,962
Exchanges	-996
Inholdings	+249
Emergencies	+306
Fixed Costs	[+123]

APPROPRIATION: Cooperative Endangered Species Conservation Fund

	2013 Full Year CR	2012 Enacted	2014 Request	Change from 2012
Section 6 Grants to States				
Traditional Grants to States	10,593	10,529	12,601	+2,072
HCP Planning Grants	9,543	9,485	7,000	-2,485
Species Recovery Land Acquisition	10,045	9,984	15,487	+5,503
HCP Land Acquisition Grants/States..	15,068	14,976	17,938	+2,962
Administration	2,724	2,707	2,974	+267
TOTAL APPROPRIATION	47,973	47,681	56,000	+8,319

Detail of Budget Changes

	2014 Change from 2012 Enacted
TOTAL APPROPRIATION	+8,319
Traditional Grants to States	+2,072
HCP Planning Grants	-2,485
Species Recovery Land Acquisition	+5,503
HCP Land Acquisition Grants	+2,962
Administration	+267

APPROPRIATION: National Wildlife Refuge Fund

	2013 Full Year CR	2012 Enacted	2014 Request	Change from 2012
TOTAL APPROPRIATION	14,043	13,958	0	-13,958

Detail of Budget Changes

	2014 Change from 2012 Enacted
TOTAL APPROPRIATION	-13,958
Payments to Counties - Current Funds	-13,958

APPROPRIATION: North American Wetlands Conservation Fund

	2013 Full Year CR	2012 Enacted	2014 Request	Change from 2012
TOTAL APPROPRIATION	35,714	35,497	39,425	+3,928

Detail of Budget Changes

	2014 Change from 2012 Enacted
TOTAL APPROPRIATION	+3,928
Wetlands Conservation	+3,928

APPROPRIATION: Multinational Species Conservation Fund

	2013 Full Year CR	2012 Enacted	2014 Request	Change from 2012
African Elephant Conservation.................	1,655	1,645	1,805	+160
Rhinoceros and Tiger Conservation	2,481	2,471	2,632	+161
Asian Elephant Conservation....................	1,660	1,645	1,645	0
Great Ape Conservation............................	2,072	2,059	2,059	0
Marine Turtle Conservation......................	1,656	1,646	1,646	0
TOTAL APPROPRIATION	9,524	9,466	9,787	+321

Detail of Budget Changes

2014 Change from
2012 Enacted

TOTAL APPROPRIATION	+321
African Elephant Conservation..................................	+160
Rhinoceros and Tiger Conservation	+161

APPROPRIATION: Neotropical Bird Conservation

	2013 Full Year CR	2012 Enacted	2014 Request	Change from 2012
TOTAL APPROPRIATION	3,809	3,786	3,786	0

APPROPRIATION: State and Tribal Wildlife Grants

	2013 Full Year CR	2012 Enacted	2014 Request	Change from 2012
TOTAL APPROPRIATION	61,698	61,323	61,323	0

Detail of Budget Changes

2014 Change from
2012 Enacted

TOTAL APPROPRIATION	0
State Formula Grants...	-7,268
Competitive Grant Program (States)...........................	+7,268

NATIONAL PARK SERVICE

Mission – As stated in its original authorizing legislation, the National Park Service mission is to "preserve unimpaired the natural and cultural resources and values of the national park system for the enjoyment, education, and inspiration of this and future generations."

Budget Overview – The 2014 President's budget current request for NPS of $2.6 billion is $56.6 million above the 2012 enacted level. The Park Service estimates total staffing would equal 21,651 full time equivalents in 2014, a decrease of 256 FTE from 2012. The 2014 President's budget request provides net programmatic increases from 2012 totaling $26.1 million to fund essential programs and emerging operational needs, plus $30.5 million in fixed cost increases.

In 2014, NPS will continue to carry on its stewardship of cultural and natural treasures of national significance and provide enriching experiences and enjoyment for all visitors including the Nation's youth. The National Park Service will maintain its commitment to protect and restore ecosystems, preserve and conserve cultural resources, provide visitors venues for physical activity and natural experiences, and assist States and local communities to develop recreational sites and facilities and preserve historic assets. Additionally, NPS will conduct construction projects that address the highest priority health and safety projects, as well as landscape scale environmental restoration projects, as in previous years. Through these activities, NPS provides an important contribution to the national economy, contributing $30.1 billion in recreation related economic output and supporting over 252,000 American jobs in 2011.

The 2014 President's budget request provides targeted increases for park operations, programs funded through the Land and Water Conservation Fund, and historic grant programs that support the President's America's Great Outdoors initiative. Additionally, a proposal to fund a portion of NPS land acquisition and recreation grants from the LWCF as a permanent appropriation will provide an additional $55.2 million to NPS.

NPS Funding

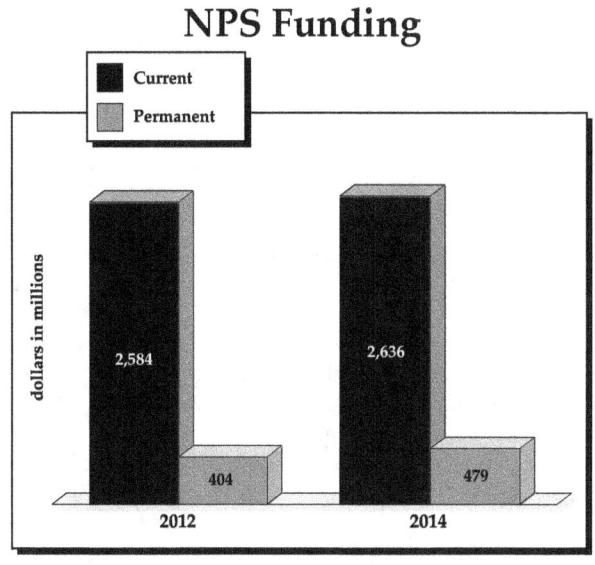

America's Great Outdoors – In 2014, a total of $2.5 billion is proposed for NPS as part of the Administration's initiative to reconnect Americans to the outdoors. This includes $2.3 billion for park operations, in the Operation of the National Park System account, a net programmatic increase of $19.5 million over 2012. The NPS will continue to engage visitors in the great outdoors and protect and interpret cultural and natural resources. The 2014 budget proposal provides several key programmatic increases, including $3.0 million to address white-nose syndrome in bats at national park units. This disease was first detected in New York State in 2006 and since then has killed millions of cave-dwelling bats and threatens bat populations in the national parks. The President's budget request also includes an increase of $2.0 million to enhance sustainable and accessible infrastructure across the national park system, ensuring access for all Americans. An additional $1.0 million, for a total $14.7 million, will be directed toward programs that foster the engagement of youth in the great outdoors. The 2014 request also continues to support important ecosystem restoration projects such as in the Everglades and Elwha River, as well as provides a $750,000 increase to NPS to participate in a multi-bureau AGO landscape initiative in the Crown of the Continent and Southwest Desert.

The 2014 budget also includes net programmatic increases of $8.2 million for current appropriations funded through the LWCF, a vital component of the America's Great Outdoors initiative. The 2014 budget proposal includes $60.4 million for Federal land acquisition, a programmatic increase of $3.4 million. This includes a total of $32.4 million for Federal acquisition projects, an increase of $1.9 million, and maintains $9.0 million in funding for American Battlefield Protection land acquisition grants for non-Federal entities. A total of $40.0 million is requested for LWCF State Conservation grants, a programmatic decrease of $5.2 million. The President's budget also requests $10.0 million to revitalize the Urban Parks and Recreation Fund, which provides matching grants and technical assistance to revitalize parks and increase access to trails, green space, and other recreational areas in economically distressed urban communities. An additional $55.2 million in permanent LWCF program funding is proposed, including $30.2 million for Federal land acquisition, $20.0 million for LWCF State Conservation grants, and $5.0 million in Urban Parks and Recreation Fund grants.

The budget also requests $1.4 million for American Battlefield Protection assistance grants and administration in the National Recreation and Preservation account, which is level with 2012. In addition, the budget requests $58.9 million for Historic Preservation Fund grants, a $3.0 million increase that would provide competitive grants to States, Tribes, communities, and non-profits to survey and nominate properties that more fully represent communities currently underrepresented on the National Register of Historic Places. A total of $10.1 million is requested for the Rivers, Trails, and Conservation Assistance program, which is essentially level with 2012. These programs support NPS stewardship of important cultural resources and ecosystems, and assist States, local communities, and other groups in developing recreational sites and facilities to protect and conserve important, non-Federal cultural and historic assets.

Park Operations – The 2014 NPS budget request for operations is $2.3 billion. This is a total increase of $48.4 million above the 2012 enacted level, consisting of programmatic increases totaling $40.0 million, and fixed cost increases totaling $28.9 million partially offset by programmatic decreases to park operations and related programs totaling $20.6 million.

Highlights of the 2014 budget request include programmatic increases that will enhance critical resource stewardship activities, including an increase of $6.0 million for NPS Cooperative Landscape Conservation-related activities for a total of $8.9 million. This increase has two components, $5.0 million for Climate Change Adaptive Management tools to support climate-related monitoring systems and the development of appropriate land, water, and wildlife adaptation strategies. The other component of the CLC increase is a request for $1.0 million to focus on the collection of landscape or watershed scale data on biological carbon sequestration and the subsequent translation of the results into management tools that can be utilized at parks. Additional resource management programmatic increases include $5.2 million to control exotic and invasive species such as zebra and quagga mussels; $5.0 million to competitively fund the highest priority, non-recurring natural resource project needs at park units; and $3.0 million as noted earlier to combat white-nose syndrome in bats and help preserve important cave habitats and bat populations. Other programmatic increases include $2.1 million to address park specific resource management and science needs at parks such as managing native bison populations; $1.3 million for NPS to expand integrative ocean and coastal stewardship activities; $1.2 million to ensure a science-based response to proposed energy development adjacent to parks; $750,000 for AGO demonstration landscapes; $700,000 to protect and restore dark night skies; $653,000 for wilderness stewardship; and $500,000 for Alaska mapping. In addition, $2.1 million will improve cultural resource stewardship activities by developing a geographic information system to better manage cultural and historic sites.

Visitor enhancement and protection increases include $920,000 to provide educational and information opportunities for visitors with visual or hearing impairments by creating accessible interpretive exhibits, as well as an additional $2.0 million for the Repair and Rehabilitation program to improve the accessibility of NPS infrastructure, as well as support projects that lead to greater water and energy efficiency at park units. The budget also proposes a $1.0 million increase to engage youth in the great outdoors through a combination of additional employment and educational opportunities, and includes an increase of $600,000 for U.S. Park Police operations to provide additional patrols and administrative support at national icons in Washington, D.C. and New York City.

Other emerging management needs addressed in the 2014 budget include a $2.0 million increase to enhance internal controls and improve financial and programmatic accountability throughout the park system, a $1.6 million increase for implementation of the Financial and Business Management System, an additional $762,000 to fund fee and rate increases for water and sewer service at park sites in the District of Columbia, and a $2.1 million increase to fund operational needs at new or recently expanded national park units, such as the Vancouver Barracks at Fort Vancouver National Historic Site, which was transferred to the NPS from the U.S. Army in 2012.

National Recreation and Preservation – This appropriation supports local community efforts to preserve natural and cultural resources. The 2014 request includes $52.0 million for these programs, a decrease of $7.8 million compared to the 2012 enacted, consisting of a programmatic reduction of $8.4 million to Heritage Partnership Programs, and fixed costs increases of $547,000.

In response to the strong public desire for additional technical assistance for public recreation and conservation projects during America's Great Outdoors listening sessions, the 2014 budget contains $10.1 million for the Rivers, Trails, and Conservation Assistance program. This amount is approximately the same as the 2012 enacted level.

Urban Parks and Recreation Fund – Based on public input at America's Great Outdoors listening sessions across the Country, the 2014 President's budget recognizes the need for additional recreational access and opportunities at the local level. The budget proposes $10.0 million for this program, which will provide direct Federal as-

sistance to eligible urban localities for rehabilitation of critically needed recreation facilities as well as encourage systematic local planning and commitment to continuing operation and maintenance of recreation programs, sites, and facilities. Of this request, $9.5 million will be for competitive grants, with $500,000 to administer the program. Additionally, a proposal to fund a portion of NPS land acquisition and recreation grants from the LWCF as a permanent appropriation will provide an additional $5.0 million for UPARR grants.

Historic Preservation – The Historic Preservation Fund supports Historic Preservation Offices in States, Territories, and tribal lands to preserve historically and culturally significant sites. The grants awarded by these offices are an important part of the America's Great Outdoors initiative, which aims to connect people with the Nation's cultural and historic assets, among other goals. The 2014 budget request for the Historic Preservation Fund is $58.9 million. Of this total, $46.9 million is requested for grants-in-aid to States and Territories, $9.0 million is requested for grants-in-aid to Tribes, and $3.0 million is requested for competitive grants targeted toward communities currently underrepresented on the National Register of Historic Places. These grants will be used to conduct the surveying, community engagement, and other pre-nomination activities to ensure that the National Register of Historic Places is representative of the full spectrum of the Nation's cultural heritage.

Construction – The 2014 request includes $160.0 million for the construction account, which funds construction projects, equipment replacement, management, planning, operations, and special projects. This is a total change of $4.6 million above the 2012 enacted level, including $878,000 in fixed costs increases. The budget funds $83.1 million for line-item construction projects, a $5.3 million increase compared to 2012. It provides funding for the highest priority construction projects critical to visitor and employee health and safety or ecosystem restoration and does not propose funding for new construction projects. The request includes $30.0 million for bridging along U.S. Highway 41, the Tamiami Trail, in Florida to increase the flow of water into the Everglades National Park. In addition, the budget includes programmatic reductions of $760,000 to the Housing Improvement Program, $228,000 for Equipment Replacement, $1.8 million to construction program management and operations, $440,000 to construction planning, and $2.4 million to management planning.

Land Acquisition and State Assistance – The total 2014 request for this account is $100.4 million, a total decrease of $1.5 million, consisting of net programmatic decreases totaling $1.8 million and fixed costs increases totaling $246,000. This includes $60.4 million for NPS Federal land acquisition, a programmatic increase of $3.4 million over the 2012 enacted level. The budget provides $32.4 million for high priority line item-acquisition projects within park boundaries, including important acquisitions within multiple NPS park sites that commemorate the Civil War. The requested funding level also includes $9.0 million for matching grants for States and local entities to acquire Civil War battlefield sites outside the national park system. The 2014 Federal land acquisition projects were selected using a strategic, merit-based process with a focus on conserving critical ecosystems, leveraging non-Federal partners, and alignment with the conservation priorities of Interior Bureaus, Federal agencies, Tribes, States, and other stakeholders. The budget also requests total funding of $3.1 million for emergencies and hardship land acquisitions, $6.4 million to acquire inholdings and facilitate land donations and exchanges, and $9.5 million for land acquisition administration.

The LWCF State Conservation Grants program provides funding to States for the purchase of lands for preservation and recreation purposes. The program is intended to create and maintain a nationwide legacy of high quality recreation areas and facilities and to stimulate non-Federal investments in the protection and maintenance of recreation resources across the United States. The State Conservation Grants program will continue to provide matching grants to States, and through States to local governments, for the acquisition and development of public outdoor recreation areas and facilities. The President's budget proposes $40.0 million for this program, a $5.2 million programmatic decrease compared to 2012.

This will provide a total of $36.4 million for grants and $3.6 million available to administer these grants.

Additionally, a proposal to fund a portion of NPS land acquisition and recreation grants from the LWCF as a permanent appropriation would provide an additional $30.2 million to NPS for Federal land acquisition projects, and an additional $20.0 million for the State Conservation Grants program.

Recreation Fee Program – This permanent funding program operates under the Federal Lands Recreation Enhancement Act. The Act authorizes NPS to collect recreation fees at selected parks and requires fee revenues be used to improve visitor services and enhance the visitor experience at those parks and throughout the national park system. The NPS estimates in 2014 it will collect $178.7 million in revenues and obligate $180.0 million in recreation fees for projects. In 2012, 49 percent of NPS recreation fee obligations addressed asset repair and maintenance projects, 14 percent addressed interpretation and visitor services, and seven percent addressed habitat restoration. The remaining 30 percent of recreation fee obligations were spent on operational activities such as law enforcement, cost of collecting fees, and visitor reservation services. The 2014 budget proposes to extend authorization for the Federal Lands Recreation Enhancement Act through 2014.

Fixed Costs – Fixed costs of $30.5 million are funded in the request.

SUMMARY OF BUREAU APPROPRIATIONS
(all dollar amounts in thousands)

Comparison of 2014 Request with 2012 Enacted

	2012 Enacted		2014 Request		Change	
	FTE	Amount	FTE	Amount	FTE	Amount
Current						
Operation of the National Park System	17,008	2,236,568	16,916	2,284,920	-92	+48,352
National Recreation and Preservation	260	59,879	262	52,035	+2	-7,844
Urban Parks and Recreation Fund	0	0	4	10,000	+4	+10,000
Historic Preservation Fund	0	55,910	2	58,910	+2	+3,000
Construction	486	155,366	456	159,961	-30	+4,595
Land Acquisition and State Assistance	111	101,897	105	100,391	-6	-1,506
LWCF Contract Authority (rescission)	0	-30,000	0	-30,000	0	0
Subtotal, Current	17,865	2,579,620	17,745	2,636,217	-120	+56,597

Comparison of 2013 Estimates with 2014 Estimates

	2013 Estimates		2014 Estimates		Change	
	FTE	Amount	FTE	Amount	FTE	Amount
Permanent						
Recreation Fee Permanent Appropriations	1,558	195,156	1,558	195,566	0	+410
Other Permanent Appropriations	464	164,455	464	168,290	0	+3,835
Miscellaneous Trust Funds	170	30,003	170	30,003	0	0
Urban Parks and Recreation Fund	0	0	0	5,000	0	+5,000
Land Acquisition and State Assistance	0	105	0	50,277	0	+50,172
LWCF Contract Authority	0	30,000	0	30,000	0	0
Subtotal, Permanent	2,192	419,719	2,192	479,136	0	+59,417
Allocation and Reimbursable						
Allocation	926	0	860	0	-66	0
Reimbursable	854	0	854	0	0	0
Subtotal, Allocation and Reimbursable	1,780	0	1,714	0	-66	0

HIGHLIGHTS OF BUDGET CHANGES
By Appropriation Activity/Subactivity

APPROPRIATION: Operation of the National Park System

	2013 Full Year CR	2012 Enacted	2014 Request	Change from 2012
Park Management				
Resource Stewardship	327,747	327,092	356,099	+29,007
Visitor Services	240,808	238,764	240,557	+1,793
Park Protection	364,685	362,113	366,529	+4,416
Facility Operations and Maintenance	684,660	682,623	687,300	+4,677
Park Support	459,692	457,057	463,081	+6,024
Subtotal, Park Management	2,077,592	2,067,649	2,113,566	+45,917
External Administrative Costs	172,664	168,919	171,354	+2,435
TOTAL APPROPRIATION *(w/o transfers)*	2,250,256	2,236,568	2,284,920	+48,352
Transfers	0	295	0	-295
TOTAL APPROPRIATION *(w/ transfers)*	2,250,256	2,236,863	2,284,920	+48,057

Detail of Budget Changes

	2014 Change from 2012 Enacted
TOTAL APPROPRIATION	+48,352
Park Management	+45,917
Resource Stewardship	+29,007
Increase Support for Cooperative Landscape Conservation	+5,998
Climate Change Adaptive Management Tools	[+4,998]
Biological Carbon Sequestration	[+1,000]
Exotic and Invasive Species Management and Control	+5,200
Park Projects	+5,000
Control and Management of White-nose Syndrome in Bats	+3,000
Resource and Science Management Needs at Parks	+2,080
Increase Support for Ocean and Coastal Resources Stewardship	+1,250
Science-based Response to Proposed Energy Development	+1,200
Protect and Restore Dark Night Skies	+700
Alaska Mapping	+500
Provide Support for America's Great Outdoors Demonstration Landscapes	+750
Provide for New Responsibilities at Parks	+100
Cultural Resources Geographic Information System	+2,110
Reduce Park Base	-2,977
Fixed Costs	+4,096
Visitor Services	+1,793
Increase Support for Youth in the America's Great Outdoors	+1,000
Provide Accessible Interpretive Media	+920

	2014 Change from 2012 Enacted
Provide for New Responsibilities at Parks	+599
Eliminate Support for National Capital Area Performing Arts Program	-2,197
Reduce Park Base	-2,241
Fixed Costs	+3,712
Park Protection	+4,416
Wilderness Area Stewardship	+653
Enhance Security at National Icons	+600
Provide for New Responsibilities at Parks	+178
Reduce Park Base	-2,441
Fixed Costs	+5,426
Facility Operations and Maintenance	+4,677
Support D.C. Water and Sewer Billing	+762
Increase Support for Challenge Cost Share Program	+610
Support Sustainable and Accessible Infrastructure	+2,000
Provide for New Responsibilities at Parks	+695
Reduce Park Base	-6,406
Fixed Costs	+7,016
Park Support	+6,024
Enhance Internal Controls and Accountability	+2,000
Implement Financial and Business Management System	+1,597
Provide for New Responsibilities at Parks	+528
Reduce Park Base	-4,288
Transfer	+200
Fixed Costs	+5,987

Detail of Budget Changes
Operation of the National Park System (continued)

External Administrative Costs .... +2,435
   Transfer .... -200
   Fixed Costs .... +2,635

Subtotals for Changes Across Multiple Subactivities
   Provide for New Responsibilities at Parks .... [+2,100]
   Reduce Park Base .... [-18,353]
   Fixed Costs .... [+28,872]

APPROPRIATION: National Recreation and Preservation

	2013 Full Year CR	2012 Enacted	2014 Request	Change from 2012
Recreation Programs...................................	590	584	594	+10
Natural Programs.......................................	13,538	13,354	13,637	+283
Cultural Programs......................................	24,836	24,764	24,771	+7
Environmental Compliance and Review.	436	430	438	+8
Grants Administration	1,758	1,738	1,933	+195
International Park Affairs	1,648	1,636	1,658	+22
Heritage Partnership Programs				
Commissions and Grants......................	16,453	16,391	8,014	-8,377
Administrative Support	986	982	990	+8
Subtotal, Heritage Partnerships........	17,439	17,373	9,004	-8,369
TOTAL APPROPRIATION	60,245	59,879	52,035	-7,844

Detail of Budget Changes

	2014 Change from 2012 Enacted		2014 Change from 2012 Enacted
TOTAL APPROPRIATION	-7,844		
Recreation Programs..	+10	Grants Administration	+195
Fixed Costs	+10	Transfer	+160
		Fixed Costs	+35
Natural Programs..	+283		
Transfer	+102	International Park Affairs	+22
Fixed Costs	+181	Fixed Costs	+22
Cultural Programs...	+7	Heritage Partnership Programs	-8,369
Transfer	-262	Reduce Heritage Area Funding.............................	-8,391
Fixed Costs	+269	Fixed Costs	+22
Environmental Compliance and Review....................	+8	Subtotals for Changes Across Multiple Subactivities	
Fixed Costs	+8	Fixed Costs	[+547]

APPROPRIATION: Urban Parks and Recreation Fund

	2013 Full Year CR	2012 Enacted	2014 Request	Change from 2012
UPARR Grants..	0	0	9,500	+9,500
UPARR Grants Administration.............	0	0	500	+500
TOTAL APPROPRIATION	0	0	10,000	+10,000

Detail of Budget Changes
Urban Parks and Recreation Fund

2014 Change from
2012 Enacted

TOTAL APPROPRIATION .... +10,000

Urban Parks and Recreation Fund .... +10,000
   UPARR Grants .... +9,500
   UPARR Grants Administration .... +500

APPROPRIATION: Historic Preservation Fund

	2013 Full Year CR	2012 Enacted	2014 Request	Change from 2012
Grants-in-Aid				
Grants-in-Aid to States and Territories	47,212	46,925	46,925	0
Grants-in-Aid to Indian Tribes	9,040	8,985	8,985	0
Competitive Survey Grants	0	0	3,000	+3,000
TOTAL APPROPRIATION *(w/o supps)*	56,252	55,910	58,910	+3,000
Hurricane Sandy Supplemental	50,000	0	0	0
TOTAL APPROPRIATION *(w/ supps)*	106,252	55,910	58,910	+3,000

Detail of Budget Changes

2014 Change from
2012 Enacted

TOTAL APPROPRIATION .... +3,000

Grants-in-Aid .... +3,000
  Competitive Grants to
    Underrepresented Communities .... +3,000

APPROPRIATION: Construction

	2013 Full Year CR	2012 Enacted	2014 Request	Change from 2012
Line Item Construction and Maint.	77,974	77,722	83,063	+5,341
Special Programs	21,861	21,791	20,803	-988
Construction Planning	7,728	7,700	7,265	-435
Construction Program Management and Operations	38,649	37,530	37,082	-448
Management Planning	14,129	14,623	11,748	-2,875
TOTAL APPROPRIATION *(w/o rescissions)*	160,341	159,366	159,961	+595
Rescission of Prior Year Balances	-4,000	-4,000	0	+4,000
TOTAL APPROPRIATION *(w/ rescissions)*	156,341	155,366	159,961	+4,595
Wildland Fire - Transfer	+15,500	-15,500	0	+15,500
Hurricane Sandy Supplemental	+348,000	0	0	0
TOTAL APPROPRIATION *(w/ transfers, rescissions, and supplemental)*	519,841	139,866	159,961	+20,095

See Appendix J for proposed 2014 construction projects.

Detail of Budget Changes
Construction Program

2014 Change from
2012 Enacted

TOTAL APPROPRIATION *(w/ rescissions)* .... +4,595

Line Item Construction and Maintenance	+5,341
Line Item Construction Program	+5,341
Special Programs	-988
Housing Improvement Program	-760
Equipment Replacement Program	-228
Construction Planning	-435
Line Item Construction Planning	-440
Fixed Costs	+5
Construction Program	
Management and Operations	-448
Denver Service Center Operations	-485
Harpers Ferry Center Operations	-720

Regional Facility Project Support	-576
Transfer	+628
Fixed Costs	+705
Management Planning	-2,875
Unit Management Plans	-1,103
Special Resource Studies	-662
EIS Planning and Compliance	-650
Transfer	-628
Fixed Costs	+168
Prior Year Rescission of Balances	+4,000
Subtotals for Changes Across Multiple Subactivities	
Fixed Costs	[+878]

APPROPRIATION: Land Acquisition and State Assistance

	2013 Full Year CR	2012 Enacted	2014 Request	Change from 2012
Federal Land Acquisition				
Federal Land Acquisition Admin	9,554	9,485	9,500	+15
Emergencies, Hardship, Relocation	3,012	2,995	3,093	+98
Inholdings, Donations, Exchanges	5,021	4,992	6,364	+1,372
American Battlefield Protection				
Program Acquisition Grants	9,041	8,986	8,986	0
Land Acquisition Projects	30,690	30,511	32,448	+1,937
Subtotal, Federal Land Acquisition	57,318	56,969	60,391	+3,422
State Assistance				
State Conservation Grants Admin.	2,907	2,790	3,590	+800
State Conservation Grants	42,296	42,138	36,410	-5,728
Subtotal, State Assistance	45,203	44,928	40,000	-4,928
TOTAL APPROPRIATION	102,521	101,897	100,391	-1,506

See Appendix F for proposed 2014 land acquisition projects.

Detail of Budget Changes

2014 Change from
2012 Enacted

TOTAL APPROPRIATION .... -1,506

Federal Land Acquisition	+3,422
Emergencies, Hardship, Relocation	+98
Inholdings, Donations,	
and Exchanges Program	+1,372
Federal Land Acquisition Projects	+1,937
Fixed Costs	+15

State Assistance	-4,928
State Conservation Grants Administration	+569
State Conservation Grants	-5,728
Fixed Costs	+231
Subtotals for Changes Across Multiple Subactivities	
Fixed Costs	[+246]

APPROPRIATION: Land and Water Conservation Fund Contract Authority

	2013 Full Year CR	2012 Enacted	2014 Request	Change from 2012
TOTAL APPROPRIATION *(rescission)*	-30,000	-30,000	-30,000	0

INDIAN AFFAIRS

Mission – The mission of the Bureau of Indian Affairs is to enhance the quality of life, to promote economic opportunity, and to carry out the responsibility to protect and improve the trust assets of American Indians, Indian Tribes, and Alaska Natives. The mission of the Bureau of Indian Education is to provide quality education opportunities from early childhood through life in Indian Country for individuals attending BIE schools.

Budget Overview – The 2014 President's budget request for Indian Affairs is $2.6 billion in current appropriations, $31.3 million above the 2012 enacted level. The BIA estimates staffing will equal 7,935 full time equivalents in 2014, a reduction of 383 FTE from 2012.

Operation of Indian Programs – The 2014 budget request for the Operation of Indian Programs account is $2.2 billion, an increase of $37.2 million above the 2012 enacted level, excluding a proposed transfer of Contract Support Costs out of OIP to a stand alone account.

Supporting Stewardship of Natural Resources and Science in Indian Country – The 2014 budget includes programmatic increases of $32.4 million for science and technical support to Tribes for the sustainable stewardship and development of natural resources. The funding will support resource management and decisionmaking, in the areas of energy and minerals, climate, oceans, water, rights protection, endangered and invasive species, resource protection enforcement, and post-graduate fellowship and training opportunities in science-related fields. Of this funding, $2.5 million will focus on projects that engage youth in the natural sciences and will establish an office to coordinate youth programs across Indian Affairs.

Improving Trust Land Management – In addition to science-focused increases for natural resources programs, described above, the 2014 budget includes $18.4 million in programmatic increases for improving trust land and water management activities. In Trust Natural Resources, BIA requests a total of $10.7 million in program increases including $3.5 million for the Rights Protection Implementation program and $2.0 million for the Tribal Man-

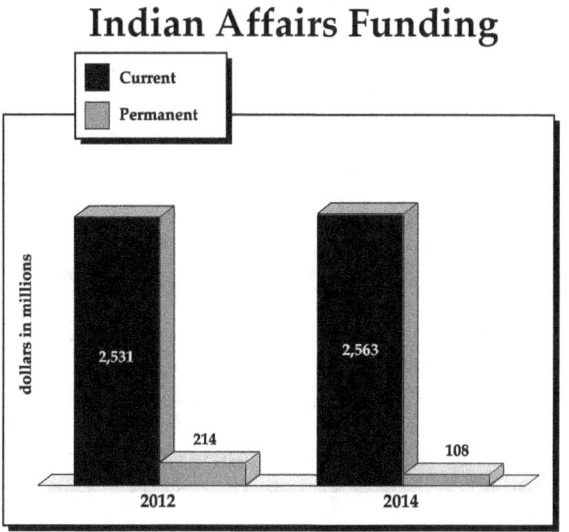

Indian Affairs Funding

Current
Permanent

dollars in millions

2,531
214
2012

2,563
108
2014

agement and Development Program to support fishing, hunting, and gathering rights on and off reservations. The budget request provides program increases of $3.1 million for the Forestry program and $500,000 for the Invasive Species program. In addition to $7.0 million of the science funding described above, an increase of $800,000 supports greater BIA and tribal participation in the Landscape Conservation Cooperatives. An additional $750,000 expands the Wildlife and Parks Program.

Within Trust Real Estate Services, a total of $7.7 million in program increases is directed toward improving trust land management activities, including a $5.5 million increase to provide a total of $7.0 million to continue authorized activities related to the Klamath Basin Restoration Agreement. The 2014 budget request also provides $1.5 million for Rights Protection Litigation Support/ Attorney Fees and $688,000 in the Real Estate Services program to meet workload demands associated with the Administration's New Energy Frontiers initiative and to assist Tribes in managing tribal trust resources. In addition, the Construction account includes an increase of $2.3 million for operation and maintenance of the Fort Peck Water System, a new water treatment plant facility.

```
┌─────────────────────────────────────────────────────────────────────────┐
│                          INDIAN AFFAIRS                                   │
│                               FACTS                                        │
│  • The Bureau of Indian Affairs was established in 1824 under the War Department and transferred │
│    to the Department of the Interior in 1849.                             │
│  • Provides services to approximately 1.7 million American Indians and Alaska Natives in 566 │
│    federally recognized Tribes in the 48 contiguous States and Alaska.    │
│  • Administers and manages 55 million surface acres and 57 million acres of subsurface minerals │
│    estates held in trust by the U.S. for individuals and Tribes.         │
│  • The Bureau of Indian Education provides education services to approximately 41,000 Indian │
│    students through 183 schools and dormitories.  The BIE also provides funding to 31 colleges, │
│    universities, and post secondary schools.                             │
│  • Employs approximately 9,000 personnel of whom about 82 percent are American Indian or │
│    Alaska Native.                                                         │
└─────────────────────────────────────────────────────────────────────────┘
```

Protecting Indian Country – The 2014 request provides programmatic increases of $19.9 million for Public Safety and Justice programs. These increases will provide $5.5 million to hire additional tribal and bureau law enforcement personnel and $13.4 million to staff recently constructed tribally-operated detention centers in Indian Country. The budget also includes an increase of $1.0 million for tribal courts, which are expected to see an increase in case loads. In addition, the budget includes $3.0 million to address the needs of Indian communities with elevated levels of domestic violence within the BIA Human Services program which will partner with the Law Enforcement program to expand services that help stem domestic violence and care for its victims.

Advancing Indian Education – The budget provides a net program increase of $537,000 for elementary and secondary school education activities funded by BIE. Increases include $2.0 million for Tribal Grant Support Costs, which fund the administrative and indirect costs of operating tribally-run schools under contract or grant authorization. It includes $15.0 million to fund a pilot program based on the Department of Education turnaround schools model and concepts. Grants will be awarded to schools that demonstrate the strongest commitment for using the funds to substantially raise the achievement of students. The increases are offset by a $16.5 million reduction in Indian School Equalization Program funds which are distributed by formula, usually based on the number of students, to BIE-funded schools for operations. Additionally, the budget funds a $2.0 million, independent evaluation of BIE programs to consider future needs and structure of the system.

The 2014 budget includes increases totaling $6.2 million for BIE-funded post-secondary programs. The budget provides an additional $2.5 million to meet the needs of growing enrollment at BIE-funded tribal colleges. Tribal colleges and universities provide local communities with the resources and facilities to teach community members the skills they need to be successful and overcome barriers to Indian higher education. To further achieve this goal, the request provides increases of $3.0 million for fellowship and training opportunities for post-graduate study in science fields and $710,000 for other higher education scholarships and adult education.

Energy Initiative – The 2014 budget request provides a total of $10.8 million to support renewable and conventional energy projects. The budget includes an increase of $2.3 million for projects to develop the renewable energy potential of hydroelectric power and solar energy leases in Indian Country. The budget also includes $1.0 million for technical assistance for alternative energy technologies for the Navajo Power Station. The primary purpose of these projects is to provide multi-source resources to meet energy needs in Indian Country.

Program Reductions and Eliminations – The 2014 OIP program decreases total $42.4 million. The budget includes a $2.6 million reduction in Law Enforcement Special Initiatives, reducing the Bureau's participation in interagency crime data sharing and activities along the southwestern border, to provide more funding for law enforcement programs on reservations. The budget includes a program reduction of $7.1 million for Information Resources Technology resulting from IT standardization across Indian Affairs and consolidation of infrastructure. As mentioned above, the budget contains a decrease of $16.5 million for ISEP formula funds as an offset for a new pilot educational program to improve student achievement at lower performing schools. There are also $3.6 million in other reductions.

In 2014, the budget proposes to eliminate $12.6 million in funding for the Housing Improvement Program. The $650.0 million Housing and Urban Development Native American Housing Assistance and Self-Determination Act program serves the same population as HIP. Tribes who receive HUD funding are not precluded from using that funding to provide assistance to HIP applicants.

Tribal Priority Allocations – Collectively, the 2014 budget proposes a total of $894.0 million in Tribal Priority Allocations, an increase of $15.5 million over the 2012 enacted level.

Contract Support Costs – In response to the *Ramah Navajo Chapter* v. *Salazar* Supreme Court decision on contract support costs funding, the 2014 budget proposes to move line-item funding for contract support to an account separate from the Operation of Indian Programs. In total, $231.0 million is provided for contract support costs, an increase of $9.8 million over 2012. The increase strengthens the capacity of Tribes to manage Indian Affairs programs for which they contract.

Construction – The 2014 budget requests $107.1 million for Construction, $16.5 million below the 2012 enacted level. Included in the Construction request is $52.3 million for Education Construction. The budget does not include funding for replacement school or replacement facility construction. Indian Affairs will continue to address the building conditions of existing school facilities in 2014 through the Facilities Improvement and Repair program rather than through new construction projects. The request includes $11.3 million for Public Safety and Justice Construction, $32.8 million for Resources Management Construction, and $10.8 million for Other Program Construction. Within Other Program Construction, the 2014 request includes $2.5 million for the Fort Peck Water System, a program increase of $2.3 million above the 2012 enacted level.

Land and Water Claims Settlements – The 2014 budget request for Indian Land and Water Claim Settlements is $35.7 million. The budget proposes the first year of current funding for the Taos Pueblo Indian Water Rights Settlement enacted as part of the Claims Resolution Act of 2010. A total of $7.8 million, including a program increase of $3.4 million, is included for the San Juan Conjunctive Use Wells and San Juan River Navajo Irrigation Project Rehabilitation, both part of the Navajo-Gallup Water Supply Project.

The budget includes $12.0 million for the Shoshone-Paiute Tribes of the Duck Valley Reservation Water Settlement, the last of five payments to satisfy this requirement. The budget also includes $6.0 million for the Navajo Nation Water Resources Development Trust Fund. The final payment for the Nez Perce/Snake River settlement was made in 2013 and is not included in the 2014 budget. The budget also includes $7.0 million for the final year of funding for agreements related to the Klamath Basin in the OIP account.

Indian Guaranteed Loan Program – The Indian Guaranteed Loan program is funded at $5.0 million, a reduction of $2.1 million. This funding level will guarantee $70.2 million in loans. Indian Affairs will facilitate the use of existing loan programs by Native Americans and Tribes by improving collaboration with other Federal agencies that provide a priority for loan guarantees to socially and economically disadvantaged or rural businesses in Indian Country.

Administrative Cost Savings – Indian Affairs will undergo a horizontal consolidation by 2014 to streamline and improve oversight operations, which will save $19.7 million and invoke management efficiencies to save an additional $13.9 million in funding. The BIA will engage in continuous consultation with Tribes to ensure tribal needs and priorities continue to be met.

Fixed Costs – Fixed costs of $16.1 million are fully funded.

SUMMARY OF BUREAU APPROPRIATIONS
(all dollar amounts in thousands)

Comparison of 2014 Request with 2012 Enacted

	2012 Enacted		2014 Request		Change	
	FTE	Amount	FTE	Amount	FTE	Amount
Current						
Operation of Indian Programs	6,050	2,367,738	5,800	2,183,774	-250	-183,964
Reimbursable Programs	935	0	906	0	-29	0
Allocations from Others	473	0	412	0	-61	0
Contract Support Costs [1]	0	[221,206]	0	231,000	0	+231,000
Construction	104	123,630	104	107,124	0	-16,506
Reimbursable Programs	6	0	5	0	-1	0
Allocations from Others	418	0	387	0	-31	0
Indian Land and Water Claim Settlements and Miscellaneous Payments to Indians	0	32,802	0	35,655	0	+2,853
Indian Guaranteed Loan Program Account	0	7,103	0	5,018	0	-2,085
Subtotal, Current	7,986	2,531,273	7,614	2,562,571	-372	+31,298

Comparison of 2014 Estimates with 2013 Estimates

	2013 Estimates		2014 Estimates		Change	
	FTE	Amount	FTE	Amount	FTE	Amount
Permanent and Trust						
Operation and Maintenance of Quarters	46	5,528	46	5,528	0	0
Miscellaneous Permanent Appropriations	275	100,041	275	100,041	0	0
White Earth Settlement Fund	0	2,500	0	2,500	0	0
Gifts and Donations	0	100	0	100	0	0
Indian Loan Guaranty and Insurance Fund Liquidating Account	0	-80	0	0	0	+80
Revolving Fund for Loans Liquidating Account	0	-600	0	0	0	+600
Indian Arts and Crafts Board	0	0	0	45	0	+45
Subtotal, Permanent and Trust	321	107,489	321	108,214	0	+725

[1] *Contract Support Costs were included in the Operation of Indian Programs account in 2012 and moved to a separate account in 2014. The non-add amount for 2012 is shown for comparison.*

APPROPRIATION: Operation of Indian Programs

	2013 Full Year CR	2012 Enacted	2014 Request	Change from 2012
Tribal Government				
Aid To Tribal Government	29,960	30,492	26,092	-4,400
Consolidated Tribal Govt Program	78,007	76,398	78,480	+2,082
Self Governance Compacts	159,472	154,836	160,812	+5,976
Contract Support [1/]	220,551	219,209	[230,000]	-219,209
Indian Self-Determination Fund [1/]	2,000	1,997	[1,000]	-1,997
New Tribes	320	314	480	+166
Small and Needy Tribes	1,959	1,947	1,947	0
Road Maintenance	25,668	25,390	25,320	-70
Tribal Govt Program Oversight	8,580	8,748	8,033	-715
Subtotal, Tribal Government	526,517	519,331	301,164	-218,167
Human Services				
Social Services	34,562	34,324	37,020	+2,696
Welfare Assistance	75,249	74,791	74,809	+18
Indian Child Welfare Act	10,628	10,850	11,241	+391
Housing Improvement Program	12,682	12,599	0	-12,599
Human Services Tribal Design	441	429	433	+4
Human Services Program Oversight	3,248	3,367	2,592	-775
Subtotal, Human Services	136,810	136,360	126,095	-10,265
Trust - Natural Resources Management				
Natural Resources, General	5,249	5,116	5,281	+165
Irrigation Ops and Maintenance	12,027	11,920	11,963	+43
Rights Protection Implementation	31,087	28,976	36,722	+7,746
Tribal Mgmt/Development Program	9,780	7,705	9,731	+2,026
Endangered Species	1,243	1,245	2,737	+1,492
Coop Landscape Conservation	1,000	200	10,000	+9,800
Integrated Resource Info Program	2,119	2,106	2,106	0
Agriculture and Range	29,234	28,836	30,595	+1,759
Forestry	44,371	43,574	48,698	+5,124
Water Resources	10,189	10,134	11,064	+930
Fish, Wildlife and Parks	11,457	11,322	14,402	+3,080
Resource Mgmt Program Oversight	6,060	6,111	5,894	-217
Subtotal, Trust - NR Management	163,816	157,245	189,193	+31,948
Trust - Real Estate Services				
Trust Services, General	16,159	10,982	15,182	+4,200
Navajo-Hopi Settlement Program	1,200	1,204	1,200	-4
Probate	12,739	12,728	11,950	-778
Land Title and Records Offices	14,466	14,413	14,522	+109
Real Estate Services	37,722	37,692	36,323	-1,369
Land Records Improvement	6,815	6,782	6,781	-1
Environmental Quality	16,492	16,507	16,491	-16
Alaskan Native Programs	1,032	1,032	1,057	+25
Rights Protection	10,892	10,883	12,353	+1,470
Real Estate Services Oversight	14,074	14,536	13,032	-1,504
Subtotal, Trust - Real Estate Services	131,591	126,759	128,891	+2,132

	2013 Full Year CR	2012 Enacted	2014 Request	Change from 2012
Public Safety and Justice				
Law Enforcement	320,734	321,944	339,764	+17,820
Tribal Courts	24,876	23,407	24,387	+980
Fire Protection	890	872	1,110	+238
Subtotal, Public Safety and Justice ...	346,500	346,223	365,261	+19,038
Community and Economic Development				
Job Placement and Training	11,599	11,502	11,227	-275
Economic Development	2,389	2,342	1,830	-512
Minerals and Mining	18,708	18,660	21,272	+2,612
Community Development Oversight ..	2,330	2,306	2,325	+19
Subtotal, Comm and Econ Dev	35,026	34,810	36,654	+1,844
Executive Direction/Admin Services	241,185	251,530	232,481	-19,049
Bureau of Indian Education				
Elementary and Secondary Programs (forward funded)	524,205	522,247	526,441	+4,194
Elementary and Secondary Programs..	123,591	122,534	123,006	+472
Post Secondary Programs (forward funded)	68,943	67,293	69,793	+2,500
Post Secondary Programs	62,506	61,435	64,992	+3,557
Education Management	21,539	21,971	18,524	-3,447
Subtotal, Indian Education	800,784	795,480	802,756	+7,276
Indian Arts and Crafts Board [2]	[1,279]	[1,279]	1,279	+1,279
TOTAL APPROPRIATION	2,382,229	2,367,738	2,183,774	-183,964

[1] *Contract Support and the Indian Self-Determination Fund were included in the Operation of Indian Programs account in 2012 and the 2013 Full Year CR and moved to a separate Contract Support Costs account in 2014. The non-add amounts are shown for comparison.*

[2] *The Indian Arts and Crafts Board was included in the Office of the Secretary account in 2012 and the 2013 Full Year CR. The IACB is proposed to be transferred to the BIA in 2014. The non-add amounts for 2012 and the 2013 Full Year CR are shown for comparison.*

Detail of Budget Changes

	2014 Change from 2012 Enacted
TOTAL APPROPRIATION	-183,964

	2014 Change from 2012 Enacted
Tribal Government	-218,167
New Tribes	+480
Road Maintenance	-320
OIP Internal Transfers	-220,940
Administrative Savings	-787
Organizational Streamlining	-1,829
Fixed Costs	+5,229
Human Services	-10,265
Social Services	+3,000
Housing Improvement Program	-12,601
Human Services Regional Oversight	-450
OIP Internal Transfers	+158
Administrative Savings	-477

	2014 Change from 2012 Enacted
Organizational Streamlining	-733
Fixed Costs	+838
Trust - Natural Resources Management	+31,948
Rights Protection Implementation	+7,500
Tribal Management/Development Program	+2,000
Endangered Species	+1,500
Cooperative Landscape Conservation	+9,800
Agriculture Program (TPA)	-566
Invasive Species	+3,000
Forestry Program (TPA)	+3,122
Forestry Projects	+3,800
Water Mgmt, Planning, and Predevelopment	+1,000
Wildlife and Parks Program (TPA)	+750

	2014 Change from 2012 Enacted
Fish, Wildlife, and Parks Projects	+2,250
Resources Management Program Oversight	+250
OIP Internal Transfers	-220
Administrative Savings	-1,454
Organizational Streamlining	-2,387
Fixed Costs	+1,603
Trust - Real Estate Services	+2,132
Trust Services	+5,500
Real Estate Services Program	+688
Litigation Support/Attorney Fees	+1,500
OIP Internal Transfers	-343
Administrative Savings	-2,473
Organizational Streamlining	-4,536
Fixed Costs	+1,796
Public Safety and Justice	+19,038
Criminal Investigations and Police Services	+5,500
Detention/Corrections	+13,400
Law Enforcement Special Initiatives	-2,550
Tribal Courts	+1,000
OIP Internal Transfers	+1,194
Administrative Savings	-3,124
Organizational Streamlining	-132
Fixed Costs	+3,750
Community and Economic Development	+1,844
Economic Development	-543
Minerals and Mining Projects	+2,900
OIP Internal Transfers	-118
Administrative Savings	-118

	2014 Change from 2012 Enacted
Organizational Streamlining	-470
Fixed Costs	+193
Executive Direction and Administrative Services	-19,049
Assistance Secretary Support	+2,234
Administrative Services (TPA)	-585
Information Technology	-7,140
Human Resources	-173
OIP Internal Transfers	-295
Administrative Savings	-3,167
Organizational Streamlining	-6,535
Fixed Costs	-3,388
Bureau of Indian Education	+7,276
ISEP Formula Funds	-16,463
Tribal Grant Support Costs	+2,000
Turnaround Pilot Program	+15,000
Tribal Colleges and Universities	+2,500
Scholarships and Adult Education	+610
Special Higher Education Scholarships	+100
Science Post-Graduate Scholarships	+3,000
OIP Internal Transfers	-642
Administrative Savings	-1,668
Organizational Streamlining	-3,035
Fixed Costs	+5,874
Indian Arts and Crafts Board	+1,279
Subtotals for Changes Across Multiple Subactivities	
Administrative Savings	[-13,268]
Organizational Streamlining	[-19,657]
Fixed Costs	[+15,895]

APPROPRIATION: Contract Support Costs [1/]

	2013 Full Year CR	2012 Enacted	2014 Request	Change from 2012
Contract Support	[220,551]	[219,209]	230,000	+230,000
Indian Self-Determination Fund	[2,000]	[1,997]	1,000	+1,000
TOTAL APPROPRIATION	[222,551]	[221,206]	231,000	+231,000

[1/] *Contract Support Costs were included in the Operation of Indian Programs account in 2012 and the 2013 Full Year CR and moved to a separate account in 2014. The non-add amounts for 2012 and the 2013 Full Year CR are shown for comparison.*

Detail of Budget Changes
Contract Support Costs

	2014 Change from 2012 Enacted		2014 Change from 2012 Enacted
TOTAL APPROPRIATION	+231,000		
Contract Support Costs	+230,000	Indian Self-Determination Fund	+1,000
Transfer from OIP	+219,209	Transfer from OIP	+1,997
Internal Transfer	+1,997	Internal Transfer	-1,997
Program Increase	+8,794	Program Increase	+1,000

APPROPRIATION: Construction

	2013 Full Year CR	2012 Enacted	2014 Request	Change from 2012
Education Construction	71,026	70,826	52,285	-18,541
Public Safety and Justice Construction	11,375	11,311	11,306	-5
Resources Management Construction	32,932	32,959	32,759	-200
Other Program Construction	9,054	8,534	10,774	+2,240
TOTAL APPROPRIATION	124,387	123,630	107,124	-16,506

See Appendix J for proposed 2014 construction projects.

Detail of Budget Changes

	2014 Change from 2012 Enacted		2014 Change from 2012 Enacted
TOTAL APPROPRIATION	-16,506		
Education Construction	-18,541	Other Program Construction	+2,240
Replacement School Construction	-17,807	Construction Program Management	+2,300
Employee Housing Repair	-600	Administrative Savings	-106
Administrative Savings	-178	Fixed Costs	+46
Fixed Costs	+44		
		Subtotals for Changes Across Multiple Subactivities	
Public Safety and Justice Construction	-5	Administrative Savings	[-552]
Administrative Savings	-5	Fixed Costs	[+153]
Resources Management Construction	-200		
Administrative Savings	-263		
Fixed Costs	+63		

APPROPRIATION: Indian Land and Water Claim Settlements

	2013 Full Year CR	2012 Enacted	2014 Request	Change from 2012
Land Settlements				
White Earth Land Settlement	625	624	625	+1
Hoopa-Yurok Settlement Fund	250	250	250	0
Water Settlements				
Pyramid Lake Water Rights Settlement	142	142	142	0
Nez Perce/Snake River				
Rights Settlement	9,450	9,435	0	-9,435
Navajo Water Resources				
Development Trust Fund	6,000	5,990	6,000	+10
Duck Valley Water Rights Settlement ..	12,000	11,980	12,000	+20
Navajo-Gallup Water Supply Project ..	4,536	4,381	7,826	+3,445
Taos Pueblo Water Rights Settlement...	0	0	8,812	+8,812
TOTAL APPROPRIATION	33,003	32,802	35,655	+2,853

Detail of Budget Changes

	2014 Change from 2012 Enacted
TOTAL APPROPRIATION	+2,853
Land Settlements	
White Earth Land Settlement Act	+1
Water Settlements	
Nez Perce/Snake River Rights Settlement	-9,435
Navajo Water Resources	
Development Trust Fund	+10
Duck Valley Water Rights Settlement.....................	+20
Navajo-Gallup Water Supply Project	+3,445
Taos Pueblo Water Rights Settlement.....................	+8,812

APPROPRIATION: Indian Guaranteed Loan Program

	2013 Full Year CR	2012 Enacted	2014 Request	Change from 2012
TOTAL APPROPRIATION	7,146	7,103	5,018	-2,085

Detail of Budget Changes

	2014 Change from 2012 Enacted
TOTAL APPROPRIATION	-2,085
Subsidies..	-2,103
Fixed Costs...	+18

DEPARTMENTAL OFFICES

Overview – The Department of the Interior protects and manages the Nation's cultural heritage and natural resources; provides scientific and other information about those resources; and honors trust responsibilities and commitments to American Indians, Alaska Natives, and affiliated island communities.

Departmental Offices provide leadership, management, and coordination activities; deliver services to Interior's bureaus and offices; and operate unique cross-cutting functions that do not logically fit elsewhere. The Office of the Secretary provides executive leadership for the Department through the development of policy, legislation, and the annual budget. The Office of the Secretary also provides administrative services such as finance, information resources, acquisition, and human resources. The Office manages the administrative appeals functions contained in the Office of Hearings and Appeals, appraises the value of lands and minerals through the Office of Valuation Services, and collects and disburses revenues from energy production on Federal and Indian lands and on the Outer Continental Shelf through the Office of Natural Resources Revenue.

The Office of Natural Resources Revenue was established within the Office of the Secretary on October 1, 2010 as part of the reorganization of the former Minerals Management Service. This placement in the Assistant Secretary – Policy, Management and Budget established ONRR as a leader in Department-wide collaboration and implementation of key initiatives to enhance assurance that Interior is collecting every dollar due to the taxpayers. The ONRR strives to improve the management and oversight of royalty and revenue collection and disbursement activities for the Interior. The Office is responsible for ensuring revenue from Federal and Indian mineral leases is effectively and accurately collected and disbursed to recipients in approximately 38 States, 41 Tribes, some 30,000 Indian mineral royalty owners, and U.S. Treasury accounts.

Several programs within Departmental Offices are funded in separate appropriations. The Office of Insular Affairs provides assistance to insular areas; the Office of the So-

Departmental Offices Funding

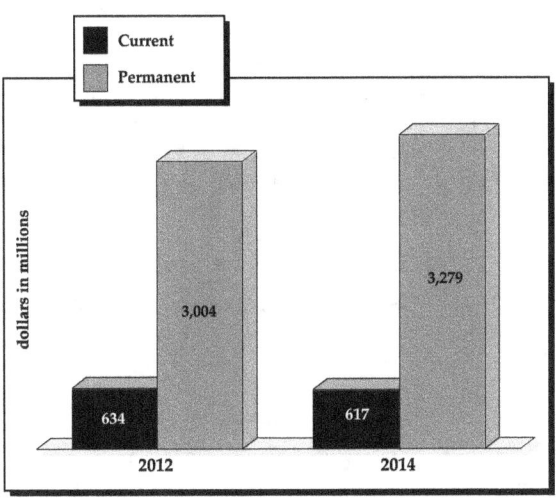

licitor provides legal services to the bureaus and offices on behalf of the Secretary; and the Office of Inspector General reviews Interior activities and conducts audits and investigations.

The Office of the Special Trustee for American Indians manages and discharges the Secretary of the Interior's responsibility for nearly $4.4 billion in trust assets for American Indians. In December 2012, the Secretary of the Interior established the Land Buy-Back Program for Tribal Nations, in the Office of the Secretary, to implement the land consolidation aspects of the Individual Indian Money Account Litigation Settlement, formerly referred to as the *Cobell* v. *Salazar* lawsuit. The settlement was authorized and confirmed by the Claims Resolution Act of 2010 and approved with finality on November 24, 2012 after appeals were exhausted through the U.S. Supreme Court. The Settlement provides $1.9 billion for a Trust Land Consolidation Fund for the Department to acquire fractional interests in trust or restricted land within ten years, at fair market value, from willing individual Indian sellers. Acquired interests will remain in trust or restricted status, and be consolidated for beneficial use by tribal communities. After consultation with Tribes in 2011 and 2012, the Department issued an Initial Implementation Plan regarding use of the Fund.

The Office of the Secretary also manages four Department-wide programs. The Payments in Lieu of Taxes program provides payments to local governments in jurisdictions where Federal lands are located; the Central Hazardous Materials Fund provides a coordinated, consistent approach to remediate Interior sites impacted by hazardous substances; the Natural Resource Damage Assessment and Restoration program coordinates all of the Department's restoration efforts for affected resources injured as a result of oil spills or hazardous substance releases into the environment; and the Wildland Fire Management program addresses wildfire on public lands. Working collaboratively with the participating bureaus, the Department coordinates wildland fire activities within Interior and with the Department of Agriculture's U.S. Forest Service. The Office of the Secretary also manages the Department's Working Capital Fund, the Interior Franchise Fund, and the agency-wide Financial and Business Management System. These Department-wide programs are discussed as a separate chapter in the Bureau Highlights.

OFFICE OF THE SECRETARY

Mission – The Office of the Secretary provides the executive level leadership, policy, guidance, and coordination needed to manage the diverse, complex, and nationally significant programs that are the Department of the Interior's responsibilities.

Budget Overview – The 2014 budget request for Departmental Operations is $268.9 million in current appropriations, which is $7.0 million above the 2012 enacted level. The Office of the Secretary estimates direct staffing will equal 1,136 full time equivalents in 2014, a reduction of 36 FTE from 2012. The budget request reflects continued support of ONRR's mineral receipts management and reforms. The budget proposes to transfer the Indian Arts and Crafts Board, its $1.3 million and 12 FTE, from the Office of the Secretary, Management Services to the Bureau of Indian Affairs. The transfer aligns the administrative and operational support of the Indian Arts and Crafts Board and the three Indian Museums it manages within Indian Affairs. Program increases include $267,000 to enhance mineral receipts modeling and reporting and $800,000 for enhanced analytical capabilities in the Office of Policy Analysis for evidenced-based evaluations Interior-wide. A Departmental Scientific Integrity Officer position will be established promoting collaboration and coordination of scientific initiatives across the Department.

America's Great Outdoors – The 2014 request includes $12.2 million for the Office of Valuation Services from the Land and Water Conservation Fund, a vital component of the America's Great Outdoors initiative. Valuation Services provides appraisal services to land management bureau land acquisition programs. In addition to this current request, the Administration will submit a legislative proposal to permanently authorize annual funding, without further appropriation or fiscal year limitation, for the Land and Water Conservation Fund starting in 2014. The proposal includes an additional $6.0 million for OVS in 2014 permanent funding to support an expanded Federal land acquisition program for Interior.

Improving Minerals Revenue Management and Accountability – The 2014 budget request includes $121.1 million for ONRR's receipts management programs, an increase of $1.6 million above the 2012 enacted level. The ONRR is responsible for ensuring revenue from Federal and Indian mineral leases is effectively, efficiently, and accurately collected, accounted for, analyzed, audited, and disbursed to recipients. Revenue distributions, which totaled $12.2 billion in 2012, benefit States, Tribes, individual Indian mineral royalty owners, and U.S. Treasury accounts.

In 2012 the Department began to enhance capabilities to perform production verification and meter inspections on offshore rigs/platforms and production facilities. It has become clear that a phased start is prudent to enable the mechanics of the program and the relationships between implementing organizations to solidify. As a result of this measured approach, ONRR will reduce the budget request by $380,000 in 2014. The request also includes a reduction of $653,000 due to program efficiencies.

The 2014 budget realigns $1.2 million from Leadership and Administration to the Office of Natural Resources Revenue related to the reorganization of the Minerals Management Service. This transfer of base budget authority has no net impact on the budget. During the reorganization, budget authority for the Western Administrative Service Center was transferred to the Assistant Secretary – Policy, Management and Budget as administrative requirements were finalized. The ONRR is the primary customer for the Western Service Center and the proposed adjustment aligns budget authority with function.

Extractive Industries Transparency Initiative – In September 2011, President Obama announced the United States' intention to implement the Extractive Industries Transparency Initiative and in October 2011, named Secretary Salazar as the U.S. Senior Official responsible for implementing EITI. In response, the Secretary committed to work with the industry and civil societies on EITI, and designated the Assistant Secretary – Policy, Management and Budget to lead the implementation effort.

The EITI offers a voluntary framework for governments to disclose revenues received from oil, gas, and mining assets belonging to the governments, with parallel disclosure by companies of what they have paid the government in royalties, rents, bonuses, taxes, and other payments. The design of each EITI framework is country-specific and developed through a collaborative process by a multi-stakeholder group comprised of government, industry, and civil society representatives. It is this voluntary framework and collaborative process that promotes EITI's principal tenet of global transparency and accountability for extractive industry revenues such as mining, oil, and gas. The EITI principles align with the Department's Open Government Initiative and the Administration's pledge of a more transparent, participatory, and collaborative government.

The Office of Natural Resources Revenue provides expertise to support the implementation of EITI in the United States. As a member of Interior's Implementation Team, ONRR supported the establishment of a multi-stakeholder group to oversee implementation of the U.S. EITI and develop a plan to achieve EITI compliance. In December 2012, Secretary Salazar announced the membership of the multi-stakeholder group, which consists of 21 members and 20 alternates representing government, industry and civil societies. Rhea Suh, the Assistant Secretary for Policy, Management and Budget convened the first meeting of the group in February 2013. The multi-stakeholder group will meet routinely to provide collaborative and consensus-based oversight of U.S. EITI implementation and act as a forum for consultation among EITI stakeholders.

The implementation of U.S. EITI provides additional oversight to the collection and disbursement of the Nation's mineral resources revenues and helps ensure the full and fair return to the American people for the utilization of these public resources. Supporting U.S. EITI advances the revenue reform efforts underway in ONRR and benefits the American public, whose interests will be better protected by a strong commitment to oversight and transparency.

Fixed Costs – Fixed costs of $8.9 million are fully funded in the request.

OFFICE OF INSULAR AFFAIRS

Mission – The Office of Insular Affairs empowers insular communities by improving quality of life, creating economic opportunity, and promoting efficient and effective governance.

Budget Overview – The 2014 OIA budget request is $92.0 million in current appropriations, a decrease of $12.3 million from the 2012 enacted level. Since a new Compact with Palau has been sent to Congress for authorization, the temporary extension of $13.1 million from 2012 has not been re-proposed, which accounts for part of the decrease from 2012. The OIA estimates staffing will equal 41 full time equivalents in 2014.

Assistance to Territories – The 2014 budget provides $89.0 million for Assistance to Territories, an increase of $1.1 million from 2012. Within this amount, Compact Impact-Discretionary funding is moved from General Technical Assistance in 2012 to its own budget line in 2014 and funded at $3.0 million to implement a comprehensive plan to mitigate the impacts and costs of Compact migration. Without the Compact Impact funds, General Technical Assistance increases $3.7 million from the 2012 level of $13.8 million. The budget also includes $3.0 million in Empowering Insular Communities to implement energy projects identified by the territories in their comprehensive sustainable energy strategies. The Water and Wastewater program funding ends with the 2014 budget request, a decrease of $790,000 from 2012. Water and wastewater improvements will be addressed within existing Covenant capital improvement resources. The 2014 request includes $3.5 million for brown tree snake control and $1.0 million for the coral reef initiative. An additional $1.0 million in funding for brown tree snake and coral reef research is included in the 2014 budget request for the U.S. Geological Survey.

Compact of Free Association – The 2014 budget provides $3.1 million for Compact of Free Association, a decrease of $259,000 from 2012, excluding 2012 Palau funding. The budget includes a $263,000 reduction for Enewetak support in the Compact of Free Association activity. The Enewetak request will maintain $236,000 in current appropriations to supplement an estimated $1.5 million in permanent funds in 2014.

Fixed Costs – Fixed costs of $474,000 are fully funded in the request.

OFFICE OF THE SOLICITOR

Mission – The Office of the Solicitor's mission is to provide high quality legal and counseling services to the Secretary and Interior's offices and bureaus, administer the Department's ethics program, help resolve legal issues among bureaus and offices as they fulfill their duties, and manage Interior's Freedom of Information Act appeals.

Budget Overview – The Solicitor's 2014 budget request is $65.8 million, a decrease of $390,000 below the 2012 enacted level. The 2014 budget request also includes internal transfers of $12.1 million from the Ethics and General Administration activities to the Legal Services activity. The internal transfer re-distributes the costs of the Office of the Solicitor between its three activities to better align placement of positions and distribution of office-wide costs with the operations of the Office. The Solicitor estimates staffing will equal 428 full time equivalents in 2014.

Salaries and Expenses – The budget includes a $3.1 million program decrease in the following areas: $1.6 million in personnel, $200,000 in travel, and $320,000 in office space. The 2013 budget request also decreases the Ethics Office by $1.0 million. In 2014, the program would decrease the up-front investment costs for an ethics case matter tracking system that was completed in 2012.

Fixed Costs – Fixed costs of $2.7 million are fully funded in the request.

OFFICE OF INSPECTOR GENERAL

Mission – The Office of Inspector General's mission is to provide independent oversight and promote excellence, integrity, and accountability within the programs, operations, and management of the Department of the Interior and its resources.

Budget Overview – The Inspector General's 2014 budget request is $50.8 million, an increase of $1.4 million compared to the 2012 enacted level. The request includes $2.0 million for consolidating office space within the Washington DC Metropolitan area and $468,000 in funding to support the Council of the Inspectors General on Integrity and Efficiency. The Inspector General estimates staffing will equal 273 full time equivalents in 2014.

Salaries and Expenses – The budget request reflects program increases to Investigations of $735,000 for the Energy Investigation Unit, Suspension and Debarment, Complex Data Analysis, and Program Integrity Division. The budget also includes decreases to Audits, Inspections, and Evaluations to reflect proposed reductions in OIG's physical footprint and an internal $2.9 million transfer realigning staff to Mission Support.

Fixed Costs – Fixed costs of $455,000 are fully funded in the request.

OFFICE OF THE SPECIAL TRUSTEE FOR AMERICAN INDIANS

Mission – The Office of the Special Trustee for American Indians provides fiduciary guidance, management, and leadership for Tribal Trust and Individual Indian Money accounts. The OST oversees and coordinates the Department's efforts to establish consistent policies, procedures, systems, and practices throughout Interior for the Indian fiduciary trust.

Budget Overview – The 2014 budget requests $139.7 million in current appropriations, $12.4 million below the 2012 enacted level. The OST estimates staffing will equal 638 full time equivalents in 2014. From the 2012 level adjusted for reprogramming, the 2014 budget decreases Executive Direction funding by $3.0 million and Program Operations and Support by $9.4 million, $8.1 million of which is a reduction in funding available for Historical Trust Accounting. In 2012, an independent third party delivered the final report on an Efficiency Study conducted of OST operations. The adjustments from the 2012 enacted reflect the OST implementation of some of the report's recommendations, including realignment of certain management responsibilities and functions to streamline the organization, eliminate overlaps in staff responsibilities, and improve efficiency resulting in savings.

The OST has operational responsibility for financial trust fund management, including receipt, investment, and disbursement of Indian trust funds and for real estate appraisals on Indian trust lands. The OST manages nearly $4.4 billion held in approximately 3,000 trust accounts for more than 250 Indian Tribes and over 387,000 open Individual Indian Money accounts. The balances that have accumulated in the trust funds have resulted generally from judgment awards, settlement of claims, land-use agreements, royalties on natural resource use, other proceeds derived directly from trust resources, and financial investment income. The Office of Historical Trust Accounting has responsibility to plan, organize, direct, and execute the historical accounting of Tribal Trust accounts and IIM accounts. The Special Trustee oversees additional trust functions of the Department carried out by the Bureau of Land Management, Bureau of Indian Affairs, and the Secretary's Offices of Hearings and Appeals and Natural Resources Revenue.

Executive Direction – The budget includes a net reduction of $3.0 million in Executive Direction reflecting implementation of reorganization recommendations in late 2012 and 2013, moving some functions to Field Operations, and the completion of other duties.

Program Operations and Support – The 2014 OST budget includes a net program decrease of $9.4 million for Program Operations and Support. The 2014 budget includes a net program decrease of $20.0 million for Program Operations and a net increase of $10.6 million for Program Support.

Field Operations, Appraisal Services, and Trust Services – The budget provides a $1.3 million net increase for Field Operations reflecting a transfer of trust investments functions from Executive Direction and a $2.2 million net increase for Trust Services to address increased workload such as increases in volume of calls to the Tribal Beneficiary Call Center and requests to the Field Offices to provide assistance to the beneficiary community. The settlement also requires, in some instances, the establishment and maintenance of additional beneficiary accounts by Trust Services.

Historical Trust Accounting – The budget includes a net $8.1 million reduction for the Office of Historical Trust Accounting. The $23.0 million funding level for OHTA is built on estimates for litigation support needs in the wake of settlement of *Cobell* v. *Salazar* and other tribal lawsuits and includes a transfer of funding to Program Management for record space. The Office addresses pending tribal cases and supports analysis of tribal claims in coordination with the U.S. Department of Justice. There are currently 66 tribal trust cases pending involving 66 Tribes. The Historical Accounting program will also work to resolve the ownership of residual balances in special deposit accounts and distribute account balances to Tribes, individual Indians, and non-trust entities.

Trust Accountability – The 2014 budget does not include funding for the Trust Accountability budget line item, a reduction of $15.5 million. Some functions formerly funded under this line item have been completed and others realigned. Risk Management is now a component of Program Management and funding for the Office of Hearings and Appeals is now included in Business Management. The budget eliminates funding for Trust Training; instead DOI University will offer training in trust management and Indian fiduciary trust certification courses for OST, BIA, and tribal personnel. The budget also eliminates the Product Development Initiative due to the completion of its mission.

Program Support – The budget includes a $12.8 million net increase for Business Management, including $8.7 million in funding for the Office of Hearings and Appeals previously carried within the Trust Accountability budget line and $4.0 million for litigation support previously carried in the Office of Trust Records. Business Management includes budget, finance, and administration, information services, external affairs, and litigation coordination. The budget includes a net reduction in Program Management of $2.2 million reflecting transfers out to Business Management, transfers in from OHTA and Trust Accountability, and increases to expand the capacity for trust review and audit. Program Management supports operations by maintaining trust records and conducting reviews and audits of trust programs. In accordance with the Indian Trust Reform Act, the Office of Trust Review and Audit conducts program compliance audit reviews of BLM, BIA, and ONRR to evaluate those organizations' management of trust resources relative to statutory requirements.

Fixed Costs – The budget includes a net reduction of $1.4 million in fixed costs. The fixed cost request reflects increases of $1.2 million in personnel related costs and a $2.5 million reduction in office space rents.

SUMMARY OF BUREAU APPROPRIATIONS
(all dollar amounts in thousands)

Comparison of 2014 Request with 2012 Enacted

	2012 Enacted		2014 Request		Change	
	FTE	Amount	FTE	Amount	FTE	Amount
Current						
Office of the Secretary	1,172	261,897	1,136	268,868	-36	+6,971
Office of Natural Resources Revenue	[640]	[119,418]	[645]	[121,060]	[+5]	[+1,642]
Assistance to Territories	41	87,901	41	88,976	0	+1,075
Compact of Free Association	0	16,460	0	3,054	0	-13,406
Office of the Solicitor	359	66,190	339	65,800	-20	-390
Office of Inspector General	288	49,392	273	50,831	-15	+1,439
Office of Special Trustee for American Indians	665	152,075	638	139,677	-27	-12,398
Subtotal, Current	2,525	633,915	2,427	617,206	-98	-16,709

Comparison of 2014 Estimates with 2013 Estimates

	2013 Estimate		2014 Request		Change	
	FTE	Amount	FTE	Amount	FTE	Amount
Permanent and Other						
Take Pride in America	0	5	0	5	0	0
Indian Arts and Crafts Board	0	45	0	0	0	-45
Geothermal Revenues, Payments to Counties	0	4,018	0	0	0	-4,018
Leases of Lands Acquired for Flood Control, Navigation, and Allied Purposes	0	26,059	0	26,790	0	+731
Mineral Leasing and Associated Payments	0	2,142,000	0	2,209,000	0	+67,000
Payments to Alaska from Oil and Gas Leases, NPRA	0	2,900	0	3,010	0	+110
National Forests Fund, Payment to States	0	8,145	0	8,265	0	+120
State Share from Certain Gulf of Mexico Leases	0	245	0	2,808	0	+2,563
Office of the Secretary - Departmental Ops	0	0	10	6,000	+10	+6,000
Trust Land Consolidation Fund 1/	3	1,900,000	11	0	+8	-1,900,000
Payments to U.S. Territories, Fiscal Assistance	0	339,627	0	314,627	0	-25,000
Compact of Free Association	0	205,100	0	281,040	0	+75,940
Tribal Special Funds	0	313,157	0	324,022	0	+10,865
Tribal Trust Fund	0	100,006	0	103,853	0	+3,847
Allocation Account - Office of the Secretary	60	0	60	0	0	0
Allocation Account - Office of the Solicitor	17	0	20	0	+3	0
Reimbursements - Office of the Secretary	289	0	289	0	0	0
Reimbursements - Office of the Solicitor	65	0	69	0	+4	0
Subtotal, Permanent and Other	434	5,041,307	459	3,279,420	+25	-1,761,887
National Indian Gaming Commission	123	19,000	115	19,000	-8	0

1/ *The Cobell Settlement Agreement, enacted by Congress as the Individual Indian Money Account Litigation Settlement in the Claims Resolution Act of 2010, establishes a $1.9 billion fund for the voluntary buy back and consolidation of fractionated land interests on Indian lands. The settlement was finalized on November 24, 2012, following action by the U.S. Supreme Court and expiration of the appeal period. As an incentive to participate in the Land Buy-Back Program, the Settlement authorizes up to $60 million of the Fund to be set aside for an Indian Education Scholarship Fund for American Indian and Alaska Native students when individuals sell fractional interests under the Land Buy-Back Program.*

APPROPRIATION: Office of the Secretary - Departmental Operations

	2013 Full Year CR	2012 Enacted	2014 Request	Change from 2012
Leadership and Administration...............	120,897	120,160	127,523	+7,363
Management Services................................	22,455	22,319	20,285	-2,034
Office of Natural Resources Revenue	120,148	119,418	121,060	+1,642
TOTAL APPROPRIATION *(w/o supps/trans)*	263,500	261,897	268,868	+6,971
Oil Spill Supplemental	+360,000	0	0	0
Other Net Transfers...............................	0	+1,000	0	-1,000
TOTAL APPROPRIATION *(w/ supps/trans)*	623,500	262,897	268,868	+5,971

Detail of Budget Changes

	2014 Change from 2012 Enacted
TOTAL APPROPRIATION	+6,971
Leadership and Administration..................................	+7,363
Science Allocation..	+800
ONRR Receipts Model Support	+267
Internal Transfers...	-974
Fixed Costs	+7,270
Management Services..	-2,034
Indian Arts and Crafts Board....................................	-1,279
Office of Valuation Services	-563
Program Reductions	-86
Internal Transfers...	-191
Fixed Costs	+85
Natural Resources Revenue...	+1,642
Program Reductions	-1,033
Internal Transfers...	+1,165
Fixed Costs	+1,510
Subtotals for Changes Across Multiple Subactivities	
Fixed Costs	[+8,865]

APPROPRIATION: Assistance to Territories

	2013 Full Year CR	2012 Enacted	2014 Request	Change from 2012
American Samoa				
Operations Grants	22,856	22,717	22,752	+35
Northern Marianas				
Covenant Grants (Mandatory)	27,720	27,720	27,720	0
Territorial Assistance				
Office of Insular Affairs	9,523	9,465	9,448	-17
Technical Assistance	13,889	18,774	17,504	-1,270
Maintenance Assistance Fund	2,251	2,237	1,081	-1,156
Brown Tree Snake	3,013	2,995	3,500	+505
Coral Reef Initiative	1,004	998	1,000	+2
Water and Wastewater Projects	795	790	0	-790
Empowering Insular Communities	2,218	2,205	2,971	+766
Compact Impact-Discretionary	5,000	0	3,000	+3,000
Subtotal, Territorial Assistance	37,693	37,464	38,504	+1,040
TOTAL APPROPRIATION	88,269	87,901	88,976	+1,075

Detail of Budget Changes

	2014 Change from 2012 Enacted		2014 Change from 2012 Enacted
TOTAL APPROPRIATION	+1,075		
American Samoa	+35		
Operations Grants	+35		
Territorial Assistance	+1,040	Brown Tree Snake Control	+505
Office of Insular Affairs	-17	Coral Reef Initiative	+2
Administrative Services	-491	Water and Wastewater Projects	-790
Fixed Costs	+474	Empowering Insular Communities	+766
Technical Assistance	-1,270	Compact Impact-Discretionary	+3,000
Maintenance Assistance	-1,156		

APPROPRIATION: Compact of Free Association

	2013 Full Year CR	2012 Enacted	2014 Request	Change from 2012
Federal Services	2,831	2,814	2,818	+4
Enewetak Support	502	499	236	-263
Palau Compact Extension	13,147	13,147	0	-13,147
TOTAL APPROPRIATION	16,480	16,460	3,054	-13,406

Detail of Budget Changes

	2014 Change from 2012 Enacted
TOTAL APPROPRIATION	-13,406
Compact of Free Association	-13,406
Federal Services	+4
Enewetak	-263
Palau Compact Extension	-13,147

APPROPRIATION: Office of the Solicitor

	2013 Full Year CR	2012 Enacted	2014 Request	Change from 2012
Legal Services	48,399	47,434	59,658	+12,224
General Administration	16,681	16,218	4,647	-11,571
Ethics	1,515	2,538	1,495	-1,043
TOTAL APPROPRIATION	66,595	66,190	65,800	-390

Detail of Budget Changes

	2014 Change from 2012 Enacted		2014 Change from 2012 Enacted
TOTAL APPROPRIATION	-390		
Legal Services	+12,224	Ethics Office	-1,043
Travel Reduction	-200	Ethics Tracking System	-1,023
Space Reduction	-320	Internal Transfers	-59
Workforce Planning	-1,586	Fixed Costs	+39
Internal Transfers	+12,112		
Fixed Costs	+2,218	Subtotals for Changes Across Multiple Subactivities	
		Fixed Costs	[+2,739]
General Administration	-11,571		
Internal Transfers	-12,053		
Fixed Costs	+482		

APPROPRIATION: Office of Inspector General

	2013 Full Year CR	2012 Enacted	2014 Request	Change from 2012
Audits, Inspections, and Evaluations	18,611	21,398	18,129	-3,269
Investigations	17,851	17,742	18,754	+1,012
Management	13,232	10,252	13,948	+3,696
TOTAL APPROPRIATION	49,694	49,392	50,831	+1,439

Detail of Budget Changes

	2014 Change from 2012 Enacted		2014 Change from 2012 Enacted
TOTAL APPROPRIATION	+1,439		
Office of Audits, Inspections, and Evaluations	-3,269	Mission Support	+3,696
Internal Reprogramming	-2,900	Internal Reprogramming	+2,900
Reducing OIG's Footprint	-591	DC Area Space Consolidation	+2,000
Fixed Costs	+222	Telecommunications Reduction	-94
		IT Contractor Support Reduction	-250
Office of Investigations	+1,012	Attrition Estimate	-816
Energy Investigations Unit	+553	Fixed Costs	-44
Suspension and Debarment	+276		
Complex Data Analysis	+276	Subtotals for Changes Across Multiple Subactivities	
Program Integrity Division	+138	Attrition Estimate	[-1,174]
Fleet Efficiency	-150	Fixed Costs	[+455]
Attrition Estimate	-358		
Fixed Costs	+277		

APPROPRIATION: Office of the Special Trustee for American Indians

	2013 Full Year CR	2012 Enacted	2014 Request	Change from 2012
Federal Trust Programs				
Executive Direction	3,316	5,046	2,026	-3,020
Program Operations and Support	149,690	147,029	137,651	-9,378
TOTAL APPROPRIATION	153,006	152,075	139,677	-12,398

Detail of Budget Changes

	2014 Change from 2012 Enacted		2014 Change from 2012 Enacted
TOTAL APPROPRIATION	-12,398		
Executive Direction	-3,020	Historical Trust Accounting	-8,076
Executive Direction	-1,865	Historical Trust Accounting	-6,986
Internal Transfer	-1,160	Internal Transfer	-1,108
Fixed Costs	+5	Fixed Costs	+18
Program Operations and Support	-9,378	Trust Accountability	-15,511
Program Operations	-19,989	Program Changes	-3,832
Field Operations	+1,314	Internal Transfer	-11,679
Program Changes	+143		
Internal Transfer	+973	Program Support	+10,611
Fixed Costs	+198	Program Management	-2,156
		Program Changes	+1,556
Office of Appraisal Services	+53	Internal Transfer	-3,806
Appraisal Services	-11	Fixed Costs	+94
Fixed Costs	+64	Business Management	+12,767
		Program Changes	+197
Trust Services	+2,231	Internal Transfer	+14,454
Trust Services	-207	Fixed Costs	-1,884
Internal Transfer	+2,326		
Fixed Costs	+112	Subtotals for Changes Across Multiple Subactivities	
		Fixed Costs	[-1,393]

DEPARTMENT-WIDE PROGRAMS

Overview–Department-wide programs support bureaus and offices through the execution of activities that are broad in scope and impact. These programs complement the many diverse activities of the Department of the Interior and help to achieve key strategic goals.

The Department's Wildland Fire Management program funds fire preparedness, suppression, and rehabilitation activities performed by the land management bureaus and the Bureau of Indian Affairs. The Payments in Lieu of Taxes program supports the activities and functions of Interior's land management bureaus by funding payments to local governments in jurisdictions where Federal lands are located. These payments assist local jurisdictions to offset costs associated with maintaining infrastructure that supports Federal lands within their boundaries. Through the Central Hazardous Materials Fund, the Department remediates hazardous substances on Interior lands, working collaboratively with bureaus and offices to approach these activities in a consistent and coordinated fashion. The Natural Resource Damage Assessment and Restoration program coordinates the Department's restoration efforts for resources injured as a result of oil spills or hazardous substance releases where endangered species or migratory birds are impacted.

The Department's Working Capital Fund is a revolving fund that finances centralized administrative and business services in lieu of operating duplicative systems and processes in each bureau and office. The Working Capital Fund provides the mechanism to collect funds for services that are provided to other Federal agencies in business areas such as payroll. The Department's request also includes appropriated funding for a Working Capital Fund account which supports Department-wide projects. The Interior Franchise Fund finances acquisition services that are provided to Departmental customers and other Federal agencies through the Interior Business Center.

WILDLAND FIRE MANAGEMENT

Mission – The goal of the Wildland Fire Management program is to achieve both a cost-efficient and a technically

Department-wide Programs Funding

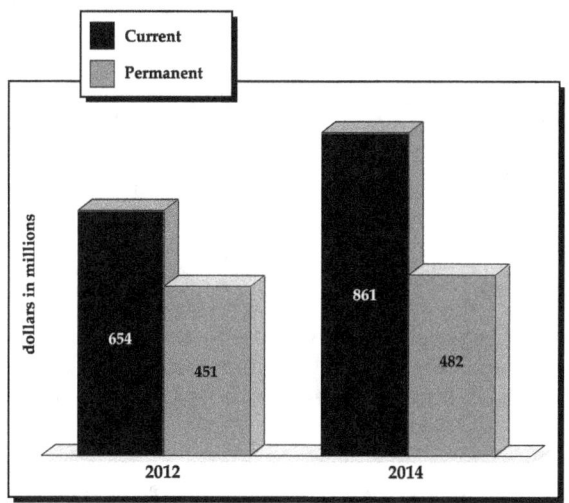

effective fire management program that meets resource and safety objectives, while minimizing both the cost of suppression and damage to resources.

Budget Overview – The 2014 budget proposes a total of $776.9 million to support the fire preparedness, suppression, fuels reduction, and burned area rehabilitation needs of the Department of the Interior. This includes $691.9 million in new budget authority in the Wildland Fire Management account, with a cancellation of $7.0 million in prior year balances, for a net request of $684.9 million in this account. An additional $92.0 million is requested in the FLAME Wildfire Suppression Reserve Fund. The 2014 total of $776.9 million, is an increase of $201.5 million over the 2012 enacted level. The Office of Wildland Fire estimates its staffing will equal 20 FTE in 2014. The estimate for Wildland Fire program staffing throughout the Department is 3,445 FTE, a decrease of 512 FTE from 2012 enacted.

The 2014 budget fully funds the inflation-adjusted 10-year average of suppression expenditures of $377.9 million, with the funding split between $285.9 million in the regular suppression account and $92.0 million in the FLAME Fund. The total request for the 10-year suppression average represents a program increase of $205.1 million over the 2012 enacted level because the full 10-year average was not appropriated in 2012 and the program relied on available balances from prior years.

The 2014 President's budget reduces funding for the Hazardous Fuels Reduction program to $95.9 million. This is a net program reduction of $88.9 million from the 2012 enacted level. The 2014 program presents an opportunity to re-evaluate and recalibrate the focus of HFR to align and support the direction in the National Cohesive Wildland Fire Management Strategy and the Federal Wildland Fire Management Policy. Affirming a commitment to the intergovernmental goals of the Cohesive Strategy, HFR program activities will be planned and implemented to mitigate increasing risks posed by wildfire. A risk-based prioritization process is used to ensure activities are implemented in the areas at greatest risk from wildfire. In 2014, the program will foster closer alignment and integration of the programmatic components of HFR into the bureaus' broader natural resource management programs. The use of risk and evidenced-based decisionmaking continues to be emphasized. To encourage this, the 2014 program includes $2.0 million to conduct additional research on the effectiveness of hazardous fuels treatments.

The budget provides a $3.0 million increase for the Burned Area Rehabilitation program to address the greater post-fire rehabilitation needs caused by the severe 2012 fire season.

Fixed Costs – Fixed costs of $7.2 million are fully funded.

CENTRAL HAZARDOUS MATERIALS FUND

Mission – The mission of the Central Hazardous Materials Fund is to protect the public health and ensure the safety of those who use Interior's lands and facilities. The Office conducts hazardous materials cleanup activities and subsequent maintenance and monitoring of the remedial actions consistent with the National Contingency Plan and with bureau land use and management plan objectives. The Office pursues aggressive cost recovery and cost-sharing actions with the parties responsible for contaminating Federal lands.

Budget Overview – The 2014 budget request for the Central Hazardous Materials Fund is $10.0 million, a decrease of $127,000 from the 2012 enacted level. The Central Hazardous Materials Fund continues to focus on contaminated sites that pose the highest risks to employees, public health and welfare, and the environment; and typically, are so costly and complex to clean up they

cannot adequately be addressed using available bureau resources. In 2014, it is anticipated that cleanup work at approximately 30 different sites will be funded. Many of these sites are the result of past industrial or mining practices by either current or previous owners. Some of the larger sites include the Crab Orchard National Wildlife Refuge, Illinois; Valley Forge National Historic Park, Pennsylvania; Red Devil Mine, Alaska; Phosphate Mines, Idaho; and Orphan Mine, Grand Canyon National Park, Arizona. The program will continue to seek the participation of the current or previous owners to minimize the cleanup cost borne by the American taxpayer. Working with legal advisors, the Central Hazardous Materials Fund will aggressively pursue cost avoidance or cost recoveries at sites with viable potentially responsible parties. The program will also monitor performance and compliance to ensure cleanup funds are being used for their intended purpose through internal control reviews. Completion of nine internal control reviews in 2014 is anticipated. The program will continue to seek opportunities to benchmark efficiencies to reduce the cost of cleanup across the Department.

Fixed Costs – Fixed costs of $21,000 are fully funded.

NATURAL RESOURCE DAMAGE ASSESSMENT AND RESTORATION

Mission – The mission of the Natural Resource Damage Assessment and Restoration program is to restore natural resources injured as a result of oil spills or hazardous substance releases into the environment. In partnership with other affected State, tribal, and Federal trustee agencies, damage assessments provide the basis for determining the restoration needs that address damage to and loss of these resources.

Budget Overview – The 2014 request for NRDAR is $12.5 million, a programmatic increase of $6.1 million from the 2012 enacted level. The increase includes $3.6 million for restoration support, $2.2 million for on-shore oil spill preparedness, and $251,000 for program management. The Interior NRDAR Fund supports natural resource damage assessment, restoration planning, and implementation at hundreds of sites nationwide in partnership with Federal, State, and tribal co-trustees. In 2014, $80.0 million is anticipated to flow into the Fund from receipts recovered through damage assessment cases, advanced cooperative assessment funds, and earned interest. By statute, receipts such as these can only be used by trustees to restore injured lands and resources or to reimburse for past assessment costs. In 2014, a current funding increase and an internal transfer from damage assessment will enable the NRDAR Program to optimize restoration of injured lands and resources using monies from the Fund. This restoration includes work in the Gulf of Mexico, where Interior is working with the Department of Commerce National Oceanic and Atmospheric Administration and the States of Alabama, Florida, Louisiana, Mississippi, and Texas to conduct a comprehensive damage assessment and develop and implement restoration related to the Deepwater Horizon oil spill. Program increases for an onshore Oil Spill Preparedness program will be used to update contingency plans, develop targeted training materials, and support field participation in Environmental Protection Agency and U.S. Coast Guard oil spill response exercises.

Fixed Costs – Fixed costs of $230,000 are fully funded.

WORKING CAPITAL FUND

Mission – The Department's Working Capital Fund provides centralized services and systems to Interior bureaus and offices and to other customers.

Budget Overview – The 2014 budget proposes $62.0 million for the appropriated portion of the Department's Working Capital Fund, essentially level with the 2012 enacted level. The 2014 budget includes an increase of $6.1 million for the Financial and Business Management System and $2.0 million to improve accountability and preservation of Interior's cultural and scientific collections. The budget request includes a reduction of $5.0 million reflecting the transition of information technology enhancement funding from the appropriated WCF to the central bill WCF. The WCF also includes a reduction of $2.5 million to the Acquisition Improvement initiative, and a decrease of $496,000 to the Service First Consolidations program compared to 2012.

Financial Integrity and Transparency – The budget request includes $58.0 million to continue the deployment of the Financial and Business Management System, an increase of $6.1 million above the 2012 enacted level. The FBMS has been deployed to the Bureau of Ocean Energy Management, Bureau of Safety and Environmental Enforcement, Office of Surface Mining, Bureau of Land Management, U.S. Geological Survey, Departmental Offices, Fish and Wildlife Service, and most recently at the beginning of fiscal year 2013, the National Park Service and Bureau of Indian Affairs. The 2014 request will fund the completion of the deployment of FBMS to the Bureau of Reclamation as well as the implementation of functional and technical improvements across the system.

Improving Stewardship of the Nation's Cultural and Scientific Collections – An increase of $2.0 million is requested to initiate the Department's Cultural and Scientific Collections Management initiative. This initiative will respond to recent Inspector General reports regarding the need to improve Interior's accountability

for and preservation of its cultural and scientific collections and museum holdings. The proposed funding will implement a multi-year corrective action plan which will improve oversight and technical assistance, identify and assess collections at non-Federal repositories, and correct identified deficiencies in accountability, preservation, and protection of Interior cultural and scientific collections.

Advancing Efficient Operations – The budget includes $2.0 million to continue the Department's Service First Consolidation initiative, slightly below the 2012 enacted level. Interior's mission is to protect and manage the Nation's natural resources and cultural heritage through programs that operate in over 2,400 locations across the Country. The Service First initiative will expand collaboration among Interior bureaus and other agencies to gain operating efficiencies, expand the use of communications and technology tools, co-locate programs, share services, and create an environment that provides incentives for improved program delivery and cost avoidance.

Information Technology Transformation – The budget request includes a reduction of $5.0 million reflecting the transition of the Department's Information Technology Transformation initiative from the appropriated WCF to the WCF centralized bill. Under this funding model, Interior will self-fund information technology infrastructure enhancements through investments from the benefiting bureaus and offices. The IT Transformation initiative will reduce costs as a result of data center consolidation, implementation of a single e-mail system, network simplification, and migration to enterprise service desks, and also from redirection of technology staff to other duties. Combining infrastructure resources and requirements will increase buying power and provide consistent access to tools and technology across the Department. The Federal Chief Information Officer has approved this long-term savings plan and has agreed to provide the Department near-term flexibility to conduct necessary planning, develop tools and mechanisms, and implement policies and procedures to realize the transformation.

In 2014, estimated collections into the WCF total $195.3 million for centralized billing and $299.1 million for direct-billed activities.

Fixed Costs – There are no fixed costs requested for funds appropriated to the Working Capital Fund.

INTERIOR FRANCHISE FUND

Mission – The Interior Franchise Fund provides business support services to Interior bureaus and offices and other Federal agencies on a competitive basis at customer discretion.

Budget Overview – The Government Management Reform Act of 1994 authorized creation of six executive agency pilot franchise funds. The Director of the Office of Management and Budget approved the Department of the Interior's application for a pilot program in May 1996 and the Interior Franchise Fund was established in the 1997 Interior and Related Agencies Appropriations Act. The 2008 Consolidated Appropriations Act provided permanent franchise fund authority.

Interior Franchise Fund activities are executed wholly within the Office of the Secretary by the Interior Business Center for a variety of Federal agency customers, primarily for acquisition services.

PAYMENTS IN LIEU OF TAXES

Mission – The Payments in Lieu of Taxes program makes payments to counties to help offset the costs of services and infrastructure incurred by local jurisdictions where certain Federal lands are located.

Budget Overview – Since the inception of the PILT program in 1977 and through 2007, PILT funding was subject to appropriation. The Emergency Economic Stabilization Act of 2008 converted PILT to a permanent classification and authorized the program through 2012. The Moving Ahead for Progress in the 21st Century Act extended the permanent authorization through 2013. The 2014 budget request proposes to extend this activity as a permanent program through 2014 at the full entitlement level. In 2012, payments of $393.0 million were made to counties, which were funded from the permanent appropriation at the full entitlement level of $393.4 million. The remaining $400,000 covered administrative costs as authorized. The 2013 PILT payment amounts for local jurisdictions will be formulated consistent with current authorization, with a scheduled payment to be made in June 2013. The Department will investigate commissioning an independent public evaluation of the PILT program, which expires at the end of 2013 and is proposed for a one-year extension. The proposed evaluation would review the PILT program, in both concept and practice, with a goal of developing options to put the program on a sustainable long-term funding path.

SUMMARY OF BUREAU APPROPRIATIONS
(all dollar amounts in thousands)

Comparison of 2014 Request with 2012 Enacted

	2012 Enacted		2014 Request		Change	
	FTE	Amount	FTE	Amount	FTE	Amount
Current						
Wildland Fire Management *(FTE DWP only)*............	24	483,589	20	684,893	-4	+201,304
FLAME Wildfire Suppression Reserve Fund..........	0	91,853	0	92,000	0	+147
Central Hazardous Materials Fund........................	5	10,133	5	10,006	0	-127
Natural Resource Damage Assessment..................	10	6,253	20	12,539	+10	+6,286
Working Capital Fund..	55	61,920	55	62,000	0	+80
Subtotal, Current.......................................	94	653,748	100	861,438	+6	+207,690

Comparison of 2014 Estimates with 2013 Estimates

	2013 Estimates		2014 Estimates		Change	
	FTE	Amount	FTE	Amount	FTE	Amount
Permanent and Other						
Payments in Lieu of Taxes	1	401,298	1	410,127	0	+8,829
Natural Resource Damage Assessment..................	0	81,950	0	71,950	0	-10,000
Working Capital Fund...	1,287	0	1,281	0	-6	0
Interior Franchise Fund...	111	0	67	0	-44	0
Subtotal, Permanent and Other	1,399	483,248	1,349	482,077	-50	-1,171

HIGHLIGHTS OF BUDGET CHANGES
By Appropriation Activity/Subactivity

APPROPRIATION: Wildland Fire Management

	2013 Full Year CR	2012 Enacted	2014 Request	Change from 2012
Preparedness	279,508	276,522	281,928	+5,406
Suppression Operations	276,508	80,904	285,878	+204,974
Other Operations				
Hazardous Fuels Reduction	145,315	183,021	95,935	-87,086
Burned Area Rehabilitation	13,025	13,025	16,035	+3,010
Fire Facilities	6,127	6,127	6,127	0
Joint Fire Science	5,990	5,990	5,990	0
Subtotal, Other Operations	170,457	208,163	124,087	-84,076
Repayment of Fire Transfers	23,000	0	0	0
TOTAL APPROPRIATION *(w/o resc/trans)*	749,473	565,589	691,893	+126,304
Rescission of Prior Year Balances	0	-82,000	0	+82,000
Net Transfers	-15,500	0	-7,000	-7,000
TOTAL APPROPRIATION *(w/ resc/trans)*	733,973	483,589	684,893	+201,304

Detail of Budget Changes

	2014 Change from 2012 Enacted
TOTAL APPROPRIATION	+126,304
Preparedness	+5,406
Fixed Costs	+5,406
Suppression Operations	+204,974
10-Year Suppression Average Adjustment	+204,974
Hazardous Fuels Reduction	-87,086
Reduce Base Funding	90,917
Research Study – Hazardous Fuels Treatments	+2,000
Fixed Costs	+1,831

	2014 Change from 2012 Enacted
Burned Area Rehabilitation	+3,010
Burned Area Rehabilitation	+3,010
Subtotals for Changes Across Multiple Subactivities	
Fixed Costs	[+7,237]

APPROPRIATION: FLAME Wildfire Suppression Reserve Fund

	2013 Full Year CR	2012 Enacted	2014 Request	Change from 2012
TOTAL APPROPRIATION	92,415	91,853	92,000	+147

Detail of Budget Changes

	2014 Change from 2012 Enacted
TOTAL APPROPRIATION	+147
FLAME Wildfire Suppression Reserve Fund	+147
10-Year Suppression Average Adjustment	+147

APPROPRIATION: Central Hazardous Materials Fund

	2013 Full Year CR	2012 Enacted	2014 Request	Change from 2012
TOTAL APPROPRIATION	10,195	10,133	10,006	-127

Detail of Budget Changes

	2014 Change from 2012 Enacted
TOTAL APPROPRIATION	-127
Central Hazardous Materials Fund...........................	-127
Program Changes...	-148
Fixed Costs	+21

APPROPRIATION: Natural Resource Damage Assessment and Restoration Fund

	2013 Full Year CR	2012 Enacted	2014 Request	Change from 2012
Damage Assessments	3,177	3,737	3,191	-546
Restoration Support....................................	1,160	613	4,797	+4,184
Oil Spill Preparedness	0	0	2,200	+2,200
Program Management.................................	1,954	1,903	2,351	+448
TOTAL APPROPRIATION	6,291	6,253	12,539	+6,286

Detail of Budget Changes

	2014 Change from 2012 Enacted
TOTAL APPROPRIATION	+6,286
Damage Assessments	-546
Internal Transfer	-570
Fixed Costs	+24
Restoration Support..	+4,184
Internal Transfer	+570
Program Change...	+3,605
Fixed Costs	+9
Oil Spill Preparedness	+2,200
Program Change...	+2,200
Program Management...	+448
Program Change...	+251
Fixed Costs	+197
Subtotals for Changes Across Multiple Subactivities	
Fixed Costs	[+230]

APPROPRIATION: Working Capital Fund

	2013 Full Year CR	2012 Enacted	2014 Request	Change from 2012
TOTAL APPROPRIATION	62,299	61,920	62,000	+80

Detail of Budget Changes

	2014 Change from 2012 Enacted
TOTAL APPROPRIATION	+80
Working Capital Fund..	+80
Financial Business Management System	+6,064
Cultural and Scientific Collections	+2,000
Service First..	-496
Information Technology	-4,992
Acquisitions..	-2,496

APPENDICES

COMPARISON OF 2012, 2013, AND 2014
BUDGET AUTHORITY*
(in thousands of dollars)

Appropriation/ Bureau/Account	2012 Enacted	2012 Actual	2013 Full Year CR	2014 Request
INTERIOR, ENVIRONMENT, AND RELATED AGENCIES				
BUREAU OF LAND MANAGEMENT				
Current Appropriations				
Management of Lands and Resources	961,900	961,900	960,361	980,228
Rescissions/reductions of new BA	-1,539	-1,539	0	0
Across-the-Board increase of new BA	0	0	+5,877	0
Account total	960,361	960,361	966,238	980,228
Construction	3,576	3,576	3,570	0
Rescissions/reductions of new BA	-6	-6	0	0
Across-the-Board increase of new BA	0	0	+22	0
Account total	3,570	3,570	3,592	0
Oregon and California Grant Lands	112,043	112,043	111,864	115,543
Rescissions/reductions of new BA	-179	-179	0	0
Across-the-Board increase of new BA	0	0	+685	0
Account total	111,864	111,864	112,549	115,543
Land Acquisition	22,380	22,380	22,344	32,618
Rescissions/reductions of new BA	-36	-36	0	0
Across-the-Board increase of new BA	0	0	+137	0
Account total	22,344	22,344	22,481	32,618
Service Charges, Deposits, and Forfeitures	32,448	32,448	31,965	32,465
Service Charges, Deposits, and Forfeitures Offset	-32,448	-32,448	-31,965	-32,465
Range Improvements	10,000	10,000	10,000	10,000
Miscellaneous Trust Funds	20,815	20,815	23,125	23,125
Subtotal, current appropriations	1,128,954	1,128,954	1,137,985	1,161,514
Budget authority	[1,130,714]	[1,130,714]	[1,131,264]	[1,161,514]
Rescissions/reductions of new BA	[-1,760]	[-1,760]	[0]	[0]
Across-the-Board increase of new BA	[0]	[0]	[+6,721]	[0]
Permanent Appropriations				
Permanent Operating Funds	95,464	56,993	65,342	61,176
Miscellaneous Permanent Payments Accounts	51,887	43,766	45,729	4,369
Miscellaneous Trust Funds	1,800	3,264	1,800	1,800
Land Acquisition	0	0	0	0
Net transfer	0	0	0	+16,308
Account total	0	0	0	16,308
Subtotal, permanent appropriations	149,151	104,023	112,871	83,653

* *Notes explaining the scoring assumptions for this table are found beginning on page A-18.*

COMPARISON OF 2012, 2013, AND 2014 BUDGET AUTHORITY
(in thousands of dollars)

Appropriation/ Bureau/Account	2012 Enacted	2012 Actual	2013 Full Year CR	2014 Request
BLM (*continued*)				
Total, Bureau of Land Management	**1,278,105**	**1,232,977**	**1,250,856**	**1,245,167**
Budget authority	[1,279,865]	[1,234,737]	[1,244,135]	[1,228,859]
Rescissions/reductions of new BA...................	[-1,760]	[-1,760]	[0]	[0]
Across-the-Board increase of new BA..............	[0]	[0]	[+6,721]	[0]
Net transfers..	[0]	[0]	[0]	[+16,308]
BUREAU OF OCEAN ENERGY MANAGEMENT				
Current Appropriations				
Ocean Energy Management	59,792	59,792	59,696	71,549
Rescissions/reductions of new BA...................	-96	-96	0	0
Across-the-Board increase of new BA..............	0	0	+365	0
Account total...	59,696	59,696	60,061	71,549
Subtotal, current appropriations........................	59,696	59,696	60,061	71,549
Budget authority	[59,792]	[59,792]	[59,696]	[71,549]
Rescissions/reductions of new BA...................	[-96]	[-96]	[0]	[0]
Across-the-Board increase of new BA..............	[0]	[0]	[+365]	[0]
Total, Bureau of Ocean Energy Management	**59,696**	**59,696**	**60,061**	**71,549**
Budget authority	[59,792]	[59,792]	[59,696]	[71,549]
Rescissions/reductions of new BA...................	[-96]	[-96]	[0]	[0]
Across-the-Board increase of new BA..............	[0]	[0]	[+365]	[0]
BUREAU OF SAFETY AND ENVIRONMENTAL ENFORCEMENT				
Current Appropriations				
Offshore Safety and Environmental Enforcement	61,473	61,473	61,375	83,263
Rescissions/reductions of new BA....................	-98	-98	0	0
Across-the-Board increase of new BA..............	0	0	+376	0
Account total..	61,375	61,375	61,751	83,263
Oil Spill Research	14,923	14,923	14,899	14,899
Rescissions/reductions of new BA....................	-24	-24	0	0
Across-the-Board increase of new BA..............	0	0	+91	0
Account total..	14,899	14,899	14,990	14,899
Supplemental - Hurricane Sandy Disaster Relief.............	0	0	+3,000	0
Account total..	14,899	14,899	17,990	14,899
Subtotal, current appropriations........................	76,274	76,274	76,741	98,162
Supplemental - Hurricane Sandy Disaster Relief.............	0	0	+3,000	0
Subtotal, current appropriations........................	76,274	76,274	79,741	98,162
Budget authority	[76,396]	[76,396]	[76,274]	[98,162]
Rescissions/reductions of new BA....................	[-122]	[-122]	[0]	[0]
Across-the-Board increase of new BA..............	[0]	[0]	[+467]	[0]
Supplemental - Hurricane Sandy Disaster Relief.............	[0]	[0]	[+3,000]	[0]

COMPARISON OF 2012, 2013, AND 2014 BUDGET AUTHORITY
(in thousands of dollars)

Appropriation/ Bureau/Account	2012 Enacted	2012 Actual	2013 Full Year CR	2014 Request
BSEE (*continued*)				
Total, Bureau of Safety and Environmental Enforcement .	**76,274**	**76,274**	**79,741**	**98,162**
Budget authority	[76,396]	[76,396]	[76,274]	[98,162]
Supplemental - Hurricane Sandy Disaster Relief	[0]	[0]	[+3,000]	[0]
Rescissions/reductions of new BA	[-122]	[-122]	[0]	[0]
Across-the-Board increase of new BA	[0]	[0]	[+467]	[0]

OFFICE OF SURFACE MINING RECLAMATION AND ENFORCEMENT
Current Appropriations

Regulation and Technology	123,010	123,114	122,813	115,055
Rescissions/reductions of new BA	-197	-197	0	0
Across-the-Board increase of new BA	0	0	+751	0
Account total	122,813	122,917	123,564	115,055
Abandoned Mine Reclamation Fund	27,443	27,443	27,399	28,013
Rescissions/reductions of new BA	-44	-44	0	0
Across-the-Board increase of new BA	0	0	+168	0
Account total	27,399	27,399	27,567	28,013
Subtotal, current appropriations	150,212	150,316	151,131	143,068
Budget authority	[150,453]	[150,557]	[150,212]	[143,068]
Rescissions/reductions of new BA	[-241]	[-241]	[0]	[0]
Across-the-Board increase of new BA	[0]	[0]	[+919]	[0]

Permanent Appropriations

Payments to United Mine Workers Association Health Plans (*AML*)	48,430	48,430	54,789	15,000
Supplemental payments to UMWA Health Plans (*General Fund*)	205,561	205,561	140,663	180,000
Payments to States in Lieu of Coal Fee Receipts (*Treasury*)	265,300	265,317	129,301	85,300
Mandatory Grants to States and Tribes (*AML*)	220,196	220,196	210,145	188,200
Subtotal, permanent appropriations	739,487	739,504	534,898	468,500
Total, Office of Surface Mining	**889,699**	**889,820**	**686,029**	**611,568**
Budget authority	[889,940]	[890,061]	[685,110]	[611,568]
Rescissions/reductions of new BA	[-241]	[-241]	[0]	[0]
Across-the-Board increase of new BA	[0]	[0]	[+919]	[0]

COMPARISON OF 2012, 2013, AND 2014 BUDGET AUTHORITY
(in thousands of dollars)

Appropriation/ Bureau/Account	2012 Enacted	2012 Actual	2013 Full Year CR	2014 Request
U.S. GEOLOGICAL SURVEY				
Current Appropriations				
Surveys, Investigations, and Research	1,069,744	1,069,744	1,068,032	1,166,855
Rescissions/reductions of new BA	-1,712	-1,712	0	0
Across-the-Board increase of new BA	0	0	+6,536	0
Account total	1,068,032	1,068,032	1,074,568	1,166,855
Other net transfers	0	+806	0	0
Account total	1,068,032	1,068,838	1,074,568	1,166,855
Subtotal, current appropriations	1,068,032	1,068,032	1,074,568	1,166,855
Other net transfers	0	+806	0	0
Subtotal, current appropriations	1,068,032	1,068,838	1,074,568	1,166,855
Budget authority	[1,069,744]	[1,069,744]	[1,068,032]	[1,166,855]
Rescissions/reductions of new BA	[-1,712]	[-1,712]	[0]	[0]
Across-the-Board increase of new BA	[0]	[0]	[+6,536]	[0]
Net transfers	[0]	[+806]	[0]	[0]
Permanent Appropriations				
Operations and Maintenance of Quarters	25	58	40	42
Contributed Funds	572	799	1,122	1,081
Subtotal, permanent appropriations	597	857	1,162	1,123
Total, U.S. Geological Survey	**1,068,629**	**1,069,695**	**1,075,730**	**1,167,978**
Budget authority	[1,070,341]	[1,070,601]	[1,069,194]	[1,167,978]
Rescissions/reductions of new BA	[-1,712]	[-1,712]	[0]	[0]
Across-the-Board increase of new BA	[0]	[0]	[+6,536]	[0]
Net transfers	[0]	[+806]	[0]	[0]
FISH AND WILDLIFE SERVICE				
Current Appropriations				
Resource Management	1,228,142	1,228,142	1,226,177	1,295,085
Rescissions/reductions of new BA	-1,965	-1,965	0	0
Across-the-Board increase of new BA	0	0	+7,504	0
Account total	1,226,177	1,226,177	1,233,681	1,295,085
Other net transfers	0	+9,000	0	0
Account total	1,226,177	1,235,177	1,233,681	1,295,085
Construction	23,088	23,088	23,051	15,722
Rescissions/reductions of new BA	-37	-37	0	0
Across-the-Board increase of new BA	0	0	+141	0
Account total	23,051	23,051	23,192	15,722
Supplemental - Hurricane Sandy Disaster Relief	0	0	+68,200	0
Account total	23,051	23,051	91,392	15,722

COMPARISON OF 2012, 2013, AND 2014 BUDGET AUTHORITY
(in thousands of dollars)

Appropriation/ Bureau/Account	2012 Enacted	2012 Actual	2013 Full Year CR	2014 Request
FWS (*continued*)				
Land Acquisition	54,720	54,720	54,632	70,833
Rescissions/reductions of new BA	-88	-88	0	0
Across-the-Board increase of new BA	0	0	+334	0
Account total	54,632	54,632	54,966	70,833
Multinational Species Conservation Fund	9,481	9,481	9,466	9,787
Rescissions/reductions of new BA	-15	-15	0	0
Across-the-Board increase of new BA	0	0	+58	0
Account total	9,466	9,466	9,524	9,787
North American Wetlands Conservation Fund	35,554	35,554	35,497	39,425
Rescissions/reductions of new BA	-57	-57	0	0
Across-the-Board increase of new BA	0	0	+217	0
Account total	35,497	35,497	35,714	39,425
Cooperative Endangered Species Conservation Fund	47,757	47,757	47,681	56,000
Rescissions/reductions of new BA	-76	-76	0	0
Across-the-Board increase of new BA	0	0	+292	0
Account total	47,681	47,681	47,973	56,000
National Wildlife Refuge Fund	13,980	13,980	13,958	0
Rescissions/reductions of new BA	-22	-22	0	0
Across-the-Board increase of new BA	0	0	+85	0
Account total	13,958	13,958	14,043	0
Neotropical Migratory Bird Conservation	3,792	3,792	3,786	3,786
Rescissions/reductions of new BA	-6	-6	0	0
Across-the-Board increase of new BA	0	0	+23	0
Account total	3,786	3,786	3,809	3,786
State and Tribal Wildlife Grants	61,421	61,421	61,323	61,323
Rescissions/reductions of new BA	-98	-98	0	0
Across-the-Board increase of new BA	0	0	+375	0
Account total	61,323	61,323	61,698	61,323
Subtotal, current appropriations	1,475,571	1,475,571	1,484,600	1,551,961
Supplemental - Hurricane Sandy Disaster Relief	0	0	+68,200	0
Other net transfers	0	+9,000	0	0
Subtotal, current appropriations	1,475,571	1,484,571	1,552,800	1,551,961
Budget authority	[1,477,935]	[1,477,935]	[1,475,571]	[1,551,961]
Supplemental - Hurricane Sandy Disaster Relief	[0]	[0]	[+68,200]	[0]
Rescissions/reductions of new BA	[-2,364]	[-2,364]	[0]	[0]
Across-the-Board increase of new BA	[0]	[0]	[+9,029]	[0]
Net transfers	[0]	[+9,000]	[0]	[0]

COMPARISON OF 2012, 2013, AND 2014 BUDGET AUTHORITY
(in thousands of dollars)

Appropriation/ Bureau/Account	2012 Enacted	2012 Actual	2013 Full Year CR	2014 Request
FWS (*continued*)				
Permanent Appropriations				
Sport Fish Restoration	625,943	626,382	668,182	606,605
Net transfers	-192,439	-192,439	-205,520	-186,089
Account total	433,504	433,943	462,662	420,516
Migratory Bird Conservation Account	47,000	56,495	52,000	66,000
North American Wetlands Conservation Fund	651	651	500	700
National Wildlife Refuge Fund	8,000	7,596	8,000	8,000
Miscellaneous Permanent Appropriations	4,366	3,898	4,198	3,760
Federal Lands Recreation Enhancement Act	5,000	5,085	5,100	5,100
Federal Aid in Wildlife Restoration	399,178	397,627	570,644	610,652
Land Acquisition	0	0	0	0
Net transfer	0	0	0	+35,497
Account total	0	0	0	35,497
Contributed Funds	4,000	2,585	3,000	3,000
Cooperative Endangered Species Conservation Fund	51,356	52,938	62,636	61,524
Net transfer	0	0	0	+28,000
Account total	51,356	52,938	62,636	89,524
Subtotal, permanent appropriations	953,055	960,818	1,168,740	1,242,749
Budget authority	[1,145,494]	[1,153,257]	[1,374,260]	[1,365,341]
Net transfers	[-192,439]	[-192,439]	[-205,520]	[-122,592]
Total, Fish and Wildlife Service	**2,428,626**	**2,445,389**	**2,721,540**	**2,794,710**
Budget authority	[2,623,429]	[2,631,192]	[2,849,831]	[2,917,302]
Rescissions/reductions of new BA	[-2,364]	[-2,364]	[0]	[0]
Across-the-Board increase of new BA	[0]	[0]	[+9,029]	[0]
Net transfers	[-192,439]	[-183,439]	[-205,520]	[-122,592]
Supplemental - Hurricane Sandy Disaster Relief	[0]	[0]	[+68,200]	[0]

NATIONAL PARK SERVICE
Current Appropriations

Operation of the National Park System	2,240,152	2,240,152	2,236,568	2,284,920
Rescissions/reductions of new BA	-3,584	-3,584	0	0
Across-the-Board increase of new BA	0	0	+13,688	0
Account total	2,236,568	2,236,568	2,250,256	2,284,920
Other net transfers	0	+295	0	0
Account total	2,236,568	2,236,863	2,250,256	2,284,920
National Recreation and Preservation	59,975	59,975	59,879	52,035
Rescissions/reductions of new BA	-96	-96	0	0
Across-the-Board increase of new BA	0	0	+366	0
Account total	59,879	59,879	60,245	52,035

COMPARISON OF 2012, 2013, AND 2014 BUDGET AUTHORITY
(in thousands of dollars)

Appropriation/ Bureau/Account	2012 Enacted	2012 Actual	2013 Full Year CR	2014 Request
NPS (*continued*)				
Construction	159,621	159,621	159,366	159,961
Rescissions/reductions of new BA	-255	-255	0	0
Across-the-Board increase of new BA	0	0	+975	0
Account total..	159,366	159,366	160,341	159,961
Supplemental - Hurricane Sandy Disaster Relief.............	0	0	+348,000	0
Rescissions/reductions of prior year BA	-4,000	-4,000	-4,000	0
Fire transfers..	0	-15,500	0	0
Fire repayment..	0	0	+15,500	0
Account total..	155,366	139,866	519,841	159,961
Rescission of contract authority (LWCF)	-30,000	-30,000	-30,000	-30,000
Urban Parks and Recreation Fund	0	0	0	10,000
Land Acquisition and State Assistance	102,060	102,060	101,897	100,391
Rescissions/reductions of new BA	-163	-163	0	0
Across-the-Board increase of new BA	0	0	+624	0
Account total..	101,897	101,897	102,521	100,391
Historic Preservation Grants-in-Aid Fund............................	56,000	56,000	55,910	58,910
Rescissions/reductions of new BA	-90	-90	0	0
Across-the-Board increase of new BA	0	0	+342	0
Account total..	55,910	55,910	56,252	58,910
Supplemental - Hurricane Sandy Disaster Relief.............	0	0	+50,000	0
Account total..	55,910	55,910	106,252	58,910
Subtotal, current appropriations..	2,583,620	2,583,620	2,599,615	2,636,217
Supplemental - Hurricane Sandy Disaster Relief.............	0	0	+398,000	0
Rescissions/reductions of prior year BA	-4,000	-4,000	-4,000	0
Other net transfers..	0	+295	0	0
Fire transfers..	0	-15,500	0	0
Fire repayment..	0	0	+15,500	0
Subtotal, current appropriations..	2,579,620	2,564,415	3,009,115	2,636,217
Budget authority	[2,617,808]	[2,617,808]	[2,613,620]	[2,666,217]
Supplemental - Hurricane Sandy Disaster Relief.............	[0]	[0]	[+398,000]	[0]
Rescissions/reductions of new BA	[-4,188]	[-4,188]	[0]	[0]
Rescissions/reductions of prior year BA	[-4,000]	[-4,000]	[-4,000]	[0]
Across-the-Board increase of new BA	[0]	[0]	[+15,995]	[0]
Net transfers...	[0]	[+295]	[0]	[0]
Fire transfers..	[0]	[-15,500]	[0]	[0]
Fire repayment..	[0]	[0]	[+15,500]	[0]
Rescission of contract authority	[-30,000]	[-30,000]	[-30,000]	[-30,000]
Permanent Appropriations				
Recreation Fee Permanent Appropriations............................	187,677	195,324	195,156	195,566
Other Permanent Appropriations...	161,217	163,376	164,455	168,290
Miscellaneous Trust Funds	25,004	44,401	30,003	30,003
Land and Water Conservation Fund Contract Authority	30,000	30,000	30,000	30,000

COMPARISON OF 2012, 2013, AND 2014 BUDGET AUTHORITY
(in thousands of dollars)

Appropriation/ Bureau/Account	2012 Enacted	2012 Actual	2013 Full Year CR	2014 Request
NPS (*continued*)				
Land Acquisition and State Assistance	105	105	105	82
Net transfer	0	0	0	+50,195
Account total	105	105	105	50,277
Urban Parks and Recreation Fund	0	0	0	0
Net transfer	0	0	0	+5,000
Account total	0	0	0	5,000
Subtotal, permanent appropriations	404,003	433,206	419,719	479,136
Total, National Park Service	**2,987,623**	**3,016,826**	**3,019,334**	**3,060,158**
Supplemental - Hurricane Sandy Disaster Relief	0	0	+398,000	0
Rescissions/reductions of prior year BA	-4,000	-4,000	-4,000	0
Other net transfers	0	+295	0	+55,195
Fire transfers	0	-15,500	0	0
Fire repayment	0	0	+15,500	0
Total, National Park Service	**2,983,623**	**2,997,621**	**3,428,834**	**3,115,353**
Budget authority	[3,021,811]	[3,051,014]	[3,033,339]	[3,090,158]
Supplemental - Hurricane Sandy Disaster Relief	[0]	[0]	[+398,000]	[0]
Rescissions/reductions of new BA	[-4,188]	[-4,188]	[0]	[0]
Rescissions/reductions of prior year BA	[-4,000]	[-4,000]	[-4,000]	[0]
Across-the-Board increase of new BA	[0]	[0]	[+15,995]	[0]
Net transfers	[0]	[+295]	[0]	[+55,195]
Fire transfers	[0]	[-15,500]	[0]	[0]
Fire repayment	[0]	[0]	[+15,500]	[0]
Rescission of contract authority	[-30,000]	[-30,000]	[-30,000]	[-30,000]
INDIAN AFFAIRS				
Current Appropriations				
Operation of Indian Programs	2,371,532	2,371,532	2,367,738	2,183,774
Rescissions/reductions of new BA	-3,794	-3,794	0	0
Across-the-Board increase of new BA	0	0	+14,491	0
Account total	2,367,738	2,367,738	2,382,229	2,183,774
Construction	123,828	123,828	123,630	107,124
Rescissions/reductions of new BA	-198	-198	0	0
Across-the-Board increase of new BA	0	0	+757	0
Account total	123,630	123,630	124,387	107,124
Indian Land and Water Claims Settlements and Miscellaneous Payments to Indians	32,855	32,855	32,802	35,655
Rescissions/reductions of new BA	-53	-53	0	0
Across-the-Board increase of new BA	0	0	+201	0
Account total	32,802	32,802	33,003	35,655
Indian Guaranteed Loan Program Account	7,114	7,114	7,103	5,018
Rescissions/reductions of new BA	-11	-11	0	0
Across-the-Board increase of new BA	0	0	+43	0
Account total	7,103	7,103	7,146	5,018

COMPARISON OF 2012, 2013, AND 2014 BUDGET AUTHORITY
(in thousands of dollars)

Appropriation/ Bureau/Account	2012 Enacted	2012 Actual	2013 Full Year CR	2014 Request
Indian Affairs (*continued*)				
Contract Support	0	0	0	231,000
Subtotal, current appropriations	2,531,273	2,531,273	2,546,765	2,562,571
Budget authority..	[2,535,329]	[2,535,329]	[2,531,273]	[2,562,571]
Rescissions/reductions of new BA	[-4,056]	[-4,056]	[0]	[0]
Across-the-Board increase of new BA	[0]	[0]	[+15,492]	[0]
Permanent Appropriations				
Operation and Maintenance of Quarters	5,533	5,699	5,528	5,528
Gifts and Donations	100	100	100	100
Miscellaneous Permanent Appropriations	98,588	103,323	100,041	100,041
White Earth Settlement Fund..	2,500	1,293	2,500	2,500
Indian Loan Guaranty and Insurance Fund				
Liquidating Account...	-80	-99	-80	0
Indian Direct Loan Program Account....................................	484	484	0	0
Indian Guaranteed Loan Program Account	2,622	0	0	0
Revolving Fund for Loans, Liquidating Account.................	-750	-551	-600	0
Indian Land and Water Claim Settlements				
and Miscellaneous Payments to Indians.........................	104,656	104,656	0	0
Indian Arts and Crafts Board...	0	0	0	45
Subtotal, permanent appropriations.....................................	213,653	214,905	107,489	108,214
Total, Indian Affairs...	**2,744,926**	**2,746,178**	**2,654,254**	**2,670,785**
Budget authority..	[2,748,982]	[2,750,234]	[2,638,762]	[2,670,785]
Rescissions/reductions of new BA	[-4,056]	[-4,056]	[0]	[0]
Across-the-Board increase of new BA	[0]	[0]	[+15,492]	[0]

DEPARTMENTAL OFFICES

OFFICE OF THE SECRETARY
Current Appropriations

	2012 Enacted	2012 Actual	2013 Full Year CR	2014 Request
Office of the Secretary - Departmental Operations................	262,317	262,317	261,897	268,868
Rescissions/reductions of new BA	-420	-420	0	0
Across-the-Board increase of new BA	0	0	+1,603	0
Account total	261,897	261,897	263,500	268,868
Supplemental - Hurricane Sandy Disaster Relief.............	0	0	+360,000	0
Other net transfers	0	+1,000	0	0
Account total	261,897	262,897	623,500	268,868
Subtotal, current appropriations	261,897	262,897	623,500	268,868
Budget authority..	[262,317]	[262,317]	[261,897]	[268,868]
Supplemental - Hurricane Sandy Disaster Relief.............	[0]	[0]	[+360,000]	[0]
Rescissions/reductions of new BA	[-420]	[-420]	[0]	[0]
Across-the-Board increase of new BA	[0]	[0]	[+1,603]	[0]
Net transfers..	[0]	[+1,000]	[0]	[0]

COMPARISON OF 2012, 2013, AND 2014 BUDGET AUTHORITY
(in thousands of dollars)

Appropriation/ Bureau/Account	2012 Enacted	2012 Actual	2013 Full Year CR	2014 Request
OS (*continued*)				
Permanent Appropriations				
Mineral Leasing and Associated Payments	2,074,836	2,050,334	2,142,000	2,209,000
National Petroleum Reserve, Alaska	2,660	4,749	2,900	3,010
Leases of Lands Acquired for Flood				
Control, Navigation, and Allied Purposes	18,871	24,343	26,059	26,790
Geothermal Lease Revenues, Payment to Counties	4,163	3,718	4,018	0
Trust Land Consolidation Fund	0	0	1,900,000	0
National Forests Fund, Payment to States	8,484	10,458	8,145	8,265
State share from certain Gulf of Mexico leases	400	314	245	2,808
Land and Water Conservation Fund	0	0	0	200,000
Net transfer	0	0	0	-200,000
Account total	0	0	0	0
Salaries and Expenses	0	0	0	0
Net transfer	0	0	0	+6,000
Account total	0	0	0	6,000
Indian Arts and Crafts Board	40	42	45	0
Take Pride in America	5	5	5	5
Subtotal, permanent appropriations	2,109,459	2,093,963	4,083,417	2,255,878
Total, Office of the Secretary	**2,371,356**	**2,356,860**	**4,706,917**	**2,524,746**
Budget authority	[2,371,776]	[2,356,280]	[4,345,314]	[2,718,746]
Supplemental - Hurricane Sandy Disaster Relief	[0]	[0]	[+360,000]	[0]
Rescissions/reductions of new BA	[-420]	[-420]	[0]	[0]
Across-the-Board increase of new BA	[0]	[0]	[+1,603]	[0]
Net transfers	[0]	[+1,000]	[0]	[-194,000]
INSULAR AFFAIRS				
Current Appropriations				
Assistance to Territories	87,997	87,997	87,901	88,976
Rescissions/reductions of new BA	-96	-96	0	0
Across-the-Board increase of new BA	0	0	+368	0
Account total	87,901	87,901	88,269	88,976
Compact of Free Association	16,465	16,465	16,460	3,054
Rescissions/reductions of new BA	-5	-5	0	0
Across-the-Board increase of new BA	0	0	+20	0
Account total	16,460	16,460	16,480	3,054
Subtotal, current appropriations	104,361	104,361	104,749	92,030
Budget authority	[104,462]	[104,462]	[104,361]	[92,030]
Rescissions/reductions of new BA	[-101]	[-101]	[0]	[0]
Across-the-Board increase of new BA	[0]	[0]	[+388]	[0]

COMPARISON OF 2012, 2013, AND 2014 BUDGET AUTHORITY
(in thousands of dollars)

Appropriation/ Bureau/Account	2012 Enacted	2012 Actual	2013 Full Year CR	2014 Request
Insular Affairs (*continued*)				
Permanent Appropriations				
Compact of Free Association	218,222	202,163	205,100	281,040
Payments to the U.S. Territories, Fiscal Assistance	248,000	312,547	339,627	314,627
Subtotal, permanent appropriations	466,222	514,710	544,727	595,667
Total, Insular Affairs	**570,583**	**619,071**	**649,476**	**687,697**
Budget authority	[570,684]	[619,172]	[649,088]	[687,697]
Rescissions/reductions of new BA	[-101]	[-101]	[0]	[0]
Across-the-Board increase of new BA	[0]	[0]	[+388]	[0]
OFFICE OF THE SOLICITOR				
Current Appropriations				
Office of the Solicitor - Salaries and Expenses	66,296	66,296	66,190	65,800
Rescissions/reductions of new BA	-106	-106	0	0
Across-the-Board increase of new BA	0	0	+405	0
Account total	66,190	66,190	66,595	65,800
Subtotal, current appropriations	66,190	66,190	66,595	65,800
Total, Office of the Solicitor	**66,190**	**66,190**	**66,595**	**65,800**
Budget authority	[66,296]	[66,296]	[66,190]	[65,800]
Rescissions/reductions of new BA	[-106]	[-106]	[0]	[0]
Across-the-Board increase of new BA	[0]	[0]	[+405]	[0]
OFFICE OF INSPECTOR GENERAL				
Current Appropriations				
Office of Inspector General - Salaries and Expenses	49,471	49,471	49,392	50,831
Rescissions/reductions of new BA	-79	-79	0	0
Across-the-Board increase of new BA	0	0	+302	0
Account total	49,392	49,392	49,694	50,831
Subtotal, current appropriations	49,392	49,392	49,694	50,831
Total, Office of Inspector General	**49,392**	**49,392**	**49,694**	**50,831**
Budget authority	[49,471]	[49,471]	[49,392]	[50,831]
Rescissions/reductions of new BA	[-79]	[-79]	[0]	[0]
Across-the-Board increase of new BA	[0]	[0]	[+302]	[0]

COMPARISON OF 2012, 2013, AND 2014 BUDGET AUTHORITY
(in thousands of dollars)

Appropriation/ Bureau/Account	2012 Enacted	2012 Actual	2013 Full Year CR	2014 Request
OFFICE OF THE SPECIAL TRUSTEE FOR AMERICAN INDIANS				
Current Appropriations				
Federal Trust Programs	152,319	152,319	152,075	139,677
Rescissions/reductions of new BA	-244	-244	0	0
Across-the-Board increase of new BA	0	0	+931	0
Account total	152,075	152,075	153,006	139,677
Subtotal, current appropriations	152,075	152,075	153,006	139,677
Budget authority	[152,319]	[152,319]	[152,075]	[139,677]
Rescissions/reductions of new BA	[-244]	[-244]	[0]	[0]
Across-the-Board increase of new BA	[0]	[0]	[+931]	[0]
Permanent Appropriations				
Tribal Special Fund	328,324	311,352	313,157	324,022
Tribal Trust Fund	100,430	100,349	100,006	103,853
Subtotal, permanent appropriations	428,754	411,701	413,163	427,875
Total, Office of the Special Trustee for American Indians.	**580,829**	**563,776**	**566,169**	**567,552**
Budget authority	[581,073]	[564,020]	[565,238]	[567,552]
Rescissions/reductions of new BA	[-244]	[-244]	[0]	[0]
Across-the-Board increase of new BA	[0]	[0]	[+931]	[0]
DEPARTMENTAL OFFICES SUMMARY				
Subtotal, current appropriations	633,915	634,915	997,544	617,206
Budget authority	[634,865]	[634,865]	[633,915]	[617,206]
Supplemental - Hurricane Sandy Disaster Relief	[0]	[0]	[+360,000]	[0]
Rescissions/reductions of new BA	[-950]	[-950]	[0]	[0]
Across-the-Board increase of new BA	[0]	[0]	[+3,629]	[0]
Net transfers	[0]	[+1,000]	[0]	[0]
Subtotal, permanent appropriations	3,004,435	3,020,374	5,041,307	3,279,420
Budget authority	[3,004,435]	[3,020,374]	[5,041,307]	[3,473,420]
Net transfers	[0]	[0]	[0]	[-194,000]
Total, Departmental Offices	**3,638,350**	**3,655,289**	**6,038,851**	**3,896,626**
Budget authority	[3,639,300]	[3,655,239]	[5,675,222]	[4,090,626]
Supplemental - Hurricane Sandy Disaster Relief	[0]	[0]	[+360,000]	[0]
Rescissions/reductions of new BA	[-950]	[-950]	[0]	[0]
Across-the-Board increase of new BA	[0]	[0]	[+3,629]	[0]
Net transfers	[0]	[+1,000]	[0]	[-194,000]

COMPARISON OF 2012, 2013, AND 2014 BUDGET AUTHORITY
(in thousands of dollars)

Appropriation/ Bureau/Account	2012 Enacted	2012 Actual	2013 Full Year CR	2014 Request
NATIONAL INDIAN GAMING COMMISSION				
Permanent Appropriations				
National Indian Gaming Commission,				
Gaming Activity Fees	17,000	18,902	19,000	19,000
Subtotal, permanent appropriations	17,000	18,902	19,000	19,000
Total, National Indian Gaming Commission	**17,000**	**18,902**	**19,000**	**19,000**
Budget authority	[17,000]	[18,902]	[19,000]	[19,000]
DEPARTMENT-WIDE PROGRAMS				
Current Appropriations				
Central Hazardous Materials Fund	10,149	10,149	10,133	10,006
Rescissions/reductions of new BA	-16	-16	0	0
Across-the-Board increase of new BA	0	0	+62	0
Account total	10,133	10,133	10,195	10,006
Wildland Fire Management	566,495	566,495	726,473	691,893
Supplemental - Fire	0	0	+23,000	0
Rescissions/reductions of new BA	-906	-906	0	0
Account total	565,589	565,589	749,473	691,893
Rescissions/reductions of prior year BA	-82,000	-82,000	0	-7,000
Transfer from FLAME account	0	+176,720	0	0
Other net transfers	0	+832	0	0
Fire transfers	0	+15,500	0	0
Fire repayment	0	0	-15,500	0
Account total	483,589	676,641	733,973	684,893
FLAME Wildfire Suppression Reserve Fund	92,000	92,000	91,853	92,000
Rescissions/reductions of new BA	-147	-147	0	0
Across-the-Board increase of new BA	0	0	+562	0
Transfer to Wildland Fire	0	-91,853	0	0
Account total	91,853	0	92,415	92,000
Natural Resource Damage Assessment Fund	6,263	6,263	6,253	12,539
Rescissions/reductions of new BA	-10	-10	0	0
Across-the-Board increase of new BA	0	0	+38	0
Account total	6,253	6,253	6,291	12,539
Working Capital Fund	62,019	62,019	61,920	62,000
Rescissions/reductions of new BA	-99	-99	0	0
Across-the-Board increase of new BA	0	0	+379	0
Account total	61,920	61,920	62,299	62,000

Comparison of 2012, 2013, and 2014 Budget Authority
(in thousands of dollars)

Appropriation/ Bureau/Account	2012 Enacted	2012 Actual	2013 Full Year CR	2014 Request
DWP (*continued*)				
Subtotal, current appropriations	735,748	643,895	920,673	868,438
Rescissions/reductions of prior year BA	-82,000	-82,000	0	-7,000
Other net transfers	0	+177,552	0	0
Fire transfers	0	+15,500	0	0
Fire repayment	0	0	-15,500	0
Subtotal, current appropriations	653,748	754,947	905,173	861,438
Budget authority	[736,926]	[736,926]	[896,632]	[868,438]
Supplemental - Fire	[0]	[0]	[+23,000]	[0]
Rescissions/reductions of new BA	[-1,178]	[-1,178]	[0]	[0]
Rescissions/reductions of prior year BA	[-82,000]	[-82,000]	[0]	[-7,000]
Across-the-Board increase of new BA	[0]	[0]	[+1,041]	[0]
Transfer to Wildland Fire	[0]	[-91,853]	[0]	[0]
Other net transfers	[0]	[+177,552]	[0]	[0]
Fire transfers	[0]	[+15,500]	[0]	[0]
Fire repayment	[0]	[0]	[-15,500]	[0]
Permanent Appropriations				
Payments in Lieu of Taxes	386,748	393,444	401,298	410,127
Natural Resource Damage Assessment Fund	70,000	125,493	90,000	80,000
Net transfers	-6,000	-7,279	-8,050	-8,050
Account total	64,000	118,214	81,950	71,950
Subtotal, permanent appropriations	450,748	511,658	483,248	482,077
Budget authority	[456,748]	[518,937]	[491,298]	[490,127]
Net transfers	[-6,000]	[-7,279]	[-8,050]	[-8,050]
Total, Department-wide Programs	**1,104,496**	**1,266,605**	**1,388,421**	**1,343,515**
Budget authority	[1,193,674]	[1,255,863]	[1,410,930]	[1,358,565]
Supplemental - Fire	[0]	[0]	[+23,000]	[0]
Rescissions/reductions of new BA	[-1,178]	[-1,178]	[0]	[0]
Rescissions/reductions of prior year BA	[-82,000]	[-82,000]	[0]	[-7,000]
Across-the-Board increase of new BA	[0]	[0]	[+1,041]	[0]
Net transfers	[-6,000]	[+78,420]	[-8,050]	[-8,050]
Fire transfers	[0]	[+15,500]	[0]	[0]
Fire repayments	[0]	[0]	[-15,500]	[0]

COMPARISON OF 2012, 2013, AND 2014 BUDGET AUTHORITY
(in thousands of dollars)

Appropriation/ Bureau/Account	2012 Enacted	2012 Actual	2013 Full Year CR	2014 Request
INTERIOR, ENVIRONMENT, AND RELATED AGENCIES SUMMARY				
Total, Interior, Environment and Related Agencies	**16,289,424**	**16,269,793**	**18,551,117**	**17,034,413**
Supplementals	0	0	+852,200	0
Other net transfers *(current authority only)*	0	+188,653	0	0
Total, Interior, Environment & Related Agencies	**16,289,424**	**16,458,446**	**19,403,317**	**17,034,413**
Grand total, current authority, regular appropriations	**[10,489,962]**	**[10,398,213]**	**[10,696,683]**	**[10,907,541]**
Supplementals	[0]	[0]	[+852,200]	[0]
Rescissions/reductions of new BA	[-16,667]	[-16,667]	[0]	[0]
Rescissions/reductions of prior BA	[-86,000]	[-86,000]	[-4,000]	[-7,000]
Net transfers	[0]	[+188,653]	[0]	[0]
Rescission of contract authority	[-30,000]	[-30,000]	[-30,000]	[-30,000]
Net, current authority	**[10,357,295]**	**[10,454,199]**	**[11,514,883]**	**[10,870,541]**
Grand total, permanent authority	**[6,130,568]**	**[6,203,965]**	**[8,102,004]**	**[6,417,011]**
Net transfers	[-198,439]	[-199,718]	[-213,570]	[-253,139]
Net, permanent authority	**[5,932,129]**	**[6,004,247]**	**[7,888,434]**	**[6,163,872]**

ENERGY AND WATER DEVELOPMENT

BUREAU OF RECLAMATION
Current Appropriations

Water and Related Resources	895,000	895,000	895,000	791,135
Across-the-Board increase of new BA	0	0	+5,477	0
Account total	895,000	895,000	900,477	791,135
Policy and Administration	60,000	60,000	60,000	60,000
Across-the-Board increase of new BA	0	0	+367	0
Account total	60,000	60,000	60,367	60,000
Indian Water Rights Settlements	0	0	0	78,661
San Joaquin Restoration Fund	0	0	0	26,000
California Bay-Delta Restoration	39,651	39,651	39,651	37,000
Across-the-Board increase of new BA	0	0	+243	0
Account total	39,651	39,651	39,894	37,000
Central Valley Project Restoration Fund	53,068	53,068	53,068	53,288
Across-the-Board increase of new BA	0	0	+325	0
Account total	53,068	53,068	53,393	53,288
Central Utah Project Completion Account	0	0	0	3,500
Mandated transfers	0	0	0	-1,000
Account total	0	0	0	2,500

COMPARISON OF 2012, 2013, AND 2014 BUDGET AUTHORITY
(in thousands of dollars)

Appropriation/ Bureau/Account	2012 Enacted	2012 Actual	2013 Full Year CR	2014 Request
RECLAMATION *(continued)*				
Utah Reclamation Mitigation and Conservation Account....	0	0	0	0
Mandated transfers...	0	0	0	+1,000
Account total	0	0	0	+1,000
Subtotal, current appropriations	1,047,719	1,047,719	1,054,131	1,049,584
Budget authority	[1,047,719]	[1,047,719]	[1,047,719]	[1,049,584]
Across-the-Board increase of new BA..............................	[0]	[0]	[+6,412]	[0]
Discretionary Offsets	[-52,767]	[-52,761]	[-39,582]	[-53,288]
Permanent Appropriations				
Colorado River Dam Fund, Boulder Canyon Project	112,537	96,433	111,098	110,053
Miscellaneous Permanent Accounts......................................	265	930	515	515
Bureau of Reclamation Loan Liquidating Account...............	-851	-17,847	-853	-869
San Joaquin Restoration Fund...	24,077	31,124	0	0
Reclamation Trust Funds	3,000	200	3,000	3,000
Federal Lands Recreation Enhancement Act	648	651	685	685
Reclamation Water Settlements Fund	60,000	60,000	60,000	60,000
Utah Reclamation Mitigation and Conservation Account....	0	0	0	7,170
Subtotal, permanent appropriations	199,676	171,491	174,445	180,554
Total, Bureau of Reclamation	**1,247,395**	**1,219,210**	**1,228,576**	**1,230,138**
Budget authority	[1,247,395]	[1,219,210]	[1,222,164]	[1,230,138]
Across-the-Board increase of new BA..............................	[0]	[0]	[+6,412]	[0]
Discretionary Offsets	-52,767	-52,761	-39,582	-53,288
CENTRAL UTAH PROJECT				
Current Appropriations				
Central Utah Project Completion Account............................	28,704	28,704	28,704	0
Across-the-Board increase of new BA..............................	0	0	+175	0
Mandated transfers...	-2,000	-2,000	-2,012	0
Account total	26,704	26,704	26,867	0
Utah Reclamation Mitigation and Conservation Account....	0	0	0	0
Mandated transfers...	+2,000	+2,000	+2,012	0
Account total	2,000	2,000	2,012	0
Subtotal, current appropriations..	28,704	28,704	28,879	0
Budget authority	[28,704]	[28,704]	[28,704]	[0]
Across-the-Board increase of new BA..............................	[0]	[0]	[+175]	[0]
Permanent Appropriations				
Utah Reclamation Mitigation and Conservation Account....	0	3,375	0	0
Subtotal, permanent appropriations	0	3,375	0	0
Total, Central Utah Project	**28,704**	**32,079**	**28,879**	**0**
Budget Authority	[28,704]	[32,079]	[28,704]	[0]
Across-the-Board increase of new BA..............................	[0]	[0]	[+175]	[0]

COMPARISON OF 2012, 2013, AND 2014 BUDGET AUTHORITY
(in thousands of dollars)

Appropriation/ Bureau/Account	2012 Enacted	2012 Actual	2013 Full Year CR	2014 Request
ENERGY AND WATER DEVELOPMENT SUMMARY				
Total, Energy and Water Development	**1,276,099**	**1,251,289**	**1,257,455**	**1,230,138**
Grand total, current authority	[1,076,423]	[1,076,423]	[1,076,423]	[1,049,584]
Across-the-Board increase of new BA	[0]	[0]	[+6,587]	[0]
Net, current authority	[1,076,423]	[1,076,423]	[1,083,010]	[1,049,584]
Grand total, permanent authority	[199,676]	[174,866]	[174,445]	[180,554]

DEPARTMENT OF THE INTERIOR

	2012 Enacted	2012 Actual	2013 Full Year CR	2014 Request
Total, Department of the Interior	**17,565,523**	**17,521,082**	**19,808,572**	**18,264,551**
Supplementals	0	0	+852,200	0
Other net transfers	0	+188,653	0	0
Total, Department of the Interior	**17,565,523**	**17,709,735**	**20,660,772**	**18,264,551**
Grand total, current authority	[11,566,385]	[11,474,636]	[11,712,912]	[11,957,125]
Supplementals	[0]	[0]	[+852,200]	[0]
Rescissions/reductions of new BA	[-16,667]	[-16,667]	[0]	[0]
Across-the-Board increase of new BA	[0]	[0]	[+66,781]	[0]
Net transfers	[0]	[+188,653]	[0]	[0]
Rescissions/reductions of prior BA	[-86,000]	[-86,000]	[-4,000]	[-7,000]
Rescission of contract authority	[-30,000]	[-30,000]	[-30,000]	[-30,000]
Net, current authority	**[11,433,718]**	**[11,530,622]**	**[12,597,893]**	**[11,920,125]**
Grand total, permanent authority	[6,330,244]	[6,378,831]	[8,276,449]	[6,597,565]
Net transfers	[-198,439]	[-199,718]	[-213,570]	[-253,139]
Net, permanent authority	**[6,131,805]**	**[6,179,113]**	**[8,062,879]**	**[6,344,426]**

COMPARISON OF 2012, 2013, AND 2014 BUDGET AUTHORITY

EXPLANATORY NOTES

Appendix A is presented to bridge the different scoring approaches used by the Appropriations Committees and the Executive Branch. As a result of these differences, the budget totals in the 2014 Interior Budget in Brief differ slightly from the presentation in the 2014 President's budget. The President's budget uses a system of budget scoring required by the Budget Enforcement Act based on "net discretionary budget authority." The Interior Budget in Brief document almost exclusively uses a system of scoring based on "current authority" to be consistent with the presentation used by the Appropriations Committees.

Current authority presents the amounts Congress appropriates each year for the Department's programs, including funds classified as mandatory under the Budget Enforcement Act which are subject to annual appropriations. Most mandatory funding is not subject to annual appropriations and is excluded from current authority.

Net discretionary amounts also exclude mandatory funding but unlike current authority, are reduced by offsetting receipts. Additionally, there can be differences in how statutory provisions included in the Appropriations Acts are displayed or scored by the Appropriations Committee as compared to the President's budget. For example, the rescission of NPS contract authority and the net receipts sharing provision in the Interior Appropriations bill are shown as reductions to current authority in the Appropriations Committee scoring tables. However, in the 2012 column of the 2014 President's Budget Appendix, these provisions are not shown as reductions to reach discretionary budget authority totals.

The difference in scoring impacts the budgets of BLM, Reclamation, and OIA. Both BLM and OIA have current authority as well as portions of appropriated accounts classified as mandatory, which are included in the Appropriations Committee scoring tables. This funding is excluded from the net discretionary totals for these bureaus in the President's Budget Appendix. Additionally, BLM and Reclamation have receipts that offset appropriated account totals. The BLM Service Charges, Deposits, and Forfeitures, BLM's Mining Law Administration in the Management of Lands and Resources, and Reclamation's Central Valley Project accounts all include discretionary offsets (receipts) that reduce discretionary totals in the President's Budget Appendix.

Scoring differences are not as significant for Interior's other bureaus relative to the size of the budget. As depicted on the table on the next page the difference in scoring approaches is $179.2 million. The Department's total budget in current authority is $11.9 billion and $11.7 billion in net discretionary authority.

EXPLANATORY NOTES (*continued*)

Budget from Current Authority to Net Discretionary Authority

	2012 Enacted	2012 Actual	2013 Full Year CR	2014 Request
Total, Current Authority	11,433,718	11,530,622	12,597,893	11,920,125
Adjustment for Mandatory Current Accounts				
Bureau of Land Management				
Range Improvements	-10,000	-10,000	-10,000	-10,000
Miscellaneous Trusts	-20,815	-20,815	-23,125	-23,125
Insular Affairs				
Compact of Free Association	-27,720	-27,720	-27,720	-27,720
Adjustment for Offsets				
Bureau of Land Management				
Mining Law Administration	-14,304	-26,152	-16,000	-23,000
Office of the Secretary				
Net Receipts Sharing	-42,000	0	-40,000	-42,000
Reclamation Central Valley Restoration Receipts	-52,767	-52,761	-39,582	-53,288
Office of Surface Mining Civil Penalties	-100	0	-100	-100
Total, Net Discretionary	11,266,012	11,393,174	12,441,366	11,740,892

Another difference in the presentation of budget materials is that the Office of Management and Budget presents the President's budget to the Congress in "millions of dollars" and the Interior Budget in Brief presents funding in "thousands of dollars," the level at which Congress appropriates. When several amounts round to millions of dollars are added or subtracted, there may be small differences between the sums of the rounded and non-rounded numbers. This may result in slight differences between the totals in the President's budget and totals in this document.

Appendix A is structured to provide two account totals where applicable. Most accounts only have one total, which reflects annual congressional action. This total includes supplemental appropriations that fund operations ongoing in nature, such as Wildland Fire operations; across-the-board rescissions; across-the-board increases such as included in Continuing Appropriations Resolution, 2013; and transfers authorized by the Interior, Environment, and Related Agencies and the Energy and Water Development appropriations bills. When applicable, accounts include an additional total line which includes one-time rescissions of prior year balances, non-recurring supplemental appropriations, transfers authorized by other Committees, and non-directed transfers. This convention provides an agency total for "normalized" activities comparable to the initial enacted appropriation actions and a separate total that reflects all other actions during the fiscal year.

2012 ACTUAL

Prior to the passage of the full-year appropriations, the Department operated under five continuing resolutions. The first continuing resolution (P.L. 112-33) provided funding through October 4, 2011. The second continuing resolution (P.L. 112-36) provided funding through November 18, 2011. The third continuing resolution (P.L. 112-55) provided funding through December 16, 2011. The fourth continuing resolution (P.L. 112-67) provided funding through December 17, 2011. The fifth continuing resolution (P.L. 112-68) provided funding through December 23, 2011.

On December 23, 2011, the President signed the Consolidated Appropriations Act, 2012 (P.L. 112-74), providing appropriations for fiscal year 2012. Division B, the Energy and Water Development and Related Agencies Appropriations Act included the following specific provisions and allowances:

EXPLANATORY NOTES (*continued*)

- **Authorization** – The Act provided an expansion of the authorization for appropriations to $30.0 million for the Las Vegas Wash wetlands restoration and Lake Mead improvement project (Sec. 203).

- **Authorization** – The Act provided an extension of the authority through 2013 for the water desalination program and authorizes $3.0 million in appropriations for each of fiscal years 2012 and 2013 (Sec. 204).

Division E, the Interior, Environment, and Related Agencies Appropriations Act, included the following specific provisions and allowances:

- **Authorization** – The Act included a provision to extend the authorization of the Chesapeake Bay Gateways program in NPS through 2013.

- **Rescission** – The Act included a rescission of $4.0 million in unobligated balances in the NPS Construction account.

- **Reorganization** – The Act continued the reorganization of BOEMRE by providing appropriations for the newly created Bureau of Ocean Energy Management and Bureau of Safety and Environmental Enforcement, and adopts the proposed transfer of the Office of Natural Resources Revenue to the Office of the Secretary.

- **Expansion of OCS Inspection Fees** – The Act included the proposed expansion for OCS inspection fees on each OCS above-water oil and gas facility and mobile drilling unit that is subject to inspection. The fee defrayed inspection costs based on the complexity of the facility as determined by the number of wells. The offset for these fee collections totaled $62.0 million.

- **OSM Permit Fees** – The Act included the proposed permit fee in the OSM Regulation and Technology account. The fee is estimated to result in $40,000 in offsetting collections in 2012.

- **Net Receipts Sharing** – The Act continued the provision to deduct two percent from the States' mineral leasing payments to help offset the administrative costs of Federal leasing programs. In 2012, the amount scored for this was $42.0 million.

- **Rescission** – The Act included a rescission of $82.0 million in unobligated balances in the Wildland Fire Management account.

- **Oil and Gas Leasing Internet Program** – The Act authorizes the Secretary to establish an oil and gas leasing internet program (Sec. 110).

- **Reorganization of the Bureau of Ocean Energy Management, Regulation and Enforcement** – The Act includes a provision provided in the 2011 Full-Year Continuing Resolution for the reorganization of BOEMRE. The provision allowed for the establishment of accounts and transfer of funds (Sec. 112).

- **Palau Compact Extension** – The Act provided for an additional one-year discretionary extension of the Compact with Palau, which expired at the end of 2009. The extension allowed for continued payments to the Republic of Palau through 2012. The extension was scored as an increase of $14.0 million in current authority (Sec. 120).

- **Hiring Authorities** – The Act included a provision providing direct hiring authorities of different types to the National Park Service, Bureau of Ocean Energy Management, and Bureau of Safety and Environmental Enforcement, as well as competitive conversion clarifications under ANILCA (Sec. 121).

EXPLANATORY NOTES (*continued*)

- **Vietnam Veterans Memorial Visitor Center** – The Act authorized the use of Federal funds for the use in building the visitor center for the Vietnam Veterans Memorial only when awarded through competitive grants (Sec. 420).

- **Service First** – The Act provided permanent authority for the Service First programs at the Department of the Interior and Forest Service (Sec. 422).

- **Claim Maintenance Fee Amendments** – The Act amended the mining claim maintenance fees authorization to ensure that each mining claim pays a proportional share of the annual maintenance fee (Sec. 430).

- **Across-the-Board Rescission** – The Act included an across-the-board rescission of 0.16 percent for all current amounts provided in Division E, the Interior, Environment, and Related Agencies Appropriations Act (Sec. 436).

- **Air Quality Permitting Authority** – The Act amended the Clean Air Act to transfer air quality permitting authority for offshore oil and gas activities in Alaska to the Bureau of Ocean Energy Management (Sec. 432).

Other legislation and transfers impacting Interior Appropriations for 2012 included:

- **Authorization** – On July 6, 2012, the Moving Ahead for Progress in the 21st Century Act (P.L. 112-141) was signed into law. The Act included the following provisions impacting the Department:

  ◊ Extension of the Federal-Aid Highways program (Title I) providing funding for Federal lands and tribal transportation programs for fiscal years 2013 and 2014.

  ◊ Extension of the Federal Aid in Sport Fish Restoration Act (Title IV, Sec. 34001-34002) through fiscal year 2014.

  ◊ Required a determination with respect to natural quiet and experience relating to over-flights in Grand Canyon National Park (Sec. 35001).

  ◊ Provision allowing for the denial of applications for air tour operations at Crater Lake National Park or Great Smoky Mountains National Park if the air tour operations adversely affect park visitors or resources (Sec. 35002).

  ◊ Extension of the Secure Rural Schools and Community Self-Determination Program for one-year (Sec. 100101).

  ◊ Extension of the Payments in Lieu of Taxes program for one-year (Sec. 100111).

  ◊ Limitation on payments from the Abandoned Mine Reclamation Fund for certified States or Indian Tribes to not more than $15 million (Sec. 100125).

- The U.S. Geological Survey received a transfer of $806,000 from the United States Agency for International Development.

- The Fish and Wildlife Service received a transfer of $9.0 million for their International Affairs program.

- The National Park Service received a transfer of $294,000 using the Service First authority provided in P.L. 112-74.

- The National Park Service received a transfer of $1,000 from the Executive Office of the President for drug trafficking deterrent actions.

EXPLANATORY NOTES (*continued*)

- The National Park Service transferred $15.5 million to the Interior Wildland Fire Management account for emergency wildland fire suppression activities as authorized under the Sec. 102 emergency transfer authority in the 2012 Interior, Environment and Related Agencies Appropriations Act (P.L. 112-74).

- The Office of the Secretary received a transfer of $1.0 million from USAID for international activities.

- The FLAME Wildfire Reserve Fund transferred $91.9 million in new budget authority and $84.9 million in unobligated balances to the Wildland Fire Management account for fire suppression activities in 2012.

- The Wildland Fire Management account received a transfer of $832,000 for wildland fire activities from the Forest Service.

2013 ESTIMATES

Continuing Resolution - At the time the 2014 President's budget was prepared, Congressional action on full year appropriations for 2013 had not been enacted and the Department was operating under a continuing resolution. On September 28, 2012, the President signed the Continuing Appropriations Resolution, 2013 (P.L. 112-175), providing continuing appropriations through March 27, 2013. The CR included the following provisions for the Department:

- **Wildland Fire** – Provides an annual rate of operations of $726.5 million for the Wildland Fire Management account and an additional $23.0 million to repay funds borrowed in 2012 under the Sec. 102 emergency transfer authority for emergency wildland fire suppression activities (Sec. 140).

- **Abandoned Mine Reclamation Fund** – Makes a technical correction to the Surface Mining Control and Reclamation Act, as amended by MAP-21 (P.L. 112-141) to clarify the authority to reallocate funds (Sec. 142).

- **Across-the-Board Increase** – Includes a 0.612 percent across-the-board increase for activities funded in the continuing resolution (Sec. 101(c)).

Supplemental Appropriations - On January 29, 2013, the President signed the Disaster Relief Appropriations Act, 2013 (P.L. 113-2) providing supplemental appropriations for response and recovery at Interior facilities impacted by Hurricane Sandy, and mitigation activities. The Act included the following amounts for the Department:

- Bureau of Safety and Environmental Enforcement, Oil Spill Research - $3.0 million.

- Fish and Wildlife Service, Construction - $68.2 million.

- National Park Service, Historic Preservation Fund - $50.0 million.

- National Park Service, Construction - $348.0 million.

- Office of the Secretary, Salaries and Expenses - $360.0 million, provides transfer authority to move these funds to any account within the Department and authority to award grants or enter into cooperative agreements to accomplish the purposes outlined in the provision.

- In addition, the Act includes a provision prohibiting the use of the funds provided in the Act from being used for land acquisition (Sec. 1096).

EXPLANATORY NOTES (*continued*)

Sequestration – On March 1, 2013, the President issued a sequestration order in accordance with section 251A of the Balanced Budget and Emergency Deficit Control Act, as amended by the Budget Control Act of 2011. Amounts displayed for 2013 in this document do not reflect reductions required in the sequestration order.

2014 REQUEST

LEGISLATIVE MANDATORY PROPOSALS

The 2014 budget includes legislative proposals, which will be submitted to the Congress to collect a fair return to the American taxpayer for the sale of Federal resources, reduce unnecessary spending, and extend beneficial authorities of law. Revenue and savings proposals will generate an estimated $3.7 billion over the next decade. The 2014 budget also includes three permanent spending proposals estimated at $8.1 billion in outlays over the next decade.

Land and Water Conservation Fund – The Department of the Interior will submit a legislative proposal to permanently authorize annual funding, without further appropriation or fiscal year limitation for LWCF in the Departments of the Interior and Agriculture. During a transition to permanent funding in 2014, the budget proposes $600.0 million in total LWCF funding, comprised of $200.0 million in permanent and $400.0 million in current funding. Starting in 2015, the fully authorized level of $900.0 million in permanent funds will be authorized each year.

Payments in Lieu of Taxes – The authorization for permanent PILT payments was extended through 2013 as part of the Surface Transportation Extension Act of 2012. The 2014 budget proposes to extend authorization of the current program for one year in 2014, while a sustainable long-term funding solution is developed for the PILT Program.

Palau Compact – On September 3, 2010, the U.S. and the Republic of Palau successfully concluded the review of the Compact of Free Association and signed a 15-year agreement that includes a package of assistance through 2024. Permanent and indefinite funding for the Compact expired at the end of 2009. The 2014 budget assumes authorization of permanent funding for the Compact occurs in 2013. The cost for this proposal is estimated at $189 million over the 2014-2023 period.

Federal Oil and Gas Reforms – The budget includes a package of legislative reforms to bolster and backstop administrative actions to reform the management of Interior's onshore and offshore oil and gas programs, with a key focus on improving the return to taxpayers from the sale of these Federal resources. Collectively, these oil and gas reforms will generate roughly $2.5 billion in net revenue to the Treasury over ten years, of which about $1.7 billion would result from statutory changes. Many States will also benefit from higher Federal revenue sharing payments.

Helium Sales, Operations and Deposits – The Department will submit a legislative proposal to authorize the Helium Fund to continue activities that support the sale of helium. Under the Helium Privatization Act of 1996, the Helium Fund is set to expire upon the repayment of the helium debt, anticipated to occur the first quarter of fiscal year 2014. The proposal would enable the sale of helium and related products and deposits of net proceeds to the Treasury. Additional revenues from this proposal are estimated at $480 million over the decade.

Transboundary Gulf of Mexico Agreement – The 2014 budget includes a legislative proposal to implement the Agreement between the U.S. and the United Mexican States Concerning Transboundary Hydrocarbon Reservoirs in the Gulf of Mexico, signed by representatives of the U.S. and Mexico on February 20, 2012. The Agreement establishes a framework for the cooperative exploration and development of hydrocarbon resources that cross the United States-Mexico maritime boundary in the Gulf of Mexico. The budget assumes bonus bid revenues from lease sales in this area will generate an estimated $50 million for the Treasury in 2014.

Return Coal Abandoned Mine Land Reclamation Fees to Historic Levels – The budget proposes legislation to modify the 2006 amendments to the Surface Mining Control and Reclamation Act that lowered the per-ton coal fee that companies pay into the AML Fund. The proposal would return the fees to the same levels that companies paid prior to the 2006 fee reduction. The additional revenue, estimated at $427 million over ten years, will be used to reclaim high priority abandoned coal mines.

Reallocate State Share of NPR-A Revenues to Priority BLM Alaska Activities – The budget proposes to temporarily halt revenue sharing payments to the State of Alaska from NPR-A oil and gas development in order to reallocate these resources to a new Alaska Land Conveyance and Remediation Fund. This fund would be used to supplement current appropriations and address priority BLM program needs in Alaska, specifically the remediation of oil and gas legacy wells in NPR-A and the completion of remaining land title conveyances to the State of Alaska, individual Alaska Natives, and Alaska Native Corporations. The regular 50/50 Federal-State revenue sharing arrangement would resume once the work on these two Alaska-specific activities is complete. This approach of temporarily suspending revenue sharing payments is similar to the approach taken by Congress to address priority site remediation needs in the Naval Oil Shale Reserve No. 3 located in the State of Colorado.

Discontinue AML Payments to Certified States – The budget proposes to discontinue the unrestricted payments to States and Tribes certified for completing their coal reclamation work. These payments can be used for general purposes and no longer contribute to abandoned coal mine lands reclamation. While the Surface Transportation Extension Act of 2012 capped annual payments to each certified State and Tribe at $15.0 million, this proposal terminates all such payments with estimated savings of $327 million over the next ten years.

Reclamation of Abandoned Hardrock Mines – The Department proposes to create a parallel Abandoned Mine Lands Program for abandoned hardrock sites, financed through the imposition of a new AML fee on hardrock production on both public and private lands to address the legacy of abandoned hardrock mines across the U.S. and hold the hardrock mining industry accountable for past mining practices. The BLM will distribute the funds through a set allocation to reclaim the highest priority hardrock abandoned sites on Federal, State, tribal, and private lands.

Reform Hardrock Mining on Federal Lands – Interior will submit a legislative proposal to provide a fair return to the taxpayer from hardrock production on Federal lands. The legislative proposal will institute a leasing program under the Mineral Leasing Act of 1920 for certain hardrock minerals including gold, silver, lead, zinc, copper, uranium, and molybdenum, currently covered by the General Mining Law of 1872. The proposal is projected to generate revenues to the U.S. Treasury of $80 million over ten years, with larger revenues estimated in following years.

Net Receipts Sharing for Energy Minerals – The Department proposes to make permanent the current arrangement for sharing the cost to administer energy and minerals receipts. Under current law, States receiving significant payments from mineral revenue development on Federal lands also share in the costs of administering the Federal mineral leases from which the revenue is generated. In 2014, this net receipts sharing deduction from mineral revenue payments to States will be implemented as an offset to the Interior Appropriations Act, consistent with the provision included in 2010 and continued in 2011, 2012, and 2013. Permanent implementation of net receipts sharing is expected to result in savings of $44 million in 2015 and $421 million over ten years.

EXPLANATORY NOTES (*continued*)

Geothermal Energy Receipts – The Department proposes to repeal Section 224(b) of the Energy Policy Act of 2005, relating to geothermal revenues. The repeal of Section 224(b) will permanently discontinue payments to counties and restore the disposition of Federal geothermal leasing revenues to the historical formula of 50 percent to the States and 50 percent to the Treasury. This results in savings of $4.0 million in 2014 and $48 million over ten years.

Federal Land Transaction Facilitation Act – The Department proposes to reauthorize this Act that expired on July 25, 2011, and allow lands identified as suitable for disposal in recent land use plans to be sold using the Act's authority. The Act's sales revenues will continue to be used to fund the acquisition of environmentally sensitive lands and the administrative costs associated with conducting the sales.

Federal Migratory Bird Hunting and Conservation Stamps – Federal Migratory Bird Hunting and Conservation Stamps, commonly known as Duck Stamps, were originally created in 1934 as the annual Federal license required for hunting migratory waterfowl. Today, 98 percent of the receipts generated from the sale of these $15.00 stamps are used to acquire important migratory bird areas for migration, breeding, and wintering. The price of the Duck Stamp has not increased since 1991, while the cost of land and water has increased significantly. The Department proposes to increase these fees to $25.00 per stamp per year, beginning in 2014. Increasing the cost of Duck Stamps will bring the estimate for the Migratory Bird Conservation account to an estimated $61 million.

Recreation Fee Program – The Department of the Interior will propose legislation to permanently reauthorize the Federal Lands Recreation Enhancement Act, which expires in December 2014. The Department currently collects over $200 million in recreation fees annually under this authority. In addition, the Department will propose a General Provision in the 2014 budget request to amend appropriations language to extend the authority through 2015.

GENERAL PROVISIONS PROPOSALS

Chesapeake Bay Initiative – The budget includes a provision to extend the authorization of the Chesapeake Bay Initiative authorized by P.L. 105-312 through 2014.

American Battlefield Protection Program Grants – The budget includes a provision to extend the authorization for the American Battlefield Protection Program grants authorized by P.L. 111-11 through 2014.

Service First – The budget includes a provision to expand the authorization for the Service First authorities which are currently authorized for the BLM, FWS, NPS, and Forest Service to encompass all the bureaus and offices of the Department of the Interior.

OFFSETTING COLLECTIONS AND FEES

The budget includes the following proposals to collect or increase various fees, so that industry shares some of the cost of Federal permitting and regulatory oversight.

Fee Increase for Offshore Oil and Gas Inspections – Through appropriations language, the Department proposes to fund inspection fees at $65.0 million in 2014 for offshore oil and gas drilling facilities that are subject to inspection by the Bureau of Safety and Environmental Enforcement. These fees will support BSEE's expanded inspection program, which will increase production accountability, human safety, and environmental protection.

EXPLANATORY NOTES (*continued*)

New Fee for Onshore Oil and Gas Inspections – Through appropriations language, the Department proposes to implement an inspection fee in 2014 for onshore oil and gas activities subject to inspection by BLM. The proposed inspection fee is expected to generate an estimated $48.0 million in 2014, $10.0 million more than the corresponding $38.0 million reduction in requested appropriations for BLM, thereby expanding the capacity of BLM's oil and gas inspection program. The fee is similar to fees already in place for offshore operations.

Onshore Oil and Gas Drilling Permit Fee – The 2014 budget proposes to continue a fee for processing drilling permits through appropriations language, an approach taken by Congress in the 2009 and subsequent Interior Appropriations Acts. A fee of $6,500 per drilling permit was authorized in 2010, and if continued, will generate an estimated $32.5 million in offsetting collections in 2014.

Surface Mining and Reclamation Permit Fee – The 2014 budget continues an offsetting collection initiated in 2012, allowing the Office of Surface Mining Reclamation and Enforcement, to retain coal mine permit application and renewal fees for the work performed as service to the coal industry. The fee will help ensure the efficient processing, review, and enforcement of the permits issued, while recovering some of the regulatory operating costs from the industry that benefits from this service. The fee, authorized by section 507 of SMCRA, will apply to mining permits on lands where regulatory jurisdiction has not been delegated to the States. The permit fee will generate an estimated $2.4 million in offsetting collections in 2014.

Grazing Administrative Fee – The 2014 budget proposes a new grazing administrative fee of $1 per animal unit month. The BLM proposes to implement this fee through appropriations language on a three-year pilot basis. The 2014 budget estimates the fee will generate $6.5 million in 2014, which will assist the BLM in processing grazing permits. During the period of the pilot, BLM will work through the process of promulgating regulations for the continuation of the grazing fee as a cost recovery fee after the pilot expires.

Marine Minerals Administrative Fee – The 2014 budget also proposes to establish an offsetting fee in the Marine Minerals program of the Bureau of Ocean Energy Management to recover costs associated with processing offshore sand and gravel mining permits. The fees are estimated to generate approximately $470,000 in revenue in 2014, and will be implemented through existing regulatory authority under the Outer Continental Shelf Lands Act.

ENERGY PROGRAMS

(in thousands of dollars)

Bureau/Program/Activity	2013 Full Year CR [1]	2012 Enacted	2014 Request	Change from 2012
BUREAU OF LAND MANAGEMENT				
Energy and Minerals Program				
Oil and Gas Management Subactivity........................	76,042	72,466	46,699	-25,767
Offsetting Collections (APD fees)	32,500	32,500	32,500	0
Offsetting Collections (inspection fees)......................	0	0	47,950	+47,950
Renewable Energy Subactivity [2]	22,826	19,703	29,061	+9,358
Soil, Water, and Air Subactivity				
Air Quality Monitoring	2,000	2,000	2,000	0
Subtotal, Appropriations and				
Offsetting Collections......................................	133,368	126,669	158,210	+31,541
Other Funding Sources				
Service Charges, Deposits, and Forfeitures Account				
Oil and Gas Cost Recoveries (non-APD) [3]...........	3,320	3,292	3,320	+28
Rights-of-Way Processing Cost Recoveries [4].......	8,450	8,424	8,450	+26
ROW Cost Recoveries - Renewable Energy [4]......	[4,225]	[4,212]	[4,225]	[+13]
Permanent				
APD Permit Processing Improvement Fund........	20,698	18,512	18,726	+214
NPR-2 Revenue	29	9	53	+44
Subtotal, Other Funding Sources..........................	32,497	30,237	30,549	+312
Subtotal, Bureau of Land Management...................................	165,865	156,906	188,759	+31,853
BLM Subtotal - New Energy Frontier Initiative [5]............	[154,066]	[145,181]	[176,936]	[+31,755]
BUREAU OF OCEAN ENERGY MANAGEMENT				
Ocean Energy Management...	60,061	59,696	71,549	+11,853
Offsetting Collections...	101,082	101,082	97,891	-3,191
Subtotal, Bureau of Ocean Energy Management....................	161,143	160,778	169,440	+8,662
BOEM Subtotal - New Energy Frontier Initiative [5]	[161,143]	[160,778]	[169,440]	[+8,662]
BUREAU OF SAFETY AND ENVIRONMENTAL ENFORCEMENT				
Offshore Safety and Environmental Enforcement	61,751	61,375	83,263	+21,888
Offsetting Collections...	59,081	59,081	58,970	-111
Offsetting Collections (inspection fees)......................	62,000	62,000	65,000	+3,000
Oil Spill Research..	14,990	14,899	14,899	0
Subtotal, Bureau of Safety and Environmental Enforcement	197,822	197,355	222,132	+24,777
BSEE Subtotal - New Energy Frontier Initiative [5]...........	[197,822]	[197,355]	[222,132]	[+24,777]
BUREAU OF RECLAMATION				
Sustainable Hydropower...	2,000	794	1,113	+319
Reclamation Subtotal - New Energy Frontier Initiative..	[2,000]	[794]	[1,113]	[+319]

ENERGY PROGRAMS
(in thousands of dollars)

Bureau/Program/Activity	2013 Full Year CR [1]	2012 Enacted	2014 Request	Change from 2012
U.S. GEOLOGICAL SURVEY				
Energy Resources - Renewable Energy	5,904	5,904	9,904	+4,000
Energy Resources - Conventional Energy	19,480	19,480	21,161	+1,681
Hydraulic Fracturing	8,578	5,578	18,613	+13,035
Subtotal, U.S. Geological Survey	33,962	30,962	49,678	+18,716
USGS Subtotal - New Energy Frontier Initiative	[33,962]	[30,962]	[49,678]	[+18,716]
FISH AND WILDLIFE SERVICE				
Consultation, Planning, and Enforcement	14,108	10,108	17,508	+7,400
FWS Subtotal - New Energy Frontier Initiative	[14,108]	[10,108]	[17,508]	[+7,400]
BUREAU OF INDIAN AFFAIRS				
Community and Economic Development				
Mining and Minerals Program (TPA)	4,206	4,208	4,021	-187
Mining and Minerals Program (non-TPA)	12,752	12,702	15,574	+2,872
Mining and Minerals Central Oversight	897	892	907	+15
Mining and Minerals Regional Oversight	853	858	770	-88
Real Estate Services	1,000	1,000	1,400	+400
Subtotal, Bureau of Indian Affairs	19,708	19,660	22,672	+3,012
BIA Subtotal - New Energy Frontier Initiative	[8,500]	[8,500]	[10,800]	[+2,300]
OFFICE OF THE SECRETARY				
Office of Hearings and Appeals	1,245	1,234	1,207	-27
Office of Insular Affairs	2,218	1,087	2,971	+1,884
Office of Natural Resources Revenue	120,148	119,418	121,060	+1,642
Subtotal, Office of the Secretary	123,611	121,739	125,238	+3,499
OS Subtotal - New Energy Frontier Initiative	[122,366]	[120,505]	[124,031]	[+3,526]
TOTAL, DEPARTMENT OF THE INTERIOR	**718,219**	**698,302**	**796,540**	**+98,238**
TOTAL, NEW ENERGY FRONTIER INITIATIVE [5]	**[693,967]**	**[674,183]**	**[771,638]**	**[+97,455]**

[1] *The 2013 Full Year CR totals do not include any funding from the Disaster Relief Appropriations Act, 2013.*

[2] *The 2014 Request includes an internal transfer of $2.0 million in base funding for geothermal energy from the Oil and Gas Management subactivity to the Renewable Energy subactivity.*

[3] *These cost recovery amounts are estimates only in the 2013 Full Year CR and 2014 Request.*

[4] *Amounts shown are 50 percent of the total Rights-of-Way cost recoveries, reflecting estimates for energy-related ROWs. It is then estimated that 50 percent of energy-related ROWs are renewable energy-related.*

[5] *The New Energy Frontier initiative subtotals include current, permanent, and offsetting collections funding for BLM, BOEM, and BSEE.*

WATERSMART

(in thousands of dollars)

Bureau/Account/Program	2013 Full Year CR	2012 Enacted	2014 Request	Change from 2013 CR
BUREAU OF RECLAMATION *				
Water and Related Resources				
WaterSMART Grants	24,500	12,233	12,000	-12,500
Basin Studies	6,000	4,928	4,734	-1,266
Cooperative Watershed Management	250	247	250	0
Shared Investment Water Innovation Program	0	0	1,000	+1,000
Title XVI Water Reclamation and Reuse Program	20,271	24,653	14,000	-6,271
Water Conservation Field Services	4,886	5,047	3,437	-1,449
Subtotal, Bureau of Reclamation	55,907	47,108	35,421	-20,486

	2013 Full Year CR	2012 Enacted	2014 Request	Change from 2012
U.S. GEOLOGICAL SURVEY				
Surveys, Investigations, and Research				
Ecosystems				
Fisheries	498	498	1,884	+1,386
Climate and Land Use Change				
Land Change Science	634	498	634	+136
Energy, Minerals, and Environmental Health				
Contaminant Biology	0	0	1,000	+1,000
Toxic Substances Hydrology	0	0	1,800	+1,800
Water Resources				
Groundwater Resources	2,685	2,685	4,512	+1,827
National Water Quality Assessment	1,100	0	3,300	+3,300
Hydrologic Research and Development	0	0	300	+300
Hydrologic Networks and Analysis	5,393	4,293	6,639	+2,346
Cooperative Water Program	1,500	0	2,000	+2,000
Core Science Systems				
National Cooperative Geologic Mapping	0	0	200	+200
National Geospatial Program	200	0	200	+200
Subtotal, U.S. Geological Survey	12,010	7,974	22,469	+14,495
TOTAL, DEPARTMENT OF THE INTERIOR	67,917	55,082	57,890	–
CHANGE FROM 2012 ENACTED	–	55,082	57,890	+2,808
CHANGE FROM 2013 FULL YEAR CR	67,917	–	57,890	-10,027

* Reclamation project details for the 2014 request are compared to the 2013 Continuing Resolution, P.L. 112-175, annualized.

YOUTH IN THE GREAT OUTDOORS

(in thousands of dollars)

Bureau/Account/Program	2013 Full Year CR	2012 Enacted	2014 Request	Change from 2012
BUREAU OF LAND MANAGEMENT				
Soil, Water and Air Management	1,111	3,611	4,861	+1,250
Recreation Resource Management	4,009	4,009	4,009	0
Wildlife Management for				
National Fish and Wildlife Foundation	0	0	1,500	+1,500
National Fish and Wildlife Foundation	1,000	1,000	1,000	0
Subtotal, Bureau of Land Management	6,120	8,620	11,370	+2,750
BUREAU OF RECLAMATION	2,800	3,800	3,800	0
U.S. GEOLOGICAL SURVEY				
Science Support	1,554	1,512	2,554	+1,042
Enterprise Information	0	90	0	-90
National Cooperative Geologic Mapping-EDMAP	600	600	600	0
Subtotal, U.S. Geological Survey	2,154	2,202	3,154	+952
FISH AND WILDLIFE SERVICE				
Refuges	4,207	4,079	4,207	+128
Fisheries	3,694	3,694	3,694	0
Migratory Bird Management	274	524	274	-250
National Conservation Training Center	4,193	4,193	6,693	+2,500
Youth Internships	1,000	1,000	1,000	0
Subtotal, Fish and Wildlife Service	13,368	13,490	15,868	+2,378
NATIONAL PARK SERVICE				
Operation of the National Park System	13,648	13,638	14,661	+1,023
Recreation Fee Program	[6,400]	[6,400]	[6,400]	[0]
Subtotal, National Park Service	13,648	13,638	14,661	+1,023
INDIAN AFFAIRS				
Operation of Indian Programs				
Bureau of Indian Affairs				
Trust Natural Resources	0	0	2,500	+2,500
Oversight Youth Office	0	0	[250]	[+250]
Bureau of Indian Education				
Post-Secondary Programs	0	0	3,000	+3,000
Subtotal, Indian Affairs	0	0	5,500	+5,500
TOTAL, DEPARTMENT OF THE INTERIOR	**38,090**	**41,750**	**54,353**	**+12,603**

LAND AND WATER CONSERVATION FUND

(in thousands of dollars)

Program/Bureau/Activity	2013 Full Year CR	2012 Enacted	2014 Current	2014 Permanent	2014 Total	2014 Total Change from 2012
FEDERAL LAND ACQUISITION						
Department of the Interior						
Bureau of Land Management............................	22,481	22,344	32,618	16,308	48,926	+26,582
Fish and Wildlife Service	54,966	54,632	70,833	35,497	106,330	+51,698
National Park Service..	57,318	56,969	60,391	30,195	90,586	+33,617
Interior Office of Valuation Services	12,770	12,692	12,168	6,000	18,168	+5,476
Subtotal, Department of the Interior.........................	147,535	146,637	176,010	88,000	264,010	+117,373
Interior Collaborative Landscape Planning......	[83,597]	[0]	[57,087]	[55,154]	[112,241]	[+112,241]
Department of Agriculture						
U.S. Forest Service..	52,842	52,521	58,000	34,200	92,200	+39,679
Collaborative Landscape Planning	[25,000]	[0]	[36,384]	[20,631]	[57,015]	[+57,015]
TOTAL, FEDERAL LAND ACQUISITION	**200,377**	**199,158**	**234,010**	**122,200**	**356,210**	**+157,052**
Total, Collaborative Landscape Planning.................	[108,597]	[0]	[93,471]	[75,785]	[169,256]	[+169,256]
OTHER CONSERVATION GRANTS						
Department of the Interior						
Fish and Wildlife Service						
Cooperative Endangered Species						
Conservation Fund [1]..................................	25,113	24,960	56,000	28,000	84,000	+59,040
National Park Service						
State Grants - Current [2]	45,203	44,928	40,000	20,000	60,000	+15,072
Urban Parks and Recreation Fund	0	0	10,000	5,000	15,000	+15,000
Subtotal, Department of the Interior.........................	70,316	69,888	106,000	53,000	159,000	+89,112
Department of Agriculture						
U.S. Forest Service						
Forest Legacy..	53,629	53,303	60,000	24,800	84,800	+31,497
TOTAL, OTHER CONSERVATION GRANTS	**123,945**	**123,191**	**166,000**	**77,800**	**243,800**	**+120,609**
TOTAL, LAND AND WATER						
CONSERVATION FUND..	**324,322**	**322,349**	**400,010**	**200,000**	**600,010**	**+277,661**
TOTAL, DEPARTMENT OF THE INTERIOR	**217,851**	**216,525**	**282,010**	**141,000**	**423,010**	**+206,485**
TOTAL, DEPARTMENT OF AGRICULTURE	**106,471**	**105,824**	**118,000**	**59,000**	**177,000**	**+71,176**

[1] *The 2012 and 2013 amounts include only the funding that is appropriated by Congress from the LWCF. The 2014 budget proposes to fund all of the Cooperative Endangered Species Conservation Fund from the LWCF.*

[2] *Excludes permanent appropriations from revenues generated by leasing activities on the Outer Continental Shelf, authorized by the Gulf of Mexico Energy Security Act, and disbursed by NPS.*

LAND ACQUISITION PROGRAM
LAND AND WATER CONSERVATION FUND

(current authority in thousands of dollars)

Bureau/State/Project	Acres	2014 Current
BUREAU OF LAND MANAGEMENT		
California		
Big Morongo Canyon Area of Critical		
Environmental Concern [1]	738	1,330
California Coastal National Monument	23	2,000
California Wilderness [1]	12,235	6,702
Coachella Fringe-Toed Lizard ACEC [1]	1,971	1,971
Dos Palmas ACEC [1]	176	850
Johnson Canyon ACEC [1]	295	1,060
Pacific Crest National Scenic Trail [1]	620	2,920
San Filpe / San Sebastian Marsh ACEC [1]	497	200
Santa Rosa and San Jacinto Mountains		
National Monument [1]	3,261	5,948
Subtotal		22,981
Colorado		
Canyons of the Ancients National Monument	1,562	1,703
Idaho		
Lower Salmon River ACEC		
Special Recreation Management Area	4,604	1,820
Montana		
Blackfoot River SRMA / Douglas Creek [2]	3,680	2,600
Subtotal, BLM line-item projects		29,104
Acquisition Management		1,898
Emergencies and Hardships		1,616
Subtotal, Bureau of Land Management		**32,618**
FISH AND WILDLIFE SERVICE		
Arkansas		
Cache River National Wildlife Refuge	1,920	5,000
Florida		
Everglades Headwaters National Wildlife Refuge		
and Conservation Area	1,250	5,000
St. Marks National Wildlife Refuge [3]	905	2,208
Subtotal		7,208
Georgia		
Okenfenokee National Wildlife Refuge [3]	990	2,408
Kansas		
Flint Hills Legacy Conservation Area	5,000	2,000

LAND ACQUISITION PROGRAM
LAND AND WATER CONSERVATION FUND

(current authority in thousands of dollars)

Bureau/State/Project	Acres	2014 Current
Montana		
Blackfoot Valley Conservation Area [2/]	7,200	4,680
Rocky Mountain Front/ Swan Valley Conservation Area [2/]	14,670	7,260
Subtotal		11,940
South Carolina		
Cape Romain National Wildlife Refuge [3/]	960	2,329
Waccamaw National Wildlife Refuge [3/]	1,045	2,536
Subtotal		4,865
Texas		
Neches River National Wildlife Refuge	1,913	3,000
Multi-State		
Dakota Grassland Conservation Area (ND/SD)	23,053	8,650
Dakota Tallgrass Prarie Wildlife Management Area (ND/SD)	6,122	3,000
Subtotal		11,650
Subtotal, FWS line-item projects		48,071
Acquisition Management		10,778
Land Protection Planning		3,434
Cost Allocation Methodology		2,003
Inholdings/Emergencies/Hardships		5,047
Exchanges		1,500
Subtotal, Fish and Wildlife Service		70,833

NATIONAL PARK SERVICE

California		
Joshua Tree National Park, Mojave National Preserve [1/]	9,558	7,595
Colorado		
Sand Creek Massacre National Historic Site	640	319
Florida		
Timucuan Ecological and Historic Preserve [3/]	262	2,031
Michigan		
Sleeping Bear Dunes National Lakeshore	37	5,269
Montana		
Glacier National Park [2/]	2	1,030
South Carolina		
Congaree National Park [3/]	355	1,428

LAND ACQUISITION PROGRAM
LAND AND WATER CONSERVATION FUND

(current authority in thousands of dollars)

Bureau/State/Project	Acres	2014 Current
Texas		
San Antonio Missions National Historic Park......................	40	1,760
Virgin Islands		
Virgin Islands National Park..	3	2,771
Multi-State		
Civil War Sesquicentennial Units (TBD)		5,500
Greenways and Blueways (TBD)..		4,745
Subtotal..		10,245
Subtotal, NPS line-item projects...		32,448
Acquisition Management		9,500
Emergencies, Hardship, and Relocation		3,093
Inholdings, Donations, and Exchanges		6,364
American Battlefield Protection Program		
Acquisition Grants..		8,986
Subtotal, National Park Service		**60,391**
OFFICE OF THE SECRETARY		
Office of Valuation Services		12,168
TOTAL, DEPARTMENT OF THE INTERIOR		
FEDERAL LAND ACQUISITION..		**176,010**
TOTAL, DEPARTMENT OF THE INTERIOR,		
COLLABORATIVE LANDSCAPE PLANNING		**[57,087]**

[1] *These projects are part of the Collaborative Landscape Planning for the Southwest Desert landscape.*
[2] *These projects are part of the Collaborative Landscape Planning for the Crown of the Continent landscape.*
[3] *These projects are part of the Collaborative Landscape Planning for the Longleaf Pine landscape.*

LAND ACQUISITION PROGRAM
LAND AND WATER CONSERVATION FUND

(permanent authority in thousands of dollars)

Bureau/State/Project	Acres	2014 Permanent
BUREAU OF LAND MANAGEMENT		
Arizona		
Agua Fria National Monument	80	111
Ironwood Forest National Monument	612	1,000
Subtotal		1,111
Colorado		
Dominguez-Escalante National Conservation Area	135	600
Idaho		
Henrys Lake Area of Critical Environmental Concern	515	1,000
Montana		
Lewis and Clark National Historic Trail/ Nez Perce NHT/Upper Missouri National Wild and Scenic River [1]	779	1,600
Oregon		
Cascade-Siskiyou National Monument	1,320	2,000
Crooked National Wild and Scenic River	101	975
Pacific Crest National Scenic Trail [1]	3,573	4,122
Subtotal		7,097
Utah		
Red Cliffs National Conservation Area	100	4,000
Wyoming		
North Platte River Special River Management Area	70	900
Subtotal, Bureau of Land Management		16,308
FISH AND WILDLIFE SERVICE		
California		
Grasslands Wildlife Management Area	475	1,000
San Diego National Wildlife Refuge [2]	1,405	11,770
San Joaquin River National Wildlife Refuge	91	1,000
Subtotal		13,770
Maryland		
Blackwater National Wildlife Refuge	247	1,000
Minnesota		
Northern Tallgrass Prairie National Wildlife Refuge	80	567
New Mexico		
Valle de Oro National Wildlife Refuge [1]	106	6,800

LAND ACQUISITION PROGRAM
LAND AND WATER CONSERVATION FUND

(permanent authority in thousands of dollars)

Bureau/State/Project	Acres	2014 Permanent
Pennsylvania		
Cherry Valley National Wildlife Refuge [1]	3,129	4,300
Rhode Island		
John H. Chafee National Wildlife Refuge	13	900
Texas		
Lower Rio Grande Valley	800	1,000
Washington		
Steirgerwald National Wildlife Refuge [1]	86	1,560
Multi-State		
Silvio O. Conte National Fish and Wildlife Refuge (CT/MA/NH/VT)	3,700	4,600
Upper Mississippi River National Wildlife Refuge (IA/IL/MN/WI)	300	1,000
Subtotal		5,600
Subtotal, Fish and Wildlife Service		**35,497**
NATIONAL PARK SERVICE		
Arizona		
Saguaro National Park	61	1,456
California		
Santa Monica Mountains National Recreation Area	317	3,737
Hawaii		
Ala Kahakai National Trail [1]	59	4,250
Oregon		
Nez Perce National Historic Trail [1]	973	1,210
Wisconsin		
Ice Age national Scenic Trail [1]	457	3,780
Multi-State		
Appalachian National Trail (CT/GA/MA/MD/ME/NH/NJ/NY/NC/PA/TN/VT/VA/WV) [1]	374	3,700
Continental Divide National Scenic Trail (CO/ID/MT/NM/WY) [1]	2,885	5,300
New England National Scenic Trail (CT/MA) [1]	206	4,000
North Country National Scenic Trail (MI/MN/NY/ND/OH/PA/WI) [1]	395	2,762
Subtotal		15,762
Subtotal, National Park Service		**30,195**

LAND ACQUISITION PROGRAM
LAND AND WATER CONSERVATION FUND

(permanent authority in thousands of dollars)

Bureau/State/Project	Acres	2014 Permanent
OFFICE OF THE SECRETARY		
Office of Valuation Services		6,000
TOTAL, DEPARTMENT OF THE INTERIOR		
COLLABORATIVE LANDSCAPE PLANNING		[55,154]
TOTAL, DEPARTMENT OF THE INTERIOR		
FEDERAL LAND ACQUISITION		88,000

[1] *These projects are part of the Collaborative Landscape Planning for the National Trails.*

[2] *These projects are part of the Collaborative Landscape Planning for the Southwest Desert Landscape.*

EVERGLADES RESTORATION

(in thousands of dollars)

Bureau/Account/Program	2013 Full Year CR	2012 Enacted	2014 Request	Change from 2012
U.S. GEOLOGICAL SURVEY				
Surveys, Investigations, and Research				
Ecosystems				
Environments	6,882	6,882	6,882	0
Invasive Species	0	0	1,000	+1,000
Subtotal, U.S. Geological Survey	6,882	6,882	7,882	+1,000
FISH AND WILDLIFE SERVICE				
Resource Management				
Comprehensive Everglades Restoration Plan				
Implementation	3,246	3,246	3,246	0
Ecological Services	2,913	2,913	2,913	0
Refuges and Wildlife	4,016	4,016	4,016	0
Migratory Birds	99	99	99	0
Law Enforcement	608	608	608	0
Fisheries	92	92	92	0
Land Acquisition				
Everglades Headwaters National				
Wildlife Refuge and Conservation Area	3,000	0	5,000	+5,000
Subtotal, Fish and Wildlife Service	13,974	10,974	15,974	+5,000
Comprehensive Everglades Restoration Plan				
Reimbursable Agreement with the U.S. Army				
Corps of Engineers	[720]	[1,390]	[500]	[-890]
NATIONAL PARK SERVICE				
Operation of the National Park System				
Park Operations	29,571	29,611	30,191	+580
Comprehensive Everglades Restoration Plan				
Implementation	4,720	4,691	4,764	+73
Comprehensive Everglades Restoration Plan				
Rental Space	410	410	410	0
Task Force	1,311	1,303	1,322	+19
Everglades Research	3,845	3,822	3,831	+9
Construction				
Modified Water Deliveries Project	8,000	7,987	0	-7,987
Big Cypress Sustainable Trail System	0	2,669	0	-2,669
Tamiami Trail Bridging	0	0	30,000	+30,000
Land Acquisition				
Everglades National Park	0	24,960	0	-24,960
Big Cypress National Park and Preserve	0	5,551	0	-5,551
Everglades Acquisition Management	700	634	700	+66
Subtotal, National Park Service	48,557	81,638	71,218	-10,420
BUREAU OF INDIAN AFFAIRS				
Operation of Indian Programs				
Seminole and Miccosukee Tribal Water Studies	390	390	390	0
TOTAL, DEPARTMENT OF THE INTERIOR	**69,803**	**99,884**	**95,464**	**-4,420**

OCEANS

(in thousands of dollars)

Bureau/Account/Program	2013 Full Year CR [1]	2012 Enacted	2014 Request	Change from 2012
BUREAU OF OCEAN ENERGY MANAGEMENT				
Ocean Energy Management	161,143	160,778	169,440	+8,662
BUREAU OF SAFETY AND ENVIRONMENTAL ENFORCEMENT				
Offshore Safety and Environmental Enforcement	182,832	182,456	207,233	+24,777
Oil Spill Research	14,990	14,899	14,899	0
Subtotal, Bureau of Safety and Environmental Enforcemt	197,822	197,355	222,132	+24,777
U.S. GEOLOGICAL SURVEY				
Surveys, Investigations, and Research				
Ecosystems	37,100	37,100	42,800	+5,700
Climate and Land Use Change	3,209	2,012	4,275	+2,263
Natural Hazards - Earthquake, Landslide,				
Global Seismic Network	14,900	14,900	14,900	0
Natural Hazards - Coastal and Marine Geology	42,221	42,821	48,954	+6,133
Energy, Minerals, and Environmental Health	2,100	2,100	2,100	0
Water Resources	17,700	15,000	15,000	0
Core Science Systems	5,000	5,000	5,300	+300
Subtotal, U.S. Geological Survey	122,230	118,933	133,329	+14,396
FISH AND WILDLIFE SERVICE				
Resource Management	194,990	210,560	200,810	-9,750
Sport Fish Restoration Account [2][3]	27,130	31,160	26,980	-4,180
North American Wetlands Conservation Fund [2]	18,130	18,110	17,980	-130
Subtotal, Fish and Wildlife Service	240,250	259,830	245,770	-14,060
NATIONAL PARK SERVICE				
Operation of the National Park System	87,332	87,332	88,582	+1,250
Everglades Restoration and Research	4,938	4,908	4,959	+51
Subtotal, National Park Service	92,270	92,240	93,541	+1,301
DEPARTMENTAL OFFICES				
Office of the Secretary				
Office of Natural Resources Revenue	60,034	59,709	60,530	+821
Office of Insular Affairs				
Assistance to Territories, Coral Reef Initiative	1,004	998	1,000	+2
Subtotal, Departmental Offices	61,038	60,707	61,530	+823
DEPARTMENT-WIDE PROGRAMS				
Natural Resource Damage Assessment and Restoration [4]				
Damage Assessments	1,600	1,600	1,600	0
Restoration Implementation	30,000	26,000	30,000	+4,000
Subtotal, Department-wide Programs	31,600	27,600	31,600	+4,000
TOTAL, DEPARTMENT OF THE INTERIOR	**906,353**	**917,443**	**957,342**	**+39,899**

[1] *Amounts included in 2013 Full Year CR do not include supplemental appropriations provided in the Disaster Relief Appropriations Act, 2013.*
[2] *Grant amounts for 2013 and 2014 are estimates until awarded.*
[3] *The 2013 and 2014 amounts are estimates of permanent authority in the Sport Fish Restoration account.*
[4] *The 2013 and 2014 amounts are estimates as of March 2013. Restoration implementation is funded by permanent receipts from legal settlements.*

MAINTAINING AMERICA'S HERITAGE

(in thousands of dollars)

Bureau/Account/Program	2013 Full Year CR	2012 Enacted	2014 Request	Change from 2012
MAINTENANCE				
Bureau of Land Management				
Management of Land and Resources ²⁄	71,490	71,120	74,061	+2,941
Oregon and California Grant Lands	10,908	10,984	10,063	-921
National Landscape Conservation System	1,754	1,754	1,754	0
Recreation Fee Program	5,018	5,099	5,124	+25
Subtotal, Bureau of Land Management	89,170	88,957	91,002	+2,045
U.S. Geological Survey				
Surveys, Investigations, and Research	26,380	30,380	26,380	-4,000
Fish and Wildlife Service				
Resource Management	158,704	159,528	160,224	+696
Federal Highway Administration	30,000	25,594	30,000	+4,406
Recreation Fee Program	1,665	1,383	1,594	+211
Subtotal, Fish and Wildlife Service	190,369	186,505	191,818	+5,313
National Park Service				
Operation of the National Park System	337,406	336,402	338,657	+2,255
Federal Highway Administration Park Roads	240,000	240,000	240,000	0
Recreation Fee Program	83,500	89,458	83,500	-5,958
Subtotal, National Park Service	660,906	665,860	662,157	-3,703
Indian Affairs				
Operation of Indian Programs	154,159	152,846	153,632	+786
Department-wide Programs				
Wildland Fire Management	6,127	6,127	6,127	0
SUBTOTAL, MAINTENANCE	**1,127,111**	**1,130,675**	**1,131,116**	**+441**
Construction				
Bureau of Land Management ²⁄	3,592	3,570	0	-3,570
Fish and Wildlife Service	23,192	23,051	15,722	-7,329
National Park Service ³⁄	160,341	159,366	159,961	+595
Indian Affairs	124,387	123,630	107,124	-16,506
SUBTOTAL, CONSTRUCTION	**311,512**	**309,617**	**282,807**	**-26,810**
TOTAL, DEPARTMENT OF THE INTERIOR	**1,438,623**	**1,440,292**	**1,413,923**	**-26,369**

MAINTAINING AMERICA'S HERITAGE
(in thousands of dollars)

Bureau/Account/Program	2013 Full Year CR	2012 Enacted	2014 Request	Change from 2012
TOTALS BY BUREAU				
Bureau of Land Management	92,762	92,527	91,002	-1,525
U.S. Geological Survey	26,380	30,380	26,380	-4,000
Fish and Wildlife Service	213,561	209,556	207,540	-2,016
National Park Service	821,247	825,226	822,118	-3,10
Indian Affairs	278,546	276,476	260,756	-15,720
Department-wide Programs, Wildland Fire	6,127	6,127	6,127	0
TOTAL, DEPARTMENT OF INTERIOR	**1,438,623**	**1,440,292**	**1,413,923**	**-26,369**

[1] *Amounts included in the 2013 Full Year CR do not include supplemental appropriations provided in the Disaster Relief Appropriations Act.*

[2] *The 2014 Bureau of Land Management Budget eliminates the Construction appropriation. Beginning in 2014, BLM construction and deferred maintenance projects will be funded in the Deferred Maintenance and Capital Improvements subactivity in the Management of Lands and Resources account.*

[3] *The amount included for the NPS Construction appropriation does not include the rescission of $4.0 million in the 2012 enacted appropriation and an identical $4.0 million in the 2013 Full Year CR. In addition, the NPS Construction amounts for 2012 do not reflect the transfer of $15.5 million to Wildland Fire Management for fire suppression activities for the later transfer of $15.5 million from Wildland Fire Management in 2013 Full Year CR to repay funds transferred in 2012.*

CONSTRUCTION PROGRAM
INTERIOR, ENVIRONMENT, AND RELATED AGENCIES

(in thousands of dollars)

Bureau/State/Project	Estimated Cost	Through 2013	2014 Request
FISH AND WILDLIFE SERVICE			
Arkansas			
White River National Wildlife Refuge			
Install Tier Two energy upgrades			
to visitor center and offices.	550	0	550
Rehabilitate habitat at Dry Lake.	600	0	600
California			
Modoc National Wildlife Refuge			
Construct seepage control at Dorris Dam.	300	0	300
Colorado			
National Black-Footed Ferret Conservation Center			
Perform emergency building stabilization.	190	0	190
Georgia			
Okefenokee National Wildlife Refuge			
Repair boardwalk and observation platform.	159	0	159
Idaho			
Kooskia National Fish Hatchery			
Rehabilitate signs and interpretive displays.	25	0	25
Illinois			
Crab Orchard National Wildlife Refuge			
Demolish buildings within Areas 9 and 7.	409	0	409
Repair Crab Orchard Dam relief well toe drain system.	525	0	525
Massachusetts			
Great Meadows National Wildlife Refuge			
Install photovoltaic system at headquarters.	362	0	362
New Jersey			
Great Swamp National Wildlife Refuge			
Install photovoltaic system.	330	0	330
Oklahoma			
Tishomingo National Wildlife Refuge			
Rehabilitate headquarters building to			
improve energy efficiency.	139	0	139
Pennsylvania			
John Heinz National Wildlife Refuge			
Rehabilitate boardwalk.	527	0	527

CONSTRUCTION PROGRAM
INTERIOR, ENVIRONMENT, AND RELATED AGENCIES
(in thousands of dollars)

Bureau/State/Project	Estimated Cost	Through 2013	2014 Request
Washington			
Abernathy Fish Technology Center			
Replace electric fish barrier.	1,610	510	1,100
Little White Salmon National Fish Hatchery			
Demolish hatchery building water reuse system.	50	0	50
Makah National Fish Hatchery			
Replace electric fish barrier.	970	0	970
Turnbull National Wildlife Refuge			
Complete Tier Two energy upgrades for Turnbull comfort station and remove power line.	210	0	210
Multi-State			
Perform seismic safety inspections.	215	0	215
Servicewide			
Dam and Bridge Safety			
Dam Safety Program Inspections			1,113
Bridge Safety Program Inspections			739
National Engineering Services			
Core Engineering Services			5,991
Environmental Compliance Management			998
Seismic Safety Program			120
Waste Prevention and Recycling			100
Subtotal Servicewide			9,061
TOTAL, FISH AND WILDLIFE SERVICE			**15,722**

NATIONAL PARK SERVICE

Bureau/State/Project	Estimated Cost	Through 2013	2014 Request
Alaska			
Wrangell-St. Elias National Park and Preserve			
Correct critical life/health/safety issues at Kennecott Mine structures, Phase Two.	TBD [1/]	6,007	1,850
Arizona			
Grand Canyon National Park			
Provide potable water to South Rim and replace failing transcanyon pipeline at Phantom Ranch.	4,046	300	3,746
California			
San Francisco Maritime National Historical Park			
Replace heating system in National Historic Landmark Aquatic Park bathhouse building.	1,644	60	1,584

CONSTRUCTION PROGRAM
INTERIOR, ENVIRONMENT, AND RELATED AGENCIES
(in thousands of dollars)

Bureau/State/Project	Estimated Cost	Through 2013	2014 Request
District of Columbia			
National Capital Parks - East			
Rehabilitate Historic Carter G. Woodson Home.	3,583	374	3,209
National Mall and Memorial Parks			
Install irrigation, drainage, a water collection system, and re-landscape the National Mall, Phase Two.	42,980	18,766	14,219
Florida			
Everglades National Park			
Construct Tamiami Trail bridging.	TBD [1/]	2,980	30,000
New York			
Vanderbilt Mansion National Historic Site			
Complete the exterior rehabilitation of the Vanderbilt Mansion and protect critical resource.	7,091	873	6,218
Pennsylvania			
Independence National Historical Park			
Repair Second Bank block hazardous walkways.	2,266	285	1,981
Washington			
Olympic National Park			
Continue ongoing restoration of Elwha River Ecosystem.	324,652	314,486	5,891
Wyoming			
Yellowstone National Park			
Replace fishing bridge water system to correct critical life/health/safety deficiencies.	12,288	415	11,873
Multi-State			
Indiana, Virginia			
Indiana Dunes National Lakeshore, Appalachian National Scenic Trail			
Demolish and remove excess structures.	2,709	217	2,492
Servicewide			
Special Programs			
Emergency/Unscheduled			3,855
Housing Improvement Program			2,200
Dam Safety			1,248
Equipment Replacement			13,500
Subtotal, Special Programs			20,803
Construction Planning			7,265
Construction Program Management and Operations			37,082
Management Planning			11,748
TOTAL, NATIONAL PARK SERVICE			**159,961**

CONSTRUCTION PROGRAM
INTERIOR, ENVIRONMENT, AND RELATED AGENCIES
(in thousands of dollars)

Bureau/State/Project	Estimated Cost	Through 2013	2014 Request
INDIAN AFFAIRS			
Education Construction [2/]			
Employee Housing Repair			
Repair critical life safety-related deficiencies in employee housing.			
Multiple Facilities			2,818
Demolition			1,000
Facilities Improvement and Repair			
Repair critical life safety items, consolidate or close under-utilized facilities, and repair education facilities for BIE-funded schools.			
Program Management			3,227
Special Programs			45,240
Subtotal, Education Construction			52,285
Public Safety and Justice Construction			
Facilities Improvement and Repair			
Address detention facilities improvement and repair needs, with emphasis on critical health and safety items identified in safety reports.			
Minor Improvement and Repair			2,206
Condition Assessments			288
Emergency Repair			370
Environmental Projects			547
Portable Offices for Law Enforcement			961
Detention Center Employee Housing			
Construct New Employee Housing			3,194
Advance Planning and Design			300
Fire Protection and Safety Coordination			
Procure fire trucks and equipment and install fire sprinklers and fire and smoke alarms in dormatories, detention centers, and other buildings.			
Fire Protection			3,274
Fire Safety Coordination			166
Subtotal, Public Safety and Justice Construction			11,306

CONSTRUCTION PROGRAM
INTERIOR, ENVIRONMENT, AND RELATED AGENCIES
(in thousands of dollars)

Bureau/State/Project	Estimated Cost	Through 2013	2014 Request
Resources Management Construction			
Irrigation Project Construction			
New Mexico			
Navajo Indian Irrigation Project			3,384
Multiple States			
Irrigation Projects - Rehabilitation			998
Engineering and Supervision			2,044
Survey and Design			292
Federal Power Compliance (FERC)			633
Safety of Dams Projects			
Rehabilitation - Expedited Actions.			15,762
Arizona			
Davis (Hawley) Dam			
Pasture Canyon Dam			
Tufa Stone Dam			
Montana			
Crow Dam			
Hell Roaring Dam			
New Mexico			
Grady Hamilton Dam			
Red Lake Dam			
Tsailie Dam			
North Dakota			
Belcourt Dam			
Gordon Dam			
South Dakota			
Antelope			
Ghost Hawk Dam			
South Okreek			
Sully 2 Dam			
Multiple States			
Expedited Issues - Mitigation of High Risks Failure Modes			406
Issues Evaluations			230
Security			316
Emergency Management Systems			1,900
Safety of Dams Inspection/Evaluations			2,000
Program Coordination			2,884
Dam Maintenance			1,910
Subtotal, Resources Management Construction			*32,759*

CONSTRUCTION PROGRAM
INTERIOR, ENVIRONMENT, AND RELATED AGENCIES
(in thousands of dollars)

Bureau/State/Project	Estimated Cost	Through 2013	2014 Request
Other Program Construction, Improvement, and Repair			
Telecommunications Improvement and Repair			856
Facilities Quarters Improvement and Repair			
Condition Assessments			41
Emergency Repair			200
Environmental Projects			350
Minor Improvement and Repairs			580
Construction Program Management			
Program Management			7,247
Facilities Management Information System			1,500
Subtotal, Other Program Construction, Improvement and Repair			10,774
TOTAL, BUREAU OF INDIAN AFFAIRS			**107,124**

CONSTRUCTION PROGRAM
ENERGY AND WATER DEVELOPMENT
(in thousands of dollars)

Bureau/State/Project	Estimated Cost	Through 2013	2014 Request
BUREAU OF RECLAMATION *(includes Central Utah Project Completion Act)* [3/]			
Arizona			
Central Arizona Project			
Spring Creek Oak Fish Barrier	1,300	70	1,230
O'Donnell Canyon Fish Barrier	337	50	287
Subtotal			1,517
Colorado River Front Work and Levee System			
Yuma Mesa Conduit Construction Improvement	3,849	3,291	558
California			
Colorado River Front Work and Levee System			
Colorado River Backwater C5 Unit	434	51	383
Colorado River Backwater C10 Unit	168	152	16
Subtotal			399
Sacramento River Division, Central Valley Project [4/]			
Red Bluff Diversion Dam	193,567	192,527	1,040
Colorado			
Orchard Mesa Irrigation District			
Canal Automation and System Improvements	16,500	2,087	4,690
New Mexico			
Aamodt Litigation Settlement			
Pojoaque Basin Regional Water System	206,566	70,687	4,664
Navajo-Gallup Water Supply Project	1,040,645	187,058	60,497
Utah			
Upper Colorado Recovery Implementation Program			
Tusher Wash Diversion Dam Fish Screen	4,100	2,100	2,000
Safety of Dams			
California			
Folsom Dam [5/]	368,000	257,707	24,600
Nebraska			
Red Willow Dam	29,030	21,226	800
Wyoming			
Glendo Dam	65,000	29,402	14,000
TOTAL, BUREAU OF RECLAMATION			**114,765**

CONSTRUCTION PROGRAM

1/ *Overall cost and scope are under review.*

2/ *There are no replacement schools or major facilities and repair projects funded in the 2014 Request. All estimates are for minor improvement and repair projects and are without forecast costs until priority rankings are finalized.*

3/ *Projects include only construction funding and therefore may differ from funding amounts shown in the Bureau Highlights of Budget Changes section of this volume.*

4/ *Includes non-Federal contributions of $12.0 million from the State of California for the Fish Passage Improvement Project at Red Bluff Diversion Dam, through 2013.*

5/ *The Bureau of Reclamation has requested a re-baselining for the estimated cost of the Folsom Dam project from $408.3 million to $368.0 million.*

RECREATION FEE PROGRAM

(in thousands of dollars)

Bureau	2012 Actual	2013 Estimate	2014 Estimate
BUREAU OF LAND MANAGEMENT			
Unobligated Balance Brought Forward and Recoveries	13,268	13,221	12,878
Plus: Fee Revenues	+17,141	+18,000	+18,500
America the Beautiful Pass	[800]	[800]	[800]
Less: Funds Obligated	-17,188	-18,343	-19,069
Unobligated Balance	13,221	12,878	12,309
Total Expenditures (outlays)	17,135	17,180	17,510
Obligations by Type of Project			
Asset Repair and Maintenance			
Facilities Routine and Annual Maintenance	3,934	4,000	4,100
Facilities Capital Improvements Health and Safety	153	18	24
Facilities Deferred Maintenance	1,012	1,000	1,000
Subtotal, Asset Repair and Maintenance	5,099	5,018	5,124
Interpretation and Visitor Services	5,997	6,000	6,130
Habitat Restoration	840	850	890
Law Enforcement	2,387	2,800	3,000
Direct Operation Costs - Cost of Collection	325	325	325
Fee Management Agreement and Reservation Services	1,012	2,150	2,300
Administration, Overhead, and Indirect Costs	1,528	1,200	1,300
Total Obligations	17,188	18,343	19,069
FISH AND WILDLIFE SERVICE			
Unobligated Balance Brought Forward and Recoveries	4,535	4,730	4,499
Plus: Fee Revenues	+5,085	+5,100	+5,100
America the Beautiful Pass	[390]	[400]	[440]
Less: Funds Obligated	-4,890	-5,331	-5,221
Unobligated Balance	4,730	4,499	4,378
Total Expenditures (outlays)	5,212	6,000	7,000
Obligations by Type of Project			
Asset Repair and Maintenance			
Facilities Routine and Annual Maintenance	802	998	1,004
Facilities Capital Improvements	404	513	448
Facilities Deferred Maintenance	177	154	142
Subtotal, Asset Repair and Maintenance	1,383	1,665	1,594
Interpretation and Visitor Services	1,765	1,808	1,810
Habitat Restoration	210	210	204
Law Enforcement	342	387	352
Direct Operation Costs - Cost of Collection	665	734	734
Fee Management Agreement and Reservation Services	78	78	78
Administration, Overhead and Indirect Costs	447	449	449
Total Obligations	4,890	5,331	5,221

RECREATION FEE PROGRAM
(in thousands of dollars)

Bureau	2012 Actual	2013 Estimate	2014 Estimate
NATIONAL PARK SERVICE*			
Unobligated Balance Brought Forward and Recoveries	103,417	103,265	104,952
Plus: Fee Revenues	+179,361	+178,687	+178,687
America the Beautiful Pass	[21,014]	[22,000]	[22,000]
Less: Funds Obligated	-182,513	-180,000	-180,000
Unobligated Balance	100,265	101,952	103,639
Total Expenditures (outlays)	206,151	135,000	151,000
Obligations by Type of Project			
Asset Repair and Maintenance			
Facilities Routine and Annual Maintenance	5,144	4,000	4,000
Facilities Capital Improvements Health and Safety	9,211	4,500	4,500
Facilities Deferred Maintenance	75,103	75,000	75,000
Subtotal, Asset Repair and Maintenance	89,458	83,500	83,500
Interpretation and Visitor Services	26,235	30,500	30,500
Habitat Restoration	12,860	13,500	13,500
Law Enforcement	1,029	1,500	1,500
Direct Operation Costs - Cost of Collection	35,442	35,500	35,500
Fee Management Agreement and Reservation Services	5,864	6,000	6,000
Administration, Overhead, and Indirect Costs	11,625	9,500	9,500
Total Obligations	182,513	180,000	180,000
BUREAU OF RECLAMATION			
Unobligated Balance Brought Forward and Recoveries	939	1,229	0
Plus: Fee Revenues	+651	+685	+685
Less: Funds Obligated	-361	-1,914	-685
Unobligated Balance	1,229	0	0
Total Expenditures (outlays)	318	2,010	685
Obligations by Type of Project			
Visitor Services	361	1,914	685
Total Obligations	361	1,914	685

* *The above information represents accounting changes per Federal Lands Recreation Enhancement Act that combine Recreation Fee, National Park Pass, America the Beautiful Pass, and Deed Restricted revenues when reporting obligations and unobligated balances for the Recreation Fee program. This table does not include other programs administered under the Recreation Fee Permanent account such as the Transportation Systems Fund, Education Expenses for the Children of Yellowstone National Park Employees, and the Payment of Tax Losses on Land Acquired at Grand Teton National Park.*

GRANTS AND PAYMENTS

(in thousands of dollars)

Bureau/Grant or Payment	2012 Actual	2013 Estimate	2014 Estimate
BUREAU OF LAND MANAGEMENT			
General Fund Payment to Counties and Native Corporations [1]	28,462	28,187	0
Payments to States and Counties from Shared Receipts including SNPLMA Payments	15,304	17,542	4,369
OFFICE OF SURFACE MINING			
Abandoned Mine Reclamation State Grants	485,496	339,446	273,500
State and Tribal Regulatory Grants	68,590	69,010	57,674
BUREAU OF RECLAMATION			
Boulder Canyon Project Payments to AZ, NV	600	600	600
Title XVI Water Reclamation and Reuse Program	24,653	20,271	14,000
WaterSMART Grants	12,233	24,500	12,000
FISH AND WILDLIFE SERVICE			
Boating Infrastructure Grants	12,238	13,070	11,834
Clean Vessel Act Grants	12,238	13,070	11,834
Coastal Wetlands Conservation	33,960	36,268	32,840
Cooperative Endangered Species Conservation Fund [2]			
Current Funds	47,681	47,973	56,000
Permanent Funds	0	0	28,000
Subtotal, CESCF	47,681	47,973	84,000
Federal Aid in Wildife Restoration Payments to States	362,761	534,271	573,293
National Fish and Wildlife Foundation	7,525	7,525	8,525
Fisheries Commissions and Boating Council	1,200	1,200	1,200
Hunter Education and Safety Grant Program	8,000	8,000	8,000
Multi-State Conservation Grant Program	6,000	6,000	6,000
Multinational Species Conservation Fund [2]	9,466	9,524	9,787
National Outreach Program	12,238	13,070	11,834
National Wildlife Refuge Fund (current and permanent) [2]	21,554	22,043	8,000
Neotropical Migratory Bird Conservation [2]	3,786	3,809	3,786
North American Wetlands Conservation Fund [2]	36,148	36,214	40,125
Sport Fish Restoration, Apportionment to States	348,776	372,486	337,267
State and Tribal Wildlife Grants [2]	61,323	61,698	61,323
NATIONAL PARK SERVICE			
American Battlefield Program Matching Grants			
LWCF	8,986	9,041	8,986
Non-LWCF	1,198	1,202	1,198
Subtotal, American Battlefield Program Matching Grants	10,184	10,243	10,184
Challenge Cost Share	390	390	1,000
Chesapeake Bay Gateway Grants	1,997	2,025	1,997
Heritage Partnership Program	16,391	16,453	8,014
Historic Preservation Grants			
Indian Tribes	8,985	9,040	8,985
States and Territories	46,925	47,212	46,925
Competitive Grants to Underrepresented Communities	0	0	3,000
Subtotal, Historic Preservation Fund Grants	55,910	56,252	58,910

GRANTS AND PAYMENTS
(in thousands of dollars)

Bureau/Grant or Payment	2012 Actual	2013 Estimate	2014 Estimate
Japanese-American Confinement Site Grants	2,995	3,004	2,995
LWCF State Conservation Grants			
Current Funds	42,138	42,296	36,410
Permanent Funds, Oil Lease Revenues	102	102	80
Other Permanent Funds	0	0	20,000
Subtotal, State Conservation Grants	42,240	42,398	56,490
Native American Graves Protection Act Grants	1,747	1,752	1,747
Urban Parks and Recreation Fund			
Current Funds	0	0	9,500
Permanent Funds	0	0	5,000
Subtotal, Urban Parks and Recreation Fund	0	0	14,500
OFFICE OF THE SECRETARY - OFFICE OF NATURAL RESOURCES REVENUE			
Cooperative and Delegated Audits of Oil and Gas Operations	12,568	12,568	12,568
Mineral Revenue Payments to States [3]	2,084,598	2,053,676	2,136,865
Geothermal Payments to Counties	3,718	4,081	0
Qualified OCS Revenue Payments to Gulf of Mexico States	314	245	2,808
OFFICE OF INSULAR AFFAIRS			
American Samoa	22,717	22,856	22,752
Brown Tree Snake	2,995	3,013	3,500
Compact of Free Association (current)	16,460	16,480	3,054
Compact of Free Association (permanent)	202,163	205,100	281,040
Coral Reef Initiative	998	1,004	1,000
Covenant Grants	27,720	27,720	27,720
Maintenance Assistance Fund	2,237	2,251	1,081
Return Federal Taxes to Guam and Virgin Islands	312,547	339,627	314,627
Technical Assistance	18,774	13,889	17,504
Water and Wastewater Projects	790	795	0
Compact Impact Discretionary	0	5,000	3,000
Empowering Insular Communities	2,205	2,218	2,971
DEPARTMENT-WIDE PROGRAMS			
Payments in Lieu of Taxes	393,044	400,898	409,727
TOTAL, DEPARTMENT OF THE INTERIOR	**4,855,934**	**4,929,715**	**4,967,845**

[1] *The budget reflects a five-year reauthorization of the Secure Rural School Act with funding through permanent appropriations in the U.S. Department of Agriculture's U.S. Forest Service Appropriations.*

[2] *Amounts shown include administrative costs.*

[3] *Payments include Mineral Leasing Associated Payments, National Forest Fund Payments to States, Payments to States from Lands Acquired for Flood Control, Navigation and Allied Purposes, National Petroleum Reserve – Alaska, royalty payments to Oklahoma, and interest on late payments. Payments are reduced by the Net Receipts Sharing provision enacted in the 2012 Appropriations Act, continued in the 2013 annualized CR, and proposed in the 2014 President's Budget. All years exclude payments made to coastal States and counties under Section 8(g) the Outer Continental Shelf Lands Act, the Gulf of Mexico Energy Security Act of 2006, BLM Rights-of-Way payments, and Geothermal Revenue Sharing Payments to Counties under the Energy Policy Act of 2005.*

RECEIPTS BY SOURCE CATEGORY

(in thousands of dollars)

Source Category	2012 Actual	2013 Estimate	2014 Estimate	Change
OFFSETTING RECEIPTS				
Onshore Energy Mineral Leasing				
Rents and Bonuses				
Oil and Gas	402,120	211,143	208,176	-2,967
Coal	413,147	588,255	644,421	+56,166
Geothermal	2,822	1,433	1,476	+43
All Other	1,030	207	207	0
Adjustments [1]	-42,302	0	0	0
Royalties				
Oil and Gas	2,711,585	2,491,405	2,591,421	+100,016
Coal	796,560	794,886	810,415	+15,529
Geothermal	12,408	10,019	10,404	+385
All Other	97,568	71,661	71,661	0
Adjustments [1]	-7,812	0	0	0
Subtotal, Onshore Energy Mineral Leasing	4,387,126	4,169,009	4,338,181	+169,172
Noncompetitive Filing Fees	34	34	34	0
Grazing Fees	15,009	13,317	13,217	-100
Timber Fees	26,375	25,233	19,553	-5,680
Recreation Entrance/Use Fees	217,507	218,123	219,014	+891
Park Concession Special Accounts and Other Fees	151,419	145,211	148,126	+2,915
Rent of Land and Structures	98,577	91,626	91,722	+96
Sale of Land, Water, Power, Buildings, etc	206,490	206,418	349,461	+143,043
Offsetting Earnings on Investments	68,961	97,211	56,803	-40,408
All Other Offsetting Receipts [2]	899,128	2,775,265	857,928	-1,917,337
Subtotal, Offsetting Receipts	6,070,626	7,741,447	6,094,039	-1,647,408
UNDISTRIBUTED PROPRIETARY RECEIPTS				
OCS Mineral Leasing				
Rents and Bonuses	681,460	1,107,596	1,250,987	+143,391
Royalties	5,923,397	5,736,229	5,682,556	-53,673
Proposed Oil and Gas Reform	0	0	60,000	+60,000
Subtotal, OCS Mineral Leasing	6,604,857	6,843,825	6,993,543	+149,718
Escrow Payout Interest	39,729	1,414	1,802	+388
Subtotal, Undistributed Proprietary Receipts	6,644,586	6,845,239	6,995,345	+150,106
NON-OFFSETTING GOVERNMENTAL RECEIPTS				
Mined Land Reclamation Fees	249,725	216,205	265,730	+49,525
All Other Non-Offsetting Receipts	736,716	734,700	693,700	-41,000
Subtotal, Non-Offsetting Governmental Receipts	986,441	950,905	959,430	+8,525
UNDISTRIBUTED INTERFUND RECEIPTS				
Non-offsetting Earnings on Investments	1,541	3,000	3,000	0
TOTAL, DEPARTMENT OF THE INTERIOR	**13,703,194**	**15,540,591**	**14,051,814**	**-1,488,777**

[1] *Adjustments consist of lease level transactions, ongoing adjustments, and settlements relating to oil and gas, coal, and geothermal. The 2013 and 2014 estimates do not include projected adjustments and settlements.*

[2] *The Cobell Settlement Agreement, enacted by Congress as the Individual Indian Money Account Litigation Settlement in the Claims Resolution Act of 2010, establishes a $1.9 billion fund for the voluntary buy back and consolidation of fractionated land interests on Indian lands. The settlement was finalized on November 24, 2012, following action by the U.S. Supreme Court and expiration of the appeal period. As an incentive to participate in the Land Buy-Back Program, the Settlement authorizes up to $60 million of the Fund to be set aside for an Indian Education Scholarship Fund for American Indian and Alaska Native students when individuals sell fractional interests under the Land Buy-Back Program.*

MINERAL REVENUE PAYMENTS TO STATES*

(in thousands of dollars)

State	2012 Actual	2013 Estimate	2014 Estimate
Alabama	4,155	4,029	4,187
Alaska	13,470	11,500	11,960
Arizona	12	12	12
Arkansas	2,067	1,925	1,985
California	101,048	99,642	103,705
Colorado	157,819	155,624	161,970
Florida	541	533	555
Idaho	4,539	4,476	4,658
Illinois	264	282	290
Indiana	4	3	3
Kansas	1,331	1,313	1,366
Kentucky	486	383	389
Louisiana	6,914	6,548	6,780
Michigan	331	310	321
Minnesota	12	9	9
Mississippi	2,598	2,059	2,092
Missouri	3,062	2,386	2,421
Montana	47,257	46,600	48,500
Nebraska	28	27	28
Nevada	10,436	10,291	10,710
New Mexico	488,150	481,356	500,985
North Dakota	64,501	65,051	67,469
Ohio	284	282	289
Oklahoma	5,372	5,286	5,498
Oregon	343	338	352
Pennsylvania	67	71	73
South Carolina	1	1	1
South Dakota	1,907	1,881	1,957
Texas	7,727	7,721	7,928
Utah	164,410	162,122	168,733
Virginia	45	42	43
Washington	11	11	12
West Virginia	235	241	247
Wyoming	995,170	981,321	1,021,336
TOTAL	**2,084,598**	**2,053,676**	**2,136,865**

* *Payments include Mineral Leasing Associated Payments, National Forest Fund Payments to States, Payments to States from Lands Acquired for Flood Control, Navigation and Allied Purposes, National Petroleum Reserve – Alaska, royalty payments to Oklahoma, and interest on late payments. Payments are reduced by the Net Receipts Sharing provision enacted in the 2012 Appropriations Act, continued in the 2013 annualized CR, and proposed in the 2014 President's Budget. All years exclude payments made to coastal States and counties under Section 8(g) the Outer Continental Shelf Lands Act, the Gulf of Mexico Energy Security Act of 2006, BLM Rights-of-Way payments, and Geothermal Revenue Sharing Payments to Counties under the Energy Policy Act of 2005.*

STAFFING [1]

(Full Time Equivalent Staff Years)

Bureau/Office	2012 Enacted	2012 Actual	2013 Estimated Usage	2014 Estimated Usage
Bureau of Land Management	10,489	10,565	10,301	10,291
Bureau of Ocean Energy Management	572	560	572	580
Bureau of Safety and Environmental Enforcement	703	615	710	763
Office of Surface Mining	503	486	503	522
Bureau of Reclamation [2]	5,381	5,280	5,384	5,388
U.S. Geological Survey	8,518	8,546	8,554	8,646
Fish and Wildlife Service	9,368	9,542	9,467	9,518
National Park Service	21,907	21,830	21,679	21,651
Bureau of Indian Affairs	8,318	8,245	8,146	7,935
Departmental Offices				
Office of the Secretary	1,521	1,408	1,460	1,495
Trust Land Consolidation Fund	0	0	3	11
Central Utah Project [2]	4	4	4	0
Office of Insular Affairs	41	38	41	41
Office of the Solicitor	441	437	439	428
Office of Inspector General	288	275	267	273
Office of the Special Trustee for American Indians	665	639	638	638
Department-wide Programs				
Wildland Fire Management	24	23	23	20
Payments in Lieu of Taxes	1	1	1	1
Central Hazardous Materials Fund	5	5	5	5
Natural Resource Damage Assessment	10	9	12	20
Working Capital Fund/Franchise Fund	1,453	1,395	1,403	1,403
National Indian Gaming Commission	123	100	115	115
TOTAL, DEPARTMENT OF THE INTERIOR	**70,335**	**70,003**	**69,727**	**69,744**
Utah Mitigation Commission	12	9	10	10
COMBINED TOTAL	**70,347**	**70,012**	**69,737**	**69,754**

[1] *All FTE numbers include direct, allocated, permanent, and reimbursable FTE.*

[2] *The Central Utah Project's four FTE are included in the Bureau of Reclamation in 2014. The 2014 estimated usage reflects the budgetary realignment of CUPCA to Reclamation.*

www.ingramcontent.com/pod-product-compliance
Lightning Source LLC
Chambersburg PA
CBHW081428310526
45790CB00020B/1673